The editors of Monthly Review Press dedicate this new series of popularly written socialist books to Leo Huberman (1903 to 1968), co-editor of *Monthly Review* magazine and co-founder of Monthly Review Press.

It is a great challenge to keep the ideas of Marxism alive and responsive to a changing world. It is just as great a challenge to present these ideas in lucid and comprehensible form to assist new people to achieve revolutionary consciousness. The appearance of this series is an invitation to new readers to learn about the liberating program of socialism, and to writers and scholars to present their work in the simple, concise, yet exciting style so characteristic of Leo Huberman's work.

THE LEO HUBERMAN PEOPLE'S LIBRARY

Books by
Leo Huberman
———★———

WE, THE PEOPLE

───────────★───────────

by

LEO HUBERMAN

WITH ILLUSTRATIONS BY
THOMAS H. BENTON

MONTHLY REVIEW PRESS
NEW YORK

Standard Book Number: SBN-85345-134-6

First Modern Reader Paperback Edition 1970

10 9 8 7 6

MANUFACTURED IN THE UNITED STATES OF AMERICA

To My Wife

CONTENTS

PART II

ILLUSTRATIONS

Preface to Revised Edition

★————————————————————————————————★

Much of the original material for this book was first published in 1932 just prior to the election of Franklin Delano Roosevelt as the thirty-second President of the United States. The fifteen years that have elapsed since that time mark the beginning of a new era in the history of our country.

The old era really ended not in 1932, but in 1929 when the crash came. From its earliest beginnings until 1929, America was the Promised Land, a land flowing with steel and oil as well as with milk and honey. It was a land of riches to which the poor of Europe came for wealth. It was a land of freedom to which the enslaved and oppressed fled.

I have tried to write the story of the extent to which the promise was—and was not—fulfilled.

The first part, Chapters I through XIV, covers the longer period from the earliest explorations through the boom of 1929. It is a stirring account of the building of a nation through the efforts of men, women, and children of stout heart in the face of great odds. It is the story of tremendous economic expansion under the dominance of the corporate form of business enterprise. It is the saga of Big Business in America, its most congenial home. It is a tale of the growing power of monopoly.

Not that this power went unchallenged. Opposition came from the farmers and from the industrial workers. The story of that opposition is included. So, too, is an account of the foreign adventures of American Big Business, by which at the end of the nineteenth century it became a world force.

The second part, Chapters XV through XX, is new material. It is a tale of bankruptcy, terror, woe, and helpless groping after a light that failed. It begins with the crash of 1929 and deals largely with the attempts of the New Deal to repair the damage and to set the wheels in motion again. But because the inevitable crash of 1929 was a crisis not *in* but *of* the system, the New Deal was bound to fail. This is, however, precisely what makes a clear understanding of the New Deal and of its desperate efforts toward Relief, Recovery, and Reform so very important. For the New Deal helped educate millions in the workings and unworkabilities of the whole system. They began to learn that mere good will, as represented by the New Deal, was not enough; that what was wanted was not a new hand but a new deck of cards.

"America was promises." But the promises have been fulfilled, in recent years, only for the men at the top. It is of crucial importance at this time that fulfillment of the promises should come for all of us. The American dream *can* become a reality. That transformation is ours to make—soon—because history will not wait.

I wish to express my deep obligation and appreciation to the following: to Dr. N. B. Heller who first taught me the importance of the role played by economics in history; to Sybil May, Dr. Otto Nathan, Aleine Austin, and my wife Gertrude, for their constant encouragement and critical review of the manuscript; and to the Viking Press and Reynal and Hitchcock for permission to use material from some of my other books published by them.

Leo Huberman

New York, January, 1947

Preface to New Printing

The revised edition of *We, the People* went out of print a few years after it was published in 1947. I had hoped I would find time to add a few chapters for a new edition which would bring the story up-to-date, but I have not succeeded. Meanwhile, I have examined the history books which are published each year hoping to find one which puts the emphasis where I think it belongs—on the workers, not the wars, on the common man, not the "leaders." None has appeared. It seemed, therefore, a good idea to wait no longer and reprint the edition of 1947. This, then, is the original book, as it was revised in 1947.

New York, March, 1964   **L. H.**

Part I

Here They Come!

———————————————————————————

From its very beginnings America has been a magnet to the people of the earth. They have been drawn to its shores from anywhere and everywhere, from near and far, from hot places and cold places, from mountain and plain, from desert and fertile field. This magnet, three thousand miles wide and fifteen hundred miles long, has attracted every type and variety of human being alive. White people, black people, yellow people, brown people; Catholics, Protestants, Huguenots, Quakers, Baptists, Methodists, Unitarians, Jews; Spaniards, Englishmen, Germans, Frenchmen, Norwegians, Swedes, Danes, Chinese, Japanese, Dutch, Bohemians, Italians, Austrians, Slavs, Poles, Rumanians, Russians—and the list is only just begun; farmers, miners, adventurers, soldiers, sailors, rich men, poor men, beggarmen, thieves, shoemakers, tailors, actors, musicians, ministers, engineers, writers, singers, ditchdiggers, manufacturers, butchers, bakers, and candlestick makers.

First came the Norsemen; then an Italian sailing in behalf of Spain; then another Italian sailing in behalf of England; then Spaniards, Portuguese, English, French; then an Englishman sailing for Holland. All of them discovered parts of America, explored a bit, then raised their country's flag and claimed the land. They returned home and told stories (some of them true) of what they had seen. People listened—and believed and came. Millions came within three hundred years, sometimes at the rate of a million a year.

This unique immigration of peoples was not accomplished without difficulties and dangers. To cross the ocean in the *Queen Mary* or the *Queen Elizabeth*, steamships over nine hundred and seventy-five feet long weighing over eighty thousand tons, is one thing. But to cross the Atlantic in a sailboat perhaps ninety feet long and twenty-six feet wide, with a tonnage of only three hundred was quite another thing. (Ordinary ferryboats on the Hudson River average about seven hundred tons.) For over two hundred years the earlier immigrants poured into the United States in just such boats as these. Remember, too, that in those days there were no refrigerators —fish and meat had to be salted to be preserved, and very often the crossing took so long a time that all the food rotted.

Here is a portion of a letter written by Johannes Gohr and some friends, describing their trip from Rotterdam to America in February, 1732 (over one hundred years after the flood of immigrants began). "We were 24 weeks coming from Rotterdam to Martha's Vineyard. There were at first more than 150 persons—more than 100 perished.

"To keep from starving, we had to eat rats and mice. We paid from 8 pence to 2 shillings for a mouse, 4 pence for a quart of water."

Gottlieb Mittelberger was an organist who came to this country in 1750 in charge of an organ which was intended for Philadelphia. Here is a part of his story:

"Both in Rotterdam and Amsterdam the people are packed densely, like herrings, so to say, in the large sea vessels. . . .

When the ships have for the last time weighed their anchor at Cowes, the real misery begins, for from there the ships, unless they have good winds, must often sail 8, 9, 10 or 12 weeks before they reach Philadelphia. But with the best wind the voyage lasts 7 weeks . . .

That most of the people get sick is not surprising, because in addition to all other trials and hardships, warm food is served only 3 times a week, the rations being very poor and very small. These meals can hardly be eaten on account of being so unclean. The water which is served out on the ships is often very black, thick and full of worms, so that one cannot drink it without loathing, even with the greatest thirst. O surely, one would often give much money at sea for a piece of good bread, or a drink of good water if only it could be had. I myself experienced that sufficiently, I am sorry to say. Toward the end we were compelled to eat the ship's biscuit which had been spoiled long ago; though in a whole biscuit there was scarcely a piece the size of a dollar, that had not been full of red worms and spiders' nests. Great hunger and thirst force us to eat and drink everything, but many do so at the risk of their lives. . . .

When the ships have landed at Philadelphia after their long voyage no one is permitted to leave them except those who pay for their passage or can give good security; the others who cannot must remain on board the ships till they are purchased, and are released from the ships by the purchasers. The sick always fare the worst, for the healthy are naturally preferred and purchased first, and so the sick and wretched must often remain on board in front of the city for 2 and 3 weeks, and frequently die, whereas many a one if he could pay his debt and was permitted to leave the ship immediately, might recover. . . .

The sale of human beings in the market on board the ship is carried on thus: Everyday Englishmen, Dutchmen, and high German people come from the city of Philadelphia and other places, some from great distance, say 60, 90 and 120 miles away, and go on board the newly arrived ship that has brought and offers for sale passengers from Europe, and select among the healthy persons such as they deem suitable for their business, and bargain with them how long they will serve for their passage money, for which most of them are still in debt. When they have come to an agreement, it happens that adult persons bind themselves in writing to serve 3, 4, 5 or 6 years for the amount due by them varies according to their age and strength. But very young people, from 10 to 15 years must serve until they are 21 years old.

The last part of this letter is particularly valuable, because it introduces us to a system then very common. Many of the people who wanted to come to America didn't have the money to pay for their passage. They therefore agreed to sell themselves as servants for a period of years to whoever would pay their debt to the captain of the ship. Frequently the newspapers carried advertisements telling about the arrival of such groups. In the *American Weekly Mercury*, published in Philadelphia, on November 7, 1728, there appeared the following advertisement:

Just arrived from London, in the ship Borden, William Harbert, Commander, a parcel of young likely men-servants, consisting of Husbandmen, Joyners, Shoemakers, Weavers, Smiths, Brickmakers, Bricklayers, Sawyers, Taylers, Stay-Makers, Butchers, Chairmakers and several other trades, and are to be sold very reasonable either for ready money, wheat Bread, or Flour, by Edward Hoane in Philadelphia.

And in the *Pennsylvania Staatsbote* for January 18, 1774, this item appeared:

German People

There are still 50 or 60 German persons newly arrived from Germany. They can be found with the widow Kriderin at the sign of the Golden

Swan. Among them are two schoolmasters, Mechanics, Farmers, also young children as well as boys and girls. They are desirous of serving for their passage money.

The contract which these unfortunates who were "desirous of serving for their passage money" had signed with the ship captain was called an indenture, and they were known as "indentured servants."

Isn't it amazing that in spite of shipwreck, rotten food, vermin, sickness, people continued to come by the thousands? Of course conditions did improve. By 1876 nearly all the immigrants came in large steamships which took only seven to twelve days to cross, instead of that number of weeks in a small sailing vessel, as heretofore. But even these furnished no pleasure cruise for steerage passengers. Edward A. Steiner tells the story of his voyage in the early 1900's.

There is neither breathing space below nor deck room above, and the 900 steerage passengers crowded into the hold . . . are positively packed like cattle, making a walk on deck when the weather is good, absolutely impossible, while to breathe clean air below in rough weather, when the hatches are down, is an equal impossibility. The stenches become unbearable, and many of the emigrants have to be driven down; for they prefer the bitterness and danger of the storm to the pestilential air below. . . .

The food, which is miserable, is dealt out of huge kettles into the dinner pails provided by the steamship company. When it is distributed, the stronger push and crowd, so that meals are anything but orderly procedures. On the whole, the steerage of the modern ship ought to be condemned as unfit for the transportation of human beings.

And a woman investigator for the United States Immigration Commission reported in 1911:

During these twelve days in the steerage I lived in a disorder and in surroundings that offended every sense. Only the fresh breeze from the sea overcame the sickening odors. . . . There was no sight before which the eye did not prefer to close. Everything was dirty, sticky, and disagreeable to the touch. Every impression was offensive.

Now obviously no human beings would go through the hardships described above unless they had very good reasons. The end of the journey would have to promise a great deal to make it worth the sorrow of parting from relatives and friends, from all the fun, comfort, and security of home. It's not easy to "pull up stakes," and most people are apt to think a very long time before they do so.

Then what made these millions and millions of people seek homes in a distant land?

Most of the immigrants came because they were hungry—hungry for more bread and for better bread. America offered that. Europe was old; America was young. European soil had been farmed for many years; American soil was practically untouched. In Europe the land was in the hands of a few people, the upper classes; in America the land was available to all. In Europe it was difficult to get work; in America it was easy to get work. In Europe there were too many laborers looking for the few available jobs, so wages were low; in America there weren't enough laborers to fill the available jobs, so wages were high.

"In Europe there were large numbers of people without land; in America there were large areas of practically free land without people." The map on page 8 will give you an idea of how vast, how huge this America was by comparison with European countries.

Not only was this land very extensive, but it was also very good. Here was some of the best farm land in the entire world; the climate and soil suitable for the production of practically every product of the temperate zone and for the grazing of millions of cattle; here were rivers thousands of miles long to water these fertile valleys; here were gold, silver, copper, coal, iron, oil—and all this bounty of nature was to be had for almost nothing. Off to America!

Here was a poor peasant living on someone else's land, in a miserable hut with a leaky roof and no windows; or a person paying heavy taxes without having anything to say in governing his country; or perhaps someone who wanted to work but could not find anything to do, so that there was always too little to eat and no prospect of ever getting enough; if such people saw no hope of ever getting out of the hole they were in as long as they stayed where they were, naturally they would jump at the chance to move to a place described in this manner by a person who had seen it with his own eyes:

Provisions are cheap in Pennsylvania. The people live well, especially on all sorts of grain, which thrives very well because the soil is wild and fat. They have good cattle, fast horses, and many bees. The sheep, which are larger than the German ones, have generally two lambs a year. Hogs and poultry, especially turkeys, are raised by almost everybody. Every evening a tree is so full of chickens that the boughs bend beneath them. Even in the humblest and poorest houses in this country, there is no meal without meat, and no one eats the bread without the butter or cheese,

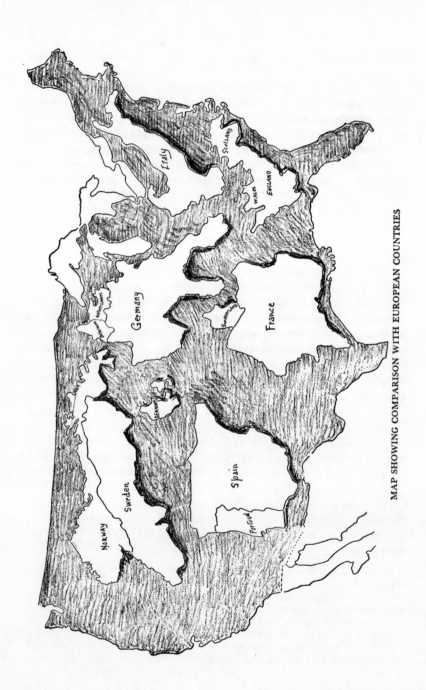

MAP SHOWING COMPARISON WITH EUROPEAN COUNTRIES

although the bread is as good as with us. On account of the extensive stock raising meat is very cheap; one can buy the best beef for three kreuzers a pound.

Of course there did come a time when most of the free land in America had been taken up. But still the immigrants poured in. James Watt had perfected his steam engine, and many other inventions followed which changed the world's way of making things. America was changing from a farm to a workshop. It happened that where formerly most of the immigrants had come from northeastern Europe—England, Ireland, Germany, Scandinavia—the new immigrants came primarily from southeastern Europe—Italy, Russia, Austria, Hungary, Poland. The new immigrants came not to take possession of and cultivate the land as in the past, but to work in the factories, the mills, and the mines. When trees were being felled, gold, copper, coal, and iron being mined, steel being made, clothing being made, railroads being built, workers were needed. And the more that came the greater was the need for more food, more houses, more bridges, more clothing, more autos, more trains, etc. As America changed from a farming country to a manufacturing and industrial country, labor moved from places where it was abundant and cheap, to America where it was scarce and dear. American manufacturers sent agents to all parts of the world to get men to work for them. America needed workers. Workers in Europe and other places needed jobs. Jobs were waiting in this new world. To America!

People came, then, and found land and jobs; at last they had enough to eat. Of course they described their good fortune in the letters they wrote to their relatives and friends at home. Everyone is interested in the adventures of those who leave home, and these letters were passed from hand to hand and eagerly read by all. A letter from America was an exciting event. Very often the people of a whole town would get together to hear some one read a letter from a friend in America. The truth alone was enough to make the stay-at-homes want to make the journey, and oftentimes some of the letters were highly colored, a little bit of truth and a great deal of imagination mixed together. An amusing story is told of an immigrant just landed, who saw a twenty-dollar gold piece on the ground, and, instead of bending for it, kicked it away with his foot.

Someone asked him: "Why did you do that? Don't you know that is real gold?"

"Of course," he replied, "but there are huge piles of gold in

America to be had for the taking, so why should I bother with one piece!"

Very often the envelope that carried the letter contained also the passage money for those back home who were still hesitant or who had no money. Here was real proof of success to be made in America. On the one hand, letters describing the abundance of good things in America; on the other hand, food becoming more and more scarce. The result was immigration, despite dangers and difficulties. Off to America!

A bigger and better loaf of bread, then, attracted most of the in-pouring hordes of people to America. But many came for other reasons. One was religious persecution. If you were a Catholic in a Protestant country, or a Protestant in a Catholic country, or a Protestant in another kind of Protestant country, or a Jew in almost any country, you were oftentimes made very uncomfortable. You might have difficulty in getting a job, or you might be jeered at, or have stones thrown at you, or you might even be murdered—just for having the wrong (that is, different) religion. You learned about America where your religion didn't make so much difference, where you could be what you pleased, where there was room for Catholic, Protestant, Jew. To America, then!

Or perhaps you had the right religion but the wrong politics. Perhaps you thought a few people in your country had too much power, or that there should be no kings, or that the poor people paid too much taxes, or that the masses of people should have more to say about governing the country. Then, oftentimes, your government thought you were too radical and tried to get hold of you to put you into prison, where your ideas might not upset the people. You didn't want to go to prison, so you had to leave the country to avoid being caught. Where to go under the circumstances? Some place where you could be a free man, where you weren't clapped into jail for talking. Probably you turned to the place Joseph described in his letter to his brother. "Michael, this is a glorious country; you have liberty to do as you will. You can read what you wish, and write what you like, and talk as you have a mind to, and no one arrests you." Off to America!

For several hundred years America was advertised just as Lucky Strike cigarettes and Buick cars are advertised today. The wonders of America were told in books, pamphlets, newspapers, pictures, posters—and always this advice was given, "Come to America." But

why should anyone be interested in whether or not Patrick Mc-
Carthy or Hans Knobloch moved from his European home to
America? There were two groups interested at different times, but
for the same reason—business profits.

In the very beginning, over three hundred years ago, trading
companies were organized which got huge tracts of land in America
for nothing or almost nothing. That land, however, was valueless
until people lived on it, until crops were produced, or animals killed
for their furs. Then the trading company would step in, buy things
from the settlers and sell things to them—at a profit. The Dutch West
India Company, the London Company, and several others were
trading companies that gave away land in America with the idea of
eventually making money on cargoes from the colonists. They
wanted profits—needed immigrants to get them—advertised—and
people came.

In later years, from 1870 on, other groups interested in business
profits tried to get people to come to America. The Cunard line, the
White Star line, the North German Lloyd, and several others earned
money only when people used their ships. They therefore sent advertisements to all parts of the world to get people to travel to
America—in their ships. They sent not only advertisements, but also
agents whose business it was to "hunt up emigrants." All the other
reasons mentioned before were operating, and along came a man
who promised to help you, gave you complete directions, aided
you in all the little details that were necessary, sometimes even
got you a passport, and finally led you to the right ship—To America!

For one reason or another, then, people were attracted to America and came of their own free will. There were others who came
not because they wanted to, but because they had to.

In the early days when America was a colony of England, that
country saw a chance to get rid of people who seemed to be "undesirable." Accordingly, hundreds of paupers and convicts were put
on ships and sent to America. Some of the latter were real criminals,
but many had been put in prison for small offenses such as poach-
ing, or stealing a loaf of bread, or being in debt. However, they
were not "good citizens" as far as England was concerned, so what
better idea could that country have than to get rid of them? Off to
America, whether they liked it or not!

There were two groups of indentured servants. There were those
who voluntarily sold themselves for a four- to seven-year term just

to get their passage paid. There was another group, however, "who were carried here against their will—hustled on board ships, borne across the sea and sold into bondage. . . . The streets of London were full of kidnappers—'spirits,' as they were called; no workingman was safe; the very beggars were afraid to speak with anyone who mentioned the terrifying word 'America.' Parents were torn from their homes, husbands from their wives, to disappear forever as if swallowed up in death. Children were bought from worthless fathers,

orphans from their guardians, dependent or undesirable relatives from families weary of supporting them."

Still another group of immigrants were brought against their will. When the early settlers found it practically impossible to make good slaves of the Indians they found here, because the red man was too proud to work under the lash, they turned to Africa, where Negroes could be obtained. For most of the eighteenth century over twenty thousand slaves were transported every year. Negro slave trading became a very profitable business. Many great English fortunes were founded on the slave trade. The Gladstone family fortune is a famous example.

SLAVE SHIP

As might be expected, the privations suffered by the whites in the sea crossing were as nothing compared to the misery of the Negroes. Here is a sample account of conditions on the slave ships:

She had taken in, on the coast of Africa, 336 males, and 226 females, making in all 562, and had been out seventeen days, during which she had thrown overboard 55. The slaves were all enclosed under grated hatchways, between decks: The space was so low, that they sat between each other's legs, and stowed so close together, that there was no possibility of their lying down, or at all changing their position, by night or day. . . . Over the hatchway stood a ferocious-looking fellow, with a scourge of many twisted thongs in his hand, who was the slave-driver of the ship, and whenever he heard the slightest noise below, he shook it over them, and seemed eager to exercise it. . . .

But the circumstance which struck us most forcibly was, how it was possible for such a number of human beings to exist, packed up and wedged together as tight as they could cram, in low cells, three feet high, the greater part of which, except that immediately under the grated hatchways was shut out from light or air, and this when the thermometer, exposed to the open sky, was, standing in the shade, on our deck at 89 degrees. . . .

It was not surprising that they should have endured much sickness and loss of life in their short passage. They had sailed from the coast of Africa on the 7th of May, and had been out but seventeen days, and they had thrown overboard no less than fifty-five, who had died of dysentery and other complaints, in that space of time, though they had left the coast in good health. Indeed, many of the survivors were seen lying about the decks in the last stage of emaciation, and in a state of filth and misery not to be looked at.

And so they came, both the willing and the unwilling. The movement began with a few people in the early 1600's, grew to hundreds, then thousands, and three hundred years later had to be measured in hundreds of thousands—in 1907 more than a million people entered the United States within the year. In the years 1903 to 1913 *every time the clock struck the hour, day and night* [*taking the average for the whole 10 years*] *100 persons* born in some foreign country, not including Canada and Mexico, landed on the shores of the United States."

What became of these swarms of people after they got here?

Beginnings

★——★

What equipment would be most essential for beginning life three thousand miles from home? According to Captain John Smith, one of the earliest settlers, the following list of supplies was most suitable for the move from England to the trackless, uncivilized region of Virginia:

List of Necessities for People Going to Virginia
Cost roughly [£ = $5, s. = 25c., d. = 2c.]

Clothing	Cost		
3 shirts	7s.	6d.
3 falling bands	1s.	3d.
A Monmouth cap	1s.	10d.
1 Waste-coat	2s.	2d.
1 suit of canvase	7s.	6d.
1 suit of Frize [frieze, a coarse woolen cloth] .	10s.	
1 suit of cloth	15s.	
3 paire of Irish stockings	4s.	
4 paire of shooes	8s.	8d.
1 paire of garters		10d.
1 dozen of points [laces for fastening clothing]		3d.
1 paire of Canvas sheets	8s.	
7 ells of Canvas to make a bed and boulster, to be filled in Virginia serving for two men ..	8s.	
5 ells of coarse Canvas to make a bed at sea for two men	5s.	
1 coarse rug at sea for two men	6s.	

Food for a Whole Year for a Man

8 bushels of meale	£ 2	
2 bushels of pease	9s.	
2 bushels of otemeale ..	6s.	
1 gallon of Aquavitae ..	2s.	6d.
1 gallon of oyle	3s.	6d.
2 gallons of Vinegar ...	2s.	

Arms for a Man

1 Armor compleat, light	17s.	
1 long peece five foot and halfe, neere Musket bore .... £ 1	2s.	
1 Sword	5s.	
1 Belt	1s.	
1 Bandilier [Bandoleer, a broad leather belt worn by soldiers over the left shoulder] ...	1s.	6d.
20 pound of powder ..	18s.	
60 pound of shot or lead Pistoll and Goose shot	5s.	

Tools for a Family of 6 Persons

2 broad axes at 3s. 8d. a peece	7s.	4d.
5 felling axes at 18d. a peece	7s.	6d.
2 steele handsawes at 16d. a peece	2s.	8d.
2 two handsaws [two-hand saws] at 5s. a peece	10s.	

List of Necessities for People Going to Virginia—Continued
Cost roughly [£ = $5, s. = 25c., d. = 2c.]

1 whipsaw, set and filed, with box, file and wrest	10s.	
2 hammers 12d. a peece	2s.	
5 broad howes [hoe] at 2s. a peece	10s.	
5 narrow howes at 16d. a peece	6s.	8d.
3 shovels at 18d. a peece	4s.	6d.
2 spades at 18d. a peece	3s.	
2 augers at 6d. a peece	1s.	
6 chissels at 6d. a peece	3s.	
2 Percers stocked at 4d. a peece		8d.
3 Gimblets at 2d. a peece		6d.
2 Hatchets at 21d. a peece	3s.	6d.
2 frowes [a wedge-shaped tool for splitting rails or staves] at 18d. a peece	3s.	
2 Hand Bills at 20d. a peece	3s.	4d.
1 Grindstone	4s.	
Nails of all sorts to the value of	£ 2	
2 Pickaxes	3s.	

Household Implements for a Family of 6 Persons

1 Iron Pot	7s.	
1 Kettell	6s.	
1 large Frying-pan	2s.	6d.
1 Gridiron	1s.	6d.
2 Skellets	5s.	
1 Spit	2s.	
Platters, dishes, spoones of wood		4s.
For Sugar, Spice and Fruit at Sea for six men	12s.	6d.
So the full charge after this rate for each person will amount to about the summe of .	£12 10s. 10d.	
The passage of each man is	£ 6	
The freight of these provisions for a man, will be about halfe a tun, which is	£ 1 10s.	
So the whole charge will amount to about	£20	

With only this small stock of goods along, after tossing about on a small sailing vessel for eight weeks or more, the settlers arrived in a strange place uninhabited except by Indians and wild beasts. Only the sea, the sky, and the never-ending wilderness.

The settlers' first thought was, of course, something to eat and a place to sleep. There were deer and other animals in the forest, fish in the streams, and trees for houses. When the trees were cut down there would be a clearing for a farm (occasionally a group of settlers were lucky enough to land at a place where the Indians had made a clearing and abandoned it). Here, then, were all the materials at hand for a crude beginning, but time was pressing. The ship on which they had come would stand by until a start was made, but very often the captain was impatient to return. Besides, the longer the ship tarried, the faster the settlers' small store of provisions would be eaten, since the sailors meant so many more mouths to feed.

John Smith knew from experience that saws would be needed, that a good sharp ax was absolutely necessary. Houses varied, of course, with the climate, the ability and amount of work of the pioneers, and the time they had for building. In some places it was necessary to get under a shelter quickly, so they lived in caves dug in the side of a hill until they could have time to chop down the trees for log houses; in other places they copied the wigwams of the Indians; but log houses were the most common.

A favorite form of a log house for a settler to build in his first "cut down" in the virgin forest, was to dig a square trench about two feet deep, of dimensions as large as he wished the ground floor of his house, then to set upright all around this trench (leaving a space for a fireplace, window, and door) a closely placed row of logs all the same length, usually 14 feet long for a single story; if there was a loft, 18 feet long. The earth was filled in solidly around these logs, and kept them firmly upright; a horizontal band of puncheons, which were split logs smoothed off on the face with the axe, was sometimes pinned around within the log walls, to keep them from caving in. Over this was placed a bark roof, made of squares of chestnut bark, or shingles of overlapping birch-bark. A bark or log shutter was hung at the window, and a bark door hung on withe [a band consisting of a twig or twigs twisted] hinges, or if very luxurious, on leather straps, completed the quickly made home. . . . A rough puncheon floor, hewed flat with an axe or adze, was truly a luxury. . . . A small platform placed about 2 feet high alongside one wall, and supported at the outer edge with strong posts, formed a bedstead. Sometimes hemlock boughs were the only bed. The frontier saying was, "A hard day's work makes a soft bed." The tired pioneers slept well even on hemlock boughs.

His shelter having been built, the settler next turned his attention to planting. Here he was helped by the Indians, who showed him how to plant maize, a sure crop that didn't require too much toil. From the Indian, also, he learned ways of hunting and fishing that were best suited to his new home. Nevertheless, he had often to look upon the Indian as a bitter enemy whose attacks were as sudden and unexpected as they were horrible. This was the reason for the laws in several of the settlements requiring that "the head of every family should keep in his house, ready to hand, a well fixed gun, two pounds of powder, and eight pounds of shot for every person under him who was able to carry arms."

As time went on and more and more white people came, the Indian found himself being pushed farther and farther back; naturally he resented this and fought to retain his land. There were cruel deeds performed by both whites and Indians which led to terrible battles, but even had they been kind to one another the ways of living of the two peoples were very different and there was bound to be a conflict. The settlers fought with the Indians, traded with them, and, as more settlers came, tried to kill them off entirely.

Captain John Mason wrote an account of an expedition of his soldiers against the Indians. He came to an Indian fort early one morning while the Indians were asleep. After putting half his men under Captain Underhill at one exit, he surrounded the other exit with the rest of his men, then set the wigwams on fire. Here is his account:

The Captain also said, "We must burn them," . . . (and immediately stepping into the Wigwam where he had been before), brought out a Fire-Brand and putting it into the Matts with which they were covered, set the Wigwams on fire . . . and when it was throughly kindled, the Indians ran as Men most dreadfully Amazed. And indeed such a dreadful Terror did the Almighty let fall upon their Spirits, that they would fly from us and into the very Flames, where many of them perished. And when the Fort was thoroughly Fired, Command was given, that all should fall off and surround the Fort; which was readily attended by all. . . . The Fire was kindled on the North East Side to windward; which did swiftly over-run the Fort, to the extreme Amazement of the Enemy, and great Rejoycing of ourselves. Some of them climbing to the Top of the Palizado; others of them running into the very Flames; many of them gathering to windward, lay pelting at us with their Arrows; and we repayed them with our small Shot; Others of the Stoutest issued forth as we did guess, to the Number of Forty, who perished by the Sword. . . . And thus in little more than one Hour's space was their impregnable Fort with themselves utterly destroyed, to the Number of Six or Seven Hundred, as some of themselves confessed. There were only Seven taken Captive and about Seven escaped. . . .
Of the English, there were two Slain outright, and about twenty wounded.

Very few human beings could look on while they forced six hundred men, women, and children to be roasted alive unless there had been real trouble between them. To the early newcomer the Indians, with few exceptions, were a source of constant fear.

It was a hard life. Some of the accounts are appalling. William Bradford, historian of the Plymouth settlement tells us: "But that which was most sad and lamentable was that in 2 or 3 months time *half of their company died,* especially in January and February being ye depth of winter and wanting houses and other comforts; . . . so as there died some 2 or 3 of a day in ye aforesaid time; that of 100 and odd persons, scarce 50 remained."

NORTH AMERICAN INDIAN

And George Percy tells us about the settlement in Virginia: "The tenth day died William Bruster Gentleman, of a wound given by the Savages, and was buried the eleventh day.

"The fourteenth day, Jerome Alikock, Ancient, died of a wound, the same day Francis Midwinter, Edward Moris Corporall died suddenly.

"The fifteenth day, their died Edward Browne and Stephen Galthorpe. The sixteenth day, their died Thomas Gower Gentleman. The seventeenth day their died Thomas Mounslic."

Impure water, rotten food, not enough food, unbearable heat, unbearable cold, slaughter by the Indians, this was too often the lot of the first settlers. Yet they persisted and others came; more permanent settlements were made and more newcomers helped to carve a country out of the wilderness. They were brave souls who left their native lands to try their fortunes in a New World; they came to a life of adventure where only the strong survived; they were a determined, courageous people.

The country which is now the United States had its beginnings on that strip of land which lies between Nova Scotia and Florida, on the eastern coast, facing Europe. It was here that Jamestown was settled in 1607, and Plymouth in 1620. By 1760 settlements dotted the whole strip, in some places far apart, in others close together. At that time, about one hundred and fifty years after Jamestown, there were more than one and a half million people here, many of whom had been born in the settlements. Though New York had been first settled by the Dutch, and though Swedes, Germans, Scotch-Irish, and French had also come over, yet the majority of the people were English, the strip of land was owned by England, and the settlements on it were called "colonies" of England. For most of those early settlers England was "home."

It was natural, therefore, to find practically all of the first settlements near the coast, on a sound or bay, or on one of the many river mouths; natural because it was essential to the colonists to be on or very near the one road that led back to where they came from; the place *to* which they could send whatever products they farmed or whatever goods they made; the place *from* which they could receive whatever they desired, be it supplies, letters, relatives, or friends. So it was that for the first hundred years of settlement, even when, as often happened, settlers moved from one part of the strip to another, their houses were built along the shores of the Atlantic, their one connection with "home."

Coming from England meant that these colonists were Englishmen, not only in name, but in habit, speech, and thought. They walked English, talked English, dressed English, thought English. It meant that English ideas of living and of working would be introduced here, and so they were—with some changes.

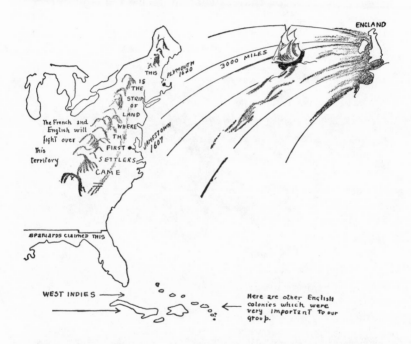

These earliest immigrants landed at different times, at different places along the eastern shore of America. They came with very definite ideas about what they would do here, how they would live, what work they would perform. But they had to modify their plans to fit in with the conditions they found—rivers, soil, coast line, mountains, climate—in short, geography. The work that was done in the various settlements depended very largely on the geography of that region. It didn't "just happen" that men farmed plantation style in the southern end of the strip of land, while other men from the northern end of the strip sailed the seven seas in whaling boats.

There were certain definite geographic reasons that forced these things to happen.

If you look at the relief map you will find that the strip of land has been divided into three sections, the Southern Colonies, the Middle Colonies, and the New England Colonies. This division is made because the people in these three different sections found special geographic conditions which forced them to do a special kind of work, and so to a certain extent determined the kind of people

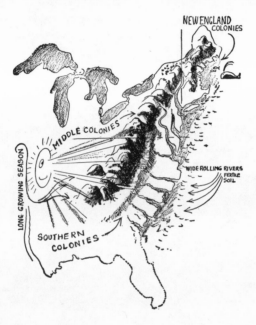

they became. Geography forced the settlements of Virginia, Maryland, North and South Carolina, and Georgia to do much the same things, so for convenience' sake we shall consider them together; in like manner, New York, Pennsylvania, New Jersey, and Delaware are taken together as the Middle Colonies, and Connecticut, Rhode Island, New Hampshire, and Massachusetts are taken together as the New England Colonies.

If you look at the relief map again you will see that it was a happy combination of mountains, sea, and sun which destined farming to become the leading industry of the Southern Colonies. Here the Appalachian Mountains, so close to the coast in the northern area, were two hundred miles back from the sea. The ocean made plentiful clouds, the clouds hitting the mountains made plentiful rain, the rain washing down the mountains for thousands of years had built a wide plain of good fertile soil. The rivers which had brought down the soil were steep near the mountains, but near the coast they were wide and rolling, deep enough for the small boats of the time to navigate for miles inland. It was far enough south for the summers to be hot, so that the growing season lasted from six months in Maryland to about nine in South Carolina. Now add to these ideal farming conditions the early discovery of a New World crop which was always in demand in the Old World, and you readily understand why the Southern Colonies became a farming group.

Tobacco! This was the breath of life in Virginia, the oldest of the Southern Colonies. Men talked, thought, and bought in tobacco. It was farming country, and other crops were also grown, but while the Southerner might have competition in the production of fruits and grains, in tobacco he was master. It was a waste of time asking him to try something else—tobacco sold very readily, there was a big profit in it, and tobacco he would grow. It becomes more and more difficult to change a person's way of doing things once that way develops into a habit. Tobacco! It was a magic word. Everything revolved around its production and it had a tremendous effect upon life in the South.

Now tobacco is a sensitive plant that exhausts the soil quickly. Nowadays, every farmer knows that it is best to move his crops around every year or every two years. So, in the field where last year he planted his corn, this year he plants oats, then next year perhaps he will plant rye, and so on. But the Southerner did not rotate his crops in this fashion (he planted tobacco year after year in the same field), nor did he manure his soil. In about three years he found that to produce the best tobacco he would have to clear more land and start again on virgin soil. Land was cheap, more land was needed to plant tobacco, so plantations kept growing. They grew so fast that, though there weren't so many settlers in Virginia in 1685 as there were in a small part of London, yet their plantations spread over an area as large as the whole of England itself.

However, it must not be supposed that all of the plantation was open field. Barely one fifth was cleared, the rest was wooded. When the planter cleared a new strip of his land he left the old strip to grow up again in underwood, so that plantations were, for the most part, wilderness, a small cleared section, and two or three fields either abandoned or given over to corn and other grains.

For the first hundred years, while there were a few very large plantations thousands of acres in extent, most of them averaged about six hundred acres. These were held by small farmers who worked the fields themselves with their families. In Virginia, up to 1700, if you went from plantation to plantation, you would usually find the landowner toiling in his field with one or two helpers, often his own sons, or an indentured servant, or possibly a Negro slave.

Up to the end of the seventeenth century one of the difficulties the tobacco planter had to face was the scarcity of labor. Tobacco raising requires many hands but these, in the 1600's, were hard to get. Some of the hired labor was supplied by free men who worked for wages, or in many cases by indentured servants. But these servants were hard to keep because after their terms of labor expired they would become tenant farmers or work for wages—and the next step was a field of their own. (Few people will work someone else's land when they can work for themselves.) This was the path many indentured servants followed in the 1600's, some few even becoming very rich men.

But the plantation-owner was not so much interested in the success of other men as he was in obtaining permanent help for himself—and in the 1700's he found the solution to his problem. Negroes—slaves for life. Here, at last, was help that would stay, had to. Now if he could buy more slaves, he could raise more tobacco, then buy more land, raise more tobacco and so on until he had a really large plantation.

Negro labor was not new to the colonists, but in the seventeenth century Negroes were not as numerous as white servants. The first shipload had arrived at Jamestown in 1619, and by 1690 there were about twenty thousand scattered throughout the colonies. They had been tried as laborers in the North, but except as house servants they did not fit into the scheme of work there. But they were suited to plantation work in southern fields and in the eighteenth century they were brought in by the thousands. Ship after ship arrived with huge quotas of Negro slaves. In some districts there were soon more blacks than whites.

This, of course, had a tremendous effect on living and working in the South. Now it was no longer easy for the small farmer or freed indentured servant to get along. Land rose in price and was gobbled up by richer plantation-owners. The poor farmer who worked in the fields with his own hands had to compete in the tobacco market with the cheaper labor of Negroes. Now, unless he had enough money to buy a few slaves for himself, he had to give up his land and move on. Often he became a "poor white" who retired into the back country to meet others like himself, or indentured servants now freed, and fast becoming "poor white." In addition, because field work was primarily done by blacks, white people could no longer do it without shame. No more could Negro slave and white man work side by side in the fields on the same terms. In the social ladder of the South, the Negro was at the bottom rung, and the white man to retain his position on a higher rung must not do work suited to blacks. So large plantations swallowed small ones, and there were two extremes in the social scale—white and black—master and slave.

The larger plantations lined both sides of the navigable rivers. Ships did not unload at some coast town, but sailed for miles inland, stopping at the private wharves of these planters. They sailed *from* Virginia with their holds filled with hogsheads of tobacco, and returned *to* Virginia with their holds filled with all kinds of manufactured articles, such as fine cloth, household goods, silver, tapestries, fine wines, ironware. Though he had on his plantation a staff of workers—carpenters, shoemakers, blacksmiths, spinners, weavers, and so on—who supplied him with essential farm articles, the planter looked to England for the finer material things. His clothes, pictures, books, and furniture came from England, and his children went to English schools. For all these things he paid in—tobacco. Sometimes he bought too much or the crop failed that year—then he didn't pay, but owed the Englishmen and promised to pay from next year's crop. The planter lived very well and was quite often in debt. All of southern life was wrapped up in the leaf of tobacco.

This, then, was the pattern for Virginia up to 1760. And while South Carolina added rice and indigo, and North Carolina added pitch and tar, and Georgia added indigo, this was their pattern also. Good soil and warm climate . . . farming country, plantation style . . . first, indentured servants, then Negro slave labor . . . importing manufactured goods and exporting staples such as rice and tobacco . . . easygoing, soft-mannered, slow-moving people who spoke with a drawl and had an aristocratic air . . . planters who felt secure in their land and took time to play. . . . This was the South in 1760. And geography helped to make it that.

Englishmen settled Virginia, and other Englishmen settled New England, yet in 1760 New Englanders and Virginians carried on totally different industries—according to their geographical setting.

Look at the relief map again. You can see at a glance that New England, being farther north, will have cooler summers and colder winters; that its growing season will be much shorter. Note how close to the coast the Appalachians are, hemming in the settlers to the sea; the rivers in New England are not broad highways as in the South, but shorter, narrower, and swifter, broken by falls in many places. What our relief map does not show, but what was very important also, is the stony soil of New England. It was good farming soil, but the settler had not only to chop down the trees to make a clearing as he did in the South, but here he had to spend many additional hours picking up boulders, before he even began the work of planting. New England is lined with fences several feet thick, piled high with stones that have meant hours of backbreaking toil for the farmer. As some joker said later, "Here the sheep's noses were sharpened for cropping the grass between the stones, and the corn had to be shot into the unyielding ground with a gun."

Thus geography determined that farming in New England was to be very different from that in the South. No large plantations, no Negro field hands, no staple crop; in New England farms were small, tilled by their owners, producing a variety of crops such as corn, hay, rye, barley, fruit. The New Englander did get a hard living from his stubborn soil, but it took all his strength, so he looked about for other more suitable industries—and found them.

A few hundred miles east of this section lay the Banks of Newfoundland, perhaps the best fishing grounds in the world. European fishermen had been making the long trip there for many, many years, and here was New England within easy reach of it. So the would-be planters turned to the sea. Soon the waters off the coast were filled with fishing boats returning with cod, salmon, herring, and mackerel. Catholic countries in Europe were a permanent market for the best grades of fish, and planters in the West Indies took the poorest grades to feed to their slaves.

The sea was the home of something else eagerly sought by daring

New Englanders—the whale. In very early Colonial days dead whales would often be washed ashore. In a period when lighting was a real problem—pine knots at first, then homemade tallow or wax candles —whale oil for the metal and glass lamps of the time was readily bought. In the head of the sperm whale was also found a yellowish and white waxy solid from which spermaceti candles were made. These were much better than the tallow candles, because their bigger flame gave out much more light. Before many years had passed Yankee skippers were sailing every body of water that was thought to hold whales. Their sturdy sailing vessels could be found on the Arctic and Antarctic, on the coast of Africa, in the Pacific, everywhere. Whalemen did not work for wages; they divided their profits into shares, according to their position on the boat. They gambled on the catch. Thus the owners might get $\frac{1}{2}$, the master $\frac{1}{15}$, each able seaman $\frac{1}{50}$, cabin boy $\frac{1}{120}$, and so on. Very often a whaling boat would go on a voyage of three years or more, never once touching land in all that time. It was a hard, adventurous, daring life. Here is a day in the log of Captain Edward S. Ray of the whaler *Orion*, off on a cruise of several years.

Tuesday, May 16

Begins with light winds at S.E. at 1 P.M. Lowered the boats in chase of whales at 2 P.M. Struck one and killed him and took him along side and commenced cutting. Got one boat stove all to pieces; at 9 P.M. the bluber tore out and the whale sunk at day light took in the head at 10 A.M. The fluke chain parte & we lost half of the boddy of the whale, Latter part light airs and calms the Land in sight latt. by Obs. 43.20.

Captain Ray says simply, "got one boat stove all to pieces," without a hint of the great danger. But whaling was packed with thrills, as we learn from this unforgettable picture:

"There she blows! There! There! There! She blows! she blows!" The wild cries rent the air and instantly all is commotion. First there was the bustle of sending away the boats, then the long hard pull to the quarry, each of the four mates exhorting his crew with picturesque epithets to win the race: "Sing out and say something, my hearties. Roar and pull, my thunderbolts! Beach me, beach me on their black backs, boys; only do that for me, and I'll sign over to you my Martha's Vineyard plantation, boys; including wife and children, boys! Lay me on—lay me on! O Lord, Lord! but I shall go stark, staring mad! See! See that white water." The rowers' backs are to the whale, it is bad form to glance around, they know not how near they are until the mate shouts to the bow oar, the harpooner, *Stand up, and let him have it!* A shock as bow grounds on blubber, a frantic "Starn all!" and the death duel begins.

Anything may happen then. At best a Nantucket sleigh-ride, waves rushing past the whaleboats with a surging, hollow roar . . . "like gigantic bowls in a boundless bowling-green; the brief suspended agony of the boat as it would tip for an instant on the knife-like edge of the sharper waves, that almost seemed threatening to cut it in two; the sudden profound dip into the watery glens and hollows, the keen spurrings and goadings to gain the top of the opposite hill; the headlong, sled-like slide down its other side; . . . the cries of the headsmen and harpooners, and the shuddering gasps of the oarsmen, with the wondrous sight of the ivory *Pequod* bearing down upon her boats with outstretched sails, like a wild hen after her screaming brood." Finally the whale slows down, exhausted, and the crew pull up on him, hand over hand on the line, and dispatch him with a few well-timed thrusts; then pull quickly out of his death flurry. At worst a canny old "sparm" sinks out of sight, rises with open jaws, directly under the boat, and shoots with it twenty feet into the air, crushing its sides like an egg-shell, while the crew jump for their lives into seething, blood-streaked foam.

Fishing of this type demanded courage and daring. New England seamen in such a school soon took their place among the best sailors in the world.

Nor did the New Englanders depend on the mother country for their boats. Everything necessary for shipbuilding was at hand and the coast with its many harbors and bays was soon dotted with busy shipyards making splendid vessels. The forests came right down to the water's edge, providing timber, masts (the finest in the world), pitch, and tar, while hemp for rope was grown in the fields. With all the raw materials at hand, the New Englanders could and did undersell every other country in the building of ships. Before long their shallops, sloops, schooners, brigantines, and ketches could be seen in ports all over the world.

For a number of years the sea was practically the only way the colonists had of getting to one another. It took many years to convert Indian trails into suitable roads, and meanwhile goods between the colonies were carried on the water. The sea was the highway and in this coastwise trade the New Englanders were the leaders.

Unlike the Southerners, they had no staple farm products that were eagerly sought in the Old World, but they could transport those staples in their ships, since the Southerners devoted themselves exclusively to the raising of tobacco and rice, without caring who did the carrying. Soon the Atlantic was covered with the boats of these enterprising Yankees who smelled out a trade anywhere and were on the spot to be a part of it. They carried masts, pitch, tar, and hemp to England. When they were not loaded with their own fish and lumber, they were carrying tobacco from the South or wheat from Pennsylvania, or sugar from the West Indies. There wasn't a port on the Atlantic that wasn't visited at some time by New Englanders looking for business. Their ships were everywhere.

Trade with the West Indies was very important to the colonies, particularly those north of Maryland. Here on these tropical islands were large plantations devoting themselves exclusively to the production of staples, such as sugar and molasses. The New Englanders were not long in discovering that the people on these islands would buy whatever the Europeans didn't need. Here, too, was a chance to obtain goods to help pay for the manufactured things that the colonies had always to buy from England. Take their own fish, lumber, grains, horses (raised especially for the West Indies) to the islands, exchange them there for sugar, molasses, indigo, and carry the latter to England and the rest of Europe. Just the kind of trading opportunity the New Englanders were on the lookout for.

The West Indies also formed one end of another interesting triangular trade. Follow the arrows in this simple picture and you will have the key to this trading situation:

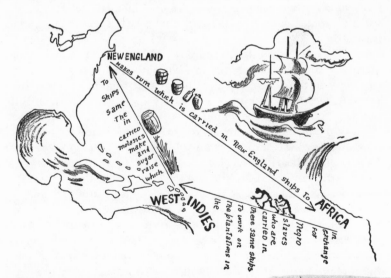

No matter where you begin on the triangle, New England ships were doing the business—and always with a full cargo. Shrewd, busy

Yankees who made themselves the best sailors in the world, knew their boats, knew the sea, and knew how to find customers!

The ships were manned by young boys to whom the sea spelled *adventure*; boys who chose between the dull routine of farm life and the lure of the ocean. Here was a chance to see the world, get high wages, and perhaps become officers. In Europe that would not have been possible, since, in many cases, officers there obtained their places through pull; here on the New England ships officers rose from the ranks and every young sailor boy had his chance. If he soon had enough of traveling or if he were not promoted, he returned to the farm, and another boy with the smell of salt air in his nostrils took his place. Those who stayed and became first mates or captains attained their positions because they knew everything about boats. Here was a fleet of ships manned by boys in their teens or early twenties, who loved their thrilling business and learned all its secrets, commanded by seamen who had begun as they, had worked hard and caught on to the tricks of seafaring, and now, with boats and the sea an open book, had become captains or mates. Small wonder that in later years many New England captains would not use the chart or sextant or other new navigation instruments and continued to reach faraway ports by "dead reckoning" alone. Small wonder since the sea and trade and ships were in the very air New Englanders breathed.

How did the Negro slave fit into the New England way of living? Hardly at all. He was unskilled labor suitable for the tobacco or rice fields of the South, but not able at that time to do the skilled jobs of the North. Fishing was not easy for savage Africans, ship-building required the best kind of skilled workmen, and the farming was so difficult that it always required the attention of the owner himself. There was no important job for the Negro. So it was that New England boats carried Negro slaves to Virginia and Maryland and North and South Carolina and the West Indies—but *not* to New England. New Englanders had no objections to using them, but they had no use for them. Later, when importing Negro slaves was forbidden, though the South thought it was quite all right to have black human beings as slaves, the New Englanders thought it was all wrong. It is plain that geography played a big part in shaping those opposite ways of thinking.

While the men were on the farm or at sea the women in New England were busy with household tasks—getting meals ready, clearing away and washing dishes, making cheese, preserving fruits, spinning, weaving, and sewing. This was the period of the home spinning wheel and loom, now found only in museums, but then very necessary and useful in making most of the clothes for the entire household. There was much work to be done, and the more help you had the better off you were. Women married quite young, sometimes as early as fourteen, and very large families of ten or more children were common. Because they worked so hard and bore so many children, very often the women died at an early age. Their husbands frequently married again and another family was started. Benjamin Franklin was the youngest son of Josiah Franklin, who had seven children by his first wife, and ten by his second. There were plenty of chores, and everybody's help was needed, from father and mother to the youngest child. The picture of the home in New England was like that painted by Defoe in 1724 of the cottages of the poor countryfolk in old England. "The women and children are always busy Carding, Spinning, etc.; so that no Hands being unemploy'd all can gain their Bread even from the youngest to the ancient; hardly anything above four years old, but its hands are sufficient to itself."

The New England pattern up to 1760: inhospitable stony soil . . . small farms tended by the owner and his sons, producing an assortment of crops . . . many small villages, and several quite large towns on the coast . . . the beckoning sea . . . the smell of fish . . . the sound of the shipbuilder's hammer . . . skilled workmen—shoemakers, carpenters, ropemakers, blacksmiths, bricklayers, weavers . . . home industries . . . rum distilleries . . . some commercial looms and forges, some indentured servants and a few Negro slaves, but primarily free white labor . . . Nature, not too bountiful, forcing hard work on the settlers . . . sturdy home-built vessels manned by skillful sailors . . . "hustlers" . . . bargain hunters in the markets of the world . . . shrewd, enterprising traders.

The Middle Colonies, lying between the South and New England, more closely resembled the pattern of the latter. Here the plain ran about one hundred miles from the coast before it met the Appalachian barrier; the soil was fertile and the growing season fairly long; the rivers were wide and deep and rainfall ample; geography, then, decreed that this be farming country—and so it was. The Middle Colonies, before long, became known as the "Bread Colonies."

Here wheat was grown extensively, also barley, rye, and fruit. Cattle, sheep, and swine were also raised. Though there were a number of very large estates comparable in size to the huge plantations of the South, yet most of the farms were small like those in New England, and the plantation system with a single staple and Negro slave labor did not exist. The Middle Colonies, like New England, had some Negro slaves, but here, too, there was little use for them and they declined in numbers. Indentured servants, on the other hand, were very numerous, and some of them, after their term of service expired and they had received their outfit of tools and barrel of corn, took up land on their own and made good.

In these Middle Colonies, too, the English were in the majority, but many other peoples made their homes here. The Dutch were the first to come to New Amsterdam (it was later taken from them by the English who re-named it New York); the Swedes settled in Delaware, and many Scotch-Irish and Germans were filling up Pennsylvania.

The Dutch carried on an extensive fur trade with the Indians, and this soon became a leading industry in this section (as well as in the other two). The Indian tasted the white man's rum and found it good; he tried the white man's guns and found them superior to his own arrows; he wanted rum and powder and brought beaver skins, deer skins, bear skins, mink skins, and gray and red fox skins to the trading post for exchange. Soon boat after boat with holds filled with furs left the Middle Colonies for Europe.

Pennsylvania and New York rivaled New England in shipbuilding and trading also. The ports of Philadelphia and New York resembled Boston in the number of vessels arriving with manufactured fineries, and leaving with flour, provisions, furs, barrel staves, horses, pork. A brisk trade was carried on with the West Indies. A merchant class—not small shopkeepers, but wealthy men owning many vessels which they sent to all parts of the world—grew up here to rival that in New England. In times of peace, business was good.

But England was very frequently at war, and the normal course of trade was apt to be interrupted. What then? These were an ingenious people and they found a way out. When England was at war with Spain or France or some other country, then these peaceful trading vessels became privateers. A privateer was a merchant vessel armed with a few guns and a "commission" from the king which gave it the right to seize and keep the enemy's ships and all "Goods, Wares and Merchandises" thereon.

The *New York Mercury* reported June 21, 1762:

Since our last a very fine Privateer Brig called The Monckton was launched at the ship-yards: she is to mount 16 guns and will be commanded by Captain Sennet: All Hearts of Oak, that have an inclination to make their Fortunes, by drubbing the Spaniards, now or never.

And in the issue of Monday, June 20, 1757, appeared this announcement of glad news:

The prizes taken by the Privateer Brig Pliny, Capt. Stoddard, of this Port, in Company with the Wasp, Capt. McNamara, of Halifax, and The King of Prussia, Capt. Roof of Rhode Island, as mentioned in our last, were a Ship called the La Amiable Jane, Monsieur Arnaud, Commander of 16 guns and 50 men; and a Snow called St. Rene of 10 guns and 30 men; They were taken on the 25th of May, about 40 Leagues to the Eastward of Bermuda on their voyage from Cape-Francois for Old France, and had been 50 days out. Their Cargoes, Indigo, Sugar, Coffee and Cotton.

It was exciting, adventurous life and very profitable—so much so that often daring captains continued privateering after the war was over. Thus did privateering become piracy. A number of colonial fortunes, both in the Middle Colonies and in New England, were built on merchant vessels turned privateers, turned pirates.

The Middle Colonies pattern up to 1760: a thriving fur trade . . . good fertile soil . . . small, well-kept farms producing a variety of crops, particularly wheat . . . towns and seaport cities . . . a few Negro slaves and many indentured servants . . . home industries, the beginning of manufacturing, but still importers of manufactured goods . . . ships and trade . . . privateers . . . Dutch, Swedes, Scotch-Irish, Germans, English.

Beginnings. From 1607 to 1760 the face of England's strip of land was changed. A wilderness was transformed into a live, active, growing country of one and a half million people. Here were farms, towns, cities; Indian trails had become roads, and the ocean and rivers were no longer the only highways between settlements. Though nine tenths of the people were farmers, home industries had always been carried on, and now manufacturing on a larger scale was beginning. Ships, their holds bursting with the raw materials of a new country, left for ports in every sea; already the thirteen colo-

PETER KETELTAS

HAS *just imported from* Briftol, *in the Snow* York, *which he will fell for ready Money or fhort Credit, Striped Blankets, fpotted Rugs, red and blue duffils,* Glocefter CHEESE, *writing Paper, fhort and long Pipes, Felt Hats, and* Taunton ALE *in Bottles :* He has alfo to fell, Cable Yarn, *two Cables, of* 8 *and* nine *Inches,* 80 *Fathoms each;* and a SHROUD HAWSER, &c.

TO BE SEEN, at the Houfe of John Dowers, at the Sign of the Ship-a-Mafting, at the Upper-End of Moravian-Street, near the Back of Spring-Garden ; A wild Animal (lately brought from the Miffiffippi) called,

A BUFFALO.

It will be expofed to Sight from Ten in the Morning 'till Noon, and from Two till Six.----Price, only SIX-PENCE.

ALL *Perfons that have any Demands on the Prize Ship the* Marfhal de Richlieu, *lately brought into this Port by the Privateer Sloop* Harlequin, *are defired to bring in their Accounts ; and thofe who have bought Goods at Vendue out of the faid Ship, are defired to make fpeedy Payment to* Peter Keteltas.-----*On Thurfday the* 22d *Inftant, will be fold at publick Vendue, at the* Merchant's-Coffee-Houfe, *the faid Prize Ship* Marfhal de Richlieu, *with all her Tackle and Apparel, as per Inventory, to be feen at the faid Coffee-Houfe.*

TO BE SOLD,

SIXTEEN hundred Acres of very good Land, laid out in two hundred Acre Lots, laying in *Dutchefs County,* Rumbout Precinct, the fartheft Lot not above three Miles from the Water Side, where is a very good Landing ; and about three Miles alfo, from a Dutch and Prefbyterian Meeting-Houfe : Any Perfon inclining to purchafe the Whole or any Part thereof, by applying to *LAWRENCE LAWRENCE,* at Stony-Creek-Mill, in *Rumbout Precinct,* may know the Conditions of Sale.

RUN-*away about the* 7th *or* 8th *of this Inftant* December, *from the Subfcriber, the three following Servant Men, viz.* Richard Welch, *by Trade a Tanner, about* 45 *Years old, and of a dark Complexion :* John Douglafs, 23 *Years old, and a Wheel-wright by Trade :* And Patrick Machree, *a Labourer. They are Strangers in the Country. Whoever takes up and fecures the above run-aways, fhall have* THREE POUNDS *Reward, or* TWENTY SHILLINGS *for each, and all reafonable Charges, paid by* ROBERT ALEXANDER.

For BRISTOL,
The Brigantine ULYSSES,
JAMES FAIRLIE, Mafter.
Has three Fourths of her Cargo engaged ; For Freight or Paffage apply to ANTHONY SARLY, or faid Mafter.

FROM N. Y. *Mercury,* DEC. 19, 1757

nies were carrying on more foreign trade than some of the old countries of Europe.

But it had not been easy. The Englishmen, Dutchmen, Scotch-Irish, Frenchman, Germans, and Swedes had finally conquered—but at a terrific price. Many who braved the awful journey never lived to see the New World; many others came and saw—and died.

The Europeans came and molded the strip, to some degree, into something they had been used to; but in great measure the nature of the strip determined the molding, and while they were doing something to the country, the country was doing something to them —Europeans were being changed into a new people—Americans!

Are All Men Equal?

Today in the United States if your rich neighbor buys a Cadillac and you want to do the same, there is nothing to stop you—if you have the money. But in colonial America you might have liked the gold and silver girdle your neighbor wore, or his colorful hatband, or his embroidered cap; you might have saved and saved until finally you had enough money to buy one or all of these things—but you dared not wear them—unless you belonged to the right class. In Massachusetts in 1653 two women were arrested for wearing silk hoods and scarfs, but because their husbands were worth two hundred pounds ($1,000) each they were allowed to go free. But woe betide the luckless poor person who dared to wear silk!

Throughout all the colonies you did or did not have certain rights according to your rank or the amount of property you owned. You did or did not do certain things according to your rank or the amount of property you owned. Rank and wealth. These had some bearing on almost everything you did at any time.

If you went to Harvard College you didn't just take any seat in the classrooms. Nor were you placed according to where your name appeared in the alphabet. Oh no. Not in colonial America. A seat was assigned you according to your rank or property.

Even in church the same arrangement was made. Seats were given out on the usual basis, best seats for those with most money, next best seats for those with some money, and poorest seats for those with little or no money. Occasionally, some of the best seats were separated from the others by a neat handmade balustrade so there would be no contact with the vulgar.

Were two persons found guilty of stealing something together? Then you would expect that both would be publicly whipped, since that was the usual punishment. Well, they might or might not be, depending upon what their rank was. Thus "in 1631, when Mr. Josias Plaistowe was convicted of stealing corn from the Indians, the court merely imposed a fine and directed that thenceforth he should be called by the name of Josias, and not Mr. as formerlie! On the other hand, his servants who had assisted in the theft were severely flogged."

Except in the poll tax states of the South today, you have the right to vote if you are a citizen with the proper age qualification. In colonial America, however, you had to be white, you had to be a man, in many communities you had to belong to a certain religious group, and you had to own so much property or have so much land. For a long time in many of the settlements there were many more people who were not allowed to vote than who were. And of course to be elected to any office in the government, to help make the laws or see that they were carried out, you had to own even more property than you needed in order to vote.

At one time in the Massachusetts Bay settlement the people who made the laws thought that workmen's wages were too high. So they passed a law fixing a certain amount which was to be the highest any employer might pay his workmen. If an employer paid more than this fixed sum or a workman took more than this fixed sum, both were to be fined five shillings. Fair enough. But the next year the court changed the law so that only the workman who took more was to be fined, the employer who paid more received no punishment.

To understand how all these things happened you must have a bird's-eye view of the people who lived in the colonies. At the top of the heap were the royal governors and their official friends, sent over by the King of England to help the colonists manage their affairs; rich merchants, rich plantation-owners, holders of large estates—these, too, helped the colonists to manage their affairs. These were the upper classes, the people who signed "Gentleman" after their names or Mr. before it. Some of them had come to the colonies with money; some of them had worked hard and had risen to the top; some of them were just lucky; some of them were friends of the governor and so got huge tracts of land for very little, or even as a favor; at any rate, no matter how they had attained that position, they were now the ruling class. These people wore the finest clothing, latest fashions imported from England; they lived in the finest houses; they had freedmen, or indentured servants, or Negro slaves working for them in one way or another; these were the people who had most of the money; these were the people who had the respect of most of the colonists because of their rank or their money; these were the people who had the power that rank and money gave; these were the people who voted, got themselves elected to high positions in the government, and ran it according to their own ideas of what was best for all the colonists; these were the people who made the laws.

The people called yeomen in old Merrie England had emigrated here and were next in rank to the upper classes. These yeomen in America were the small farmers who formed the largest group in the colonies. They were the people who did most of the hard work; they were the people who in the North sailed ships all over the world, caught fish in near-by waters, and tracked the whale in far-off seas; they were the people who did the fighting, later, when there was fighting to be done; these people, because they did own farms, had the right to vote; sometimes they used that vote to fight against the class of merchants and planters above them; these people were hard working, ambitious, and anxious to raise themselves to the group above.

Next came the free laborers, both skilled and unskilled. The skilled worker was sometimes able to save up enough money to buy a bit of property. This meant that he would be allowed to vote and in general better himself. But until they owned some property these free blacksmiths, carpenters, tailors, ropemakers, and those unfortunates without a trade had two groups above them, and so were quite far down in the social scale.

Beneath them were the indentured servants. Their happiness during their term of service depended on the type of master they had. Some were fortunate in getting kind masters who didn't work them too hard and perhaps even helped them get a good start when their term was over. But from the great number of advertisements for runaway servants that appeared in the newspapers we are led to believe that indentured servants had a very hard time. The master might whip them whenever he liked; he might give them the shabbiest clothes and the poorest kind of food; he could say whether or not they might be married; while they were in his service they were no better than slaves. Some servants were even branded by their masters. If they ran away and were caught they might have to serve five days for every one they had been gone—this in addition to a terrible beating. Some of the indentured servants worked very hard,

THE COLONIAL SOCIAL LADDER

were fortunate, and went step by step up the scale until they became wealthy landowners. But the majority of them had no such luck. At the end of their terms they were given a suit of clothes, some corn, and a few tools. They faced a hard life. Most of them left for the back country where land was cheap. Many of their descendants are today in the hills in the South, living miserable, poor, ignorant lives, just managing to keep from starving. They live on what they

raise, shoot, or steal. They might have been better off if Negro slavery in the South had not made it a disgrace for white people to do field work. These people are today called "poor whites" and "hillbillies."

The Negro slaves at the bottom of the scale had very little chance to better themselves. They were slaves for life, and even in those few cases where they were set free, nevertheless, their black skins kept them from ever rising far. With them, as with the indentured servants, everything depended on the type of master they had; a kind master might mean a good comfortable home without much worry, which was more than many poor whites could look forward to. A cruel master might mean horrible punishment, a wretched life, and a miserable death.

But wasn't this division into classes the same sort of thing that many of these people objected to in the Old World? Yes, it was a system modeled after that in Europe. The idea that a small group of rich people, the aristocracy, should run the government and make the laws had long been in practice there. It was true that the distinctions were not as sharp, that here in the colonies you could rise from one class to another more quickly than you could in Europe. That was a very important difference, but, nevertheless, until you climbed to the top of the heap yourself, you were ruled from above. The wealthy upper classes made the laws so it's easy to see why those laws favored the rich.

Did no one challenge the right of the rich to manage things? The small farmers who had the right to vote sometimes did. But the real challenge came from the frontier. The frontiersmen demanded a say in running things. They demanded the right to help make the laws for themselves. The American idea of all men being equal first came from the frontier. This idea had been talked of in Europe before, but it was first put into practice in America. It was a very, very important notion which later affected the whole world.

Where the last settlement ended and the wilderness began, where the edge of civilization met the beginning of savagery, this was the frontier line. Here at the farthest clearing, land was either free or very cheap. Here where the wilderness came right up to your door you could start life all over again.

And that is what happened. To the frontier line came the dissatisfied, the indentured servants, the adventure-lovers, the ambitious who saw no chance to rise in the older settlement. To the frontier, too, came the newer immigrants, hungry for a piece of land of their own. In the older settlements land was expensive and the best land had already been taken up, but here at the farthest edge on the frontier line, good cheap land was obtainable. Thousands of newly arrived Germans and Scotch-Irish went into the back country of Pennsylvania, down the valley into the neighboring colonies of Virginia, Maryland, and the Carolinas. On February 15, 1751, Gabriel Johnston, Governor of North Carolina, wrote to the secretary of the Board of Trade, "Inhabitants flock in here daily, mostly from Pennsylvania and other parts of America, who are overstocked with people and some directly from Europe, they commonly seat themselves towards the West, and have got near the mountains."

Massachusetts men moved to the back country of New York or Connecticut, and Connecticut men moved into Pennsylvania. America was on the move. Restless, roving men took their whole families and moved west to the frontier. It was a "promised land" for the oppressed, the downtrodden, the poor. Land—that was the key to independence and wealth. These people were land hungry.

As more and more people came, the frontier line kept moving westward. The Indian found the line creeping up on him, pushing him farther and farther back. The fur trader left the edge of the settlements and followed the Indian trails to the wilderness. The white hunter and trapper did the same. With these people the Indian had no quarrel except when they cheated him in a trade—which they often did. They carried on the same work he did; they did not destroy his home. But as the edge of the farming settlements moved on and on, the Indian saw his trees cut down and his wilderness home replaced by the white man's clearing. This had been going on long enough for him to understand that farming and hunting could not go on in the same place together, that as the white farmer moved in, he, the hunter, had to move out. The Indian knew this and fought every step of the settlers' advance.

The frontier line was bloodstained. The stockades around the houses in the older settlements could fall into ruins (by 1760 there were many people in the coast towns who had never even seen an Indian), but on the frontier the palisades with their loopholes shoulder high for the rifles, were in constant use. The rifle of the frontiersman was always within easy reach. His wife and children, both boys and girls, must not stray too far from the house; they must learn very early to pay attention to slight noises. No matter what they were doing—building or planting or playing—their ears must be ever alert. Indian attacks were sudden, still, and swift, and the penalty for carelessness or unpreparedness was a horrible death.

Life at the frontier was dangerous and hard. There were none of the soft refinements of civilization. It was life in the raw, fighting savages, chopping down trees, planting corn, making furniture—work, hard work and lots of it. This pioneer life made you tough, if you lived. Only the strongest did live. And here there could be no class rule—one man was as good as another. Rich man and poor man

FRONTIERSMAN

were on the same terms. Here a man was successful according to what he himself did, not for what his father or grandfather was. The frontiersman faced hard work all the time; he had to tackle and conquer difficult obstacles at every turn. He succeeded, and carried his head high. He grew independent. The frontiersman heartily believed that "a fool can put on his own coat better than a wise man can do it for him." Having mastered the wilderness, the frontiersman was not now ready to take orders from any upper class. He would be his own boss.

So it was the frontiersman who led in the fierce struggle against rule by a few. There were many such fights. The upper classes, so long the rulers of the old settlements, now used to it, and liking it, were not ready to give up their power. Allow these rough, uneducated, coarse people, who dressed and lived like savages, to question their authority? Absurd! They would teach these vulgar, unrefined upstarts to respect their betters. The rich merchants and landowners of the coast would never turn over their lawmaking power to uncouth backwoodsmen unless they were forced to do so.

There were different local reasons for the many quarrels in the several colonies, but the opposing sides in all of them were practically the same—the upper classes of the older coast settlements in the East against the struggling frontiersmen in the growing West. High taxes, unjust taxes, trouble over ownership of the land, sometimes these were the causes. Often bitter feeling would arise because the West felt that the East was not sending enough soldiers to help fight the Indians. In other places the West demanded the right to send more of its own people to take part in making the laws. In Pennsylvania, although the coast section had less than half the people, nevertheless, it elected twenty-four of the thirty-six lawmakers—two thirds of the whole number.

Occasionally, the angry backwoodsmen banded together and marched on the coast towns with their rifles in their hands, demanding with guns the satisfaction they could not get with words. This happened in 1676, when Nathaniel Bacon led the frontiersmen of Virginia in an attack on Governor Berkeley at Jamestown. Here and there other armed attacks occurred. The rich merchants and landowners saw their Old World idea of upper-class rule of the few challenged by the American frontiersmen with their New World idea of the equality of man. It was a long, hard, bitterly fought contest which has not been settled even yet.

The march to the West continued. Hunger for land brought new settlers, and desire for better land brought old settlers. By 1750 the English had advanced as far as the Appalachian Mountains. Their

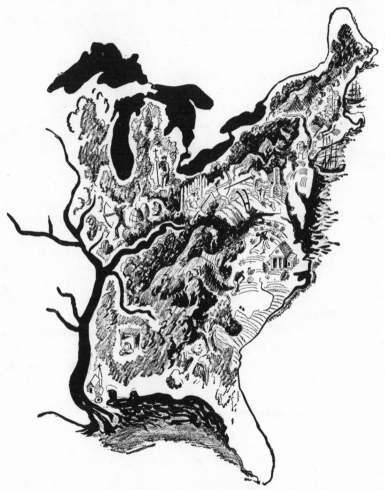

EAST AND WEST IN 1760

hunters had already crossed over to the other side and reported that the land was good. The frontier line was still moving. Before long the mountains would be crossed and settlements begun in the valley beyond. But now the Indians found help in attempting to stop these moving English. On the other side of the mountains, over the whole Mississippi Valley, from Canada to New Orleans, French fur traders and missionaries had been roaming for more than a hundred years. Several French forts had already been erected in the valley even before the first Jamestown settlers came over. And now the English were threatening to move over into this territory claimed by the French.

England and France had long been enemies. This was not their first fight, nor was it to be their last. They had fought in Europe and in Asia. They had been competing for the Indian fur trade in America for many years. Because the French were fur traders like themselves, because the French lived with the Indians, married among them and learned their habits, the Indians sided with them against the English—all but one tribe, and that was the most powerful, the Iroquois in New York. One Frenchman, Duquesne, said to these strong warriors, "Are you ignorant of the difference between the king of England and the king of France? Go see the forts that our king has established and you will see that you can still hunt under their very walls. They have been placed for your advantage in places which you frequent. The English, on the contrary, are no sooner in possession of a place than the game is driven away. The forest falls before them as they advance and the soil is laid bare, so that you can scarce find the wherewithal to erect a shelter for the night." All this was true, since the French were mainly traders and hunters. They had very few large farming settlements like those of the English. But the Iroquois would not go over to the French side. They had never forgiven the French for the time, many years ago, when Champlain, a Frenchman, helped their enemies, the Hurons, in a fight against the Iroquois. Then, too, Sir William Johnson, the Indian agent appointed to look after the affairs of the Six Nations, understood the Iroquois and knew how to handle them so they would be friendly. So these fierce, powerful Indians helped the English settlers and the British soldiers sent by the King of England, in their Seven Years' War against the French hunters, the French soldiers, and their Indian allies of other tribes.

In 1763 the war was over. France surrendered, England took from her all of Canada and all of the land from the Appalachians to the Mississippi except New Orleans at its mouth. Now the frontiersmen got ready to go over into the land for which they had just been fighting.

The frontier was to be moved still farther west. The rich fertile valley on the other side of the mountain was theirs for the taking.

Then, like a thunderbolt, came the Proclamation Act of 1763 from His Majesty the King of England, forbidding them to go into the territory they had just won. The frontiersmen were stunned.

CHAPTER IV

Molasses and Tea

★————————————————————————————————————★

And well they might be. They had fought against the Indians all their lives; they had seen their friends and relatives shot down by these same Indians; they had just fought a war for seven long years so that they might move beyond the mountains and take a piece of the fertile land there; and now they were told that the fertile land was not open to them, that it was to be reserved for the very same Indians who had always been their bitterest enemies.

The fur traders, too, were hit by the law. They had been carrying on a profitable business with the Indians, and now they were told that they could no longer trade without a license, that their business had to be done at a military post where it could be supervised.

Land speculators, also, were injured by the Proclamation. They had formed great land companies which had managed to acquire many acres of land beyond the mountains, hoping to sell it when more people moved there and the price went up. Now came the law which forbade the granting of lands or the making of settlements beyond the mountains. It is easy to see why land speculators, fur traders, and new settlers were very much disturbed by the Proclamation of 1763 which was signed by the King of England.

But what had the King of England to do with the frontiersmen, the Indians, and the western lands of a country three thousand miles from London?

All the settlements on the strip along the coast, beginning with Jamestown in 1607 had been made on land claimed by England. (The Dutch had claimed and settled New York, but in 1664 it was taken from them by the English.) Massachusetts, Virginia, Pennsylvania, New Jersey, all of them right through the thirteen, were "colonies" of England. That little island just off the western coast of Europe had built up a very strong navy and was making conquests

48

everywhere. All over the world the power of England was beginning to be felt. Islands in the West Indies, Gibraltar in Europe, parts of India in Asia, these, too, were colonies of the mother country, England. The British Empire in the 1700's was already a world-wide organization.

But why did England engage in war after war with other countries in order to get more and more colonies? Of what value were colonies to her? What was the advantage in building a bigger and bigger empire?

It was believed at that time by many people that countries were rich or poor according to the amount of gold and silver they had. One way of acquiring bullion was to be lucky enough to find new lands inhabited by Indians who knew where the mines were and who could be persuaded, by force if necessary, to give up what they had found. The Spaniards had tried that in South America with great success. But even the Indians couldn't locate mines every day, so a better, surer method had to be found. The answer to the problem seemed to lie in selling goods. So long as a country sold things, money would flow in. But England was not the only country that had figured that out. Spain, Holland, and France had thought of the same thing, and naturally all of them wanted to sell, sell, sell. But if all of them were interested only in selling, the scheme wouldn't work. Some market had to be found. The answer was more and more colonies. Let the mother country be the heart of the Empire and let every colony be a market for its goods.

Colonies could serve another purpose also. There were some things every mother country had to buy. It would be sad if any gold left the mother country in payment for these purchased goods. But if the colonies could furnish the raw materials that the mother country needed, then the gold need never leave the Empire, to make a rival mother country rich. The trick, then, was to build up a strong empire of mother country and colonies, an empire which was self-sufficient, one that did not have to depend on outside countries for anything. It might look like a wheel in which the hub is the mother country, whose business it is to make things which are to go to the colonies on the rim of the wheel. They in turn produce raw materials which they send to the mother country. The spokes of the wheel would be the trade routes lined with boats carrying goods to and from mother country and colonies.

A beautiful scheme with a very plain purpose—to make the

mother country rich. But, as you can readily see, the plan would work *only if the trade of the colonies were under the control of the mother country.* That was very important.

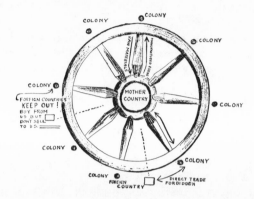

In the seventeenth and eighteenth centuries the English Parliament was made up of rich landowners, merchants, and manufacturers. Of course they believed in the mother-country colony scheme outlined above. One of their committees, the Lords Commissioners for Trade and Plantations, had reported that "the great object of colonization upon the continent of N.A. has been to improve and extend the commerce and manufactures of this kingdom." This the Parliament believed very strongly. Accordingly, in the 156 years from 1607 to 1763 it had passed a series of laws which were meant to control the trade of the colonies to the advantage of the mother country.

One set of laws provided that all goods (with a few exceptions) that were sent to the colonies from Europe or Asia had to be sent to England first, then be reshipped. This would prevent direct trade between the colonies and foreign countries.

Holland cloth . . . → to England . . . → to America
instead of Holland cloth . . . → directly . . . . . → to America

In like manner certain colonial products, such as tobacco, rice, indigo, masts, turpentine, tar, pitch, beaver skins, pig iron, and a few others (the list increased with time) had to be sent to England only. Other products might be sent anywhere. The English wanted these things for themselves, but they could not possibly use the whole amount that was produced in the colonies. Nevertheless, they wanted to have their hands on this colonial commerce, and, if possible, enter into it and thus make a profit.

Virginia tobacco → to Eng. merchant → to Fr. snuff manufacturer
instead of
Virginia tobacco → directly . . . . . → to Fr. snuff manufacturer

Some of the islands in the West Indies belonged to France and some belonged to England. The French islands were able to produce sugar and molasses more cheaply than the British islands. The commercial colonies on the North American strip did a great deal of business with the islands in the West Indies. Molasses was particularly important to them because they used it in the making of rum. Rum, in turn, was used in the slave trade, in the fur trade, and in the fishing business. (It was customary at the time for seamen to get a daily allowance of rum.) Naturally, the New England and Middle Colonies' ships traded with those islands where they could buy molasses cheapest. But according to the Empire idea they should have been trading with the British islands. Accordingly, in 1733, Parliament passed the "Molasses Act," which provided that heavy duties had to be paid on all foreign sugar and molasses imported into the colonies. (Incidentally, seventy-four members of Parliament at the time were owners of plantations in the British West Indies.)

French molasses—cheaper than British molasses→to New Englander,
but French molasses + heavy tax becomes dearer than British molasses
to New Englander

The colonists were forbidden to manufacture caps, hats, woolen, or iron goods. All the raw materials for these things were on hand in America; yet the colonists were expected to send these raw materials to England to be manufactured, then buy them back in the form of manufactured goods. English manufacturers interested in making things did not mean to have competition from their own colonies.

Colonial raw materials . . . → to England, manufactured
there . . . → sent back to America
instead of Colonial raw materials . . . → manufactured in America

To make sure that Empire trade was handled by Empire boats, another set of laws, the Navigation Acts, passed as early as 1651, provided that all goods to and from the colonies had to be carried in English or colonial ships manned mainly by English or colonial sailors. The Dutch, who were very busy rivals of England in the carrying trade, were thus cut out of any Empire business.

French ships . . . → **|** Empire wall—Keep out!
Dutch ships . . →

If you examine these laws you can readily see how careful Parliament was that a strong trading empire be built up—with the mother country, England, well taken care of. Sir Francis Bernard, the royal governor to Massachusetts, outlined the whole scheme very clearly in this way: "The two great objects of Great Britain in regard to the American trade must be (1) to oblige her American subjects to take from Great Britain only, all the manufactures and European goods which she can supply them with. (2) To regulate the foreign trade of the Americans so that *the profits thereof may finally center in Great Britain,* or be applied to the improvement of her empire."

It all looked very rosy—for the mother country. Unfortunately, however, the colonists were not quite so unselfish as to think that the colonies existed merely for the sake of the mother country but stubbornly held that the colonies existed for the sake of the colonists.

The people in the colonies had not crossed three thousand miles of ocean in order to help build up an empire. They had not fought with savage Indians, suffered from want of food, worked long and hard to build homes, so that people in England should benefit. That had never occurred to them. They had come over here because they wanted to help themselves in one way or another. Then why hadn't England and the colonists clashed during the years from 1607 to 1763? Both peoples disagreed on the very reason for the existence of the colonies, yet things had not come to a head until 1763. Why?

Because laws passed are not necessarily laws obeyed. Some of the trade laws passed by Parliament benefited the colonists. These laws they obeyed. Other trade laws hurt their pocketbooks. Those laws they obeyed only in part or disregarded entirely. (Americans today follow in the path of their colonist forefathers. They continue to disregard unpopular laws. It's an old American custom.)

The law that forced Empire goods to be carried in English or colonial boats benefited the colonists. It enabled them to build ships and carry goods without having to compete with the ships of foreign countries which had had a start on them. Of course it also helped to build up a strong British navy. But the colonists needed the protection of a strong navy. In those days the ocean wasn't the peaceful highway that it is today. Even in peace time colonial boats might be seized by Spanish or French privateers or by the many pirate boats that infested the seas. That meant not only that the boat and its cargo would be stolen, but also that the sailors might be killed or made slaves. The Barbary pirates, on the Mediterranean south of Europe, were particularly dangerous. The British Navy, however, had battled with these pirates and had forced them (with the aid of presents to the pirates amounting to about $300,000 every year) to agree to let British Empire boats alone. Colonial vessels engaged in sending wheat and flour and fish to ports in the Mediterranean were given passes by the British Admiralty. Ships that had these passes were allowed to go untouched by the pirates. The eighty to one hundred ships that did business regularly in the Mediterranean had to have this protection or they could not have carried on.

Then, too, every time the British Navy was successful in a new conquest and more colonies were added, that meant more places where colonial boats might trade without competition from outsiders. For these benefits the colonists were, of course, very grateful. Laws that helped them in this way were laws to be obeyed.

The heavy tax on sugar and molasses imported from the foreign West Indies was a different matter entirely. Colonial merchants paid from 25 to 40 per cent less for French molasses than for British. The tax would force them to buy the higher priced product. There was a way out of the difficulty and many colonial merchants took it.

Smuggling. Some of the leading merchants in the colonies (as in England) became smugglers. More than one colonial fortune depended upon this forbidden trade. Because so many men were bringing in the foreign molasses without paying the duty, smuggling was not considered wrong. "Of the 14,000 hogsheads of molasses imported into Rhode Island each year, 11,500 came from the foreign West Indies paying no duty. Of the 15,000 hogsheads imported into Massachusetts in 1763 all but 500 came from the foreign islands."

Smuggling was easy. The colonies were three thousand miles from England; their coast line was long and irregular; British officials were very easygoing; the customhouse officers whose business it was to keep an eye open for smugglers either kept that eye closed or opened it just wide enough to see a present for themselves.

The colonists did not take into account what would help the British Empire to grow or what would make English merchants or British West Indian plantation owners rich. They were interested

SMUGGLERS

in becoming rich themselves. If they could make a living by obeying
Empire laws, well and good. If, in order to make a living, Empire
laws had to be broken, well—it was better that holes be put into
English laws than into American pocketbooks.

If profits could be made by trading with the French islands in
time of peace, then even more money could be made in time of war,
and the northern merchants seized the opportunity. While the British Empire was engaged in a death struggle against the French in the
Seven Years' War, while colonial soldiers were fighting side by side
with British soldiers against the French and Indians, colonial ships
were hurrying to the French islands with provisions that were
sorely needed by the French. During a war it is customary for the
fighting sides to exchange prisoners. Colonial vessels obtained passes
from the governors of the colonies, giving them the right to go to
the French colonies for an exchange of prisoners. Oftentimes these
"flags of truce" (the popular name for such boats) would carry a
few French prisoners and a great quantity of provisions. The British
Navy was trying to starve out the French, yet colonial boats went
right through their blockade with food for the enemy. James Hamilton, Governor of Pennsylvania, wrote that in 1759 and 1760 "a very
great part of the principal merchants of Philadelphia were engaged
in this trade with the French West Indies." The Seven Years' War
might have been a five years' war if the colonists hadn't helped to
feed the enemy.

For people who had the British Empire at heart, France was the
enemy in India, Europe, North America, or the West Indies. For
the colonists, however, France in Canada and west of the Appalachian Mountains was a bitter enemy and they would help to crush her;
but France in the West Indies was a place where profitable trading
might go on. The colonists did not have the British Empire at heart.
They did not think of themselves as Englishmen, nor even as Americans. A colonist thought of himself as a Virginian or a New Yorker
or a Massachusetts man. The colonies were not one country; they
were thirteen countries. They were jealous of one another and were
having disputes all the time.

Sometimes they would quarrel over boundaries, sometimes over
competition in business. Whenever the mother country asked them
to do something, they would very often pass the buck to the other
colonies. Each colony would wait to see how much the others were
doing, and all of them tried to do as little as the slowest. It was

very difficult to get them to act together even in the face of the common enemy, the French or the Indians. Thus in the fall of 1763 there was a serious uprising by the Indians led by the Indian chief Pontiac. Amherst, the commander-in-chief of the British armies here, asked New York, New Jersey, Pennsylvania, and Virginia to furnish troops. New York said we'll do our share only if you ask New England to help. New Jersey followed New York's example. Because not enough soldiers were supplied, Gage, who was the commander-in-chief after Amherst, finally did ask the New England colonies to help. Massachusetts refused, not being willing to take orders from New York. New Hampshire refused because Connecticut and Massachusetts had not done their share. Rhode Island refused. Finally Connecticut agreed to raise a small body of soldiers. Virginia did its share. New York raised a little over one half of the troops desired, and New Jersey agreed to furnish three hundred instead of the six hundred asked. Meanwhile the fight against Pontiac was going on.

The British army commanders were enraged that they had to plead with the colonists to supply soldiers, instead of being able to force them to do so. But the colonists would not take orders easily. They had had a good deal of practice in quarreling with the British in their many disputes with the royal governors. Though the British Parliament passed trade laws dealing with its North American possessions, most of the other laws that governed the different colonies were made by the colonists themselves. Every colony elected its own group of lawmakers. In addition, for all the colonies but Rhode Island and Connecticut, a royal governor was appointed by the king to help make the laws. There were many quarrels between the colonists' lawmakers and the royal governor. They thought first of the colonists, and he thought first of England and the Empire. The colonists wanted this, the royal governor said no. The royal governor wanted that, the colonists said no. In most cases the colonists won their point, primarily because they paid the royal governor his salary. If he did not behave, his money was held up or his salary was reduced. The colonists held the whip hand. They drifted into the habit of having their own way. These quarrels with the royal governors who represented the British Government in America gave the colonists practice in standing up for what they thought were their rights.

From 1607 to 1763 these thirteen jealous colonies fought thirteen separate quarrels with the mother country. But the argument in each case was the same. Every twenty years the colonies doubled their populations. Colonial trading and farming were growing tremendously. The colonists wanted to expand—and everywhere ran into British control, whose purpose was the good of the mother country or the Empire. Because they were three thousand miles away from England; because in many cases they had come to America to get away from European customs or laws that annoyed them or kept them from making a decent living; because, once here, they had learned to take care of themselves in spite of attempts by royal governors to meddle; because they had grown used to breaking Empire laws that displeased them—because of all these things the colonists had been growing more and more independent. While England thought the colonies existed for her sake, the colonies felt that they existed for their own sakes.

Nevertheless, up to 1763 they had been content to remain part of the Empire. Up to that time very few colonists had thought of breaking away from England. Yet on July 4, 1776, thirteen years later, America said in effect: We no longer will belong to your Empire. We are going to govern ourselves. What had happened?

For seven years England had been fighting a fierce war with the French. The end of the war increased the size of her Empire tremendously. More islands in the West Indies, all the land from the Appalachians to the Mississippi (except New Orleans at its mouth), the whole of Canada, these were the huge additions to her American colonies. It was all very impressive, but it would need a great deal of attention. This new territory had to be cared for, and that would cost a great deal of money. British taxpayers were already complaining about the high cost of England's many wars, so something had to be done about it. Something had to be done about the smuggling that went on in the colonies also. And something had to be done about keeping the Indians quiet and satisfied so that their fur trade would not be given to the French, with whom they were friends. It seemed very clear to the members of Parliament that England's hold on her American colonies was much too loose, that the tie with the Empire had to be tightened.

The Indians had been alarmed at the movement west by the colonists. Excited by the French, they were on the warpath all the time. The colonial fur traders were in many cases a dishonest band of knaves who were not satisfied with the profits they could make honestly. They used rum to make the Indians drunk and then cheated them. The fur trade was important to the English, and so they wanted to keep the Indians contented. Besides, it was just as well not to allow the colonists to move too far away from the coast where they would be out of reach of the British Government. Furthermore, if profits were to be made on western lands when prices went up, Englishmen wanted to have a big share.

The Proclamation of 1763 was the answer to all this. Parliament did not intend to prevent the colonists from moving over the mountains forever; the plan was to make peace with the Indians until the fur trade could be controlled. In a few years moving west might be permitted again. But the Proclamation did not state this and the western settlers, colonial fur traders, and members of land companies were impatient. The Proclamation made them feel that they had been cheated. They were in a rage against the English.

While the Seven Years' War was going on, business in the colonies was excellent. The French, sorely needing provisions, were willing to pay high prices for them; the British Army in America meant so many more mouths to be fed. As a result American farmers and planters increased the size of their farms and sold everything they raised at a great increase in price. Shopkeepers, selling their goods at high profits, increased their stocks. Merchant ships did a huge business. Many people gathered tremendous fortunes overnight. Money was easy to get and people grew accustomed to living in better style than ever before. But, as always happens, this wartime, make-believe prosperity did not last. When the war ended in 1763 the crash came. The army was disbanded, the French suddenly stopped buying, and prices fell. Merchants, farmers, and shopkeepers found themselves oversupplied with goods, with prices shooting downward. Workmen were thrown out of work. Times were very bad. It was just the right moment to move west and start life all over again. But here was the Proclamation, that hated English law. Of course, many people went in spite of it—it was too powerful a movement to be stopped by any law—but the colonists were angry just the same.

Even after the war the British were afraid that the eighty five thousand defeated French might again make trouble. They knew that the Indians would. It was useless, they felt, to depend on the colonies for an army. They were tired of fighting colonial wars while the colonists were passing the buck instead of doing their best to help. Forts would be needed in the West and a regular army of at least ten thousand soldiers was necessary. Since the war had been fought partly to help the colonists, it was only fair, thought Parliament, that the colonists should help to pay the heavy expenses of that war. And, since the new standing army and the forts were to be used for colonial protection, it was only fair that the colonists should help pay for them also.

So Parliament went ahead with its plans for raising money and for putting a complete stop to colonial smuggling. In 1764 the "Sugar Act" was passed. It was the old "Molasses Act" dressed up in new clothing. The tax on French molasses, formerly sixpence per gallon, was reduced to threepence. Duties were put on other imports such as silks, coffee, and wine. The money raised was to go toward paying the expenses of the new army in America. There was to be *no more smuggling*. The British Navy was to patrol the American coast and seize all ships that broke the law. Customs officers were no longer allowed to stay in England while some hired person did their work for them in America. Royal governors were ordered to do their full duty. Anybody who helped to catch the smugglers would receive a share of the captured goods. Informers were to be given rewards. Parliament meant business. This new law had teeth in it.

But that was not all. In 1765 the British government passed the Stamp Act in order to raise money to help pay the expenses of the troops in America. It provided that all cards, dice, pamphlets, newspapers, advertisements, college diplomas, almanacs, marriage licenses, and many legal papers were to have stamps stuck on them.

Although this form of taxation is now taken for granted in the United States (the government's blue stamp on the top of bottles of liquor and packages of cigarettes and playing cards is familiar to all of us), it met with great resistance in the colonies in 1765. In England the Stamp Act had been a law for several years. People had grown into the habit of using stamps without making any fuss. If stamps were all right in England, thought the members of Parliament, why not in her colonies—particularly since the money collected was to be spent for the colonies. But the members of Parliament were mistaken—stamps were not all right in America in 1765.

Proclamation Act in 1763. Sugar Act in 1764. Stamp Act in 1765. Hard times in the colonies.

The stage was set for trouble, and it was not long in coming.

The quarrel between the frontiersmen and the upper classes had not stopped. The workers in the towns had begun to join in this fight for more power. The rich merchants and planters still ran the governments in all the colonies, but the poorer classes everywhere were beginning to question their right to rule.

Now an interesting thing happened. The rich merchants in the commercial colonies were greatly annoyed by the British navy boats ever on the watch to prevent smuggling. Since many of them had their whole fortunes tied up in the foreign West Indies trade, this new watchfulness of the Navy was a terrific blow to their business. Makers of rum were also hit by the blow at the smugglers. Some merchants and rummakers lost all their money, and others felt they would lose theirs also unless something was done about the hated Sugar Act.

The passage of the Stamp Act gave the merchants the chance which they sought. They stirred up the poorer classes into believing that England's new laws were the cause of their troubles. Lawyers, hit by the Stamp Act, made exciting speeches about the "rights of Englishmen." Editors of newspapers, also hit by the Stamp Act, wrote long pieces in their papers against England's "unjust laws." The common people, down and out most of the time, and now thrown out of work because of the hard times, welcomed any chance to better their own conditions. They were led to believe that England was their enemy and her laws ought not to be obeyed.

The trade laws had hurt the merchants, but this new Stamp Act hurt everybody. Never before had England tried to make the colonists pay taxes directly. It was difficult to get excited about indirect taxes like duties collected at the ports, but the Stamp Act was different. Here were the hated stamps for everyone to see.

Workmen in towns formed themselves into groups called "The Sons of Liberty." They wrecked the houses of stamp agents and dumped their furniture into the gutter. They seized the stamps and piled them high in the streets, then burned them. There were riots in New York, Boston, Charleston, and other big towns. "The Sons of Liberty" were thoroughly aroused; the plain people, with characteristic courage, were translating speeches and writings into deeds.

The merchants, too, took quick action. They thought of an excellent way to force Parliament to change its mind. They had been buying English goods all the time to sell in the colonies. Now they

RADICALS OF THE 1770's

joined together in a plan not to import any more things from England. It was a clever scheme because, if they stopped buying English goods, then English manufacturers, losing all that business, would soon bring pressure on Parliament to repeal the Stamp Act.

General Thomas Gage, who was head of the British troops in America, described what happened, in a letter to Conway, one of the king's secretaries of state, written December 21, 1765, from New York.

> The Plan of the People of Property has been to raise the lower Classes to prevent the Execution of the Law . . . with the view to terrify and frighten the people of England into a Repeal of the Act. And the Merchants having Countermanded the Goods they had written for unless it was repealed, they make no Doubt that many Trading Towns and principal Merchants in London will assist them to accomplish their Ends.
>
> The Lawyers are the Source from whence the Clamors have flowed in every Province. In this Province nothing Publick is transacted without them, and it is to be wished that even the Bench was free from Blame. The whole Body of Merchants in general, Assembly Men, Magistrates, etc., have been united in this Plan of Riots, and without the Influence and Instigation of these the inferior People would have been very quiet. Very great Pains were taken to rouse them before they Stirred. The Sailors who are the only People who may be properly Stiled Mob, are entirely at the Command of the Merchants who employ them.

The lower classes, whose major quarrel was with the wealthy, were, as Gage keenly observed, being wheedled into fighting the battle for the rich. An old, old story.

The merchants' plan of nonimportation succeeded. Household spinningwheels and looms worked overtime making clothes for the colonists so that English goods would not be bought. Colonists promised to give up the very elaborate funerals they were used to having, so that English cloth would not be needed. "Don't buy English goods!" became a popular American cry.

Business in England was bad at this time, anyway. Now, with the Americans not buying, it grew steadily worse. English merchants wrote to Parliament, begging that the laws which had made all the trouble be given up. One such letter ran, "Our trade is hurt; what the devil have you been doing? For our part we don't pretend to understand your politics and American matters, but our trade is hurt; pray remedy it, and a plague on you if you won't." Parliament saw the point. The Stamp Act was repealed in 1766.

Here is how the news was received in America:

Glorious News.

BOSTON, Friday 11 o'Clock, 16th *May* 1766.

THIS Inftant arrived here the Brig Harrifon, belonging to *John* Hancock, Efq; Captain *Shubael Coffin*, in 6 Weeks and 2 Days from LONDON, with important News, as follows.

From the LONDON GAZETTE.

Weftminfter, *March* 18th, 1766.

THIS day his Majefty came to the Houfe of Peers, and being in his royal robes feated on the throne with the ufual folemnity, Sir Francis Moli- neux, Gentleman Ufher of the Black Rod, was fent with a Meffage from his Majefty to the Houfe of Commons, commanding their atten- dance in the Houfe of Peers. The Commons being come thither accordingly, his Majefty was pleafed to give his royal affent to

An ACT to REPEAL an Act made in the laft Seffion of Parliament, in- tituled, an Act for granting and applying certain Stamp-Duties and other Duties in the Britifh Colonies and Plantations in America, towards further defraying the expences of defending, protecting and fecuring the fame, and for amending fuch parts of the feveral Acts of Parliament relating to the trade and revenues of the faid Colonies and Plantations, as direct the manner of determining and recovering the penalties and forfeitures therein mentioned.

Alfo ten public bills, and feventeen private ones.

When the KING went to the Houfe of Peers to give the Royal Affent, there was fuch a vaft Concourfe of People, huzzaing, clapping Hands, &c. that it was feveral Hours before His Majefty reached the Houfe.

Immediately on His Majefty's Signing the Royal Affent to the Repeal of the Stamp-Act, the Merchants trading to America difpatched a Veffel which had been in waiting, to put into the firft Port on the Continent with the Account.

There were the greateft Rejoicings poffible in the City of London, by all Ranks of People, on the TOTAL Repeal of the Stamp-Act,—the Ships in the River difplayed all their Colours, Illuminations and Bonfires in many Parts.— In fhort, the Rejoicings were as great as was ever known on any Occafion.

It is faid the Acts of Trade relating to America would be taken under Con- fideration, and all Grievances removed. The Friends to America are very pow- erful, and difpofed to affift us to the utmoft of their Ability.

Capt. Blake failed the fame Day with Capt. Coffin, and Capt. Shand a Fort- night before him, both bound to this Port.

It is impoffible to exprefs the Joy the Town is now in, on receiving the above, great, glorious and important NEWS—The Bells in all the Churches were immediately fet a Ringing, and we hear the Day for a general Rejoicing will be the beginning of next Week.

PRINTED for the Benefit of the PUBLIC, by *Drapers*, *Edes* & *Gill*, *Green* & *Ruffell*, and *Fleets*. The Cuftomers to the Bofton Papers may have the above gratis at their refpective Offices.

[Facsimile of an original in the library of the Mass. Hist. Society.—ED.]

REPEAL OF THE STAMP ACT

The "glorious news" was not to last. Parliament was determined to make the colonists share the expenses of the Empire in America. It was determined also to keep in the minds of the colonists the fact that it had the right to tax them. Patrick Henry, a frontiersman, who was one of the lawmakers in Virginia, had argued that only the colonists' own lawmakers, not Parliament, had the right to tax them. Other colonists said the same thing. This was so much nonsense, thought the members of Parliament.

They made a new set of laws. The duty on molasses was again lowered. The Townshend Acts, passed in 1767, laid duties on glass, lead, tea, and a few other things sent to America. This was again an indirect tax, the kind the colonists had always been used to in the past. Parliament did not expect any further trouble.

But there were some troublemaking parts to the new laws. Many British officers had been afraid to do their duty in cases against colonists who were guilty of breaking laws, because the angry people oftentimes hurt them or their property. Other British officers felt they could do nothing because the colonists paid them their salaries. One part of the new laws said that some of the money collected through the duties was to be used to pay the salaries of the royal governors and other British officials in America. The colonists immediately recognized this blow at their power. Another part provided that more customs officers and more navy boats were to be sent to America to help stop smuggling. And customs officers were given the right to break into any house, shop, or cellar, to look for and seize smuggled goods. The colonists strongly objected to this direct blow at their liberties.

The people were again aroused. Nonimportation again. More riots, more burnings, and continued smuggling. On June 10, 1768, John Hancock's sloop, *Liberty*, arrived in Boston Harbor with wine from Madeira. The officer at the port refused to allow the wine to be landed until the duties were paid. He was offered a bribe. When he refused to accept it, he was thrown into the cabin of the ship and kept there while the wine was quickly landed. A month later customs officers seized the vessel. The mob rioted, attacked the officers, and threw stones at their houses. More British soldiers were then sent to Boston.

The British were trying with all their might to stop smuggling. Benjamin Franklin wrote a paper called "Rules for Reducing a Great Empire to a Small One." With bitter sarcasm he described what England's revenue officers were doing. "Scour with armed boats every bay, harbor, river, creek, cove, or nook throughout the coast of your colonies; stop and detain every coaster, every woodboat, every fisherman; tumble their cargoes and even their ballast inside out and upside down; and if a pennyworth of pins is found unentered, let the whole be seized and confiscated."

British revenue boats were increasingly watchful, but the smuggling could not be entirely stopped. The coast line was too long and the people were actively on the side of the smugglers. In July, 1769, a mob at Newport, Rhode Island, burned the British revenue sloop, *Liberty,* because it had just captured two vessels accused of smuggling. Informers who squealed on the smugglers were oftentimes beaten up. In Boston the mob seized an informer, covered him with tar and feathers, then walked him through the busy streets; in New York three other in-

A LIST of the Names of *thofe*
who AUDACIOUSLY continue to counteract the UNIT-
ED SENTIMENTS of the BODY of Merchants thro'out
NORTH-AMERICA ; by importing Britifh Goods
contrary to the Agreement.

John Bernard,
　　(In King-Street, almoft oppofite Vernon'sHead.
James McMafters,
　　　　　(On Treat's Wharf.
Patrick McMafters,
　　　　(Oppofite the Sign of the Lamb.
John Mein,
　　(Oppofite the White-Horfe, and in King-Street.
Nathaniel Rogers,
　　(Oppofite Mr. Henderfon Inches-Store lower End
　　King-Street.
William Jackfon,
　　At the BrazenHead, Cornhill, near the Town-Houfe.
Theophilus Lillie,
　　(Near Mr. Pemberton'sMeeting-Houfe, North-End.
John Taylor,
　　(Nearly oppofite the Heart and Crown in Cornhill.
Ame & Elizabeth Cummings,
　(Oppofite the Old Brick Meeting-Houfe, all of Bofton.
Ifrael Williams, Efq; & Son,
　　　(Traders in the Town of Hatfield.
And, *Henry Barnes,*
　　　(Trader in the Town of M　ero'.

formers were also given coats of tar and feathers. The feeling of the people against informers reached down even to school children. In Boston, on Thursday morning, February 22, 1770, some schoolboys got into a quarrel with an informer named Richardson. "He retreated to his house nearby to the shrill jeers of 'Informer! Informer!' Here he was joined by his wife and a man; and the two sides pelted each other with rubbish until the better marksmanship of the children was clearly established. Then from inside the house, Richardson fired several times into the crowd, killing Christopher Snider, an eleven-year-old boy, and wounding the little son of Captain John Gore."

Think how excited the people must have been if feeling was high enough for a man to shoot at a crowd of schoolboys! The "Sons of Liberty" were active everywhere, singing songs about liberty and freedom. They made it hot for any merchants who continued to buy from England in the face of the nonimportation agreement. In Edes and Gill's *North American Almanack* for 1770 there was printed this list of the names of merchants who continued "to import British Goods contrary to the Agreement." (page 65)

More stone throwing, more tar and feathers, more wrecking of property. Many people who sided with England were afraid to get into trouble, so they kept quiet. Lieutenant Dudingston, the British commander of the revenue vessel *Gaspee* had made himself hated by both smugglers and non-smugglers because he did his duty of patrolling the coast too well. One day the *Gaspee* was chasing a colonial vessel when it ran aground on a narrow spit of land near Providence, Rhode Island. That night a band of colonists seized the crew and set the vessel on fire. The king asked some people to find out who the guilty persons were. Although at least a thousand people knew the names of those who had taken part in the affair, not a single person could be found to inform against them.

In Boston, March, 1770, only a few weeks after the shooting of Christopher Snider, five people were killed by British soldiers after a fight that started with the throwing of a few snowballs. Though the soldiers were later brought to trial and found not guilty, nevertheless the leaders of the excited colonists seized their chance to keep the fires hot. They printed handbills of the "Boston Massacre." On the following page is one that appeared at the time.

By this time most of the rich merchants who had started the trouble in the first place were beginning to feel very sad at the new turn of affairs. England had passed laws that hurt their business. They had wanted those laws repealed. They had excited the people in order to get what they wanted. But the lower classes—the mob—were going too far. To disregard unpopular laws was one thing, but to tear down houses and burn ships was another. Rich property owners were very much alarmed at the way the mob was destroying property. These small farmers, mechanics, voteless and landless people who were shouting the loudest and fighting the hardest for the "rights of man" were the very ones who had the least to say in running their own government. Many merchants saw far greater danger in the mob's taking power than in the laws of Parliament. Gouverneur Morris expressed the feelings of the rich when he wrote, "The heads of the mobility grow dangerous to the gentry and how to keep them down is the question."

In 1770 Parliament repealed the Townshend Acts except for a small tax on tea. Now the merchants were ready to call quits. They wanted things to quiet down so they could go back to business. Lower-class excitement was too dangerous.

From 1770 to 1773 there was less trouble. Business improved. Many merchants paid the small tax on tea. Others, particularly the merchants of New York and Philadelphia, still found it fairly easy to smuggle in tea in spite of the many navy boats watching the harbors. Smuggled tea was cheaper for the people who drank it, and the profits to the tea merchants were greater. Business was good.

It was true that Samuel Adams, one of the hot-headed leaders of the plain people, was still doing all he could to stir them up. In the *Boston Gazette,* on October 5, 1772, he wrote, "Is it not High Time for the People of this Country explicitly to declare whether they will be Freemen or Slaves. . . .Let us . . . calmly look around us to consider what is best to be done. . . . Let it be the topic of conversation in every social Club. Let every Town assemble. Let Associations and Combinations be everywhere set up to consult and recover our just Rights."

It was also true that in other colonies men who thought as Adams did were attempting to keep the people aroused. They had even formed "Committees of Correspondence" which wrote one another all the time

AMERICANS!
BEAR IN REMEMBRANCE
The HORRID MASSACRE!
Perpetrated in King-ftreet, BOSTON,
New-England,
On the Evening of March the Fifth, 1770.
When FIVE of your fellow countrymen,
GRAY, MAVERICK, CALDWELL, ATTUCKS,
and CARR,
Lay wallowing in their Gore!
Being bofely, and moft inhumanly
MURDERED!
And SIX others badly WOUNDED!
By a Party of the XXIXth Regiment,
Under the command of Capt. Tho. Prefton.
REMEMBER!
That Two of the MURDERERS
Were convicted of MANSLAUGHTER!
By a Jury, of whom I fhall fay
NOTHING,
Branded in the hand!
And difmiffed,
The others were ACQUITTED,
And their Captain PENSIONED!
Alfo,
BEAR IN REMEMBRANCE
That on the 22d Day of February, 1770:
The infamous
EBENEZER RICHARDSON, Informer,
And tool to Minifterial hirelings,
Moft barbaroufly
MURDERED
CHRISTOPHER SEIDER,
An innocent youth!
Of which crime he was found guilty
By his Country
On Friday April 20th, 1770;
But remained Unfentenced
On Saturday the 22d Day of February, 1772.
When the GRAND INQUEST
For Suffolk county,
Were informed, at requeft,
By the Judges of the Superior Court,
That EBENEZER RICHARDSON's Cafe
Then lay before his MAJESTY.
Therefore faid Richardfon
This day, MARCH FIFTH! 1772,
Remains UNHANGED!!!
Let THESE things be told to Pofterity!
And handed down
From Generation to Generation,
'Till Time fhall be no more!
Forever may AMERICA be preferved,
From weak and wicked monarchs,
Tyrannical Minifters,
Abandoned Governors,
Their Underlings and Hirelings!
And may the
Machinations of artful, defigning wretches,
Who would ENSLAVE THIS People,
Come to an end,
Let their NAMES and MEMORIES
Be buried in eternal oblivion,
And the PRESS,
For a SCOURGE to Tyrannical Rulers,
Remain FREE.

about exciting things happening in each colony. In this way all the fighting groups—the radicals—kept in touch with one another.

Nevertheless, these common people, who thought they were fighting for the right to manage their own affairs without interference from Parliament, could not have gone very far without the help of the powerful, rich merchants. But these merchants now thought it was better for them not to line up on the same side with the lower classes. The merchants had started the ball rolling, but they wanted to stop playing as soon as it was taken out of their hands. They no longer wanted to join together in the common quarrel against England. The two groups were separating.

At this time Parliament did a very stupid thing. The merchants and the radicals had parted company. It was Parliament's Tea Act of 1773 that made them join together again.

The East India Company, a very large, powerful British business, was in financial difficulties. Unless Parliament helped immediately, the East India Company would fail. It had seventeen million pounds of tea in its warehouses. This would bring in a lot of money if it were sold. Where to sell it? The colonies, of course! Weren't huge quantities of Dutch tea being smuggled into New York and Philadelphia? The idea behind the new Tea Act was to make the colonists buy East India Company tea rather than smuggled tea. Smuggled tea was cheap, but East India Company tea would be cheaper.

Before 1773 the East India Company brought its tea to England, then sold it *at a profit* to a London merchant; the London merchant then sold it *at a profit* to the American merchant; the American merchant then sold it *at a profit* to the American shopkeeper; the American shopkeeper then sold it *at a profit* to the colonial tea drinker. Four profits were paid before the tea finally reached the person who drank it. No wonder East India Company tea cost more than Dutch tea.

The new Tea Act changed all this. It gave the East India Company the right to send its tea in its own ships, open its own warehouses in America, and sell directly to the American shopkeeper. By cutting out two profits its tea could be sold for about one-half the former price. It would be cheaper not only than tea on which American merchants paid a duty, but even than smuggled tea.

Before the Tea Act
East India Tea Company . . . → London merchant . . .→ American merchant . . . → American shopkeeper . . . → American tea drinker.

After the Tea Act
    East India Tea Company . . . (2 profits taken out here) . . . → American shopkeeper . . . → American tea drinker.

Parliament's plan would help the East India Company to sell its seventeen million pounds of tea and it would mean cheaper tea for the colonists. An excellent idea for all—except the American merchants, who would shortly be out of the tea business. Smugglers of Dutch teas saw their profitable business gone. Merchants with tea in their warehouses saw themselves stuck with all of it when the cheaper Company tea landed.

There was one way out and the merchants took it. They again united with the radicals, the people who were not willing to give in to England in any way. Now Samuel Adams had the chance for which he had been waiting.

East India Company tea would be cheaper, and naturally the colonists would buy it. But the merchants whose pocketbooks would thus be hurt, and the radicals who were fighting against Parliament's right to tax without the consent of the colonists, did not want this to happen. The tea must not be landed!

Before long, articles appeared in the newspapers warning the people against the East India Company. One favorite argument stated that, though the tea would be very cheap at the beginning, once the company had put everybody else out of business, it would then raise its prices as high as it pleased. "Reclusus" gave this warning in the *Boston Evening Post*, October 18, 1773. "Though the first Teas may be sold at a low Rate to make a popular Entry, yet when this mode of receiving Tea is well established, they, as all other Monopolists do, will meditate a greater profit on their Goods, and set them up at what Price they please."

Another writer warned that other British companies might do the same thing, and then what would become of the colonists? In the *Pennsylvania Chronicle*, November 15, 1773, "Would not the opening of an East India House in America encourage all the great Companies in Great Britain to do the same? If so, have we a single chance of being anything but Hewers of Wood and Drawers of Waters to them?"

Several people now argued not only against East India Company tea, but against any tea drinking at all. In the *Pennsylvania Journal*, October 20, 1773, "An old Mechanic" recalled with a sigh "the time when Tea was not used, nor scarcely known amongst us, and yet people seemed at that time of day to be happier, and to enjoy more health in general than they do now."

Do you recognize the busy hands of Samuel Adams and the merchants?

Now large mass meetings were held in all the big ports. The common people listened to stirring speakers who told them about their rights. Very few speeches about the money the merchants would lose if Company tea landed; many speeches about "no taxation without representation" and about Liberty and Freedom. *The tea must not be landed!*

In Boston, in November, 1773, three Company tea ships arrived in the harbor. The radicals would not let the tea be landed. Governor Hutchinson would not let the ships return without unloading. On the night of December 16, 1773, a party of men jumped aboard the ships, ripped open the chests, and dumped the tea into the harbor. This "Boston Tea Party" cost the East India Company about $75,000.

Tea ships arrived in Charleston, New York, Annapolis. The mobs were ready for them. In Charleston, the tea was placed in damp cellars; in New York, on April 22, 1774, there was another "Tea Party"; in Annapolis, when the brig *Peggy Stewart* arrived with more than a ton of dutied tea for the firm of T. C. Williams & Company, both tea and ship were burned while a great crowd looked on.

When the news of the Boston Tea Party reached Parliament, it took swift action. Seventy-five thousand dollars worth of British property destroyed. That was going too far. The colonists must be taught a lesson. Parliament decided on very severe punishment. The port of Boston was to be closed until the tea was paid for; no more town meetings could be held without permission from the governor; British officers who were accused of murder while seeing that British laws were enforced were to have their trials in England (far away from excited colonists). General Gage was appointed governor of Massachusetts. More troops were sent to Boston.

"The die is cast," wrote George III to Lord North; "the colonies must either triumph or submit." In America, Samuel Adams and his followers had the ear of the people. They were absolutely against giving in to the demands of Parliament. In England, Lord North and his followers controlled Parliament. They were determined to punish the colonists. A fight to a finish was in the air.

The "Committees of Correspondence" were very active. A meeting of men chosen from the different colonies was planned.

On September 5, 1774, the First Continental Congress met in Philadelphia. Shall Boston be made to pay for the tea, or shall we back her up in her refusal to do so? Long speeches by those in favor of going slowly, of giving in to the demands of Parliament. Other long speeches by the radicals in favor of resistance, of accepting England's challenge. Finally, after fifty-two days of argument the radicals win. The "Continental Association" is decided upon. The colonists are to try nonimportation again, also nonexportation. Committees are to see that no one breaks the agreement. Another meeting will be held the next year.

In February, 1775, General Gage began to make active preparations for the trouble to come. He wanted to improve the fortifications of Boston Harbor. It was useless to ask the workmen of Boston to do the job, so Gage sent agents to other cities to bring back men and materials. But the Committees of Correspondence were on the alert. When Gage's messengers reached New York they found that the news of their mission had preceded them. In vain did they offer jobs to the carpenters and bricklayers there. The craftsmen of New York refused to make weapons which were to be used against their fellow workers of Boston. Gage was checkmated by working-class solidarity.

Only a spark was now needed to set off the explosion. Which side would furnish it?

On April 19, 1775, General Gage sent a body of British soldiers to seize some military supplies of the colonists at Concord. Paul Revere and Rufus Dawes sped through the countryside, spreading the news. When the troops reached Lexington on the road to Concord, they were met by a small band of colonists. A shot was fired and the war was on.

Who fired the first shot? Nobody knows. The *Salem* (Massachusetts) *Gazette*, on April 25, 1775, recorded:

. . . upon which the Troops huzzaed, and immediately one or two officers [British] discharged their pistols which were instantaneously followed by the firing of four or five of the soldiers and then there seemed to be a general discharge from the whole body: eight of our men were killed, and nine wounded. . . .

That's the American story.

The *London Gazette*, on June 10, 1775, reported:

. . . who upon their arrival at Lexington, found a body of the country people under arms on a green close to the road; and upon the King's Troops marching up to them in order to inquire the reason of their being so assembled, they went off in great confusion and several guns were fired upon the King's Troops from behind a stone wall and also from the meeting-house and other houses, by which one man was wounded, and Major Pitcairn's horse shot in two places. . . .

That's the British story.

Which side was to blame? Take your choice.

The Second Continental Congress met in Philadelphia on May 10, 1775, less than a month after the Battle of Lexington. George Washington was appointed commander of the Continental Army. Before he had time to reach his army, more battles between British soldiers and American colonists had been fought.

The war had begun in earnest. Committees of radicals were seizing power. Royal governors and other British officers fled from their posts as fast as they could. People who still sided with England, called Loyalists or Tories, were oftentimes beaten up. Others were tarred and feathered. Some were even hanged.

It was a very exciting, dangerous time. A group of radicals whose number was small, but whose organization was good, was stirring up things and taking control wherever it could.

Many people did not know which side to take. There was a large number of Tories. Some of them had been on the colonial side at first, but then went over to the English side as soon as the colonists had begun to wreck property; some had stayed on the colonial side until the Boston Tea Party; some had even been members of the First Continental Congress and had not become Tories until after the Battle of Lexington. It was very difficult to decide to which side to belong. Some remained undecided until a mob of hotheaded colonists forced a decision; some decided too late and their property was destroyed and they had to run for their lives. During the war and after it had ended, more than one hundred thousand Tories, among whom were many of the best educated and wealthiest people in the colonies, fled to Canada or England to save themselves; their property was seized or destroyed.

It was still a quarrel between colonies and mother country within the British Empire. Then came a very important change.

THE WAR HAD BEGUN IN EARNEST

On January 10, 1776, Thomas Paine published a pamphlet called *Common Sense*. It was written in very plain, outspoken language that the common people could understand. To many of them Paine's ideas were new; to others the idea of *independence* had already occurred. Paine urged the people that the time had come for the final step—complete separation from England.

Common Sense became the best seller of the day. Within three months more than one hundred and twenty thousand copies were sold. All over the colonies people were quoting from it:

> Europe, and not England, is the parent country of America. . . . Everything that is right or reasonable pleads for separation. The blood of the slain, the weeping voice of nature cries, 'TIS TIME TO PART. Even the distance at which the Almighty hath placed England and America is a strong and natural proof that the authority of the one over the other was never the design of heaven. . . . A government of our own is our natural right. . . . Wherefore what is it that we want? Why is it that we hesitate? From Britain we can expect nothing but ruin . . . nothing can settle our affairs so expeditiously as an open and determined DECLARATION FOR INDEPENDENCE.

This was strong talk, made to order for the common people. In the Continental Congress there was a long argument about separating from England. Some members still hesitated to take that final step. Others said it must be done. Samuel Adams argued: "Is not America already independent? Why not then declare it?"

In June, 1776, the members asked a committee to write the paper declaring America's independence from England. Thomas Jefferson, one of the committee members, was given the job.

He wrote the paper and presented it to Congress. A few changes were made, and then, on July 4, 1776, Congress adopted the Declaration of Independence. It said in part: " . . . that these united colonies are, and of right ought to be, free and independent states . . . and that all political connection between them and the state of Great Britain is, and ought to be, totally dissolved. . . ." The colonies had left the Empire.

The "United States of America" was born.

"In Order to Form a More Perfect Union"

★——★

When, on July 4, 1776, the thirteen colonies announced to the world that they were thirteen states independent of the British Empire, England said you can't do that, and the Revolutionary War was on. It takes lots of money to fight a war. Soldiers have to be fed, clothed, housed (or "tented"), and paid. Cannon, rifles, and bullets must be provided. All of which takes money.

Governments usually raise money by taxing the people. But one of the chief reasons for the fight against England was the colonists' objection to taxes, so Congress felt that would be a bit too risky. It began to print paper money. Its printing presses turned out hundreds, then thousands, then millions of paper dollars—with no gold or silver to back them up. It is in just such a war period when the whole peace economy has to be transformed and put on a war basis, and when the entire social organization is undergoing rapid changes, that runaway inflation is apt to occur. Soon paper dollars were worth practically nothing at all. One colonist made a blanket for his dog out of paper dollars. Another used them as wallpaper for his barbershop. Sugar sold at four dollars a pound and linen at twenty dollars a yard. In 1779 Sam Adams paid two thousand dollars for a suit of clothes and a hat.

Revolutionary time is topsy-turvy time. Mr. George Washington, Commander-in-Chief of the American armies, found it very, very hard, with paper dollars, to get food or clothing or men. Many of the soldiers in his army were poor farmers who had to hurry home when harvest time came. Others deserted simply because conditions were so awful. How Washington wished for a real army, one that would stay together until the war was won! On December 20, 1776, he wrote a letter to the president of Congress about his soldiers ". . . who come in, you cannot tell how, go, you cannot tell when, and act, you cannot tell where, consume your provisions, exhaust your stores, and leave you at last at a critical moment. These, Sir, are the men I am to depend upon. . . ."

Washington had reason to complain. It is quite a job to fight battles with an army that's here one minute and gone the next. But the soldiers' side of it is also easy to understand. Here are a few bits from a diary kept by Dr. Waldo, a surgeon from Connecticut who was with the American Army at Valley Forge in the winter of 1777:

"Dec. 14th. . . . Poor food—hard lodging—Cold Weather—fatigue— Nasty Clothes—Nasty Cookery. . . . Here comes a bowl of beef soup —full of burnt leaves and dirt.

Dec. 25th, Christmas. We are still in Tents—when we ought to be in huts—the poor Sick, suffer much in Tents this cold Weather. . . ."

But why all this suffering—men freezing for want of clothing, starving for want of food? It would not have happened if the whole country had stood behind the soldiers. Unfortunately for Washington and his men, all the people were not united in the fight against England. Perhaps one third of the Americans were Tories, loyal to the king and the Empire. Many of them fled the country; many others remained to help the British with food and clothing, or even to fight in the British Army against their fellow Americans.

Other Americans didn't much care which side won. They wanted to be left alone, to go on living and working without trouble. They were ready to sell food or supplies of any kind to whichever side paid—in good hard metal.

The Revolution had been started by a small group of determined men who knew what they wanted and tried to persuade hesitating colonists to see things their way. When the explosion came, after Lexington and the Declaration of Independence, this little group continued their shouting, their organizing, their planning. While others were doubtful, they acted. Many undecided colonists were swept along with the crowd to the rebel side. Probably two thirds of the people in the states were against England. But not all of them were fighting mad. Not all of them were ready to give up their comfort to help win the war. The men in the Army, for the most part, were the plain people, the small farmers, the frontiersmen—in short, the poorer classes. There were some rich, of course—George Washington, Charles Carroll, and others—but in the main it was the lower classes that shouldered the guns.

Everything goes higgledy-piggledy in wartime. Washington, American, was fighting Howe, British, in Pennsylvania, an American state—yet Washington's men were starving and freezing at Valley Forge, while the British had plenty of food and clothing in Philadelphia! An onlooker might have thought that Washington, not Howe, was in the enemy's country.

While some American farmers were doing the fighting in the American Army, for which they were paid in worthless paper dollars, other American farmers were selling food to the enemy, for which they were paid in precious gold or silver. While some American merchants had their ships captured by British privateers and so lost their fortunes, other American merchants, turned privateers during the war, captured British ships and gained fortunes. Abraham Whipple, on his ship the *Providence,* came upon a fleet of English ships bound from the West Indies to England. He disguised his vessel and boldly entered the fleet as though his was another English ship. Then after dark, every night, for ten successive nights, he pulled up alongside one of the vessels, boarded and captured it! Next he put a prize crew of his own men in command—and secretly sent the captured boat back to Boston. Eight of these captures reached Boston and Mr. Whipple sold their cargoes for more than $1,000,000. Some adventurous Americans designed boats especially for speed, the better to capture British merchantmen. During the war, Congress or the separate states gave privateers' commissions to more than five hundred boats, and about ninety thousand seamen served on them.

One would have supposed that the powerful British would conquer America in one, two, three order, but they didn't. One important reason was that their soldiers didn't have their hearts set on winning. Just as there were deserters in the American Army, so, too, there were deserters in the British Army. Some of these deserters even joined the American Army against their own side. (Often they were paid by Americans to substitute for them in Washington's army.) It might have been different if the landlords and merchants of England, in whose interest the war was being fought, had rushed to do the fighting. But they didn't. The British had trouble getting men. They asked for volunteers, but not enough came; they snatched beggars, people out of work, and thieves from the streets and forced them into the Army; they opened the jail doors to those prisoners who would join the Army, "three British regiments being composed entirely of lawbreakers released from prison. But all these methods failed to produce enough men for the task of saving America for the landlords and merchants of England." Finally, to fill the ranks in their army the British had to hire German soldiers from German princes who owned them. The price was fifty-five dollars for every German killed and twelve dollars for every one wounded. What could be expected from such an army?

The UNITED STATES

Of AMERICA in CONGRESS Aſſembled,

TO ALL to whom theſe PRESENTS ſhall come, ſend GREETING

Know Ye,

THAT We have granted, and by theſe Preſents do grant Licence and Authority to

Mariner, Commander of the　　　　　　called the　　　　　　of the

Burthen of　　　　　　Tons or thereabouts, belonging to

mounting　　　　　　Carriage Guns, and navigated by　　　　　　Men,

to fit out and ſet forth the ſaid　　　　　　in a warlike Manner, and by and with the ſaid

and the Officers and Crew thereof, by Force of Arms to attack, ſubdue, ſeize and take all Ships and other Veſſels, Goods, Wares and Merchandizes, belonging to the King or Crown of Great-Britain, or to his Subjects, or to Others inhabiting within any of the Territories or Poſſeſſions of the aforeſaid King of Great-Britain, or any other Ships or Veſſels, Goods, Wares or Merchandizes to whomſoever belonging, which are or ſhall be declared to be Subjects of Capture by any Ordinance of the United States in Congreſs aſſembled, or which are ſo deemed by the Law of Nations. And the ſaid Ships and Veſſels, Goods, Wares and Merchandizes ſo apprehended as aforeſaid, and as Prize taken, to bring into Port, in Order that Proceedings may be had concerning ſuch Captures in due Form of Law, and as to Right and Juſtice appertaineth. AND We requeſt all Kings, Princes, States and Potentates, being in Friendſhip or Alliance with Us, and Others to whom it ſhall appertain, to give the ſaid all Aid, Aſſiſtance and Succour in their Ports, with his ſaid Veſſel, Company and Prizes, We engaging to do the Like to all the Subjects of ſuch Kings, Princes, States and Potentates, who ſhall come into any of our Ports. AND We will and require all our Officers whatſoever, to give to the ſaid all neceſſary Aid, Succour and Aſſiſtance in the Premiſes. This Commiſſion ſhall continue in Force during the Pleaſure of the United States in Congreſs aſſembled, and no longer.

IN TESTIMONY whereof, We have cauſed the Seal of the Admiralty of the United States in Congreſs aſſembled, to be hereunto affixed.

WITNESS His Excellency　　　　　　Eſquire, Preſident of the United States in Congreſs aſſembled, at　　　　　　this Day of　　　　　　in the Year of Our Lord One Thouſand Seven Hundred and and of our Sovereignty and Independence the

PRIVATEER COMMISSION

In addition, the British generals either would not or could not use their brains. It is hard to decide which to believe. In carrying on the war they made one mistake after another. In the summer of 1777, for example, General Howe had his army in northern New Jersey. He wanted to take Philadelphia, about a hundred miles away. Instead of marching his men directly to Philadelphia, he put his army on boats and sailed to the Chesapeake Bay. He had sailed three hundred miles and now had fifty more to march to reach Philadelphia. And directly across his path lay the ragged army of Washington, which he had wasted so many weeks trying to avoid! Now there was nothing left to do but fight. At Brandywine and Germantown he fought and easily defeated the Americans. What can one think of such nonsense—taking a roundabout sea voyage of three hundred miles plus a land march of fifty miles, instead of going straight to the point one hundred miles away?

The American side went up, then down. A brilliant victory— then a crushing defeat. Good news—bad news. Victory on water— defeat on land. "Stick-to-it" George Washington and a handful of faithful followers—dissatisfied, grumbling deserters. Things looked very black. Then a bit of startling, wonderful news. Benjamin Franklin had been sent abroad to obtain help from France. The French did not love the Americans, but they hated the English. They seized the chance to strike at their old enemies, and sent money, supplies, ships, and men, to help the Revolutionary Army. Later Spain and Holland, also enemies of England, joined the Americans against the English.

In 1781, the British general, Cornwallis, found himself in Yorktown, Virginia, with the American Army under Washington in front of him and the French fleet behind him. No way out. He surrendered.

At this time there came into power in England a group of people who had been doubtful about fighting the colonists in the beginning, and who were very much against England's continuing this unhappy war against America and Europe. They wanted peace. The British Army was told to return home. The War for Independence was over. America had won its liberation from colonial slavery.

In 1783 the treaty of peace between England and the "United States of America" was signed. The new country was given all the land from the Great Lakes to Florida, and from the Atlantic to the Mississippi, except New Orleans, which went to Spain. Washington disbanded his army, and soldiers and general went back to their homes. A new nation . . . the United States of America. . . .

The American Revolution was much more than a war against England. The war ended in 1783, but the Revolution continued. The war meant a change in the government of the people of the United States, but the Revolution meant a change in their ways of living together. Some of the things for which the lower classes had been fighting before the war began were won during the Revolutionary period. Everywhere in America there was much talk about liberty, freedom, equality, and the rights of man. The Declaration of Independence had declared, "We hold these truths to be self-evident: *that all men are created equal.*" Now laws were passed which aimed at making that true in real life as well as on paper.

From England had come the system of entail and primogeniture, a device to keep land in the same hands for all time. Land which was entailed could not be sold outside the family—it could not even

be given away. Under the law of primogeniture if a man died leaving no will, all his lands were turned over to his eldest son—nothing at all went to the other children. It was a clever system which made it possible to have forever a rich powerful few who would increase their power as they kept and increased their lands. But such an unfair scheme couldn't last when men were talking about justice and equality. You could not have laws which forced property to go entirely to the eldest son and at the same time talk about "all men are created equal." New ways of thinking, Revolutionary ideas, forced these old, old laws to be given up.

The Declaration of Independence was written in 1776. Ten years later every state but two had given up entails. In fifteen years every single state had given up primogeniture. The Revolution freed the

United States from English rule, but, perhaps even more important, it helped to free the United States from Old World ideas of upper-class rule. Eldest sons and younger sons—later, even daughters—all were to be equal. Instead of great big estates in the hands of a few, forever, the American system was to be small lots owned by the farmer who worked on his own fields for himself.

During the war the Revolutionists had seized the property of the Tories. Many of these people, loyal to the King of England, had been among the richest men in the colonies. They had owned huge estates. The Fairfax estate in Virginia covered six million acres. The Phillipse estate in New York extended for three hundred square miles. Sir William Pepperell could ride along the coast of Maine for thirty miles and never once go off his own land. All this land and much more was taken away by the fighting colonists. Was it then sold in large blocks to other men of great wealth? Not at all. In line with the idea of breaking up big holdings owned by a few, these huge estates were sold in small lots to many different people. The land owned by one Tory, Roger Morris, of New York, was seized by the state and sold to two hundred and fifty people. The land taken from another Tory, James deLancey, was broken up into two hundred and seventy-five lots and sold. During the Revolutionary period, a great deal of land changed hands and the old system of large estates was being broken up. This important change, like independence, came out of the Revolution.

Another important gain came in the added number of people who were given the right to vote. Not until fifty years later were *all* white men, twenty-one years of age, citizens of the United States, given that right. Before and during the Revolutionary period you had to own property to have that right. But after the Revolution the amount of property you had to own was lowered very much, so that many more men were given the vote. It seems like a small thing, but raising the common man from a nonvoter to a voter raised him a few rungs up the social ladder. A new voter carried his head higher than before. It was the Revolutionary spirit which helped to bring about this change.

What of Negro slavery at a time when men were talking liberty, freedom, and equality? While slavery was not entirely given up at this time, nevertheless several important steps were taken toward either freeing the slaves or helping them. "The first anti-slavery society in this or any other country was formed on April 14, 1775, five days before the battle of Lexington, by a meeting at the Sun Tavern on Second Street in Philadelphia." One state government after another passed laws forbidding the importation of slaves— Rhode Island and Connecticut in 1774, Delaware in 1776, Virginia in 1778, and Maryland in 1783. In 1780 Pennsylvania passed a law "which declared that no negro born after that date should be held in any sort of bondage after he became 28 years old, and that up to that time his service should be simply like that of an indentured servant or apprentice." By 1784, in Massachusetts, Connecticut, and Rhode Island, laws were passed which provided for the gradual and complete abolition of slavery. Even in the very large slaveholding state of Virginia, laws were passed in 1782 which made it easier to free Negroes there. Within eight years, more than ten thousand slaves were freed in Virginia alone.

Many of the settlers had come to America to follow their own religions. But as late as 1770, in nine of the colonies, there was a church established by law, so that Congregationalists living in Maryland had to help support the Episcopal church there; Episcopalians living in Massachusetts had to help support the Congregationalist Church; and even those with no church affiliations at all saw some of their tax money going to pay the expenses of the state church. The new spirit in the air brought a change in these old laws, also. Just after the Revolution had begun, the established church was overthrown in five states. Though it was not for another fifty years that complete freedom of religion came to all of America, nevertheless a good beginning was made during this time of many changes.

Perhaps the best indication of the revolution in people's thinking was the Northwest Ordinance of 1787. According to the treaty with Great Britain in 1783, the territory west of the Appalachians to the Mississippi belonged to the United States. The huge strip of land north of the Ohio River was called the Northwest Territory. Here, then, was a real test of the ideas of the time—what laws would be made for the new territory, still uninhabited?

If the United States had followed in the footsteps of England and the other European countries, it would have treated this territory over the mountains as a colony, with the old thirteen seaboard states as the mother country. But the spirit of equality then in the air was directly opposed to the mother country colony idea. So Congress made a startling proposal: As soon as five thousand people lived in the territory, they could elect *their own* legislature and make *their own* laws; when the population reached sixty thousand they could enter the Union as a *state equal to the original thirteen states in every way.* Nor was that all. There was to be freedom of religion. In every township, a strip of land was to be set aside to be used for public education. There was to be *no slavery.* No primogeniture; when a man died leaving no will, his property was to be divided

equally among his sons and daughters. The Northwest Ordinance was a signpost of the spirit of the times.

One of the most significant meanings of the word revolution is "change." The American Revolution brought tremendous changes in the social life of the people here—changes that did not come to older European countries for many years afterward, changes that very early gave to the United States the reputation of being a "free country."

The first constitution of the United States was the Articles of Confederation. It was agreed to by the Continental Congress in 1777, but it was not finally ratified and in force until 1781, the year the war ended. It was a loose association of sovereign states in which the powers of Congress were strictly limited. That was to be expected, since the Articles were drafted at the very moment when the Americans were trying to rid themselves of a strong government which had meddled with their affairs too much. Naturally they would hesitate about setting up another strong government in its place. They were fighting to support their own governments against an outside one. The lawmaking body of Virginia, of Massachusetts, of New York, of your own state, that was one thing, but beware of a strong outside government—that was quite another thing. So the thirteen states joined together under the Articles of Confederation and made sure that Congress, the government of all the states, should have very little power. Congress was not to be another Parliament—it was not to command, it was to beg. Each state would elect its own lawmakers. This group of lawmakers, the legislature, was to have power to run the state. Congress was not to meddle.

Such a system might be expected from a people whose experience with a strong outside government had been so unhappy that they were fighting a war to become free of it. Yet before very long a group of frightened, anxious people was shouting for a strong government all over again. And only four short years after the treaty of peace had been signed this same group set about making the machinery of just such a government. What had happened?

Many things had happened, all of them bad in the eyes of the wealthy—the money-lenders, manufacturers, merchants, bond-holders, speculators, slaveholders. It was, for the rich, what some historians have called a "critical period."

Query: When does a person not want to be paid a debt?

Answer: When the debt is being paid in depreciated paper dollars.

If A lends B $100 in good hard money, worth $100 anywhere, anytime, he doesn't want to be paid back in paper dollars which go down in value, until $100 worth becomes $25 worth, or $10 worth, or $0 worth.

B, a poor man, hard up, in debt, and anxious to stay out of a filthy jail, wants more money to be printed so he can pay his debts more easily. A, money-lender, becomes a hard-money man, while B, money-ower, becomes a paper-money man.

In 1786, in seven of the thirteen states, the legislatures passed paper-money laws. The money-owers were happy; the money-lenders grumbled.

John Weeden, owned a butcher shop, in Newport, Rhode Island.

One day one of his customers, John Trevett, came in and bought some meat. Trevett asked the price, and then offered to pay with Rhode Island paper dollars. Weeden refused to take the paper money and Trevett brought him to trial before a court of five judges. Weeden won the case. The members of the legislature were enraged at the judges and ordered them to come and explain. Then they voted that they were not satisfied with the judges' reasons. At the next election only one of the judges was re-elected.

The money-lenders were sick of paper money. They wanted a strong central government that would keep these state legislatures from printing worthless paper money. Congress, under the Articles of Confederation, could not do that.

During the years of fighting between England and America, trade with England had stopped. The manufactured things formerly bought from England had to be made at home. So some people in the states started the business of making them. Their business was growing, prices were high, everything was satisfactory. Then the war ended. Manufactured goods from England and other countries of Europe poured into America. Europeans had been making things long before the Americans had begun; European workmen worked for lower wages than American workmen; European goods were therefore cheaper—and the people here bought these cheaper goods. American manufacturers saw their business slipping away. They wanted Congress to put a tax on manufactured goods coming into the country, so they could undersell the Europeans. Congress had no power to do so. It had to ask every state for permission to lay the tax. One state, Rhode Island, said no, and Congress was helpless.

American manufacturers were sick of foreign goods. They wanted a strong central government that would tax foreign goods so high that American goods would be cheaper. Congress, under the Articles of Confederation, could not do that.

Before the Revolution, American merchants had had special favors given them because they were part of the British Empire. They could carry goods to the British West Indies or other parts of the Empire and sell them there. Now they were out of the Empire and England took away their special favors—they could trade with her colonies only under the same rules that applied to other outside countries, which meant very little trade. During the war, when France and Spain were on the American side, they gave American merchants special rights to trade at their ports. Now the war was over, those rights were taken away and both countries closed many of their ports to ships from the United States.

American merchants were sick of "this-port-is-closed-to-you" laws. They wanted a strong central government that would make laws about commerce for every one of the united states, that would say to England and France and Spain, and so on, if you won't let us do so-and-so in your ports, then you may not do so-and-so in our ports. American merchants wanted a strong central government that would hit back at the merchants of those foreign countries that were hitting at them. Congress, under the Articles of Confederation, could not do that.

Many Americans had loaned money to Congress to carry on the war. In return, they were given government bonds, promises to pay back. Many officers in the Army had also received these bonds, as wages. But Congress was having a very hard time raising money to pay back what it owed. Congress had no right to tax the people. It had to beg for money from the different states. Because it looked as though Congress might never be able to pay its debts, the bonds, like paper money, went down in value. Bonds dropped to one tenth of what they had been worth, so you could buy a hundred-dollar bond for as little as ten dollars. Speculators bought bonds as the price dropped. If ever Congress raised enough money to pay back what it owed, these speculators would make a great deal of money. They would be getting full value for every bond which they had bought at less than full value—one hundred dollars for ten dollars.

People who had loaned money to Congress in exchange for bonds, soldiers who had received bonds as wages, and speculators who had bought bonds at a low price, all these holders of government promises to pay were sick of seeing their bonds drop in value. They wanted a strong central government that would have the power to collect taxes and so raise money to pay back what it owed—*in full*. Congress, under the Articles of Confederation, could not do that.

There was another kind of speculator. This kind bought western lands at a low price, hoping to sell at a high price when people moved west. But Congress had no army on the frontier to protect the settlers from the Indians and this might keep many people from going west and buying land.

Speculators in western lands were sick of seeing their western lands unprotected. They wanted a central government that would be strong, one that would raise an army which would protect people on the frontier. Congress, under the Articles of Confederation, could not do that.

Other men also had reason for wanting an army ever on hand. Southerners who owned slaves were always afraid that the Negroes would band together and attack their white masters. Slaveholders wanted a central government that would be strong, one that could send a well-trained army immediately to any place where there was an uprising of Negro slaves. Congress, under the Articles of Confederation, could not do that.

Money-lenders, manufacturers, merchants, bondholders, speculators, slaveholders—all of them wanted a strong central government. They were the people with money, the rich, and they wanted a strong central government that would protect their property and enable them to add to it by carrying on business safely and easily.

In 1786 things began to happen that frightened this group into wanting that strong central government *right away*.

In the elections of that year the people who wanted paper money won in seven states and lost in Massachusetts, New Hampshire, Connecticut, Virginia, Maryland, and Delaware. Times were bad; money was hard to get. The people who owed money were in danger not only of having their property taken away from them, but also of being thrown into a dreadful, dirty jail. In New Hampshire a mob of several hundred men marched on the legislature with clubs, stones, swords, and guns, and demanded relief. "Print paper money, and lower the taxes"—these were their demands.

In Massachusetts there were uprisings which were much more alarming. Taxes there were very high, and the poor had no money to pay what they owed. In several of the paper-money states, "stay laws" had been passed to hold up the collection of debts; in others, debts could be paid in cattle or in farm products. The poor people of Massachusetts wanted relief of this kind—relief of any kind that would help them out of the predicament in which they found themselves. When their state legislature went home without passing any laws to help them, the poor banded together and rioted.

In the *New York Packet* for September 11, 1786, there appeared this item of news from Springfield, Massachusetts: "On Tuesday the 29th [of August] . . . the day appointed by law for the sitting of the Court of Common Pleas . . . in Northampton, there assembled in the town from different parts of the county four or five hundred people some of whom were armed with muskets, the others with bludgeons, with the professed intention to prevent the court from proceeding to business. . . ."

It is easy to understand why the mob did not want to let the court go ahead with its business. It was to the court that money-lenders brought their cases against the money-owers; it was the court that ordered the poor farmer to give up his small farm to the person to whom he owed money; it was the court that sent the poor man to a miserable debtor's jail.

At Great Barrington another mob closed the court, broke open the jails, searched houses, and chased people out of town.

Later, about one thousand men, armed with muskets, swords, and clubs, led by Daniel Shays, formerly an officer in the Revolutionary War, continued the rioting; they closed the courts for several months. Shays' Rebellion was serious business. The upper classes throughout the country were thoroughly frightened at this armed uprising of the poor people. There was no money in the treasury to pay the state troops, so a number of rich people contributed enough to do so. Shays and his followers headed for Springfield, where there was a public storehouse containing seven thousand new muskets, thirteen thousand barrels of gunpowder, stoves, camp kettles, and saddles. They were stopped by the state troops, a few shots were fired, and the group dispersed.

General Knox wrote a letter to George Washington in which he anxiously told of the dangerous ideas of the Shaysites. He wrote that they believed ". . . that the property of the United States has been protected from . . . Britain by the joint exertions of all and therefore *ought to be the common property of all*."

Chills went up and down the spines of the wealthy. A strong central government was needed—immediately.

It wasn't surprising then, that a meeting was held in 1787 to revise the Articles of Confederation. Of the fifty-five members chosen to attend the meeting, by the legislatures of twelve states (Rhode Island refused to send any), not one member represented the small-farming or mechanic class—almost all were either money-lenders, merchants, manufacturers, bondholders, speculators, or slaveholders.

The meetings were held in Philadelphia, beginning in May and ending on September 17, 1787. The members thought it best to keep their work secret, so they met behind closed doors. One of the members was Benjamin Franklin, now quite an old man. He was very popular and was often asked out to dinner, where he told excellent stories. The members, being very careful, asked one of their number to accompany Mr. Franklin to all of his dinner parties; it was this member's duty to stop the old gentleman whenever he started on any story that touched on the secrets of the meeting.

Though they had been sent to Philadelphia merely to fix up and perhaps add to the old Articles of Confederation, the members soon gave up that idea and began work on a new plan of union for the thirteen states—one that would provide for a strong central government. They made the Constitution of the United States.

For the men of property, all would be well under the Constitution, the new plan of government. No more could states print paper money; no more could states pass laws giving people more time to pay their debts, or allowing debts to be paid in goods or cattle—contracts were to be kept without change (cheering news to money-lenders). Under the Constitution, Congress, the central government of all the states, was to have real power, no more need to beg. Congress was given control over both foreign trade and trade between states; with foreign countries, it could make treaties which would apply to all of the thirteen states as one. Now at last taxes could be laid on foreign goods and trade agreements could be made with foreign countries (cheering news for manufacturers and merchants). Congress would need money to pay government debts—it was given the right to collect taxes (cheering news for speculators). No more could hotheaded revolutionists like Shays stop the courts from sitting and attack property—Congress would have an army and a navy ready to put a stop to any future rebellions (cheering news for all property-holders).

The meeting in Philadelphia, now called the Constitutional Convention, dragged on for four weary months. There were many arguments between the members from the different states. Should large states have more to say in the national government than small states? Should Negro slaves be counted as white people? Should Congress have the right to stop the importation of Negro slaves? On these questions and many others the members quarreled long and hard. But on one thing practically all of them were agreed—the common people, the people with little or no property, *must not have too much power.*

How could that be arranged?

The government would be divided into three main parts. Only the House of Representatives, one half of one of those parts, would be elected directly by the people. In the selection of all the other parts there would be no direct line to the people. It would be something like "The House that Jack Built"—this is the Senate of the United States, elected by the state legislators, who are elected by the people; this is the President of the United States, who is elected by electors, who have been chosen in one way or another by the state legislators, who have been elected by the people; this is the Supreme Court of the United States, appointed by the President, who is elected by electors, who have been chosen in one way or another by the state legislators, who have been elected by the people. Small danger of the common people ever getting complete control under such an arrangement.

But still more could be done to make sure. Let each of the three parts of the government have the power to "check and balance" the other. Then let all of the parts be selected for different periods of time:

Congress
{ House of Representatives—elected directly by the people for two years
  Senate—elected indirectly by the people for six years (one third every two years) }

President—elected more indirectly by the people for four years
Supreme Court—selected more indirectly by the people for life

Let Senators and the President be older than Representatives. Older people are less likely to do rash things.

How would all this work? Suppose the common people are highly excited and want dangerous laws passed. At the two-year election they refuse to re-elect the old Representatives and one third of the Senators—there still remain the other two thirds of the Senate and the Supreme Court to see that no new "unsafe" laws are rushed through. In every way the Constitution seemed to provide protection for property against danger from the lower classes.

The old toasts of the Revolutionary army officers, "Here's cement to the Union," and "A hoop to the barrel," would be realized in this new plan. The Constitution began with the words, "We, the people of the United States, in order to form a more perfect union. . . ." It provided for a central government that would be strong; a government that would combine thirteen separate, quarreling states into one country. If the Constitution were accepted by the people, there would be a real tie-up, the States of America would truly become, in fact as well as in name, the United States of America.

But there were rocks ahead for those who had worked so hard on their ship of state. According to the Articles of Confederation, before the new plan could become law it would have to be sent to every state legislature and be approved by every single one of them. The fathers of the Constitution knew there was small chance for their plan under such an arrangement, so they boldly wrote into the Constitution that special meetings be called in every state to decide on it, and that as soon as nine of the thirteen states had approved it, the Constitution would become the law of the land.

That daring stroke brought them safely past the first rock, but there were still others ahead. From September 17, 1787, to July, 1788, all over the country, a bitter fight was carried on between those for the Constitution and those against. Not all rich men were for it, not all poor men were against it. But in general, the line-up was money-lenders, manufacturers, merchants, speculators—the rich —on the "yes" side, and small farmers, mechanics—the poor—on the "no" side. Not all the people had the right to vote; others did not care to; not more than one fourth of all the white men over twenty-one voted either for or against.

The rich had a better organization; they had more able men; they had more money to spend; they had more to gain if their side won; they worked harder to win. The poor were less well organized; they were scattered in country districts; they had fewer "great names" on their side; they had no money to carry on. Nevertheless, the vote was very close. Rhode Island and North Carolina voted against it. In three other states it looked as though the "noes" would win, but after all kinds of speechmaking and trickery, the "yeas" won out.

In Pennsylvania, for example, several "noes," feeling that the "yeas" were putting something over on them, purposely stayed away from a meeting of the legislature. This meant that the bills the "yeas" wanted to pass could not be voted on because a quorum would not be present. Whereupon the "yeas" broke into the lodgings of the "noes," dragged them through the streets to the meeting-house, and held them there by force until the vote was taken.

The closeness of the vote in some of the state meetings shows how bitter the struggle was:

	For	Against
In New York	30	27
In New Hampshire	57	47
In Massachusetts	187	168
In Virginia	89	79

On June 21, 1788, the ninth state, New Hampshire, accepted the Constitution and the new plan became the law of the land. The thirteen states were tied together by a strong central government.

In 1789 George Washington was elected the first President of the United States.

Feb. 24
read.
this
ch.!

A Rifle, An Ax—

★————————————————————————————★

And a bag of corn. These were the weapons in a fierce battle—
a fight that took courage, a struggle in which only the strong survived. Unlike the usual run of battles, this was not a fight of one
organized army against another; it was a more thrilling war between
men, women, and children on the one side, and the uncharted wilderness on the other.

In 1770, before the Revolution, the English General Gage had
written home about the Americans that "it is the Passion of every
Man to be a Landholder, and the People have a Natural Disposition
to rove in search of good Lands, however distant."

Lord Dunmore, another Englishman, agreed with Gage in his
analysis. He wrote of the Americans, "They acquire no attachment
to Place: But wandering about Seems engrafted in their Nature . . .
they . . . for ever imagine the Lands further off, are still better than
those upon which they are already settled."

Gage and Dunmore were right. What else could have happened
when a land-hungry people with a roving disposition found some
of the best farm land in the world could be theirs for very little or
no money? How long would a person who had not fitted into the
life of his home town remain there when he might move west and
start all over again? Gay, energetic youngsters anxious for "something to happen" saw the contrast—at home everything always the
same, no excitement, no change, but at the frontier line—Indians,
wild animals, gunplay, danger, adventure—would they take time
to think twice about leaving? Or down-and-outers, owning nothing,
working long and hard, but always seeing the debtor's jail staring
them in the face, how would such men feel about a fresh beginning
in a new country? Take a farmer who had farmed his land so long
that the soil had become starved, or was poor or stony soil to begin

with—now comes the news of wonderful virgin soil never before plowed, how long before he'd wave good-by to the old farm and set out for the new? An immigrant escaping from the misery of the Old World arrives in the New, wants to buy a farm, but finds that the land on the coast is too expensive; in the West, however, land is very cheap. Would he hesitate about moving west?

How long before all these people would turn to the West? The answer is easy. From 1770 to 1840 the movement west grew from

a handful of people to hundreds of thousands. Swarms of land seekers poured into the Mississippi Valley. It became a stampede. Single men packed up and left, families packed up and left, whole towns packed up and left. America was on the move. In 1770 there were five thousand people west of the Appalachians; in 1840 there were eight million. Millions and millions of acres of land were occupied by the moving horde. The map shows how immense this added territory was.

How the people pressed into the Mississippi Valley! There were all sorts and conditions of people, walking, on horseback, pushing carts, in wagons, on boats. The *Salem* (Massachusetts) *Mercury* for

Tuesday, December 23, 1788, reported this item of news from Virginia: "A gentleman who left Kentucky the 18th of September informs—that he met on his way 1,004 people, in one party, bound to Kentucky."

Robbstown is a village in Pennsylvania lying directly on the western highway to Pittsburgh. In one month, from October 6 to November 6, 1811, it reported that 236 wagons with men, women, and children, and 600 sheep, had passed through on their way to Ohio. This is the record for only one month in only one town.

"Reports from Lancaster (Pennsylvania) state that 100 moving families had been counted going through the town *in a week*, and that the turnpike was fairly covered with bands of emigrants. At Zanesville (Ohio) 50 wagons crossed the Muskingum in one day."

"At Easton, Pennsylvania, which lay on the favorite westward route for New Englanders, 511 wagons with 3,066 persons passed in a month. They went in trains of from 6 to 50 wagons each day."

Never before had the world seen such a movement. It was a never-ending stream. Towns grew and villages sprang up almost overnight. "Mount Pleasant in Jefferson County, Ohio, was in 1810 a little hamlet of 7 families living in cabins. In 1815 it contained 90 families numbering 500 souls, had 7 stores and 3 taverns, a meeting-house, a school-house, a market-house, a machine for spinning wool, a factory for making thread, and 40 artisans and mechanics representing 11 trades."

In 1817 John Calhoun said, "We are great, and rapidly—I was about to say fearfully—growing." Perhaps fearfully was the correct word.

The figures alone shout the story. Michigan had:

in 1810 ▪
    4,000 people
in 1820 ▬
    8,000 people
in 1830 ▬▬
    31,000 people
in 1840 ▬▬▬▬▬▬▬▬▬▬▬▬▬▬▬
    212,000 people

This in only thirty years! It was astounding. The broadening line, moving, moving, ever moving to the West.

From the size of this tremendous westward movement it would be natural to suppose that going west was the easiest job in the world.

Not at all. Most of these moving people were moving primarily because they had little or no money, so plush seats in speedy railroad trains that could make the journey in twenty-four hours were not for them; besides, railroad trains as we know them simply did not exist for anyone, money or not. The superb concrete roads familiar to us were not even dreamed of; trucks and automobiles with cushioned shock absorbers, comfortable springs, and rubber tires, were

seventy-five years in the future. No, for these early pioneers, going west was what they wanted to do, but not because it was easy to do it. The Appalachian Mountains, though not as high as the Rockies, were nevertheless a real barrier. The ranges average only about three thousand feet high, but they are about three hundred miles wide and are long and unbroken. You find a gap in one range and then you must go north or south for miles to find another pass through the next range. Nowhere are the gaps opposite one another through all the hills.

Rivers which cut through the mountains were, of course, a great help. But the traveler had to ford the streams, and getting his family and cattle across was not very simple. Occasionally a summer rain would swell a mountain creek into a rushing torrent. Then crossing was very dangerous. Always there was the fear of attack by the Indians. Once safely past the mountains, the going was a little easier. Then the whole family, husband, wife, children, and cattle could board a raft or keelboat on a river and float with the current downstream. Unfortunately, because so many people were making the journey westward, it was difficult to procure a boat right away. Since everybody was on the move, workmen were hard to find. Often a traveling family would have to wait weeks before its boat was built. And always, even while floating down the river, there was the danger of surprise attacks by the Indians on the shore. For this reason many flatboats were entirely enclosed on all sides so that they looked like floating forts. There were loopholes on both sides for the rifles of the emigrants.

Later, in those sections of the country where the Indians had been removed, the boats presented a more peaceful picture. James Hall traveled west in the 1820's. He tells what he saw on the Ohio River:

Today we passed two large rafts lashed together, by which simple conveyance several families from New England were transporting themselves and their property to the land of promise in the western woods. Each raft was 80 or 90 feet long, with a small house erected on it; and on each was a stack of hay, round which several horses and cows were feeding, while the paraphernalia of a farm-yard, the ploughs, waggons, pigs, children, and poultry, carelessly distributed, gave to the whole more the appearance of a permanent residence, than of a caravan of adventurers seeking a home. A respectable-looking old lady, with spectacles on nose, was seated on a chair at the door of one of the cabins, employed in knitting; another female was at the washtub; the men were chewing their tobacco, and the various family avocations seemed to go on like clockwork. In this manner these people travel at slight expense. They bring their own provisions; their raft floats with the current; and honest Jonathan, surrounded with his scolding, grunting, squalling and neighing dependants, floats to the point proposed without leaving his own fire-side; and on his arrival there, may step on shore with his house, and commence business. . . .

The rivers of the West were dotted with the arks, flatboats, and barges of men, women, children, and their livestock, all piled on together. Oftentimes when a family saw a spot that looked like a good place to settle, they stopped, broke up their boat, and built their house with the planks.

Wherever the road was wide enough, wagons were used. But many people couldn't afford even the crude, uncomfortable wagons of the time. To see whole families walking hundreds of miles on foot was a common sight. Often it was pitiful to behold. "A family of 8 on their way from Maine to Indiana walked all the way to Easton, Pa. [about 415 miles], which they reached late in February, dragging the children and their worldly goods in a hand cart. A blacksmith from Rhode Island made his way in the dead of winter across Massachusetts to Albany [about 200 miles]. In a little cart on 4 plank wheels a foot in diameter were some clothes, some food and two children. Behind it trudged the mother with an infant at the breast and 7 other children beside her." It took courage to face hardships like that.

Roads were very poor. Here is a typical western story, which indicates how miserable they were:

A traveler in Ohio in the 1820's, while riding horseback over the muddy roads, came to one very bad spot. He espied a beaver hat lying with the crown upwards in the mud. Imagine his surprise at seeing it move! The traveler's flesh began to creep, but he got up enough nerve to poke the hat with his riding whip. Lo! beneath it appeared a man's head—not a ghost, but a living, laughing head which turned to the traveler and said: "Hullo stranger! Who told you to knock my hat off?" The traveler was so astonished that for a moment or two he did not realize that the head belonged to a man up to his neck in the mud. Soon, however, he came to and said "I'll alight and try to pull you up out of the mud."

"Oh, never mind," said the other. "I'm in rather a bad fix, it is true, but I have an excellent horse under me, who has carried me through many a worse place than this. We shall get along."

No, moving west was not easy. It was a life full of hardships. Even later, when the National Road was built and steamboats took the place of flatboats and the Indians were finally pushed far enough back to be less dangerous, even then the journey had its difficulties and dangers. Yet hordes of people continued to push west. Though occasionally land companies helped emigrants to get to lands that they wanted to sell, and sometimes groups of neighbors from eastern towns would band together and travel in one body, nevertheless the West was filled up, in the main, by separate families. Husband, wife, and children, hungry for land of their own, this was most often the unit that braved the dangers of travel, climbed the mountains, trudged over the trails, floated down the rivers, and carved a home out of the dense wilderness.

Don't suppose that, having once reached a place and settled down, the travelers stayed put. Oh, no. They must be up and moving again as soon as news reached them of good land farther west. They moved, settled down, packed up, sold to a newcomer, and moved on again. Moving was in their blood. J. M. Peck, who traveled in the West in the 1830's wrote a book called *A New Guide for Emigrants to the*

West. In it he wrote that moving "has become almost a habit in the West. Hundreds of men can be found, not 50 years of age, who have settled for the 4th, 5th, or 6th time on a new spot. To sell out, and remove only a few hundred miles, makes up a portion of the variety of backwoods life and manners."

Rutherford B. Hayes, who later became President of the United States, tells the story of having passed the house of a man who moved so often that even his animals had the habit; every year in the spring his chickens would come up to him and cross their legs, ready to be tied for their regular journey west.

The family of Abraham Lincoln moved from Pennsylvania to Kentucky, where he was born in 1809. In 1816, when Lincoln was seven, his family crossed the Ohio in a raft to Indiana. In 1830, when

Lincoln was twenty-one, his family moved again, from Indiana to Illinois. This was typical of life in the West.

Wave after wave rolled westward. The frontier line kept moving on.

First the buffalo and the deer traveling by wonderful animal instinct over the shortest possible routes through the gaps in the mountains to the salt springs; then the Indian follows the buffalo road; the white trader comes next on the trail of the Indian; then the hunter follows the same trail in his search for game; after the hunter comes the pioneer farmer, who makes his clearing, builds his log cabin, and allows his cattle to graze on the wild range; before long another wave of emigrants rolls along, and the pioneer farmer, craving more elbowroom, sells out to the newer settlers and moves farther west to pioneer again in another spot, while the purchaser improves on his log cabin, puts in a brick chimney and glass windows, and clears more land; another wave of settlers reaches this spot; the improved land has gone up in value and the owner is ready to sell out and repeat the same thing all over again a few hundred miles west. What was frontier line a short while ago now becomes a region of extensive farms, well-built houses, good roads, schools, factories, cities—civilization—meanwhile a new frontier line has been created for the West.

It was, of course, the first group of settlers, the trail blazers and the pioneer farmers who closely followed them, who did the real fighting with both the Indian and the wilderness. Theirs was the hard, dangerous life. The brave deeds of Daniel Boone, the most famous of the trail blazers, are known to every American schoolboy. There were many others whose experiences were also exciting. William Cooper, one of the early pioneers of the wilderness, tells his story: "In 1785 I visited the rough and hilly country of Otsego, where there existed not an inhabitant nor any trace of road. I was alone 300 miles from home, without bread, meat, or food of any kind; fire and fishing tackle were my only means of subsistence. I caught trout in the brook and roasted them in the ashes. My horse fed on the grass that grew by the edge of the waters. I laid me down to sleep in my watch-coat, nothing but the melancholy Wilderness around me."

When the backwoodsman and his family finally reached the spot where they decided to build, there was plenty of hard work ahead. They had to have food and shelter immediately. The land must be cleared of trees, the logs cut to suitable lengths for a cabin, a well dug for water, and the ground plowed for planting. Wild animals and unfriendly Indians were often lurking about in the dense wood. The pioneer needed tools. He had a rifle, an ax, and a bag of corn. His rifle served two purposes; it was protection against the Indians, and also the means of procuring food. The pioneer family often existed for long stretches of time on the meat of deer, wild turkey, and other animals killed by the ever-present rifle. The backwoodsman soon learned to be quick and accurate with the rifle— he became a "dead shot." When he met his enemy at close quarters he could use his dirk with equal skill.

The ax, of course, was absolutely essential for chopping down the trees. It was very carefully looked after. An ax weighed from three to four and a half pounds. The handle, which was invariably made of shellbark hickory, was oval in shape, and about two feet four inches in length; it always had scratched upon it a one - or two-foot measure, for the purpose of measuring off the "rail cuts" or the cabin logs. The lower part of the handle was always made smaller than the upper, so as to give it a slight degree of elasticity; this not only increased the power of the ax, but also saved the hand from a jar in using it. Grindstones were scarce, but every house was provided with a whetstone. Finally, it was a rule, never to be violated, to warm the blade or edge in winter, before proceeding to chop wood; otherwise it might break.

Indian corn was very important to the first settlers. They had so much to do and so little time in which to do it. Corn could be planted either by tilling the soil a little or even without tilling it at all; once planted, it took very little care while growing; once grown, it need not be harvested immediately; while other grains have to be gathered at just the right moment, corn might remain standing for several months; the same amount of farm work on corn as on wheat gave twice as much corn; the whole family ate it, and if there were horses, cows, hogs, or sheep, they too, fed on it. Nothing could have taken its place, neither wheat nor barley nor potatoes—it was the perfect grain for the pioneer.

The backwoodsman and his family could chop down the trees themselves; they could measure the cabin logs and notch them, themselves; but for the actual building of their cabin they needed help. When everything was ready, the neighbors for miles around —men, women, and children—would ride in on horseback. It was a chance for a "get-together" so welcome to lonely people miles away from one another. The men would pile log upon log, then put up the roof. The house was raised. Meanwhile, liquor would flow freely. Alcohol seemed necessary to the pioneer. Whenever backwoodsmen came together, for a wedding, a funeral, a husking, or a logrolling, there was always plenty to drink.

Because there were both a cabin and a farm to be looked after, and a thousand and one tasks to be performed, men usually married early. Help was always needed and families were very large; they would have been even larger if so many babies hadn't died young for want of a doctor or because so little was then known about the cure of children's diseases. Boys and girls, as soon as they became men and women, married and went farther west to begin homes for themselves.

There was work for everybody. Daniel Drake in his *Pioneer Life in Kentucky* tells us of the jobs he had as a young boy:

I have already spoken of grating and pounding corn, toting water from a distant spring, holding the calf by the ears at milking time, going to the pond at wash days. . . . To chop, split, and bring in wood, keep up the fire, pick up chips in the corn basket for kindlings in the morning, and for light through the long winter evenings, when "taller" was too scarce to afford sufficient candles, and "fat" so necessary for cooking, . . . were regular labors. . . . To slop the cows, and, when wild, drive them into a corner of the fence, and stand over them with a stick while mother milked them, was another. Occasionally I assisted her in milking but sister Lizzy was taught that accomplishment as early as possible seeing that it was held by the whole neighborhood to be quite too "gaalish" for a boy to milk.

But life was not all work and no play. True enough, the times when the backwoodsman could play were few and far between, but they did come. The cornhusking frolic was one of these occasions. It was a race to remove the dry husks from the corn; two sides would be chosen and the team that finished first was declared the winner. Drake, who took part in many of these races, described them:

When the crop was drawn in, the ears were heaped into a long pile or rick, a night fixed on, and the neighbors notified, rather than invited, for it was an affair of mutual assistance. As they assembled at night-fall the green glass quart whiskey bottle, stopped with a cob, was handed to every one, man and boy, as they arrived, to take a drink. Two men, or more commonly two boys, were by acclamation declared captains. They paced the rick and estimated its contractions and expansions with the eye, till they were able to fix on the spot on which the end of the dividing rail should be. The choice depended on the tossing of a chip, one side of which had been spit upon; and in a few minutes the rick was charged upon by the rival forces. As others arrived as soon as the owner had given each the bottle, he fell in, according to the end that he belonged to. . . . The heap cut in two, the parties turned their backs upon each other, and making their hands keep time with a peculiar sort of time, the chorus of voices on a still night might be heard a mile. The oft-replenished whiskey bottle meanwhile circulated freely and at the close the victorious captain, mounted on the shoulders of some of the stoutest men, with the bottle in

one hand and his hat in the other, was carried in triumph around the vanquished party amidst shouts of victory which rent the air. Then came the supper, on which the women had been busily employed, and which always included a "pot-pie" . . . by midnight the sober were found assisting the drunken home.

It was a hard life and it made a rough, strong people. It was a quiet, lonely life which had its effect on the pioneer. When he joined his fellows in a wolf hunt, a cockfight, or later in the Saturday gathering at the store, there was very apt to be hard drinking, all kinds of practical jokes and rough games. Brawls or wrestling matches were brutal affairs. The opponents might scratch, pull one another's hair, try to choke one another, bite off noses, and even gouge out eyes. They would think it very funny to "hoop up in a hogshead a drunken man, they themselves being drunk, put in and nail fast the head, and roll the man down a hill a hundred feet or more."

Even when he "got religion" the frontiersman became highly excited. The circuit rider (the preacher who went from settlement to settlement) would occasionally hold a big "revival" to which men, women, and children flocked from miles around. Then queer sights could be seen. As the preacher delivered his fiery sermon, many of his listeners would jump up and shout, others would bark, and some would get so excited that they would roll on the ground in spasms, or "jerks."

The Westerner was hospitable. His manners were rough, and though he appeared to be ungracious, nevertheless the lost or weary traveler could always find a welcome at his rude cabin. He had little, but he was ready to share it. His "I reckon you can stay" did not sound very inviting, but he was a man of few words and didn't stand on ceremony. James Hall, traveling through the woods, was helped over a stream by a backwoodsman. He tells what happened, "After drinking a bowl of milk, which I really called for by way of excuse for paying him a little more for his trouble, I asked to know his charge for ferrying me over the water, to which he good humoredly replied, that he 'never took money for helping a traveler on his way.'

"'Then let me pay you for your milk.'

"'I never sell milk.'

" 'But,' said I, urging him, 'I would rather pay you. I have money enough.'

" 'Well,' said he, 'I have milk enough, so we're even; I have as good a right to give you milk, as you have to give me money.' "

The pioneer had the difficult job of changing his old habits to fit into his new surroundings. The frontier line was "the meeting point between savagery and civilization." The pioneer farmer had to give up his civilized ways and actually become, for a time, a savage. He took off his civilized clothing and put on the hunting shirt and the moccasin. He gave up his civilized home and lived in a log cabin. Before long, he plowed Indian fashion with a sharp stick and he planted Indian corn. He gave up the civilized way of fighting and shouted the war cry and scalped his enemy in true savage style. All these things he did, not because he wanted to, but because he had to in order to live. The wilderness forced these things; not to have fitted himself into this kind of life would have meant certain death. Little by little he transformed the wilderness, but in the meantime he had himself been transformed. He was a new person. Many of those qualities we think are typical of Americans in general were the result of this frontier life.

What were the things this battle with the wilderness taught the pioneer?

It taught him to be independent. With his own hands, relying on his own strength, he had faced a strange situation and conquered it. He fed himself, sheltered himself, clothed himself. When he left the East he broke his ties with his old home. It is an interesting fact that while the people east of the mountains faced Europe and thought of the land in the West as the "back country," the pioneer faced west and called the East the "back country." He knew what he wanted and set out to get it; he did not like interference of any kind. He had proved that he was able to take care of himself. He was his own master.

It gave him a feeling of self-confidence; his had been a hard fight against tremendous odds, and he had won out; the failures either went back home or died, but the pioneer who stayed and lived and succeeded was proud of himself. He had fought an uphill fight and come out on top; he was ready to tackle anything. He believed in himself and in his ability to get along. His was a young country. He had the confidence and enthusiasm of the young.

He believed that one man was as good as another. In most of

these new western states the right to vote was given to all white men alike. The pioneer learned to measure men not by who they were, but by what they could do. Into the West poured Germans, Scotch-Irish, French, men from all parts of the world. In the West they were all equal; rich or poor, educated or uneducated, coarse or refined, to all the task was the same. If you made a go of it, no matter who you were, you were equal to the next man.

In a crowded meeting in the West certain officials were trying to force their way through to the platform. "Make way there," they cried. "We are the representatives of the people."

"Make way yourselves," came the quick retort. "*We are* the people."

Men who could answer in that fashion knew their own strength; they would kowtow to no one.

People who must meet new situations learn to be inventive. At the same time they learn not to be afraid of the new. The pioneer became a Jack-of-all-trades. He had to learn to fit himself to the unusual. He did—so he was not afraid to try anything once.

The pioneer lived a plain, simple life; he had a passionate hatred for pomp; he disliked ceremony; he was direct in his manner; he believed in equality and freedom; he was independent, proud, boastful, energetic, unafraid, eager to succeed. The life in the wilderness helped to make him what he was.

As the swarm of land seekers pressed farther and farther west, what happened to the Indians who had roamed through these forests for hundreds of years? They could not stop the moving horde; they fought, were defeated, and were pushed back. They fought again, were again defeated, and were pushed back still farther. The government made treaties with them. It promised to pay them for the land taken by the settlers, and offered them the land farther west. The Indians, helpless, signed the treaties and moved on. Before the ink on the last treaty was dry, the first advance of the oncoming throng of backwoodsmen was on their heels. They again appealed to the government. A new treaty was made. . . . The Indians would be paid for the land just taken, and a strip of land farther west was to be theirs *forever*. . . . Came the onward rush of settlers . . . more treaties . . . more promises. . . . Then a great warrior would unite all the tribes for one last stand against the whites. A short Indian war . . . defeat. . . . Move on, Red Man.

It was a wonderful valley of rich fertile soil into which these crowds of settlers had flocked. Stories of its marvelous fertility grew with the telling. After a backbreaking day on his stony farm, how the mouth of the New Englander must have watered as he read newspaper stories about the wonderful soil in the West:

A man returning East was reported to have been asked whether such things were true as that if a crowbar were planted, tenpenny nails would sprout overnight. Denying this, he said, "But this I can bear witness to . . . that just before I left the Muskingum, one day, horseback, having taken some pumpkin-seed into my hand at the door of a house, several of which I dropped, turning about to speak to a person then passing, so instantaneous was their growth—so surprisingly rapid their extension and spread, that before I turned back, the seed had taken root in the earth to such a degree that I was dangerously encompassed about with enormous serpentine vines, which threatened keeping pace with my utmost exertions to escape being tied in, as I immediately clapped spurs to my horse and with difficulty was disentangled."

That is, of course, a tall story of the kind Westerners were very fond of telling. Nevertheless, it *was* magnificent country and the soil was marvelously rich. Virgin soil, suitable climate, plenty of rain, a gigantic network of rivers—in short, a farmer's paradise. The land was first offered for sale by the government at two dollars an acre, in lots of 640 acres each, half to be paid for immediately, the other half at the end of a year. This did not work out well because the new settlers were poor; very few of them had $640 to start with, nor could they hope to raise the other $640 in one year.

The frontiersmen protested and the government made a new arrangement. At first, lots of 320 acres, then later lots of 160 acres were offered, still at two dollars an acre. Now, however, the government made payments much easier; the settler need pay only one quarter of the price of his farm to start with (within forty days of buying) ; then he had two years more before his second payment was due, and the third and fourth payments could be made the third and fourth year. This meant that a man needed only eighty dollars to start life on a 160-acre farm in the West. This seems like a small sum, and so it is—today. But to most of the buyers of western lands then, eighty dollars was a lot of money. Added to it was the cost of traveling west (horses or oxen, wagon, the food while on the journey) , and also money needed to tide the family over the first year before crops started growing. As a result, the pioneer farmer, moving west to better his living condition, found himself saddled with a debt of several hundred dollars to begin with. If, as frequently happened, he had bought more than a 160-acre farm, his debt was even greater.

All through the early nineteenth century the price of public lands was a subject for argument in the Congress of the United States. It wasn't long before the frontiersman wanted to know why he had to pay anything at all for the land. Hadn't he worked hard to change the land from wilderness to cleared farm? Hadn't he fought the Indians on the frontier line, thus protecting the people behind him in the East? Two dollars per acre was unfair. He didn't want to pay it if he could, and he couldn't pay it even if he wanted to. In 1820 the price was reduced to one dollar and a quarter an acre cash payment (forty-two years later the public land in the West was free to settlers) .

The pioneer had borrowed the money he needed from people back home, or later, from banks. The West was settled largely by money-owers. You would expect a bitterness to grow up between these money-owers and the money-lenders. It did. The debtor West, faced with the problem of paying back the money it owed, learned to hate the moneyed classes of the East. The bank loaned the money to the pioneer, at interest; if he was unable to pay back, the bank often found it necessary to take his land and house away from him. This was a bitter pill to a man and his family who had worked and worked and worked on that land. The money-owing West was united in its hatred of the money-lending East. Both sections had different ways of living, according to the geography of each region. As always, the ideas of both the interior and the coast peoples were determined by the way they made their living.

Since practically all the people in the pioneer West lived by farming, they could not sell to one another but had to have an outside market. After the first year or two the backwoods farmer raised more than enough food for himself and his family. His barn was filled with grain and flour, for sale to whoever would buy it. Often the backwoodsman also had hogs for sale. The money he needed to pay his taxes and to repay what he owed was in those things he wanted to sell. The problem, then, was to get his produce to market.

Travelers on the poor roads of the time would often come upon hundreds of hogs being driven to the market towns on the coast. It was quite a job, but the farmer seized upon it as one way to get money.

Sending grain to the cities on the Atlantic coast took considerable time and cost a great deal. "Even in the country where I reside, not eighty miles from tidewater," said Tucker of Virginia in 1818, "it takes the farmer one bushel of wheat to pay the expense of carrying two to a seaport town."

Grain is easily distilled into whisky; grain is bulky, whisky is light; a pack animal which could carry only about four bushels of grain as grain, could carry about twenty-four bushels of grain in the form of whisky. Naturally, many farmers turned their grain into whisky; it was one way out of their difficulty. In Pennsylvania alone, in 1790, there were about five thousand distilleries. Virginia and North Carolina also had some. When the Congress of the United States, while Washington was President, passed a law putting a tax on whisky, the back country farmers refused to pay it. The houses of the collectors were wrecked or burned. In the Whisky Rebellion that followed, a few people were wounded and some were killed. Transportation of their produce to market was a very important problem to the Westerners.

Because it was so important to them, the western settlers made a tremendous noise about it. They kept shouting for roads—more and better roads—for canals, for any good route which would make travel and transportation easier, quicker, and cheaper. They wanted roads and canals that would connect them with the East and with one another. For years and years practically all Westerners who went to

Congress had this need for internal improvements on the tips of their tongues. They made speeches to one another, to Easterners, to anyone who would listen. First they asked, then they demanded.

From 1800 to 1840 three ways of helping travel and transportation of freight were talked about at different times. First, there was the cry for improved roads. The first great highway built by the government, the National Road, was a turnpike to the west. (It was begun in 1808 at Cumberland in Maryland, reached Wheeling in West Virginia in 1817, extended to Columbus, Ohio in 1833, and finally reached Vandalia in Illinois in 1852.)

Later came the period of canal-building. Which way did the canals run? To the west.

Still later, railroads were invented. In what direction did they run? Toward the west.

The "over the mountains" country had to have an outlet for its goods. The Westerners had to sell what they raised or they could never hope to pay their debts, or rise in the world.

When the pioneers filled up the Mississippi Valley, that river and its many branches were a great help to farmers sending their flour, grain, pork, and whisky to market. The Ohio and the Mississippi were soon dotted with keelboats, flatboats, broadhorns, and barges. Freight was floated downstream to New Orleans at the mouth of the Mississippi. This was by far a better and cheaper way for the farmer to send his goods to market, than over the poor roads to the eastern cities. The Mississippi was the western farmer's outlet to the sea—he had to have it.

Up to 1800, New Orleans and the Louisiana territory west of the Mississippi were owned and controlled by Spain, in the sixteenth and seventeenth centuries a great country, but weak and powerless by 1800. In 1795 Washington made a treaty with Spain which gave Americans the right to trade through New Orleans. The Westerners could use the highway which they needed so sorely.

In 1800 Spain was secretly forced to give up Louisiana to France, then ruled by Napoleon Bonaparte. In 1802 the port of New Orleans was closed to Americans and the news was out that France now owned Louisiana. This was very serious; it meant ruin for American farmers. Spain was dying, but France was very much alive. It was one of the strongest countries in Europe. Something must be done— quickly.

Thomas Jefferson, then President of the United States, was alive to the danger. He wrote at this time: "There is on the globe one single spot the possessor of which is our natural and habitual enemy. It is New Orleans, through which the produce of three-eighths of our territory must pass to market. . . ."

Jefferson had been born on the Virginia frontier. He knew the temper of the backwoodsmen; he learned of the preparations they were making to raise an army to keep the port open. Jefferson hated war. He immediately sent messages to Livingston, the American minister to France, instructing him to try to buy New Orleans. James Monroe was then sent as another minister to France, to show the West that the government was doing all it could.

Napoleon, in the meantime, had sent an army to the French island of Santo Domingo, to put down a revolution led by Toussaint L'Ouverture, a native black. The French Army was defeated and Napoleon was quick to learn that expeditions to the New World might not always be profitable. At the same time he was planning to continue again his war against England. He knew that England's navy, so much stronger than his own, would certainly take Louisiana. Accordingly, even before Monroe arrived, he offered to sell to the United States for $15,000,000, not only New Orleans, but all of Louisiana!

We bought.

On December 20, 1803, the Stars and Stripes were hoisted in New Orleans. Another vast empire, stretching hundreds of miles west of the Mississippi, lay at the feet of the droves of land seekers.

Nor was that all. Next, Florida was purchased from Spain in 1819. Then in 1821 Moses Austin, a Connecticut Yankee, obtained a very large piece of land in Texas which then belonged to Mexico. In return he was to bring with him three hundred families to settle there. This was the beginning of the American rush. Mexico wanted its huge strip of land to be filled up with honest farmers, so it offered Texas land at twelve and one-half cents an acre—while the government of the United States was charging one dollar and twenty-five cents an acre, ten times as much. You can easily imagine the result. What if they did have to promise to be loyal to Mexico? What if they were supposed to be Catholics?—land-hungry Americans were being offered rich fertile soil for a mere song. Is it surprising to learn that in ten years, by 1830, about twenty thousand people had poured into Texas? Shortly afterward a war for independence was fought between

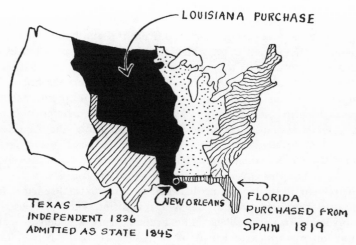

LOUISIANA PURCHASE

TEXAS
INDEPENDENT 1836
ADMITTED AS STATE 1845

NEW ORLEANS

FLORIDA
PURCHASED FROM
SPAIN 1819

the Texans and Mexico. In 1836 Texas declared itself the "Lone Star Republic" and asked for admission into the United States. Here was a territory larger than France, Belgium, Switzerland, and Denmark, waiting to be added to the fast-growing country of the United States. What a rich prize for a land-hungry people!

Before very long products from American farms on both sides of the Mississippi were being loaded on the huge flatboats. Timothy Flint traveled through the valley of the Mississippi from 1815 to 1825. At New Madrid, one of the towns on the river, on one spring day, he counted one hundred boats on their way to New Orleans:

You can name no point from the numerous rivers of the Ohio and the Mississippi from which some of these boats have not come. In one place there are boats loaded with planks from the pine forests of the southwest

of New York. In another quarter there are the Yankee notions of Ohio.
From Kentucky, pork, flour, whiskey, hemp, tobacco, bagging and bale-
rope. From Tennessee there are the same articles, together with great
quantities of cotton. From Missouri and Illinois cattle and horses, the
same articles generally from Ohio, together with peltry and lead from
Missouri. Some boats are loaded with corn in the ear and in bulk; others
with barrels of apples and potatoes. Some have loads of cider, and what
they call "cider royal" or cider that has been strengthened by boiling or
freezing. There are dried fruits, every kind of spirits manufactured in
these regions. . . .

The West was growing. The rivers were busy with its commerce.

After settlers lined the banks of the Ohio and the Mississippi, a
floating country store—a flatboat fitted with shelves, counters, and
seats—would occasionally wend its way downstream. As soon as the
boatman-shopkeeper espied a cluster of cabins on the banks, he
would blow a horn. Then, children, men, and women would stop
work, hurry to the riverbank, and board the boat. The dry goods,
china, shoes, bonnets, fine clothing, tinware—every sort of article or
tool—were a welcome sight to the pioneer farmers. They sometimes
paid in money, but more often they would trade pork, flour, or
vegetables for whatever they bought. When all the purchases were
completed, the floating storekeeper started along to tie up again
at the next group of cabins.

Navigation of a 60-by-20-foot flatboat or of a 70-by-9-foot keelboat
on the Ohio or the treacherous Mississippi was a very difficult job.
The Mississippi was, not without reason, called the "wicked river."
Its channels changed frequently (a town might be right on the
river one year and miles inland the next) ; its swift current undermined the banks constantly; its treacherous sand bars were many.
Then there were other pitfalls. Perhaps the most dangerous were
the trunks of trees embedded in the muddy bottom of the river and
sticking up like spears. Some of these logs, called "planters" were
solidly fixed and the boatmen soon learned their location. But other
trunks would bob up and down constantly. A boat might be floating
along peacefully, with nothing in sight, then suddenly run full tilt
into a rising, jagged limb. Many a river boat was wrecked in this
fashion. The river boatmen learned the treacherous ways of the
mighty Mississippi; they learned where the dangerous tree trunks
and sand bars were; they learned every turn of the crooked river
and its wild habits. But new dangers constantly arose and fatal ac-
cidents occurred frequently. The floating corpse of a dead boatman

or the rotten hulks of wrecked boats told the traveler the gruesome
tale of the wild river's brute force.

Handling a boat on such waters required great skill. Men were
necessary who would know every peculiarity, every trick, every snag
of the mighty, wicked river. Soon there appeared the professional
river boatman, a picturesque figure in his bright red flannel shirt and
coarse brown linsey-woolsey trousers with hunting knife and tobacco
pouch hanging from a leather belt. He was honest, reckless, and
brave, in love with his difficult job because of its many dangers and
exciting thrills; he was rude and coarse; a free spender, a heavy
fighter, and a hard drinker. How he loved to tell tall stories and brag
of his own mighty strength! Mark Twain, in his *Life on the Mississippi*, has one of these colorful boasters tell the world who he is:

Whoo-oop! I'm the old original iron-jawed, brass-mounted, copper-
bellied corpse-maker from the wilds of Arkansas! Look at me! I'm the
man they call Sudden Death and General Desolation! Sired by a hurri-
cane, dam'd by an earthquake, half-brother to the cholera, nearly related
to the smallpox on the mother's side! Look at me! I take nineteen alliga-
tors and a bar'l of whiskey for breakfast when I'm in robust health, and
a bushel of rattlesnakes and a dead body when I'm ailing. I split the ever-
lasting rocks with my glance, and I squench the thunder when I speak!
Whoo-oop! Stand back and give me room according to my strength!
Blood's my natural drink, and the wails of the dying is music to my ear.
Cast your eye on me, gentlemen! and lay low and hold your breath, for
I'm 'bout to turn myself loose! . . . Whoo-oop! I'm the bloodiest son of
a wildcat that lives.

No inferiority complex here—but you would have agreed that
the boat man was really quite a guy if ever you saw him and his
fellows forcing a boat upstream on the Mississippi or Missouri. Many
of the flatboats and barges were floated downstream to New Orleans,
their goods unloaded, and the boat sold there—upstream travel was
too difficult. But some boatmen did make the trip back against the
mighty current. A swift keelboat might take only *six weeks* to float
downstream from a town on the Ohio to New Orleans, but it would
need at least *four months* to make the same journey upstream. The
boats were huge and unwieldly, the current was very swift, and often
the wind, too, was blowing the wrong way. Usually at least twenty
to thirty hands were necessary. Iron-tipped poles pushed by very
strong men, would send a boat upstream only about ten miles in a
day. Wherever it was possible, men walked along the shore and
pulled the boat with a long rope.

MISSISSIPPI BOATMEN

Another more dangerous and more tiring method was called "warping." A cable about half a mile long was carried out by a yawl in advance of the boat, and fastened to a tree. The hands on board then drew the boat up to the tree. Meanwhile, another yawl had gone on ahead with a second cable, to be fastened to a tree still farther upstream. More heavy hauling while the first yawl coiled its used cable and went on above to repeat the process all over again. Six miles was a good day's progress. Warping required endless patience and brute strength.

A boat that could make the upstream trip with less trouble and more speed was badly needed both for freight and for passengers.

Then came the steamboat. The steamboat did the trick, but not immediately. At first the steamboat-builders, Easterners, made some very bad mistakes. Their boats did very well on the Hudson in New York, and on the ocean, so they designed their river boats along the same lines. These steamboatmen should have known better than to build deepwater vessels for western river use. From 1811 to 1816, their first boats, with their heavy boilers and low-pressure engines set in their deep round hulls, were designed to ride *in* the water. That was a fatal error. Western rivers were full of shoals, sand bars, snags. A steamboat was needed that would ride *on* the water. To send the boat upstream in face of the mighty current, a high-pressure engine set in a boat that wouldn't draw too much was necessary.

A river boatman was the first to realize this. Three years of experience with boats on the Mississippi had taught Henry Shreve that the best river boat was the one that drew the least water. He had learned that the keelboat hull was the best suited to western river use. It sat on the water without going down more than a few feet. Shreve's 148-foot *Washington* was simply a keelboat driven by steam. Instead of low-pressure engines set in a deep round hull, the *Washington* had double high-pressure engines set, not in its flat shallow hull, but on the main deck above. A Westerner had dared to try something new. A river boatman had finally designed a boat that was really suited to the river. Before Shreve's design, the steamboats could go upstream, but only in the deepwater part of the Mississippi between New Orleans and Natchez. Now at last the Mississippi was conquered for its entire length. The era of the river steamboat had come.

The flatboat and barge did not disappear immediately. They hung on for years, but there was no question about which was superior when round trips from Pittsburgh to New Orleans could now be measured in days instead of in months, as before.

For some years, however, there was very great question about the safety of those early steamboats. And well there might be. One disaster followed another. Snagged—sunk by ice—worn out—burned —wrecked by boiler explosion. This was the fate of steamboats whose average life was less than four years. Here are some interesting figures. In two years, sixty-six boats ended their careers. Of this number, only fifteen wore out and had to be scrapped. Of the remaining fifty-one, seven were lost in the ice, fifteen shot up in flames after their bursting boilers exploded, five were wrecked in collisions, and twenty-four were snagged. But all were replaced.

It was a very difficult task to pilot these huge boats, some of them more than twice the size of the longest flatboat, on the treacherous, muddy waters of the West. Mark Twain, who learned to be a steamboat pilot himself, was filled with awe and amazement at the wonderful memory the steamboat pilot needed. On twelve hundred miles of river he had to know the location of every shoal, every curve, every planter, the depth of the water for practically the whole length, the names of towns, points, bars, islands, bends, and a few hundred other things; and he had to know this well enough to pilot his boat not only in the daytime, but on a pitch-black night as well. The wonder of it was that there actually were a number of men who did manage to learn all this. Small wonder that the pilot was a much more important person than even the captain of a river steamboat. He was paid the highest wages and he took orders from no one.

The West was filling up, the farmers of the Mississippi Valley had quantities and quantities of produce to sell, and the river was soon covered with steamboats. River towns had yards where men worked day and night building boats. By 1840, steamboats had become very grand affairs indeed. Two or three hundred feet long, with one massive deck above another; the first, or main deck was crowded with freight; here, too, were the gear lines, snubbing posts, every contraption the deck hand needed to hustle the cargo on and off the boat; the deck for passengers had separate staterooms, a busy bar, an outside promenade, a long, overdecorated, thickly carpeted saloon brilliantly lighted, with every kind of gewgaw and doodad.

Boiler explosions, which were frequent, would wreck all this splendor, and kill many people besides. Sometimes the boiler iron was not strong enough, or the parts were badly put together. Often explosions came simply as a result of carelessness or of the desire for more speed. It was very dangerous to let the water get too low in the boilers, but hot steam was made more easily when there was little water, and hot steam meant more speed. Occasionally the water got too low, the steam was made too fast, and the boiler exploded. Then iron and wood hurtled through the air, decks were ripped open, men and women were tossed hundreds of yards, others were scalded to death or drowned. Steamboat explosions were horrible, gruesome affairs.

In spite of this danger, exciting races were frequent. Then the engine room was a busy place. Speed and more speed. Put oil on the wood, even weigh down the safety valve—do anything to get the boilers hot. The race must be won!

The story is told of a gray-haired old lady who boarded a steamboat for the first time in her life. She was going from Kentucky to New Orleans with several barrels of lard to be sold there. Her head was filled with tales of snags, collisions, fire, the danger of racing with its risk of bursting boilers. She went up to the captain and said, "I want you to promise me, Captain, before we start, that you won't run any races. You have no right to risk lives, blow up a boiler or something, just to beat some other boat."

The captain promised.

A few days later, a rival boat nosed alongside and a race was on. The Kentucky lady's boat was being beaten. She dashed up to the captain, her eyes bright with excitement, and shouted: "Captain, you can take back your promise! Don't let that boat beat us!"

"Madam," answered the captain, smiling, "we're doing the best we can. But we're going to lose out because the other boat is putting oil on her wood—see the black smoke—and we haven't any oil. We can't beat her on wood alone; can't get the boilers hot enough."

"Captain, where's my lard?" screamed the old lady.

"Your lard? Why, it's in the hold. It's perfectly safe."

"Safe!" shrieked the lady. "Safe, hell! Captain, make your boys bring up that lard this minute, and put it on the wood and get your old boilers hot! If we lose this race I swear I'll never travel with you again! What are you standing there for, looking at me? Make your boys jump, or I will!"

As more and more people poured into the West, trade on the river grew to an amazing extent. In 1819, 136,300 tons of produce, valued at $16,772,000 was floated down the Mississippi to New

Orleans; in 1860 the figure had jumped to 2,187,000 tons valued at $185,211,000. Other river towns grew by leaps and bounds. Pitts-

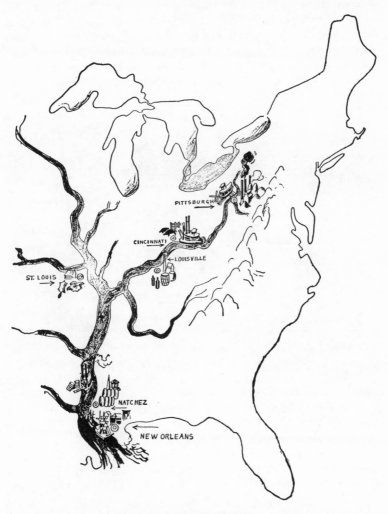

MAP OF RIVER TOWNS

burgh, Louisville, Cincinnati, Natchez, and St. Louis became big cities and kept growing.

By 1815 businessmen in the East had awakened to the fact that

there had been a deluge of people into the Mississippi Valley; that
these people—millions of them and still increasing—had farm
produce to sell; also that there were manufactured goods that
they had to buy; that here at their own back door, so to speak,
there existed a wonderful market. Now at last eastern shippers,
manufacturers, importers, merchants, all of whom had been looking toward Europe for trade, turned around and faced the
West. They joined the Westerners in their cry for ways of carrying
freight cheaply.

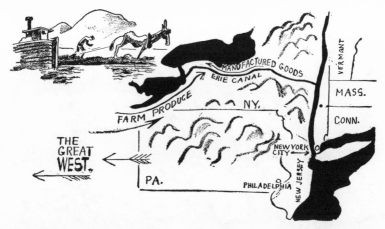

In 1817 New York State began work on the Erie Canal, which was
to connect Albany on the Hudson River with Lake Erie. Eight
years later the work was finished and goods from the Ohio Valley
could be sent from Buffalo to Albany, then down the Hudson to
New York City. Here, at last, was a direct, cheap tie-up of West with
East. The West sent its farm produce to the East and the East sent
its manufactured goods to the West. Before the canal was built it
cost one hundred dollars to send a ton of freight from Buffalo on
Lake Erie to New York City, and it took twenty days to travel between
the two places. After the canal was built it cost only eight dollars to
send the ton of freight, and it took only six days. This was exactly
what the West had wanted, had needed so badly. The traffic showed
it—within ten years the tolls on the freight on the canal more than
paid what it had cost to build.

This link with the heart of the country did wonders for New
York. No small part of that city's tremendous growth was due to

its position at the outer end of the cheap waterway from the West. New Orleans at one end, New York at the other, these were the West's water routes to the sea. Now other coast cities—Boston, Philadelphia, Charleston—all jealous of New York's successful canal, started a mad scramble to get in on the growing trade of the interior.

Year	East of the Appalachians	West of the Appalachians	Per cent of each East	West
1790	3,700,000	221,000		
1800	4,600,000	638,000		
1810	5,600,000	1,500,000		
1820	6,500,000	3,000,000		
1830	7,900,000	4,900,000		
1840	8,800,000	8,100,000		

That this tie-up with the West became very important to the cities on the Atlantic coast is shown by the wild schemes that were tried to rival the Erie Canal.

In Pennsylvania, for example, in 1826, an attempt was made to connect Philadelphia on the coast with Pittsburgh, the growing river town on the Ohio River. A splendid idea, but difficult to carry out. The distance between the two cities was only about four hundred miles, but there were the Appalachians to be crossed. Nothing daunted, the canal builders worked out an elaborate scheme of horse-drawn railroad cars (replaced by steam locomotive in 1834), inclined planes up and down the hills, then canal, then more inclined planes. The canalboats were loaded on railroad cars and by means of several sixty-horsepower engines, these cars were pulled by ropes up to the tops of the mountains and down the other side. In one stretch of only thirty-six miles, the boats were raised and lowered some twenty five hundred feet. Nor was that all. On the last lap of one hundred miles of canal there were sixty-six locks. To such crazy lengths were the people of the East led for a share of the increasing western trade.

How the West had grown! The approximate figures above show the amazing story of the increase in the population.

With the added population in the West came increased power and importance in many ways. The western idea of votes for all white men over twenty-one had seeped through to the old East, where even ordinary laborers and mechanics were winning the right to vote. In 1828 these working-class groups in the East joined with the West in voting for President of the United States.

The West was made up of farmers who had much the same interests. They were poor and in debt, they needed money, they wanted to sell their goods. When election time came, they turned to one of their own sons, a man who knew their problems. They elected a Westerner, an erstwhile poor man like themselves, who had grown up with the frontier; a rough man like themselves, who had worked with his own hands; a brave man like themselves, who had fought the fight against the Indians; a strong man like themselves, who knew what he wanted and went for it; an uneducated coarse, courageous, hot-tempered, two-fisted fighter, one of their own kind who lived as they did, thought as they did, and stood for what they stood for.

Now they had proven their strength.

The election of Andrew Jackson in 1828 was a great triumph for the West.

From 1770 on, the pioneer families followed the blazed trails over the mountains and found a wilderness. Swarms of land-hungry people thronged after them. With rifle, ax, and bag of corn they fought a grim uphill battle—and won an empire.

A Strange, Colorful Frontier — The Last

★————————————————————————————————————★

Less than one hundred years ago, in 1856 and 1857, two shiploads of camels, seventy-five in all, were landed in Texas for the use of the United States Army. One train of them marched into San Antonio, and another herd made the long trip to California. In 1858 an inhabitant of faraway Los Angeles wrote that "General Beale and about fourteen camels stalked into town last Friday week and gave our streets quite an Oriental aspect." General Beale, commander of the camel corps, was enthusiastic about them. He reported to the secretary of war that "they are the most docile, patient, and easily managed creatures in the world and infinitely more easily worked than mules." Nevertheless, in spite of the commander's enthusiasm, no more camels were bought and they soon disappeared.

But why had they been bought at all? What need of camels in the United States?

The answer lies in a speech made by Congressman Bates of Missouri in 1828. He said that all the land "between the Missouri and the Pacific, save a strip of cultural prairie not above two or three hundred miles wide . . . is waste and sterile, no better than the Desert of Sahara, and quite as dangerous to cross."

Bates probably got his mistaken information from the geography books of the 1820's to 1850's. Schoolboys of that period, studying from Morse's *System of Geography* or Goodrich's *Comprehensive Geography and History*, found maps that showed all the land from the Missouri to the Rockies as "The Great American Desert." These geographers, in turn, probably got their information from military reports of the period. Major Stephen Long's report of his expedition of 1819-20 was in part responsible for the fiction of the Great American Desert. He said of this region: "In regard to this extensive section of country, I do not hesitate in giving the opinion that it is almost wholly unfit for cultivation, and of course uninhabitable by a people depending upon agriculture for their subsistence. This region, however, viewed as a frontier, may prove of infinite importance to the United States, inasmuch as it is calculated to serve as a barrier to prevent too great an extension of our population westward."

And Zebulon Pike reported on his expedition to the Rockies, begun in 1806: "These vast plains of the western hemisphere may

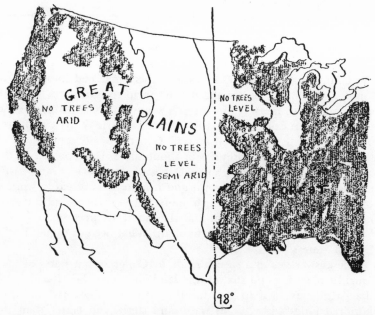

become in time as celebrated as the sandy deserts of Africa. . . . But from these immense prairies may arise one great advantage to the United States, viz: The restriction of our population to some certain limits and thereby a continuation of the Union. Our citizens being so prone to rambling and extending themselves on the frontiers will, through necessity, be constrained to limit their extent on the west to the borders of the Missouri and Mississippi. . . ."

America's recent experience with drought and erosion in the "dust bowl" makes it appear that Long and Pike were able prophets. But only half of what they said was accurate. They were wrong about this region being a desert—though it has since proven unsuited, in large part, to crop agriculture, it is admirably suited to ranching. However, they were right in believing that it would serve as a barrier to the westward movement. That is exactly what happened. Look at the map.

By 1840 the advancing horde of settlers had pushed about as far as the 98° line, and here for a while they stopped. Why?

East of the 98° line the rivers served as convenient highways for the traveler. West of that line the rivers were not easily navigable. The emigrant continuing west must leave his boat and go on by foot or wagon.

East of the 98° line the pioneers found well-watered land covered with trees. Here were fertile soil, water for the cattle or for a mill, and timber for houses, barns, fences, and fuel. Beyond the 98° line the oncoming settlers found oceans of grassy prairie rolling west to the region of little rainfall and dry plains. The absence of trees made them think the land was not fertile. Tough prairie sod was a new and unknown problem. They were used to timberlands and here there were no trees, only tall grass. "East of the Mississippi civilization stood on three legs—land, water, and timber; west of the Mississippi not one but two of these legs were withdrawn—water and timber—and civilization was left on one leg—land."

East of the 98° line the frontiersmen found a dangerous enemy in the Indian. But this eastern Indian was not a horseman, he had a settled village life and his whole tribe could be practically wiped out in his own home. West of the 98° line, the Plains Indian was a much more formidable foe. He was a nomad, wandering about as he pleased. He was a marvelous horseman, could drop his body upon either side of his horse, screening himself from his enemies' weapons while hanging by his heel over the horse's back. He carried a shield which was made of buffalo hide so hardened and tough that no arrow or bullet could go through it unless it was hit at a right angle. He could tear along on his fleet horse with his bundle of one hundred arrows so conveniently placed that he could keep one or more in the air all the time—with force enough behind each arrow to drive the shaft entirely through the body of a buffalo!

This perfect fighting machine, the Plains Indian, could keep eight arrows in the air at once. How the frontiersman, with only one shot in his rifle, must have welcomed the invention of the Colt six-shooter in 1836! Here was a weapon that could shoot bullets as fast as the Indian could shoot arrows. It was needed.

So it was that the log cabin line which had moved steadily westward came to about the 98° meridian and halted. Here on the edge of the Great Plains, settlers came to a region of less rainfall, no timber, more difficult traveling, and more dangerous Indians; they were given the mistaken idea of the existence of a sandy desert—and they stopped.

But although the farmer had stopped, the advance guard of the moving frontier line had long penetrated this vast region. Washington Irving, in his excellent book, *The Adventures of Captain Bonneville*, published in 1837, tells us that "The Rocky Mountains and the ulterior regions, from the Russian possessions in the north, down to the Spanish settlements of California, had been traversed and ransacked in every direction by bands of hunters and Indian traders; so that there is scarcely a mountain pass or defile that is not known and threaded in their restless migrations, nor a nameless stream that is not haunted by the lonely trapper."

There were beaver in the streams, mink, fox, bear, and other animals in the mountains, and buffalo on the plains. From the Missouri River to the Pacific coast stretched the vast territory covered by the daring hunter and the brave trapper. He was thoroughly at home in the Far West. "Drop him in the midst of a prairie, or in the heart of the mountains and he is never at a loss. He notices every landmark; can retrace his route through the most monotonous plains, or the most perplexed labyrinth of the mountains; no danger nor difficulty can appall him, and he scorns to complain under any privation."

St. Louis was the base of supplies. There traders loaded their boats with merchandise—guns, beads, trinkets, blankets, knives, alcohol—pushed up the Missouri, met the Indians and trappers, and exchanged their goods for the valuable furs and buffalo robes. At convenient points in the wild interior were some hundred trading posts where this same exchange of goods was carried on. Furs were brought to market in packs which weighed about one hundred pounds each. The number of furs in a pack varied. It might contain ten buffalo robes, eighty beaver, fourteen bear, or one hundred and twenty fox skins. Great care was taken in wrapping the furs into a pack so they would be protected from the weather.

There was bitter competition for the fur trade. Manuel Lisa's Missouri Fur Company, Astor's American Fur Company, the British Hudson Bay Company, the Rocky Mountain Fur Company, these and many smaller companies employed hunters and trappers to work for them by the year. They were given regular wages (hunters about $400 a year, and common camp men $200) and furnished with guns, knives, horses, and traps. They covered certain territory assigned to them by the company agent and were under his orders while they were in service. The year's catch of these hired trappers belonged to the company.

The free trappers were a more independent class. According to Captain Bonneville, "they come and go . . . when and where they please; provide their own horses, arms, and other equipments; trap and trade on their own account and dispose of their skins and peltries to the highest bidder."

Once a year, in June or July, the yearly rendezvous was held at some designated place in the mountains. It was a very picturesque affair.

To this rendezvous repair the various brigades of trappers from their widely selected hunting-grounds, bringing in the product of the year's campaign. Hither also repair the Indian tribes accustomed to traffic their peltries with the company. Bands of free trappers resort hither also to sell the furs they have collected. [Here was held the trappers' annual holiday, where] they engaged in contests of skill at running, jumping, wrestling, shooting with the rifle, and running horses. And then their rough hunters' feastings and carousals. They drank together, they sang, they laughed, they whooped; they tried to outbrag and outlie each other in stories of their adventures and achievements. . . .

The caravans of supplies arrived at the valley just at this period of gallantry and good fellowship. . . . Bales were hastily ripped open and their motley contents poured forth. A mania for purchasing spread itself through the several bands . . . rifles, hunting-knives, scarlet cloth, red blankets, garish beads, and glittering trinkets were bought at any price. . . . A grand outbreak of wild debauch ensued among the mountaineers— drinking, dancing, swaggering, gambling, quarreling and fighting. Alcohol . . . is dealt out to the trappers at $4 a pint. When inflamed by this fiery beverage, they cut all kinds of mad pranks and gambols, and sometimes burn all their clothes in their drunken bravadoes. A camp, recovering from one of these riotous revels, presents a serio-comic spectacle; black eyes, broken heads, lack-lustre visages. Many of the trappers have squandered in one drunken frolic the hard-earned wages of a year; some have run in debt and must toil to pay for past pleasure. All are sated with this deep draught of pleasure and eager to commence another trapping campaign; for hardship and hard work, spiced with the stimulants of wild adventure, and topped off with an annual frantic carousal, is the lot of the restless trapper.

Kit Carson, Jedediah Smith, William Ashley, Thomas Fitzpatrick,

Jim Bridger and a score of others—hunters and trappers in the Far West, pathfinders and trail blazers. Theirs was a wild, dangerous life, but they learned to take care of themselves; theirs was a hard, lonely life, but they learned to love it. They gave up their civilized ways and adopted the dress, habits, and manners of the Indian. With horse and two pack animals, with rifle and ammunition, with traps, and knives, with coffeepot, frying pan, and blanket, with alcohol and tobacco, the hardy trapper was ready for his year in the mountains.

Who owned this vast expanse of territory over which hunter and trapper roamed? Part of it, the Louisiana territory, belonged to the United States. Another part, the Oregon territory, was claimed by both England and the United States. South of Oregon and west of Louisiana stretched the huge territory belonging to Mexico, which had won its independence from Spain in 1821.

Neither the Spaniards nor the Mexicans had made any very large settlements in this area. There were a few thousand Mexicans scattered in settlements in California, and about three thousand in the neighborhood of Santa Fe. Every year long Mexican pack trains carried supplies from the city of Veracruz on the Gulf, over two thousand miles of river, mountain, and desert to these faraway settlements. Only those things that pack animals could carry could make the long journey. The people in Santa Fe wanted many things which they could not get. What they did get was apt to be expensive because of the long, difficult journey. Here was an excellent market for goods. Enter the American trader.

In 1822 there came into being the Santa Fe Trail, the route of the American caravans carrying dry goods, notions, and hardware from the bend of the Missouri River to Santa Fe, to be exchanged there for gold, silver, and beaver skins. Josiah Gregg, one of the traders, published his *Commerce of the Prairies, or the Journal of a Santa Fé Trader* in 1845. It is a well-written story about an exciting business. From it we learn that the starting-point for the 750-mile trip was Independence, Missouri, where the traders were wont to "purchase their provisions for the road, and many of their mules, oxen, and even some of their wagons—in short, load all their vehicles and make their final preparations for the long journey across the prairie." A few days out and Gregg relates "we encountered a region of very troublesome quagmires. On such occasions it is quite common for a wagon to sink to the hubs in mud [each wagon carried from three to five thousand pounds of cargo and was drawn by eight to twelve mules or oxen]. . . . To extricate each other's wagons we had frequently to employ double and triple teams, with 'all hands to the wheels' in addition—often led by the proprietors themselves up to the waist in mud and water."

Eleven days out brought the party to Council Grove, one hundred and fifty miles from Independence. Here it was the custom for all caravans to band together, choose a captain, and complete their final organization. Very careful arrangements for guard duty had to be made because enemy Indians lined the route, friendly Indians would steal whatever they could, and the danger of stampeding the animals was great. There was one stretch of desert between the

Arkansas and Cimarron rivers, where there was danger of losing the way. "This tract of country may truly be styled the grand 'prairie ocean'; for not a single landmark is to be seen for more than forty miles—scarcely a visible eminence by which to direct one's course. All is level as the sea, and the compass was our surest, as well as principal guide." After 1822 the route became a beaten path, and even today wheel ruts still mark the course of the old Santa Fe Trail. The first year $15,000 worth of merchandise was carried to Santa Fe. By 1843 it had grown to $450,000, and some of the American traders were no longer finishing at Santa Fe, but were going right on south to Chihuahua and west to California. Though farming settlements had stopped at the 98° line, trappers' trails and the traders' Santa Fe Trail were pointing the way onward to the Pacific coast, to California and Oregon.

As early as 1796 Yankee sea captains had become acquainted with the California coast settlements and the possibilities of profitable

trade there. They carried cotton goods, knives, gunpowder, and rum
to California, and traded them there for furs; then they carried the
furs to China, exchanged them for Chinese goods, and returned to
Boston, New York, and Philadelphia. Profits were enormous. "One
captain in a few hours collected 560 otter skins in exchange for
goods that cost him less than two dollars and sold the lot in Canton
for $22,400." Oh, yes, Yankee captains were very familiar with
California.

Trappers, hunters, and traders also had made the journey to the
coast settlements. Some of them, like some of the sailors from the

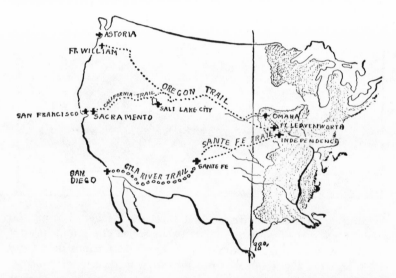

American ships, liked the country and decided to stay. They sent
messages back home to their friends about the fine soil and beautiful
climate of California and Oregon. Restless settlers on the edge of
the Great Plains, where there was little rainfall and no timber, were
very much interested in reports of faraway California and Oregon.
There on the Pacific slope it seemed there was rain again, trees again,
familiar farm land again. The American passion for moving was in
their veins. Discontented farmers on the Atlantic coast listened
eagerly to wondrous tales of far-off California. Missionaries thought
it was their duty to go to Oregon and make Christians of the Indians
there. It didn't seem to matter to these homeseekers that there lay
before them a five-months' trek over two thousand miles of plain,

mountain, desert, and mountain again—they were off to California and Oregon.

Fortunately for emigrants, the paths to California and Oregon were known by the trappers and hunters. These hardy mountain men were soon acting as guides to hundreds plodding across the Oregon Trail and its branch route to California. On December 10, 1843, Jim Bridger sent a letter to his friend, Pierre Chouteau, Jr.: "I have established a small fort with a blacksmith shop and a supply of iron in the road of the emigrants on Black's Fork of Green River which promises fairly. They, in coming out, are generally well supplied with money, but by the time they get there are in want of all kinds of supplies. Horses, provisions, smith-work, etc. bring ready cash from them and should I receive the goods hereby ordered will do a considerable business in that way with them. . . ." The trapper was giving up his old business of hunting furs, and was going into the new one of caring for the wants of emigrants moving across his old hunting grounds. The log cabin line of settlers had stopped at the 98° line—but only for a breathing spell, before it made the long journey across the plains to the Pacific.

Though the emigrants found a highway across the continent already established, it was no easy journey. Even if everything went well, the trip was long, hard, tiresome. If anything went wrong— it might very easily mean death. Perhaps the most gruesome experience of any group that made the long journey was that of the Donner Party of eighty-seven people in 1846. As far as South Pass they went with a larger caravan. Here they decided to try a short cut and went on alone. They found themselves in the Sierra Mountains in the dead of winter. One of the rescue party tells part of the horrible experience:

In this critical situation the presence of mind of Mr. Eddy suggested a plan for keeping themselves warm, which has been common among the trappers of the Rocky Mountains when caught in the snow without a fire. It is simply to spread a blanket on the snow when the party (if small) with the exception of one sit down upon it in a circle closely as possible, then place their feet upon one another in the centre, room being left for the person who has to complete the arrangement. As many blankets as necessary are then spread over the heads of the party, the ends being held down by pieces of wood or snow. After everything is completed the person outside takes his place in the circle. As the snow falls it closes up the pores of the blanket while the breath of those underneath soon causes a comfortable warmth. It was with a great deal of difficulty that Mr. Eddy succeeded in getting them to adopt this simple plan which was undoubt-

edly the means of saving their lives at this time. In this situation they remained thirty-six hours.

On the twenty-fifth about 4 P.M. Patrick Dolan died. He had been for
some time delirious and escaped from under the shelter when he stripped
off his hat, coat, and boots and exposed himself to the storm. Mr. Eddy
tried to force him back but his strength was unequal to the task. He,
however, afterward returned of his own accord and lay outside the shelter.
They finally succeeded in dragging him inside. On the 26th Lee Murphy
died after being delirious and kept under the shelter only by the united
efforts of the party.

In the afternoon of the 25th they succeeded in getting fire started in
a dry pine tree. Having been four entire days without food and since the
month of October [now December] on short allowance there were now but
two alternatives left them——either die or keep life in the living by eating
the bodies of the dead, slowly and reluctantly they adopted the alternative.

On the 27th they took the flesh from the bodies of the dead and on
that and two succeeding days they remained in camp drying the meat and
preparing to pursue their journey.

Of the eighty-seven who started the trip thirty-nine died.

But the fertile farms of beautiful California and Oregon were a
real prize, and hundreds braved the dangers of the 2,000-mile walk.
By 1846 there were seven hundred Americans in California, with
more coming. That same year there were about ten thousand Americans in Oregon, with more coming. Missionaries failed to convert the
Indians there, but succeeded in acquiring good farms. Already the
Americans in Oregon were raising more wheat than they needed
for their own use, and were exporting some to the Sandwich Islands
and other places.

Now an interesting thing happened. Texas had broken away from
Mexico and had become a state of the United States. But the United
States now had a dispute with Mexico over the boundary line of
this new state. The United States had another dispute with England over the boundary line of Oregon. Two quarrels, one with
England, one with Mexico. With England, a strong country, we
settled the quarrel peacefully. With Mexico, a weak country (which
owned California as well as New Mexico) we went to war.

Many Americans thought war with Mexico was wrong. Senator
Corwin of Ohio said: "If I were a Mexican I would tell you: 'Have
you not room in your own country? . . . If you come into mine, we
will greet you with bloody hands and welcome you to hospitable
graves.' " Another Congressman, also from Ohio, called it, "a war
against an unoffending people without adequate or just cause, for
the purpose of conquest. . . . I will lend it no aid, no support what-

ever. I will not bathe my hands in the blood of the people of Mexico, nor will I participate in the guilt of those murders which have been and will hereafter be committed by our army there."

A young Congressman from Illinois, Abraham Lincoln, afterward President of the United States, was also against war with Mexico. Later he voted that the war against Mexico had been "unnecessarily and unconstitutionally commenced by the President."

In two years the war was over. The American Army was victorious. In 1848 the United States took from Mexico what is now California, Nevada, Utah, Colorado, Arizona, and New Mexico, a vast territory greater in area than the British Isles, France, pre-Hitler Germany and Italy combined.

A week before the treaty of peace was signed gold was discovered on the ranch of John A. Sutter near Sacramento, in California. Then there followed such a rush of people to this spot as the world had never before seen. America had always been the home of moving, restless people hungry for land. This was different. Not land, but gold. Not only farmers, but mechanics, lawyers, preachers, gamblers, teachers, sailors, businessmen. Not only from the United States, but from South America, Europe, Asia, Africa, Australia—people from the whole world were on their way to the diggings! The "forty-niners" poured in from everywhere, across the overland trails, around the Horn, across the Isthmus of Panama. By 1850 there were 92,000 people in California; in 1860, 379,000. And such a mixture! "Take a sprinkling of sober-eyed earnest, shrewd, energetic New England businessmen: mingle with them a number of rollicking sailors, a dark band of Australian convicts and cut-throats, a dash of Mexican and frontier desperadoes, a group of hardy backwoodsmen, some professional gamblers, whiskey dealers . . . and having thrown in a promiscuous crowd of broken-down merchants, disappointed lovers, black sheep, unfledged dry-goods clerks, professional miners from all parts of the world . . . stir up the mixture, season strongly with gold-fever, bad liquors, faro, monte, rouge-et-noir, quarrels, oaths, pistols, knives, dancing and digging, and you have something approximating California society in early days."

Many who came to California found no gold but remained to farm. Others did a thriving business selling supplies to the throngs of newcomers. Still others found no gold but continued to search for it. They were a restless, adventurous set who roamed over the mountains much as the hunters and trappers had done before. In-

MUSHROOM TOWN

stead of beaver traps, they carried picks and pans. They were hunting, not beaver, but gold.

In 1858 they found it at Pikes Peak near Denver, Colorado. Then followed another rush to the new gold fields. On the canvas of the oncoming horde of wagons was printed in large letters, "Pike's Peak or Bust!" Many came, and a few found gold. Some stayed to farm. Others were soon homeward bound with a new sign on their returning wagons, "Busted, By Gosh!"

Nevertheless, when prospectors again found gold in Idaho and Montana, and silver in Nevada, fortune seekers again rushed to the new diggings. Rumors flew around about a new "strike" here and another one there. There was constant movement all through the mountain country. As the fortune hunters rushed to the latest "find" new camps would spring up overnight. Often the gold or silver was there and a camp grew into a city. In other places, where the talk about gold was taller than the piles to be found, camps would be born one week and die the next. The mining country was covered with dead towns where deserted cabins and abandoned diggings told the story of high hopes and miserable failure.

Nevertheless, all this activity served to advertise the West. Not in the United States alone, but all over the world, wild tales circulated about the life there. At the same time, other interesting happenings helped to focus attention on the West.

United States troops were stationed in army posts all over this huge territory. Emigrants were still streaming to the Pacific coast and others were heading for the mines. It was the business of the army to keep the Plains Indians quiet—a difficult job. The Indians were pushed onto reservations where government agents were assigned to look after them. Food was rationed out to every Indian at United States government expense.

But the Plains Indian knew of a better food supply—the buffalo. Herds of these big animals roamed the country from the Missouri to the Rockies, from Mexico to Canada. A herd of buffalo was unlike anything else anywhere. There were herds which numbered not hundreds or thousands, but hundreds of thousands, and occasionally millions. Emigrant trains would stop and gaze in wonder as the ground for miles around would be covered by a moving horde, pushing north in summer and south in winter. The whole plains country was an immense buffalo range.

To the Indian the buffalo was indispensable. It was his food, clothing, and shelter. Gregg, the Santa Fe trader, said of it: "This animal furnishes almost the exclusive food of the prairie Indians, as well as covering for their wigwams and most of their clothing; also their bedding, ropes, bags for their meat, etc.; sinews for bow-strings, for sewing moccasins, leggings, and the like." The Indian's life was wrapped up in the buffalo.

But buffalo skins were in demand, and buffalo tongues were considered a great delicacy. Traders and emigrants shot them and sent the hides east on the railways, just built to the edge of the 98° line. In the late 1860's the Union Pacific was being built across the

plains to the Pacific. Later other transcontinental roads were constructed. Railroad workers meant more eaters and killers of buffalo. Hunting parties from the East and even from Europe journeyed to the West to kill buffalo. Many thousands were killed for their skins, others were killed merely for the sport (so-called) of killing. The carcasses of dead buffalo were strewn over the plains.

The slaughter was terrific. By the late 1870's the buffalo were gone—and with them went any more danger from the Indians. Now they had to accept reservation life. The Indian menace was over.

But before the buffalo were exterminated and the Indians cooped up, a spectacular business sprang up in the West. For many years, long-horned cattle of Spanish origin had found a perfect home in southern Texas. Here the climate was mild, grass was plentiful, and water ample. The cattle were left alone and the herds grew to tremendous proportions. By 1866 there were probably about four million cattle in Texas. Because they were so plentiful they were very cheap—in Texas. They were offered at five dollars and six dollars a head and yet there were no buyers—in Texas. But in the East, where there were many more mouths to be fed, cattle were selling for fifty dollars a head. Even as far west as Kansas and Missouri the price was as high as thirty dollars a head. In 1866 it occurred to several Texans that they had a gold mine right at home in the shape of thousands of five-dollar cattle which could be made into thirty-dollar cattle. The trick was to drive the cattle north to meet the last outpost of the east-to-west railway. Five-dollar cattle which reached the depot of the railroad found their thirty-dollar market there. What a chance! Cattlemen took it. In fifteen years over 4,000,000 cattle made the long drive north to the railheads.

Fortunately for the cattle-owners, Texas longhorns were hardy animals that could stand the hardships of a trek of several hundred miles, go long stretches without water, and have strength left to cross rivers whose beds were frequently quicksand. Fortunately for the cattle-owners, there arose a type of horseman, skillful, daring, quick, and hard, who could control these wild, nervous animals ever liable to stampede. Handling cattle on the trail was a man-size job. You had to know your stuff.

After a few years of firsthand experience the cowboys learned the safest and best way of managing the cattle on the long drive. In the spring, the twenty five hundred to three thousand cattle which made up the usual-size herd on the trail, would be led through a chute where they received their road brand. Then the twelve to sixteen men working in pairs opposite each other would string them out in a long line. The old experienced hands would take their positions at the "point" in front, where they could direct the line of march and set the pace. Next came the "swing," then the "flank," and last of all the "dragmen." "Bringing up the drag" was a job usually assigned to beginning cowboys. It was the worst place in the line because the lazy or lame cattle that brought up the rear moved so very slowly; then, too, dragmen were sure to eat a lot of the dust kicked up by the herd. The "horse wrangler" was usually a boy learning the art of being a cowboy. He had charge of the *remuda*, the band of horses, six or eight for each man, which usually trailed along ahead of the herd. The "chuck wagon" in charge of the cook, went in advance to the stream where camp was to be formed and dinner eaten. The foreman, or trail boss, was anywhere and everywhere, wherever he was needed.

As soon as the cattle were "road broken," twelve to fifteen miles could be made a day. The greatest danger was from a stampede,

COWBOY

that awful moment when the cattle, suddenly frightened, would break away in a mad dash at terrific speed. Then it was that the cowboy showed his true mettle and earned his pay many times over; then it was that a good horse and a clear head were essential; not until the herd had been turned and were back on the trail in good order again was there any relief from the strain.

When the end of the trail was reached, when the cattle had been turned over to their new owner and were in the loading chute being

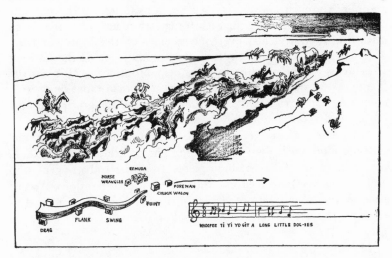

crowded into the cars, then the cowboys let loose. They had reached the cow town after sixty or ninety days of hard work, from daybreak to dark on the trail, eighteen long hours of tenseness and strain every day. No wonder they painted the town red. No wonder they blew the lid off in the saloon gambling rooms and dance halls. Abilene, the first cow town, and Wichita, Ellsworth, and Dodge City, later cow towns, were very much like the mushroom mining towns in their wild, rough, lawless life. They were outposts on the frontier where hard men met together to drink, gamble, and "raise hell" in general.

Texas cattle made the long drive to the railheads and were sold at high prices. Certain trails became well-established routes. The famous Chisholm Trail, stretching about six hundred miles north from San Antonio, was crowded with cattle on their way to Abilene on the Kansas Pacific Railway. This trail was a favorite because it was level, the rivers across it could be forded easily, and lots of grass lined the route. Later when the Santa Fe Railway extended a line farther west to Dodge City, the cattle followed the Western Trail there.

It soon became clear to cattlemen that not only Texas, but practically the whole area of the Great Plains, was suitable pasturage for their cattle. Then Texas and the Southwest became the breeding grounds, while the central and northern plains became the feeding grounds. Young steers were driven north to fatten on the millions of acres of range lands lush with forage. In a few years the range cattle industry stretched over one quarter of the continent from Texas to the Canadian border and from the edge of the farming settlements on the 98° line to the Rocky Mountains. This was the famous Cow Country. All these millions of acres of range lands were owned by the government, but they were free for grazing to anybody's cattle.

The cattle industry grew to immense proportions. People in the East ate more meat than ever before. The slaughter of the buffalo meant large-size orders, at high prices, from the Indian agent who had to have meat to feed the Indians on the reservations. At this time meat was put into cans and refrigeration was invented. The cattle of the Cow Country were finding a market as far away as Europe.

The late 70's and early 80's were "boom" times.

Men bought more and more cattle and turned them out to graze on the open range. Stories of the great wealth made by the cattle kings circulated throughout the East, and newcomers came to share in the profits. In faraway Scotland and England companies were formed to go into the cattle business in a really big way. Some of the companies gathered together as much as $1,000,000 to spend for cattle. It all looked so simple. You bought steers at $5.00, turned them loose on government land where the water and the grass were free; you watched them fatten and then sold out at $50 a head. But—

The rush to the Cow Country sent prices of cattle sky high.

The old Texas longhorn was admirably suited to trailing because he was such a tough animal, but his meat was tough eating. Finer, more expensive breeds had been introduced to the range; they were better meat, but they were not as well adapted to foraging for themselves. So many people had bought cattle that the range was soon overstocked.

A drought or a severe winter would mean death to many of these high-priced cattle. Both came. Cattle died by the thousands. The losses were terrific.

The boom times of the early 1880's became the "gloom" times of the late 1880's.

A great change came over the cattle business. The invention of barbed wire in 1868, and its sale throughout the Cow Country beginning in 1874, meant cutting up the open range into private ranches. Men bought, leased, or stole government land and ran a barbed-wire fence around to keep out the other fellow. The open range was gone, and the stock farm took its place. The cowboy, that colorful and picturesque figure that belonged to the early days of the long drive and the exciting roundup, was also gone; he became nothing more than a hired hand with less and less of his time given to cattle and more of it given to mending fences, haying, and other farm tasks. The hardy native cattle which knew how to forage for themselves were gone; expensive blooded bulls which must be carefully protected and fed in winter took their places on the fenced in stock farm.

Perhaps the chief cause of the changing of life in the Cow Country from an exciting adventure to a carefully organized business was the advance of the farmer. In 1840 he had stopped at the 98° line and made a leap to the Pacific. After 1860 many things happened which carried him on to face the new prairie and plains frontier.

A new homestead law was passed by Congress which gave 160 acres of western land *absolutely* free to anyone who settled on it for five years and cultivated it. Not at two dollars an acre, not at one dollar and a quarter an acre, but *free*.

Railroads built to the plains country and beyond to the Pacific, made the hardships of reaching this new frontier a thing of the past. Now new settlers could be deposited right on the land they were going to homestead. The railroad companies wanted as many people as possible in the West because that would bring them business. They therefore advertised the new country as a farmers' paradise (which it was not). Their highly colored stories of the wonderful fertility of the land and its amazing productivity made hopeful farmers lose their old notion of the Great American Desert. Loan companies met the oncoming settler and loaned him money (at very high rates of interest) to start his farm. The rush began. New settlers poured in from the 98° line, from farther east, from Europe. The last frontier was coming to an end.

The invention of barbed wire made homesteads of 160 acres possible. In a land without timber, overrun with cattle, the problem of fencing becomes very important. No fence meant cattle all over your farm land. Wooden fences were impossible—too expensive. The barbed-wire fence was cheap and effective. It solved the problem.

The farmer in the tall-grass country, on the prairie plains, won for himself the best agricultural land in the United States. The farmer who moved farther west into the short-grass country was confronted with the problem of getting enough water. The old-fashioned homemade well of "back home," with its "old oaken bucket" was of no use in the dry plains region. The water was too far down and the soil was too hard. The problem was solved in the 1870's by the use of metal drills which could bore a hole three hundred feet deep. But raising water hand over hand in the old way was too difficult a job where the well was so deep. A better way had to be invented. It had to be a cheap way because homesteaders were usually poor people. That problem was solved by the use of the windmill. It was very cheap and would raise the water as long as the wind blew. And how the wind does blow on the plains!

The story is told of a visitor on a ranch in the West who found the wind blowing much too hard and too long to suit him. He wasn't used to it. He went to a cowboy and asked in despair, "Does the wind blow this way all the time?"

"No," answered the cowboy; "it'll maybe blow this way for a week or ten days, and then it'll change and blow like hell for a while."

The windmill became a familiar sight on the plains. It helped to solve the water problem for some of the farmers and ranchmen. In other parts of the West irrigation and dry farming were the solution. There are still great areas of the plains which will never be suitable for farming, but which can be and are being used for cattle and sheep raising.

When the reaper, the disk plow, and other farm machines were invented, they found their greatest use on the Great Plains where the firm soil was free from stones or stumps of trees. The absence of trees however, was for some of the settlers a frightening experience.

It was to Beret, in the beautiful story called *Giants in the Earth*: "The broad expanse stretching away endlessly in every direction seemed almost like the ocean—especially now when darkness was falling. It reminded her strongly of the sea and yet it was very different. . . . This formless prairie had no heart that beat, no waves that sang, no soul that could be touched . . . or cared. . . . How will human beings be able to endure this place? she thought. Why there isn't even a thing that one can *hide behind!*"

The movement of settlers into the Great Plains continued. In 1890, for the first time, a solid band of states connected the Atlantic and the Pacific. The end of the frontier had come.

The Manufacturing North

★──★

"The custom of making these coarse cloths (woolen and linsey-woolsey) in private families prevails throughout the whole Province, and in almost every House a sufficient quantity is manufactured for the use of the Family without the least design of sending any of it to market, for every home swarms with children, who are set to work as soon as they are able to Spin and card; and as every family is furnished with a Loom, the Itinerant Weavers who travel about the Country, put the finishing hand to the work."

Governor Moore said this of New York on January 12, 1767. It was equally true of the other Northern Colonies. From the earliest settlements there until well after the Revolutionary War, most of the clothing worn by most Americans was "homespun." But, as he pointed out, it was made for the use of the family, not to be sent to market for sale. In the same way, many other necessities, such as soap, candles, furniture, leather goods, and gunpowder, were either made at home or by local craftsmen for the people in the immediate neighborhood. Manufacturing in the broader sense, of making things in great quantities to be sold outside or sent abroad, had not yet developed here.

In the Southern Colonies, practically nothing was manufactured. Southerners found it more profitable to put their labor into the production of rice and tobacco than to bother even with home industries. What Beverly said of Virginia was equally true of the other Southern Colonies: "They have their clothing of all sorts from England . . . tho' their country be overrun with wood yet they have all their wooden ware from England; their cabinets, chairs, tables, stools, chests, boxes, cart-wheels and all other things even so much as their bowls and birchen brooms."

Both North and South imported from Europe fine tools, beautiful glassware, handsome silks and brocades, luxuries of every description. Even after the War for Independence the United States was still in the main what England had wanted it to be, a country which exchanged its raw materials for the manufactured goods of other nations. Most of our labor went into farming or shipping; only a little went into manufacturing, and that little was devoted largely to the making of things for home use.

England, on the other hand, had from an early date turned to manufacturing for export. As the mother country in a growing empire, she was a supply center of manufactured goods for her colonies. When the Industrial Revolution came to England she saw an excellent chance to continue and strengthen her position as a leading manufacturing country. The invention of the new machines gave her a great advantage over other countries—if only she could keep the plans from being discovered elsewhere. You can readily imagine how jealously she guarded her secrets.

From 1765 to 1789 a series of strict laws was passed by Parliament. The new machines, or plans or models of them, must not be exported from the country . . . skilled men who worked the machines were not to leave England . . . under penalty of a heavy fine and imprisonment. England alone was to benefit from the new machinery; England was to become the workshop of the world.

But there was a hitch in this well-arranged scheme. Parts of machines were smuggled out, and workers slipped out unseen. Parliament soon found that while it might prevent a man from carrying out of the country a plan of a machine in his pocket, it could do nothing to prevent a man from carrying out of the country a plan of a machine in his head. To the United States secretly, in 1789, came Samuel Slater, formerly a worker in English factories. He carried plans of the new machinery—in his mind. At Pawtucket, Rhode Island, he set up the first complete mill for spinning yarn on the Arkwright plan; the machines he designed and constructed from memory. The Industrial Revolution was thus brought to America.

But people seldom make big changes until they are forced to do so. We always try to keep at anything that is pleasant and profitable so long as it continues that way. In 1800, eleven years after Slater's first mill, there were only eight cotton factories in the whole country. Manufacturing had not yet taken hold. Why?

Largely because we could import goods cheaper than we could make them ourselves, and also because farming and shipping were more profitable than ever before. Take the story of the good ship Betsy. In 1797, this boat of less than a hundred tons was taken around the world by a crew of thirty boys, of whom the oldest was twenty-eight years of age. Together they had "chipped in" $8,000. They came home from their trading trip with a profit of $120,000. Why go into manufacturing?

In 1793 war broke out between France and England, and soon practically every country of western Europe was taking part in the fight. It was a wonderful chance for our farmers and merchants and they seized it. "While the great commercial nations were fighting one another for the carrying-trade of the world, America ran away with the bone over which they were quarreling."

Our ships, their holds jammed full to the brim with breadstuffs, meats, and other supplies, raced back and forth over the ocean. Profits were enormous. The warring nations were ready to pay fantastic prices for grain, meat, cotton, wool, any raw material. Flour jumped from $5.41 to $9.12 a barrel. Why turn to making things ourselves when farm products brought such high prices and our boats returned laden with low-priced manufactured goods? We stuck to farming and trading and we liked it. American shipping skyrocketed from 202,000 tons in 1789 to 1,425,000 tons in 1810 —and every single ton was built in the United States.

It was a golden era, but it came to an end about 1808. England issued orders that no neutral ship could trade with France or her allies, and France issued orders that no neutral ship could trade with England or her allies. Our ships tried to break the blockade, but it was dangerous business. About sixteen hundred American ships were captured.

Thomas Jefferson, then President of the United States, advised Congress to pass the Embargo Act, a plan to make both France and England give up their blockade. We were to keep all our ships from sailing into foreign parts—the idea was that without our supplies the warring nations would soon starve. We tried it. Europe was cut off from our goods, but at the same time we were cut off from hers. Later when we went to war with England (1812-14) our foreign trade was almost entirely destroyed. From 1808 to 1814 our imports of manufactured goods dropped lower and lower. Now we were forced to learn to make things for ourselves.

Now traders and merchants, whose ships were lying idle in the harbors, were faced with the problem of what to do with their extra money. What to do with their surplus money is always a pressing problem for the people who have it. They might put it into the bank and draw the regular rate of interest. Or they might take a big chance and try their hand at manufacturing. Shipping, for the time being, was dead; manufacturing was new, but looked promising. Factories here would have to supply the country with those goods which formerly came from England and the rest of Europe, now cut off by the war. It looked like an opportunity to make big profits and some merchants made the plunge. They took the capital which they had accumulated in trading and put it into factories and machinery. Mills shot up as if by magic. "Establishments for the manufacture of cotton goods, woolen cloths, iron, glass, pottery and other articles sprang up with a mushroom growth." It was in this period that the factory system of manufacturing first took hold in the United States.

It came first to New England and the Middle Atlantic States, because there would-be manufacturers found what they needed.

Power to run machines? Right at their own back door, so to speak, water power was everywhere available from both the small and large streams with their swift currents and many falls. In the rushing rivers they could see motors for their machines.

Good harbors to receive raw materials and send out finished goods? Good harbors were plentiful in New England and in the Middle Atlantic States.

Roads or canals to the growing West, where there was such great need for manufactured goods? At this very time, in New England and the Middle Atlantic States, turnpikes, bridges, and canals were being built as never before.

Nearness to big cities whose dense population meant both a market for goods and a source of labor? The biggest cities of that day were in New England and the Middle Atlantic States.

All this added up to why the northeast region was exactly the place chosen by most beginning manufacturers. Later ones naturally drifted there, too, especially when the need for coal and iron became great, because both these essentials were found in or near this region. To Massachusetts, New Hampshire, Rhode Island, and Connecticut, then, came cotton and woolen mills, and factories of firearms, clocks, watches, and so on; to Pennsylvania, New York, and New Jersey came iron furnaces, silk mills, and factories making shoes, hats, nails, buttons, and a host of other things. The Industrial Revolution had come to America.

Many wise people had written that manufacturing on a large scale could not come to America so long as there was an abundance of good land to be had for very little money. This was the view of Benjamin Franklin, who wrote in 1760: "Manufactures are founded in poverty. It is the multitude of poor without land in a country . . . who must work for others at low wages or starve, that enables undertakers [promoters] to carry on manufacture. . . .

"But no man who can have a piece of land of his own, sufficient by his labor to subsist his family in plenty, is poor enough to be a manufacturer [worker], and work for a master. Hence, while there is land enough in America for our people, there can never be manufactures to any amount or value."

This argument sounds reasonable; yet Franklin was partly wrong. Why? Because he did not foresee the Industrial Revolution.

"The carding, roving, and spinning machines were all so simple to operate that the only adults needed in the mill were the overseers and repair mechanics. Almy and Brown who started [in 1791] with 9 children, were employing in 1801 over 100 *between the ages of 4 and 10*. They could not leave the children without at least one adult person present, so they put all their machinery into one room where they needed only a single overseer."

Children, then, were one way out of the difficulty of lack of labor. Harriet Martineau, an English traveler in America in 1834-36 tells us of another. "It is not the custom in America for women (except slaves) to work out-of-doors. It has been mentioned that the young men of New England migrate in large numbers to the West, leaving an over-proportion of female population, the amount of which I could never learn. . . . Suffice it that there are many more women than men in from six to nine States of the Union. There is reason to believe that there was much silent suffering from poverty before the institution of factories; that they afford a most welcome resource to some thousands of young women. . . ."

Women followed spinning wheels and looms from their homes to the factories; gradually they entered other industries as well. By 1860 women were working in as many as one hundred different trades. The employment of women and children did not have its beginnings in this country. It began in England, where they had been hired to work in the factories primarily because their wages were lower than men's. Here, too, they were hired for that reason, but primarily because man labor was more scarce. Alexander Hamilton, the first secretary of the treasury of the United States, in his "Report on Manufactures," had argued for the establishment of factories because it would give work to women and children. He said: "It is worthy of particular remark that, in general, women and children are rendered more useful, and the latter more easily useful, by manufacturing establishments than they would otherwise be. Of the number of persons employed in the cotton manufactories of Great Britain, it is computed that four-sevenths nearly are women and children— of whom the greatest proportion are children, and many of them of a tender age."

Readers of the *Massachusetts Spy* in the 1820's and 1830's were familiar with the HELP WANTED advertisements in the cotton mills, which usually called for "families of 5 or 6 children each." The "family" type of labor was very widely used in the mills in New England.

Every member of the family above the age of 7 or 8 worked in the factory. Slater's labor force in 1816 was typical of a "family" mill. It was made up of

    1 family with 8 members working
    1 family with 7 members working
    2 families each with 5 members working
    4 families each with 4 members working
    5 families each with 3 members working
    8 single men
    4 single women

The houses or tenements, which these families occupied in the mill towns were very often owned by the manufacturer or company that owned the mill. Other millowners preferred the "boarding-house" arrangement for working girls only. A visitor to the United States in 1836 tells about them.

The manufacturing companies exercise the most careful supervision over these girls. I have already said, that, twelve years ago, Lowell did not exist; when, therefore, the manufactories were set up, it also became necessary to provide lodgings for the operatives, and each company has built for this purpose a number of houses within its own limits, to be used exclusively as boarding-houses for them. Here they are under the care of the mistress of the house, who is paid by the company at the rate of one dollar and a quarter a week [from ⅓ to ½ of their wages] for each boarder, that sum being stopped out of the weekly wages of the girls. These housekeepers, who are generally widows, are each responsible for the conduct of her

boarders. . . . Each company has its rules and regulations. . . . I will take
those of the Lawrence Company . . . May 21, 1833 . . . Article 2: "All
ardent spirits are banished from the company's grounds, except when prescribed by a physician. All games of hazard and cards are prohibited
within their limits and in the boarding-houses. . . . Article thirteenth
directs, that every female employed by the Company shall live in one of
the Company's boarding-houses, attend regularly at divine service, and
rigidly observe the rules of the Sabbath. . . . Article fourteenth . . . pre-
scribes that the doors shall be shut at ten. . . ."

As more factories sprang up, there came the shortage of labor
which Franklin had predicted. Even girls were difficult to get. The
manufacturers sent agents into the country districts to round up
farm girls to come to the mill towns to work. The agents were paid
so much per head for every working girl they brought back. The
Lowell *Voice of Industry* on January 2, 1846, complained about the
methods used by these agents.

Observing a singular-looking, "long, low, black" wagon passing along
the street, we made inquiries respecting it, and were informed that it was
what we term a "slaver." She makes regular trips to the north of the state,
cruising around in Vermont and New Hampshire, with a "commander"
whose heart must be as black as his craft, who is paid a dollar a head for
all he brings to the market, and more in proportion to the distance—if
they bring them from such a distance that they cannot easily get back.
This is done by "hoisting false colors," and representing to the girls, that
they can tend more machinery than is possible, and that the work is so
very neat, and the wages such, that they can dress in silks and spend half
their time in reading. Now is this true? Let those girls who have been thus
deceived, answer.

There was another method whereby Americans made up for the
scarcity of workers. Failing to secure hand labor to do the work,
they invented machines to do it for them. Machines were being invented everywhere, but the laborsaving devices made by Yankee ingenuity were so many and so important that all Europe turned its
attention in this direction. Whitworth and Wallis said, in their official reports to the British Government (1854):

. . . it is much to the credit of the American inventor, that he is able so
to meet the necessities of his case, and supply the want of fingers, which
are at present so scarce. . . .
. . . Of this we have an illustration in the machine for the manufacture
of the seamless grain-bags, the loom for which is described as a perfect
self-actor, or automaton, commencing the bag, and continuing the process
until the work is complete.

For another curious illustration of this automatic action we have the manufacture of ladies' hair pins at Waterbury. . . . These pins are made at the rate of 180 per minute.

The reader is referred also to the automaton machine for shanking buttons. . . . These operations are completed at the rate of 200 a minute, the only attendance required being that of one person to feed this automaton with the blanks and the wires. . . .

It may suffice to refer to the improvements effected in spinning-machinery, by which one man can attend to a mule containing 1,088 spindles, each spinning three hanks or 3,264 hanks a day; so that, as compared with the operations of the most expert spinner in Hindoostan, the American operative can perform the work of 3,000 men.

Many industries were completely revolutionized by the great number of laborsaving devices developed during 1790-1860. There were some very important inventions that changed the whole method of work, and also countless little gadgets added to old machines to improve them. The records of the United States Patent Office show what happened. For twenty years, from 1790 to 1810, it issued, on the average, seventy-seven patents every year; in the ten years from 1850 to 1860, this figure had jumped to twenty three hundred a year.

In 1812 when Eli Whitney obtained a contract from the government for the manufacture of ten thousand muskets, he had already hit upon still another scheme to do away with the need of skilled craftsmen, and at the same time speed up production. It was the plan of interchangeable parts so common today. Whitney said he would make the same parts of different guns, as the locks, for example, as much like each other as the successive impressions of a copperplate engraving.

We know from Dwight's *Travels in New England and New York* that Whitney did carry out his plan: "In the Manufactory [Eli Whitney's at New Haven, Conn.] muskets are made in a manner which I believe to be singular . . . machinery is employed for hammering, cutting, perforating, grinding, polishing, etc., etc.

"The proportion, and relative position, of the several parts of the locks are so exactly alike; and the screws, springs, and other limbs are made so similar; that they may be transferred from one lock and adjusted to another without any material alteration."

Thus with the labor of women and children, and of men in their off season from farm work, and with the aid of innumerable inventions of machinery, manufacturing had made its beginnings in northeastern United States. With the heavy inpouring of immigrants following the 1820's it began to take a firmer hold there. Immigrant labor made possible the growth of the factory system on a larger scale than ever before. There were certain heavy industries in which the labor of women and children could not be used. Man labor was needed and the immigrants helped to supply it. By 1860, 21 per cent of the population of both Massachusetts and Rhode Island was of foreign birth! Factory jobs were waiting for them as soon as their boat docked. They needed the jobs and the jobs needed them.

If any immigrants had worked in English mills they were probably agreeably surprised at conditions here. In England there was always a plentiful supply of labor, so from the very beginning, workers were given starvation wages for long hours in unhealthy factories. In America where there was always a shortage of labor, workers were given fairly high wages to lure them into the mills. Men workers received on an average of 83¢ to $1.00 per day, women workers about $2.00 to $2.50 per week, and children from $1.50 to $2.00 per week. (These wages were about one-third to one-half higher than those in England.) But although conditions here were better than those in England, this was not a workers' paradise—not by a long shot.

In the early 1800's in the textile factories of New England work started at 5:00 in the morning and stopped at 7:30 in the evening. At 8:00 A.M. a half-hour was allowed for breakfast and at 12:00 noon another half-hour for dinner. These were the hours for every worker, young or old, man, woman, or child.

Frequent attempts were made to cheat the workers. One very common practice was to pay only part of the wages due in cash, and the other part in bills which were good for purchases only at stores owned by the manufacturer or company. The catch lay in the fact that very often the prices for goods in the company stores were much higher than in other stores—nevertheless, the workers *had* to buy there.

Another shady scheme in widespread use was that of holding back workers' pay, which meant that they worked a month and were paid for only two weeks—with two weeks' pay always owing to them. In this way workers were made more dependent upon the factory and were therefore less likely to leave. "In the Cocheco Manufacturing Company if they left without 2 weeks notice they were to forfeit 2 weeks pay. The employers, however, were not bound to give any warning of discharge." Nor did they pay the discharged worker in less than two weeks from the time of his discharge.

As more and more immigrants entered the factories, conditions grew steadily worse. When laborers were easy to get, millowners could become tyrants in the use of their power. They could force men, who needed the jobs which they had to offer, to do just as they commanded. In 1851, on the gate of one of the Lowell mills, this sign was hung out just before Election Day:

WHOEVER, EMPLOYED BY THIS CORPORATION, VOTES THE BEN BUTLER 10 HOUR TICKET ON MONDAY NEXT, WILL BE DISCHARGED.

If only your job stood between you and starvation, you were very apt to do as your boss ordered.

As more factories sprang up, the price of manufactured goods went down. Manufacturers, in business for profits, tried in every way to decrease expenses. One effective way was through the use of improved machinery. Another way was to make the workers tend more machines for the same wages. Both methods were used. In the cotton industry, for example, between 1840 and 1860, the cotton consumption per spindle increased 50 per cent; the number of spindles tended by each worker increased $33\frac{1}{3}$ per cent (thus a worker who formerly managed six machines now watched eight) ; in this way the number of yards produced by each worker was over 26 per cent greater than before—yet wages were only 2 per cent higher.

Capitalists were in business to make money. Their idea was to get as high a price as they could for goods which cost them as little as possible. Profits were greater when costs were lowest. The lower their workmen's wages, the less their goods cost to produce, and the higher their profits. Capital and labor were in for a long, very bitter struggle about the question of wages. That struggle has continued up to and including the present day.

By 1860 northeastern United States had become the manufacturing center of the United States. Shipping and farming continued to be carried on as before, but manufacturing was growing by leaps and bounds. It was a region ideally suited to manufacturing; here were water power, wood, coal, iron, and other necessary metals; here was capital to be invested; here was a growing market constantly added to by inpouring hordes of immigrants; here was a great merchant marine skilled in the carrying trade; here were no "don'ts" such as were common in Europe, no restrictions of any kind by an unfriendly government—anyone could go into any business at any time, any place, without any apprenticeship, admission, or license; the lid was off—here was every opportunity for business on a grand scale.

Now look at some telling figures:

Year	Value of manufactured goods in the U. S. (at least two-thirds from northeastern U. S.)
1810	$ 198,613,471
1840	483,278,215
1860	1,885,861,676

The Agricultural South

★━━★

In what direction was this growing stream of manufactured goods headed? Who bought the ever-swelling volume of factory-made things? Part of it went south, as we learn from the pen of an excited Southerner: "We want Bibles, brooms, buckets and books, and we go to the North; we want pens, ink, papers, wafers and envelopes, and we go to the North; we want shoes, hats, handkerchiefs, umbrellas, and pocket knives and we go to the North; we want furniture, crockery, glassware and pianos, and we go to the North; we want toys, primers, school books, fashionable apparel, machinery, medicines, tombstones, and a thousand other things and we go to the North for them all."

Hinton R. Helper, who wrote this in 1857, was trying to point out to the Southerners that buying from the North was helping to make the South poor and the North rich. He wanted Southerners to make things themselves, for themselves. That seems a good idea. Why hadn't the South, like the North, turned to manufacturing?

The answer lies partly in the fact that the South had found that it could raise a product that everyone wanted. Ordinarily, a farmer has two great worries—one is raising his crop, and the other is selling it. This was not true of the farmer who raised cotton in the South. Selling raw cotton was no problem at all. Clothing made of silk, wool, or linen was expensive, but clothing made of cotton was cheap enough to be sold to the poorest of the poor. The new textile machines in England, France, and northern United States were hungry for raw cotton. Southerners turned practically all their time and energy to what promised to be the most profitable business in America, the raising of raw cotton to feed to the machines to make clothing for the whole world. By 1860 Cotton was King in the South.

COTTON PICKERS

And well it might be. No place on the entire earth was better suited to the raising of cotton. Did the cotton plant need warm weather? The South had a long growing season, hot in summer both day and night. Was dry weather necessary at picking time? The South was a region of dry autumns. Did insects plague the farmer? The South had short, frosty winters which destroyed these pests. Everything was ideal—perfect climate, fertile soil, and plenty of rain at the right time. The result? The two million pounds of cotton produced in the South in 1789 had jumped to two thousand million pounds in 1860. Cotton was King in the South.

Rice and tobacco, the great staples of the South in the past, continued to be grown. Sugar, too, was tried with success in Louisiana, near the mouth of the Mississippi. But most southern planters turned their attention to cotton. A traveler through the South in 1827 had cotton brought to his attention so often that he could never forget it. He wrote a letter to a friend describing his journey:

When I took my last walk along the wharves in Charleston [South Carolina], and saw them piled up with mountains of Cotton, and all your stores, ships, steam and canal boats crammed with and groaning under, the weight of Cotton, I returned to the Planters' Hotel, where I found the four daily papers as well as the conversation of the boarders, teeming with Cotton! Cotton!! Cotton!!! . . . From this I continued on, meeting with little else than cotton fields, cotton gins, cotton waggons. . . . I arrived in Augusta [Georgia] and when I saw cotton waggons in Broad Street, I whistled! . . . But this was not all; there was more than a dozen tow boats in the river, with more than a thousand bales of cotton on each; and several steam boats with still more. . . . And Hamburg (as a Negro said) was worser according to its size; for it puzzled me to tell which was the largest the piles of cotton or the houses. I now left Augusta; and overtook hordes of cotton planters from North Carolina, South Carolina, and Georgia, with large gangs of Negroes bound to Alabama, Mississippi, and Louisiana, "where the cotton land is not worn out." Besides these I overtook a number of empty cotton waggons returning home, and a great many loaded with cotton going to Augusta.

The letter writer continues his story. He travels through Alabama, Mississippi, Louisiana, and Arkansas, and everywhere he sees cotton, hears cotton, and dreams cotton for seventy days and nights! Cotton was King in the South.

The graph on the next page shows the amazing growth in the amount of cotton produced in the South from 1791 to 1860.

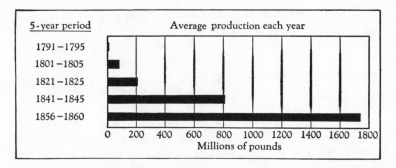

5-year period	Average production each year
1791–1795	
1801–1805	
1821–1825	
1841–1845	
1856–1860	

0   200   400   600   800   1000 1200 1400 1600 1800

Millions of pounds

In the 1790's, the rich planter who wanted to raise cotton on a large scale was faced with the problem of getting labor, just as the northern capitalist was. There were many men who were poor and wanted to grow cotton, but they did not want to grow it for anyone else. So long as there was plenty of unoccupied land which was theirs, practically for the taking, they would not work for another man for wages. While the northern manufacturer solved his labor problem through the use of women, children, men in their off season, laborsaving machinery, and immigrants, the southern planter turned to Negro slaves.

The first shipload of Negro slaves had reached this country in 1619. For many years the supply was not very plentiful. The Negroes and white indentured servants worked in the fields alongside their white masters. Until the 1690's there were more white servants than Negro slaves in the South. At that time many planters in South Carolina turned to the production of rice in the swampy lands along the coast. Growing rice meant hard work in a hot climate where malaria was frequent. Gangs of Negroes, driven by a white overseer or foreman, were judged most suitable for the steady all-year-round routine of the rice fields. More and more Negroes were imported. The tobacco growers, too, had turned to Negro slave labor in the absence of white labor that would stay put. By the end of the eighteenth century there were many more Negro slaves than indentured whites in the South.

The employment of slave labor meant the growth of the plantation system in the South.

Southern slaveholders grew rice, tobacco, sugar, or cotton because, like the northern capitalists, they wanted to make money. They had, on the one hand, a crop that could be easily sold, and on the other hand, a special kind of labor to grow that crop. There grew up, as a natural result, the plantation system.

How did a plantation differ from a farm? On the plantation, one single staple, such as tobacco, rice, sugar, or cotton was raised, all for sale. On the farm a variety of things, such as wheat, corn, hay, cheese, and pork might be produced, some for sale and some for family use. On the plantation, the laboring force was large, the larger the better. On the farm, the laboring force was small, the hired hands helping the farmer in his own work. On the plantation the large gang of laborers worked in a steady routine day in and day out all year round, always under careful supervision. On the farm the routine was not so regular, and there might be whole weeks when work would slacken.

Southerners had adopted the plantation system because it best suited the combination of their particular staple crops and Negro slave labor.

Negroes fresh from Africa were slow to learn the white man's ways; their descendants in the United States were not educated. Because Negroes were given no opportunity to learn, their masters mistakenly believed that they could not learn. Slaveowners believed with Cairnes, the English economist, who wrote in 1861: " . . . the difficulty of teaching the slave anything is so great, that the only chance of turning his labor to profit is, when he has once learned a lesson, to keep him to that lesson for life. Where slaves, therefore, are employed, there can be no variety of production. If tobacco be cultivated, tobacco becomes the sole staple, and tobacco is produced whatever be the state of the market and whatever the condition of the soil."

Slave labor tended to force "one-crop" cultivation on the South. The slave's work had to be a steady routine all the time, with all the planning done for him. This worked out well with cotton, which required attention and labor for practically all the year. It would not have been satisfactory with corn and other grains, which involved several months of nothing to do. Where you could lay off your hands during such a slack season there would be little loss, but the slaveholder could not do that. He had bought his slaves, and he had to feed, clothe, and shelter them all the time, whether there was work or not. The slaveholder knew that he could not make a profit unless he organized the work on his plantation in such a way that all his slaves, young and old, had steady jobs.

Cotton provided all-year work and allowed for organization on a large scale. Slaves worked only because they had to. When the master's eye was off their hands, their hands were apt to be off their work. Slave labor, therefore, needed careful watching. Somebody, either the planter himself or a hired overseer, had to do that watching. It was a matter of simple arithmetic to the planter to see that the more workers he could bunch together under the eye of one overseer, the cheaper it would be for him. Here again the cotton plant worked out well. Where a single laborer could cultivate thirty to forty acres of Indian corn, he could manage only about five to ten acres of cotton. This meant, of course, that the distance between hands in cotton production was much less than in corn. The slaveholder saw that his costs would be less and his profits greater if his gang of Negroes was as large as could be taken care of by one man. It was silly to pay an overseer for handling eight or ten men when he could just as easily manage thirty or thirty-five men. The cotton plant permitted large-scale organization.

It was very clear to slaveholders that the larger your gang, the lower your expenses per man and the greater your profits; there grew up, then, the idea of buying more Negroes to raise more cotton to buy more Negroes to raise more cotton, and so on. Slaveholders saw that the road to greater profits was the plantation system of using large gangs of Negroes in a steady routine, under the supervision of an overseer, in the production of a single crop for sale. J. S. Buckingham, an English traveler in the South in 1842, describes a plantation that he visited:

The slaves are all up by daylight; and everyone who is able to work, from 8 or 9 years old and upwards, repair to their several departments of field labour. They do not return to their houses either to breakfast or dinner; but have their food cooked for them in the field, by Negroes appointed to that duty. They continue thus at work till dark and then return to their dwellings. There is no holiday on Saturday afternoon, or any other time throughout the year, except a day or two at Christmas; but from daylight to dark, every day except Sunday, they are at their labour. Their allowance of food consists of a peck, or two gallons, of Indian corn per week, half that quantity for working boys and girls and a quarter for little children. This corn they are obliged to grind themselves, after their hours of labour are over; and it is then boiled in water and made into hominy, but without anything to eat with it, neither bread, rice, fish, meat, potatoes, or butter; boiled corn and water only, and barely a sufficient quantity of this for subsistence.

Of clothes, the men and boys had a coarse woollen jacket and trousers once a year, without shirt or any other garment. This was their winter dress; their summer apparel consists of a similar suit of jacket and trousers of the coarsest cotton cloth. . . . No instruction was allowed to be given in reading or writing, no games or recreations were provided, nor was there indeed any time to enjoy them if they were.

On this particular plantation the hands worked Saturday afternoon, while on others it was a holiday. Different masters and overseers decided that on the basis of which was most profitable to them in the end. Some masters found that by permitting the Negroes to rest on Saturday afternoons as well as on Sundays, they could get more and better work out of them the rest of the week; other masters found that no Saturday rest brought more cotton. Some masters found that kind treatment, prizes for good work, a little extra food occasionally, a treat of tobacco now and then, any or all of these things, brought more cotton; other masters found that very strict treatment, an ever-watchful eye, no extras, and many "don'ts" brought more cotton. The treatment of Negroes varied, then, according to the master and his idea of what would be most profitable for him.

Where an overseer was put in charge of the plantation and told that his wages depended upon the amount of cotton he produced, then work was apt to be very hard and whipping more frequent. A writer in the *Columbia South Carolinian* thought that owners who used this system were making a mistake in that their slaves were certain to be overworked.

Planters may be divided into two great classes, viz., those who attend to their business and those who do not. And this creates corresponding classes of overseers. The planter who does not manage his own business must, of course, surrender everything into the hands of his overseer. Such a planter usually rates the merits of the overseer exactly in proportion to the number of bags of cotton he makes, and of course the overseer cares for nothing but to make a large crop. To him it is of no consequence that the old hands are worked down, or the young ones overstrained; that the breeding women miscarry and the sucklers lose their children; that the mules are broken down, the plantation destroyed, the stock neglected, and the lands ruined; so that he has the requisite number of cotton bags, all is overlooked; he is employed at an advanced salary, and his reputation increased.

On most plantations clothing for the field hands was similar to that on the plantation which Buckingham saw. The food on some was perhaps a little bit better, very often bacon as well as corn being part of the regular diet. A plantation street of Negro cabins was not much to look at. The wooden huts usually consisted of a single room about twenty feet square, where a whole family, or even several families slept. Often there were little or no furniture, broken windows, leaky roof, rotting logs, no drainage and no privy. Once or twice a year all the cabins both inside and out might be white-washed. Food, clothing, and shelter for his hands were an expense and the planter tried to keep it as low as possible. On small planta-tions the average cost of all expenses of food, clothing, and shelter for a Negro for a year, was $30 to $40. On large plantations the aver-age cost was only $15. The average for young and old throughout the whole cotton belt was about $20 per year!

This very low figure would have been even lower if the planter did not have to buy nearly everything he used. It is easy to under-stand why the South, a farming section, should buy manufactured goods from the North. But why should the South, a farming section, buy from the Northwest, pork, flour, corn, and other products of the farm? Why didn't the planters themselves produce the food and other farming supplies which they needed? The planter's profits lay in the production of cotton, so the Negroes were taught to grow cotton—and nothing else. Year after year cotton, and only cotton, was grown (in tobacco sections it was only tobacco; in rice sec-tions only rice; and so on). The South became a region of one-crop cultivation.

This works very well for several years, but eventually the land becomes exhausted and will grow no more cotton. A writer described what happened in an "Address to the Farmers of Georgia for 1839": "The farmers of Georgia could not have pursued a more fatal course than they have done for the last 30 years. The growing of cotton on broken [worn-out] lands is the most ready way that can be adopted to destroy them. Hence we have thousands of acres that were once fertile . . . now worthless to the last degree—nothing but sterile red clay full of gullies."

Another Southerner, editor of an agricultural paper, wrote in 1860: "The system is such that the planter scarcely considers his land as a part of his permanent investment. It is rather a part of his current expenses. He buys a wagon and uses it until it is worn out, and then throws it away. He buys a plow, or hoe, and treats both in the same way. He buys land, uses it until it is exhausted and then sells it, as he sells scrap iron for whatever it will bring. It is with him a perishable or movable property. It is something to be worn out, not improved."

Now this is not the way sane farmers usually treat their land. And yet the Southerners were not all crazy. How could they afford to carry on this way? C. C. Clay, a Southerner, made a speech in which we find the answer: "Our . . . planters, after taking the cream off their lands, unable to restore them by rest, manures, or otherwise, are going farther West . . . in search of other virgin lands."

The West. Acres and acres of rich, fertile land. Virgin soil, never before farmed. Why manure old worn-out land in Virginia, South Carolina, North Carolina, or Georgia when it was cheaper to buy new, rich, bottom lands in Alabama, Mississippi, Louisiana, Texas? Not only the poor farmer, not only the adventure seeker, not only the restless soul made the trek west. Large planters, too, pulled up stakes, and with all their household goods and their throng of Negroes following, joined the scrambling mass moving to the better cotton lands.

Follow the arrow on the map. Cotton was first grown in the South Atlantic States, North Carolina, South Carolina, and Georgia; then it spread to the Gulf States, Alabama, Mississippi, Louisiana, Texas, and Arkansas. The figures shout the story. In 1824 the older South Atlantic States produced almost twice as much cotton as the newer Gulf States, but by 1841 it was the other way around.

Slave labor and the planter's desire for profits tended to force one-crop cultivation, and one-crop cultivation tended to force expansion to new lands. The new Southwest began to look like the old Southeast.

For many of the farmers and planters moving to the new cotton lands, it wasn't a question of wanting to, it was a question of having to, because they could not grow cotton as cheaply or as well on the older, used land. As more people journeyed west, land in the East went down in value until in many places it was worth practically nothing. A traveler tells the story of meeting a Virginian on horseback with a bag of hay for a saddle, without stirrups, and the leading-line for a bridle, and he (the traveler) said, "Stranger, whose house is that?"

"It is mine," was the reply.

They came to another, "Whose house is that?"

"Mine, too, stranger."

To a third. "And whose house is that?"

"That's mine, too, stranger; but don't suppose that I'm so darned poor as to own all the land about here."

Particularly in Virginia, the oldest of the states, was the drop in land value noticeable. Here and there men gave away their old lands and houses, or even abandoned them. In 1829, three years after the death of Thomas Jefferson, Monticello, his magnificent home, with two hundred acres of land, was sold at public auction for only $2,500.

Where land could no longer be farmed intensively, it was very expensive to own a number of Negroes, because then the profit of their labor might not equal the expense and trouble of their upkeep. For a time it seemed as though John Randolph's remark about Virginia would come true, that "if the slaves did not run away from their masters, the masters would have to run away from their slaves." In Virginia and Maryland, where the tobacco lands were exhausted, slavery would probably have died out. But Congress passed a law forbidding the importation of slaves after 1808; at the same time there came a cry from the new cotton lands in the Southwest for more and more Negroes. What happened as a result? Prices of slaves shot skyward. The average value of a good field hand about the time of the invention of the cotton gin (1793) was $200.

By 1815 it was $250;
By 1836 it was $600;
And in 1850 it was $1,000.

With prices shooting up in this fashion, it became profitable in Virginia and Maryland to raise not cotton or tobacco, but Negroes. The former slave-working states became slave-breeding states.

"Henceforth slaves were seldom kept in these states for the sake of raising crops, but crops were often cultivated for the sake of raising slaves. . . . The Negroes in Virginia, Maryland, and Kentucky were frequently kept at some light employment, perhaps earning enough to pay for their subsistence, until they had reached maturity, when they were sold to traders who took them south."

Frederic Olmsted, traveling in the South in the 1850's, received a letter from a Southerner telling him about slave breeding: "In the States of Maryland, Virginia, North Carolina, Kentucky, Tennessee and Missouri as much attention is paid to the breeding and growth of Negroes as to that of horses and mules. Further south, we raise them both for use and for market. Planters command their girls and women (married or unmarried) to have children; and I have known a great many Negro slaves to be sold off because they did not have children. A breeding woman is worth from one-sixth to one-fourth more than one that does not breed."

By 1860 the price of a first-class field hand was from $1,500 to $2,000. While the value of land went sliding downward the value of slaves went shooting upward. While horses, mules, cattle, and sheep were worth less and less, slaves were worth more and more. In the latter part of the 1850's, the Gadsen estate sold sixty-seven head of cattle, nineteen sheep, and a stallion, and received only $929.50 for the lot. Just one prime field hand almost anywhere in the South would have brought more than that. The change was noticeable in the wills that people left. Where formerly the safest and best property to leave your children was land and livestock, by the 1850's the safest and most valuable property to leave your children was slaves.

A person was rich or poor according to the number of slaves he had. Whenever a planter had any extra money he bought more slaves. Thomas R. Cobb wrote in 1857: "In a slaveholding state, the greatest evidence of wealth in the planter is the number of his slaves. The most desirable property for a remunerative income is slaves. The best property to leave to his children, and from which they will part with greatest reluctance, is slaves. Hence the planter invests his surplus income in slaves."

Most people think of the South before 1860 as a region of many slaveholders. That was not true. It is obvious from the high prices of slaves that few people would have the money to buy them. The number of slaveholders in the South was really amazingly low. In

1850 there were between 6,000,000 and 7,000,000 whites in the South, but less than half a million of them owned slaves. The 3,000,000 to 3,500,000 Negroes were owned by less than 6 per cent of the people. The following table shows the startling figures:

CLASSIFICATION OF THE SLAVEHOLDERS—1850

Holders of	1 slave		68,820
Holders of	1 and under	5	105,683
Holders of	5 and under	10	80,765
Holders of	10 and under	20	54,595
Holders of	20 and under	50	29,733
Holders of	50 and under	100	6,196
Holders of	100 and under	200	1,479
Holders of	200 and under	300	187
Holders of	300 and under	500	56
Holders of	500 and under	1,000	9
Holders of	1,000 and over		2

Aggregate number of slaveholders in the U. S. 347,525

Notice that all the owners of fifty or more slaves numbered less than eight thousand. These slaveholders, though small in number, were strong in power. They were the wealthy aristocrats of the South. They managed the affairs of their section, got themselves elected to important positions in the state and national governments, and made laws favorable to slavery and slaveholders. They owned or controlled the southern newspapers; and doctors, lawyers, ministers, teachers, professors, and the poorer classes learned to accept their ideas as The Truth. They were the ruling class and, as always happens, they used their power as far as possible to spread ideas favorable to their own group.

In both Southeast and Southwest their plantations were on the richest, most fertile soil. In the East they had bought up the best coastland and had forced the poorer people into the mountains. In the West, theirs were the Mississippi River bottoms with their deep rich soil, ideal for the plantation system with its large gangs of Negroes. The not-so-good land, or the hillsides where the workable fields were scattered, making plantation routine more difficult— these were left to be occupied by the small farmer.

In the West, after the hard work of clearing the land and getting things started was over, then the planter and his gang of Negroes appeared. The pioneer who had made the clearing was offered a high price for his land, so high that he was induced to sell and move west to pioneer all over again. If he would not sell, he soon found it difficult to compete with the organized slave labor of the planter who had become his neighbor.

A southern writer in a country newspaper complained bitterly about this:

The cotton-growing portion of the valley of the Mississippi, the very garden of the Union, is year by year being wrested from the hands of the small farmer and delivered over to the great capitalists. The white yeomen . . . are either forced into the sandy pine-hills or are driven West to clear and prepare the soil for the army of Negroes and Negro-drivers which forever presses on their heels, to make their industry unprofitable and their life intolerable.

All the great cotton lands were first opened up by industrious settlers, with small means and much energy. No sooner is their clearing made, and their homestead growing into comfort, than the great planter comes up from the East, with his black horde, settles down on the district, and absorbs and overruns everything. This is precisely the process which is going on, day by day, over the greater portion of Louisiana and Mississippi. The small farmers, that is to say, the mass of the white population, are fast disappearing. The rich bottom lands of that glorious valley are being concentrated in the hands of the large planters.

In the desolate, forlorn mountain country of West Virginia, Kentucky, and North Carolina, the "poor whites" lived on soil so worn out that it was practically impossible to get along at all. They were so poor, so down and out, that they were scorned even by the Negroes. Some of them moved so far from civilization that their customs today are much the same as they were in 1800. All of them lived ignorant, wretched, lonely lives.

F. L. Olmsted learned of them in 1860:

I asked him if there were no poor people in this country. I could see no houses which seemed to belong to poor people.

"Of course not, sir—every inch of the land is bought up by the swell-heads on purpose to keep them away. But you go back on to the pine ridge. Good Lord! I've heard a heap about the poor folks of the North, but if you ever saw any poorer people than them, I should like to know what they live on. Must be a miracle if they live at all. I don't see how these people live, and I've wondered how they do a great many times. Don't raise corn enough, great many of them, to keep a shoat alive through the winter. There's no way they can live 'less they steal."

Some of the poor whites and others not so poor objected to the rule of the very rich men in the state governments. It was the old quarrel between the many poor and the few rich. In North Carolina the wealthy planters had kept their control by managing to have their slaves counted as people when votes were needed. Olmsted talked to a man who lived in the western part of North Carolina, and learned of the hatred between the poor mountaineers and the rich plantation owners:

"There ain't no account of slaves up here in the west, but down in the east part of this State, about Fayetteville, there's as many as there is in South Carolina. That's the reason the West and the East don't agree in this State; people out here hates the eastern people."

"Why is that?

"Why, you see they vote on the slave basis, and there's some of them nigger counties where they ain't more'n four or five hundred white folks, that has just as much power in the Legislature as any of our mountain counties where there'll be some thousand voters."

Between the poor whites on the lowest level and the very rich owners of large plantations on the highest, came the great mass of Southerners who lived on their own farms or small plantations. Some of them were fairly well off, owned a few slaves, and wished they had more. The others were quite poor, owned little if any land and few if any slaves—though they hoped to some day. In the meantime, what was a person to do who needed help but didn't have the money to buy a slave or slaves? He might hire help. If there was a choice between hiring a poor white or a Negro slave, the slave was usually chosen. Poor whites were not steady, and they were apt to leave just when they were most needed, whereas a slave had to work and had to stay. Then, too, there were certain jobs, such as getting water for the house or taking care of cattle, which a hired white man considered beneath him. If you asked him to do any such objectionable work, he would get mad and tell you he "wasn't a nigger."

Slave hiring was quite common. A slaveowner who needed money would hire out his slaves to a farmer who needed help. The money, of course, was turned over to the master. Prices for hired slaves were high or low according to how badly they were needed and the number available. In the southwestern states where the large cotton and sugar plantations were always crying for more hands, the prices were higher than in the older Atlantic states where slaves were more plentiful and their labor less profitable. Look for the high-priced states in the table of yearly prices paid for hired agricultural slave labor in 1860.

	Men	Women	Youth (children of both sexes not younger than 14 years)
Virginia	$105	$ 46	$39
North Carolina	110	49	50
South Carolina	103	55	43
Georgia	124	75	57
Florida	139	80	65
Alabama	138	89	66
Mississippi	166	100	71
Louisiana	171	120	72
Texas	166	109	80
Arkansas	170	108	80
Tennessee	121	63	60

Slaves were hired not only for farm labor, but for other jobs also. Sometimes they were hired as ditchdiggers, railroad workers, or long-shoremen. Occasionally Negroes who had been taught to work around the master's house as servants instead of as field hands might be hired out as coachmen, butlers, or cooks. In the *Richmond Daily Enquirer* for May 13, 1853, there appeared this advertisement for Negro slaves to be employed in a hotel at a fashionable summer resort:

> Fifty Servants Wanted for the Springs, viz. Dining Room Servants, Chambermaids &c; Persons having such for hire will call immediately.—Toler and Cook.

The following advertisement gives us an idea of how Negroes rated in some white men's eyes:

> Sheriff's Sale. I will sell at Fairfield Court House, 2 Negroes, 2 Horses and 1 Jennet, 1 pair of Cart Wheels, 1 Bedstead, 1 Riding Saddle. Sheriff's Office Mon. 19, 1852.

Bedsteads, cart wheels, riding saddles, Negroes—all bunched together, all just so much property. At public auctions the Negroes were put up on the block, carefully inspected, then bid for just as though they were a watch or a lamp or any article at auction. Here is a description of one of these sales. "About a dozen gentlemen crowded to the spot while the poor fellow was stripping himself, and as soon as he stood on the floor, bare from top to toe, a most rigorous scrutiny of his person was instituted. The clear black skin, back and front, was viewed all over for sores from disease; and there

was no part of his body left unexamined. The man was told to open
and shut his hands, asked if he could pick cotton, and every tooth in
his head was scrupulously looked at."

Some whites became slave traders, just as other men were cattle
traders. They dealt in Negroes, bought and sold them, as you might
do with horses or cattle. The advertisement of one of these dealers
appeared in the *Richmond Enquirer* for May 8, 1835:

> Negroes! Negroes! I have stationed myself at the Boll-
> ingbrook Hotel in Petersburg to buy Negroes. Persons
> wishing to sell, either in Town or adjoining counties,
> will do well to give me a call, as I expect to pay liberal
> prices for such as are likely, of both sexes, from 12 to 30
> years of age—Mechanics and house servants in particu-
> lar—Any information directed to the subscriber will be
> attended to promptly.—Richard R. Beasley.

From another ad that appeared in the *Charleston Courier*, April
12, 1828, we learn that families of slaves might occasionally be
sold separately, never to see one another again:

> As valuable a family . . . as ever was offered for sale,
> consisting of a cook about 35 years of age, and her
> daughter about 14 and son about 8. The whole will be
> sold together or a part of them, as may suit a purchaser.

Was it possible to make slaves of 3,000,000 to 4,000,000 human
beings without serious uprisings? In some districts in the South there
were many more Negroes than whites. Occasionally a section might
be as high as 90 per cent Negro and only 10 per cent white. On some
plantations there were several hundred Negroes and only the overseer and one or two white helpers, with no other whites for miles
around. Was it possible to keep the Negroes from revolting against
their white masters? No, it was not possible. There were many revolts though American history books hardly ever mention them.
There were fierce uprisings led by desperate, brave men who were
prepared to sacrifice their lives, if necessary, to end the brutal slave
system. These revolts were not successful and they were put down
with ferocious cruelty. The southern whites were quick to act whenever the slaves dared to challenge their supremacy. And in the day
to day pattern of life which they imposed on the Negroes they took
every precaution to keep the idea of such challenge from entering
the minds of the slaves.

The whites were careful to make certain that the Negroes never got hold of pistols or dangerous weapons of any kind. That was one way of keeping them down. Another more effective way was to bring up the Negroes to respect and fear the white man, to make them feel that they were inferior to the whites. The black man, slave or free (there were a good many free Negroes in Virginia and Maryland), was to "be kept in his place." Harriet Martineau tells one of the ways of getting this over to the Negroes. "At the American Theatre in New Orleans, one of the characters in the play which my party attended was a slave, one of whose speeches was, 'I have no business to think and feel.' "

Religion, too, was a weapon used by white masters to help make Negroes believe that it was just and proper for them to be slaves. Bishop Meade of the Church of England in Virginia wrote a book of sermons which he recommended to white ministers preaching to black slaves. Here are some extracts from that book:

. . . Having thus shown you the chief duties you owe to your great Master in heaven, I now come to lay before you the duties you owe to your masters and mistresses here upon earth. And for this you have one general rule, that you ought always to carry in your minds; and that is to do all service for them as if you did it for God Himself.

Poor creatures! You little consider, when you are idle and neglectful of your master's business, when you steal, and waste . . . when you are saucy and impudent, when you are telling them lies and deceiving them, or when you prove stubborn and sullen and will not do the work you are set about without stripes and vexation,—you do not consider, I say, that *what faults you are guilty of towards your masters and mistresses are faults done against God Himself, who hath set your masters and mistresses over you in his own stead,* and expects that you would do for them just as you would do for Him. . . . I tell you that *your masters and mistresses are God's overseers and that if you are faulty towards them, God will punish you severely for it in the next world.* . . .

The church's contribution to the preservation of the slave system was not unimportant. To thus identify, in the slave's mind, his master with God was the crowning glory.

By 1860 the South had become a great agricultural section producing four staple crops—sugar, tobacco, rice, and cotton, particularly cotton. It was, of necessity, an expanding region where planters and farmers were ever on the move toward new lands which they had to have because their one-crop cultivation exhausted the soil. The four million black slaves who did most of the plantation labor were owned by a very small number of persons who had most of the money. A few thousand wealthy aristocrats had practically complete control over the social, political, and industrial life of all the people. The very wide gap between this group at the top and the poor whites at the bottom was filled with farmers and townsmen of various degrees of wealth, mostly poor people.

The United States in 1860 . . . one country but two sections . . . North and South, unlike in almost every way.

Land Lords Fight Money Lords

★——★

There had to be a fight. Perhaps it need not have been a long war which killed so many people, but disagreement and bitter feeling were bound to come. The country was called the United States, but that was true only in name, not in fact. Northern and southern states worked differently, thought differently, lived differently. In the North there were small-scale farming, shipping, and increasing manufactures, all done by free white labor; in the South there was one-crop agriculture with Negro slave labor. The two sections, so unlike in their whole manner of living, were sure to split. The northern merchant, manufacturer, and banker classes rising to new power with the Industrial Revolution, *had* to come to grips with the southern landholding classes. That struggle went on for over sixty years and finally ended in the Civil War.

The two sections quarreled because what was good for the manufacturing North was bad for the agricultural South, and vice versa.

The protective tariff was a case in point. When the tariff argument was carried on in the halls of Congress, it was very clear that Congressmen were for or against the tariff according to whichever section they represented. John Randolph of Virginia gave the southern point of view against the protective tariff: "It eventuates in this: whether you as a planter will consent to be taxed, in order to hire another man to go to work in a shoemaker's shop, or to set up a spinning jenny. . . . No, I will buy where I can get manufactures cheapest; I will not agree to lay a duty on the cultivators of the soil to encourage exotic manufactures; because, after all, we should only get much worse things at a higher price, and we, the cultivators of the soil, would in the end pay for all. . . . Why pay a man much more than the value for it, to work up our own cotton into clothing when, by selling my raw material, I can get my clothing much better and cheaper from Dacca."

The people who spoke for the manufacturers did not dwell too long on the fact that the protective tariff would mean money in their pockets. Oh, no. They were interested in the tariff largely because it would keep the factories running, which in turn would mean jobs at high wages for workers. It was the ordinary laborer, then, who was helped most by the tariff—said the spokesmen for the manufacturers. Daniel Webster of Massachusetts put it this way: "This is therefore a country of labor. . . . Now what is the first great cause of prosperity with such a people? Simply, employment . . . where there is work for the hands of men, there will be work for their teeth. Where there is employment, there will be bread. . . . Constant employment and well-paid labor produce, in a country like ours, general prosperity, content, and cheerfulness."

For many years in Congress, representatives of the northern manufacturers argued with the representatives of the southern planters over this question of the protective tariff. The quarrel grew so bitter that in 1832 South Carolina threatened to break away from the United States because the tariff was too high. Congress avoided the split then by passing a new law which lowered the tariff rates every year for ten years. The tariff, however, came up for debate again and again and continued to be a cause of much hard feeling between the manufacturing North and the agricultural South.

Then there was another question on which both sections could not agree. The Westerners, you remember, were always clamoring for good roads and canals to be built at government expense. This idea suited northern manufacturers and merchants because they wanted to sell things to the West. What could be better than fine roads or well-built canals over which western food products might be carried east to be exchanged for their manufactured goods? The North was very much in favor of government-built highways.

Not so the South. Trade between states in the South was very small; the South had no market to look for in the West; the South had no manufactured goods to send from the coast to the Mississippi; to Southerners, the natural and best route for commerce was down the Mississippi and out through New Orleans, a southern port; the South, then, was very much against the use of government money for east-to-west road building. Because Southerners saw no great need of such internal improvements, they soon found that the Constitution gave the government no power to spend its money on schemes of this sort. The North, of course, found in the same Constitution, that the government did have that power. The gulf between the cotton-growing South and the manufacturing North was growing wider.

To add to the growing friction came the fierce attack on slavery by the Abolitionists.

They were a group of people who thought that Negro slavery was wrong and should not be permitted in the United States. They were never a very large group, but they were powerful out of all proportion to their small number. Perhaps this was the case because they were terribly in earnest, certain they were right, ready to speak, write, and work for the cause. They were, of course, bitterly hated in the South, and even in the North they were looked upon as troublemakers. Nevertheless, in spite of the fact that occasionally their property was wrecked by angry mobs, that some of their leaders were put into prison, that others were dragged through the streets, and one of them even shot to death—in spite of all this, they carried on. You get an idea of how determined they were from the printed words of William Lloyd Garrison, one of their leaders: "I am in earnest—I will not equivocate—I will not excuse—I will not retreat a single inch—and I will be heard."

The Abolitionists stirred up trouble between North and South. They organized antislavery societies, wrote papers and books against slavery and distributed them everywhere—even smuggled some into the South, where they were forbidden by law. They organized the Underground Railroad, a series of houses or way stations where runaway slaves were hidden, then helped to escape to Canada. Here and there they gathered together crowds to rescue runaway Negroes who had been caught by slave-catchers. Everywhere they tried to drive home the idea that slavery was bad and must be given up.

There had been a time when the Abolitionists might have made headway in the South. As a matter of fact, between 1782 and 1790 more than ten thousand Negroes were freed in Virginia alone. This was the period just following America's War for Independence, when there was much talk of liberty, equality, and freedom, and— what was very important—it was the period when worn-out tobacco lands made owning slaves no longer profitable. It was quite easy to convince a slaveholder, who was losing money on his slaves, that slavery was evil and should be abolished. But it was a different story after cotton became King in the South and the prices of slaves shot sky high. When slaves became valuable property, Southerners could see nothing wrong with slavery.

In fact, many of them began to think of it as a positive good. Newspaper editors, teachers, and political leaders united in trying to prove by every kind of argument that Negro slavery was not only necessary, but good. Ministers quoted from the Bible to prove that it was God's will.

The horrors that the northern Abolitionist saw in slavery were not visible to the Southerner. He could not understand people who said it was wrong for one man to own another. He was born into and brought up in surroundings of white masters and Negro slaves and he became accustomed to it. It seemed the natural way for whites and blacks to live together. The books and newspapers he read, the plays he saw, the sermons he heard, every part of the society in which he moved about fixed in his mind that white people were superior to black people. He was soon used to the idea that white must be master and Negro must be slave. Besides, Negroes were his property, costly property, too, and to talk wildly about freeing the slaves meant nothing more than the destruction of his property. Southerners hated Abolitionists, with a fierce, burning hatred.

They hated the Abolitionists as meddlers. They wanted the Abolitionists to mind their own business. They were furious at being told by Northerners that their treatment of Negroes was wrong. The Negro population in the South was large and Southerners felt that "keeping them in their place" was the only safe way of handling them. Northerners with their handful of Negroes, made a great noise about how awful conditions in the South were, but what of their own section? Did Northerners take in the Negroes and treat them as their equals? Not at all. When a school for free Negroes was started in Canaan, New Hampshire, in 1835, "three hundred men appeared with a hundred yoke of oxen and pulled the schoolhouse into a neighboring swamp."

In 1833, when Miss Prudence Crandall admitted a few colored girls into her boarding school at Canterbury, Connecticut, her angry neighbors tried to boycott her. When that failed to stop her they organized a mob and attacked her. As she still persisted, they got the Legislature to pass a special law making it a crime to admit Negroes to any school. Then they threw her into prison for breaking the law.

Southerners grew more and more angry as northern attacks on

slavery continued. They wanted the Northerners to put their own house in order. Senator Hammond of South Carolina reminded Northerners that they too had slaves. He said:

In all social systems, there must be a class to do the mean duties, to perform the drudgery of life . . . we call them slaves. We are old-fashioned at the South yet; it is a word discarded now by ears polite; I will not characterise that class at the North by that term; but you have it; it is there; it is everywhere; it is eternal . . . The difference between us is that our slaves are hired for life and well compensated; there is no starvation, no begging, no want of employment among our people, and not too much employment, either. Yours are hired by the day, not cared for, and scantily compensated, which may be proved in the most deplorable manner, at any hour in any street of your large towns. Why, sir, you meet more beggars in one day, in any single street of the city of New York, than you would meet in a lifetime in the whole South. Our slaves are black, of another inferior race; . . . your slaves are white, of your own race; you are brothers in one blood.

Was Negro slavery in the South better or worse than mill slavery in the North?

The *Daily Georgian* of Savannah ran an article in 1842 on this very point, "Could our words reach the ears of the misguided people who are so much imposed on by the arch-leaders of the abolition movement, we would beg them to free the White Slaves of Great Britain and of the manufacturing states of the North, before they interfere in the domestic institutions of the South."

These Southerners argued that in hard times the northern mill worker was thrown out of his job and left to starve or freeze for want of food, clothing, and shelter; that when he grew old and could no longer work there was no one to look after him or his family. Negro slaves, on the other hand, were never hungry or cold; in sickness or old age they were taken care of; they never had to worry, because they knew they would always be provided for. A Virginian put it this way: "In the Southern system of society the laborer is sure of raiment, and of food; for if the profits of the master do not enable him to give these, the master must use his capital; and if neither his profits nor his capital will allow him to do it, then he must transfer him to some one else who is able to provide him with these comforts; and thus in any event the laborer is assured of the physical comforts and necessaries of life."

J. K. Paulding, a traveler in the South in 1836, thought there was something in this southern argument. He compared the workers in England, and the peasants in Germany and Russia, with the white laborers in the United States. "These latter he found 'as respects the essentials of comfort, far beyond the rest of the world.' Yet they worked harder than slaves, and were often thrown out of employment and deprived of bread, all because they had no master to care for them and shield their families from hunger, cold, and distress."

The quarrel over slavery grew more and more bitter. Now and then the governor of some northern state would have a dispute with the governor of some southern state about giving up a runaway or stolen Negro. A long-drawn-out wrangle would ensue, with the people in both states getting more and more excited. Then that excitement would die down and another squabble would start somewhere else. A clash would come over some Abolitionist attack on slavery, like *Uncle Tom's Cabin*. Southern states would pass laws forbidding the printing and distribution of such books or pamphlets. Southern postmasters would destroy any antislavery material of this kind. Northern states would make it hot for slave-catchers after runaways. Disagreement. Excitement. Brawls. Mobs. The conflict over slavery was driving a wedge between the manufacturing free-labor North and the agricultural slave-labor South.

In both North and South in the early days farming had been the chief industry. But while the South stuck almost entirely to one-crop agriculture, the North had added both commerce and manufacturing to its many-crop agriculture.

Every foreign visitor to the United States was struck with the great difference between the two sections—always in favor of the North. When you left the South and entered the North a great change was visible. You went from a slow-moving, sleepy atmosphere to a fast, busy one; you left behind the worn-out abandoned fields with their crumbling mansions and entered a region of well-kept, efficiently run farms, and growing towns and cities; you forgot the endless view of cotton fields when you saw the many mills, the mines, the canals, the railroads, the shops, the colleges, the banks. While southern rich men had been putting all their money into one thing—cotton—northern rich men had been putting all their money into different things, factories, mines, banks, railroads. While southern capital went into more Negroes, or into luxurious living for a few rich planters, northern capital went into more and more business schemes which built up the North and gave huge profits to the capitalists.

In every industry the North was ahead of the South. In manufacturing, of course, there was no comparison. Northern factories made—at a profit—the things the South used; or northern ships brought the things from Europe and northern merchants sold them to the South—at a profit. In a meeting of Southerners at New Orleans in 1855 Captain Pike described how dependent the South was on the North. "From the rattle with which the nurse tickles the ear of the child born in the South to the shroud that covers the cold form of the dead, everything comes to us from the North. We rise from between sheets made in Northern looms, and pillows of Northern feathers, to wash in basins made in the North, dry our beards on Northern towels, and dress ourselves in garments woven in Northern looms; we eat from Northern plates and dishes; our rooms are swept with Northern brooms, our gardens dug with Northern spades, and our bread kneaded in trays or dishes of Northern wood or tin; and the very wood which feeds our fires is cut with Northern axes, helved with hickory brought from Connecticut and New York."

Was there a demand for coal, iron, or copper? Then northern mines supplied it.

Did the growing Northwest have food to sell and manufactured goods to buy? Then Northerners built canals and railroads to tap that trade. By 1860 most of the northwestern commerce had left the rivers running to southern Gulf ports and was transferred to the canals and railroads running to northern Atlantic ports. The Northwest was being bound to the North by bands of steel.

Did anyone want to borrow money? The place to go was to the North, which owned most of the banks of the country.

But what of farming? Surely the South took the lead there. Not at all. "Though the South grew all the rice, all the sugar-cane, all the hemp, and five-sixths of the tobacco, the crop of hay harvested each summer by the farmers in the North brought them more than twice as much money as came to the planters in the South from all the rice, hemp, sugar-cane and tobacco combined."

About two thirds of the livestock on farms was raised in the North.

In 1850, the value of an acre of land in the South averaged about $9.00, while in the North it averaged about $25.

Cotton, of course, was the big crop in the South. It was true that in 1860 the value of the cotton exported from the United States was more than half the value of all our exports. Nevertheless, H. R. Helper, himself a Southerner, had this to say about cotton from the South: "The truth is, however, that the cotton crop is of but little value to the South. New England and old England, by their superior enterprise and sagacity, turn it chiefly to their own advantage. It is carried in their ships, spun in their factories, woven in their looms, insured in their offices, returned again in their own vessels, and, with double freight and cost of manufacturing added, purchased by the South at a high premium. Of all the parties engaged or interested in its transportation and manufacture, the South is the only one that does not make a profit."

This may have been true or it may have been exaggerated. But it was true that the North sold just its boots, shoes, leather goods. and iron for more than the South received for all its cotton. These facts were tremendously important. They foreshadowed the victory of northern businessmen over southern landholders.

The North had gone ahead of the South in every field except politics. Both sides fought for control of the government. It was Congress that made a high or low tariff or voted government money to help fishermen or to build roads. If southern landholders elected the President and won more seats in Congress, then the laws that would be passed would favor the South. If the candidates of the northern merchants and manufacturers won the elections, then laws would be passed that favored the North. This was clear to both sides.

By playing politics very skillfully, the southern leaders had been quite successful during the whole period from Washington's time in 1789, down to 1860. If it was possible to elect a Southerner as President, they did that. If that was not possible, they backed a northern man who was friendly to the South. From Washington to 1860 most of the presidents were Southerners or on their side; like-wise most of the judges of the Supreme Court; and either the House of Representatives, or the Senate, or both, were in their control. This was the reason that the tariff from 1822 to 1860 (with the exception of the year 1842) was made lower and lower. In the government, at least, the South was in the saddle.

If the South had not held the reins of government, the jig would have been up for it long before 1860. In the Senate of the United States every state, large or small, had two votes. As the territory in the West filled with people and came into the Union as states, a contest developed between North and South. Should the new state be slave or free? Each section wanted to add to its side the two new votes of the incoming state. There were some people who were down on slavery but were quite willing to let it exist, if it were not allowed to spread farther. It was fortunate for the South that it had control of the government, because it was thereby able to expand into the West. By the year 1850 nine free states and nine slave states had been carved out of the western land. The balance had been kept even —after many stormy arguments by representatives of both sides.

For the South, of course, expansion to new lands was necessary, apart from reasons of politics. Fresh land was essential to cotton growing with slave labor. If there should come a time when South-erners could no longer spread westward, it would mean the end of planter rule. Unfortunately for the South, that time came by 1860.

Not the Northerners, but Nature was the cause. Look at the map.

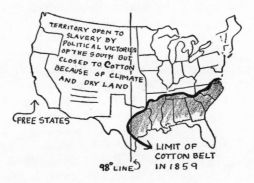

TERRITORY OPEN TO SLAVERY BY POLITICAL VICTORIES OF THE SOUTH BUT CLOSED TO COTTON BECAUSE OF CLIMATE AND DRY LAND

FREE STATES

98° LINE

LIMIT OF COTTON BELT IN 1859

West of the 98° line was arid land, too dry for cotton growing. The South had won the right to move there with its slaves, but it was land on which cotton would not grow. Nature had fixed the limit of the cotton kingdom.

On the other hand, there was no limit to "the amount of capital that could be accumulated, the variety of machines that could be invented, and the number of people who could be sustained by manufacturing." The victory had to be to the North.

"King Cotton had lost his scepter and nothing but a severe jar was necessary to overturn his throne." When their opponents, the Republican party, won the election in 1860, and Abraham Lincoln became President, southern cotton planters saw the handwriting on the wall. Now that they had lost their political power also, they felt there was nothing left to them but to withdraw from the Union. They knew what the victory of northern merchants and manufacturers meant, and they feared the result. In December, 1860, South Carolina, and shortly afterward ten other slave states, declared themselves no longer part of the United States. Representatives from the seceding states met together and formed the "Confederate States of America." The Union was broken in two.

In vain did Lincoln try to reassure the slaveholders that his government would "not interfere with the institution of slavery in the states where it exists." The eleven seceded states had made their choice. They wanted to be a separate country, with their own government making their own laws; they wanted to live as they saw fit without northern interference.

The whole South did not withdraw. The four border slave states of Delaware, Maryland, Kentucky, and Missouri, having few slaves, growing little or no cotton, and resembling the North as much as the South, would not leave the Union. Even among the states that did secede not all the people wanted to leave the Union. The mountaineers of Virginia broke away from their state, formed a new one, called West Virginia, and remained loyal to the Union. In the back country districts, in the mountain regions where slaves were few and farms were small, in those areas which had always been opposed to the rich planters, secession was not popular. The South was led into leaving the Union by the wealthy, slaveholding plantation-owners.

In the North there were many people who were satisfied to let the South go its own way. Not Mr. Lincoln. He thought the country must remain one, the Union must be preserved, even if there had to be fighting to force the slave states back.

On April 12, 1861, war broke out. For four long years the fighting continued with terrific loss of life on both sides. First each side asked for volunteers, then men were drafted into the armies. This caused bitter feelings in both South and North. In both sections drafted men were allowed to hire substitutes to serve for them. In the South the draft laws had many loopholes through which owners of large plantations or those who owned more than fifteen slaves could escape from serving. (This in a war brought on by these same people.) In the North a drafted man could get out of serving by paying the government $300. Small wonder that many poor people called it "a rich man's war and a poor man's fight."

After two years of fighting, with the South still refusing to rejoin the Union, President Lincoln issued his Emancipation Proclamation which was to free the slaves in those states fighting against the Union. Later the slaves were freed in the neutral border states also. Two billion dollars' worth of property was thus taken away from southern planters.

In April, 1865, General Lee of the South surrendered to General Grant of the North. The Civil War was over.

The South was in ruins. Sheridan, one of the northern generals, had boasted that "if a crow flew from Shenandoah Valley to Harper's Ferry he would have to take his lunch with him." The damage done to southern property was terrific; the number of killed and wounded was tremendous; the cost in money was eight billion dollars—enough to have paid for all the slaves four times over.

Nevertheless, in this "second American Revolution," Negro slavery was overthrown—and with it the rule of the slaveowners. No longer were four million human beings to be held in bondage.

No longer could the landowners of the South stand in the way of the capitalists of the North. Union armies had swept across their plantations; all their property in Negroes had been destroyed in one fell swoop; the money they had loaned to the Confederacy was completely lost; their leaders who had been government officers must obtain permission from Congress before they could again hold office. Gone were their wealth and power.

The northern capitalists, on the other hand, now had in their grasp everything for which they had been fighting for sixty years. No more fuss about the protective tariff—they put over the highest one ever; no more question about government money being spent for internal improvements—railroad companies were given thousands of acres of government land and huge sums of government money; no more high wages to workers—manufacturers could go abroad and hire laborers under contract for less than they had to pay Americans; no more private banks printing paper money that went up and down in value—money-lenders were able to secure a national banking system which made their loans and interest on their money safe.

Merchants, manufacturers, and bankers, had fought and won their battle for leadership against the landholders who had stood in their way. They knew what they wanted. Now they were in a position to get it.

Materials, Men, Machinery, Money

★——★

A few years ago at a meeting of the American Institute of Chemical Engineers a wonderful machine capable of making 442 electric light bulbs a minute was exhibited. Unscrew a bulb and look it over. Imagine making seven of these every second!

This was just one of a long series of amazing inventions which played such an important part in the Industrial Revolution. That revolution, by 1865, had caused many changes in man's way of living. But it has been during the period since the Civil War to the present day that changes of far-reaching importance have come with startling rapidity. The United States Industrial Commission declared (way back in 1902) that "the changes and progress made since 1865 have been greater in many directions than during the *whole history of the world before.*"

Therefore, Abraham Lincoln, who was shot in 1865, about two hundred and sixty years after the first settlement in Jamestown, would be much more at home in the America of those early days than in the America of today. The world of *even one thousand years ago* would be easier for him to understand than would the world today.

If he were to walk through the White House today, he would be full of wonder at such ordinary things as the telephone, electric lights, steam heat, even safety matches. Outside the White House, he would be speechless as he saw automobiles whiz by on the well-paved roads, skyscrapers towering into the air, trolley cars on the streets, and airplanes in the sky. In his day, most of the people in the United States were still farmers, though manufacturing had begun; today more people are employed in manufacturing than in farming. In his day only 16 per cent of the people lived in cities of 8,000 or over—and there were only 141 such cities; today, 50 per cent of the people live in cities of 8,000 or over—and there are 1324 such cities. In his day the difference between rich and poor was not great; today that difference is tremendous. In his day there were less than five millionaires; today, there are thousands of millionaires and even some billionaires. In his day a man who wanted a fresh start in life could move to the frontier where land was free; today there is no frontier and land is expensive. In his day most businesses were owned by individuals or partners; today most businesses are owned by corporations. In his day the worker was all important, with the tool as an addition to him; today the machine is all important, with the worker as an addition to it.

Truly an amazing transformation. How was it brought about?

Largely through the combination of materials, men, machinery, and money.

The materials, or natural resources, of the United States were in many ways beyond comparison. Coal and iron were perhaps most essential to the changing world. Of coal, the United States had half the known deposits in the world. Of iron, its output was enormous; in 1929, over 40 per cent of the world's supply came from the United States. Not only were the deposits large, but they were easy to get at. In Minnesota, for example, no drills nor dynamite were necessary —the iron lay upon the surface ready to be scooped up and dropped into the waiting cars. With oil, copper, lead, and zinc the story was the same—a more than plentiful supply. One third of the continent was covered with timber. No other region anywhere contained as large an area of level fertile land making possible the production of cotton, wheat, corn, and cattle. Nearly three million square miles of land extending from the Atlantic to the Pacific, the only great nation of the world fronting on two oceans. In the heart of this huge territory ran a network of twenty seven thousand miles of navigable rivers and canals which, added to the four thousand miles of shore line on the Great Lakes, was longer than the ice-free seashores of the whole continent of Europe.

Nature had indeed been generous. Here was an empire of astounding riches. Here were the materials for development on a scale hitherto unheard of.

In Europe, a king might own this vast storehouse of riches; or acres and acres might have been in the possession of some family of nobles for hundreds of years; or the church could count large blocks of land among its possessions.

LUMBERMEN

In America, on the other hand, about one half of the country had been taken up by individual farmers—land-hungry people who had followed the setting sun in their westward march of two hundred years. The other half of the country belonged to the people of the United States—with the government having the power to dispose of it. Up to 1860 that government was largely controlled by the land-lords of the South. But 1865 saw their downfall and the victorious money men of the North in their place. Forest, plain, and mountain could now be made to yield their treasures—under the guiding hand of northern capitalists.

What kind of men were they?

They were daring businessmen who had their eyes open to the main chance; canny schemers with the imagination to see and the wit to take advantage of changing situations which might afford a profit; they were not idealists who had notions so dear to their hearts that they would not modify them to suit new conditions that might crop up; they were practical men, money-makers with a vengeance, men who would stop at nothing in their desire for more and more profits. One of them, Commodore Vanderbilt, showed his feelings toward any agency which might be in his way, when he roared, "Law! What do I care about law? Hain't I got the power?"

He was right. He and his kind did have the power.

There was another larger group that came under the heading of Men. This was the army of labor, the men, women, and children who did the actual work of digging, building, making. These were the people who chopped away at chunks of coal deep down in the bowels of the earth; these were the people who by steady toil from dawn to dusk carefully nursed their crops through blizzard, heat, drought, and flood; these were the people who drove red-hot rivets into steel girders, while dangerously perched hundreds of feet in the air on the framework of some skyscraper; these were the people who tended the speeding machines in factories. Many of them were newly arrived immigrants from faraway countries.

In home workshops, in college laboratories, and in the labora-tories of great manufacturing plants labored another group of workers—the inventors of new machines. Some of them had no equip-ment other than a vivid imagination and a will to succeed; others had years of scientific training behind them. The amazing number of their inventions was added to, in no small measure, by the inven-tions of factory workers whose intimate acquaintanceship with the machine they operated made them quickly understand its defects and how it could be improved. The work of all these inventors is clearly shown in the records of the Patent Office. From 1850 to 1860 an average of 2,370 patents was awarded each year; from 1920 to 1930 that number had jumped to about 44,750 a year. Of all the patents awarded by all countries of the world from 1871 to 1932, no less than 30 per cent had been awarded by the United States government. Here certainly was a triumph for Yankee ingenuity.

With good reason the present era is sometimes called the Age of the Machine. You have only to look about you to see in how many ways machinery enters into all our lives—whatever we eat, wear, live in, read, play with, ride in—everything we do is touched at some point by machines. It is impossible to estimate how much the use of machinery has multiplied man's strength and skill. The years after 1865 were the years of the greatest development of the machine.

Money, too, played an important part in changing America. The materials were here, the capitalists knew what they wanted to do, and they needed money to put labor and machinery to the work of doing it. Their schemes were so gigantic that no one man had enough money to begin the jobs. At the beginning there wasn't enough available money in all the United States to carry out the plans. So people in Europe, who had extra money and wanted more, sent it here to be used and returned—with a large profit attached.

Materials, men, machinery, and money—all together they made the United States the richest country of the world. The capitalists who came into power with the Civil War were the driving force. They combined the natural resources, the labor, and the capital, and made modern America. They developed the country—sometimes by fair means, sometimes by foul means. They became rich. They became powerful. More and more the wealth of the country became concentrated in the hands of these few. Their power grew with their riches. They became the real rulers of the United States.

What were some of the important changes between Lincoln's time and our own?

There was the revolution in transportation.

The Civil War stimulated our industrial growth in every way but perhaps its greatest effect was on the transportation system. For four years supplies and troops had to be carried from place to place as quickly as possible. The railroads did the job—the first great war in which they played an important role. War-time necessity forced their early development, and peace-time expansion stimulated that development further.

In 1860 there were thirty thousand miles of railroad track in the United States.

In 1880 there were ninety thousand miles—three times as much.

In 1930 there were two hundred and sixty thousand miles—more than enough for five double tracks around the earth!

The first rails were made of hemlock topped with straps of iron. In an era of plodding oxen and slow canal boats the first locomotive ever run on a track in America was quite a sight. The villagers in Honesdale, Pennsylvania, turned out in full force to see the "Stourbridge Lion," just imported from England, make its first run. The wheezy locomotive with its steam-belching boiler on a framework set on wheels of oak was a strange object. It puffed and it puffed and finally rumbled down the track at the magnificent speed of four miles an hour.

A few years later an excited passenger on another line wrote to a friend, "Yesterday we attained the astounding speed of twelve miles an hour. If ever anyone goes any faster he'll have to go to Kentucky and charter a streak of lightning!"

In the early days most of the railroads were short lines. If you made a journey of any considerable distance you had to change frequently from one line to another. At one time, in order to go from New York to Buffalo (about four hundred miles) eleven changes had to be made. The railroad lines often were in cahoots with the innkeepers en route to give them business. Schedules were arranged so that travelers had to stay for lunch or dinner or overnight between changes of railroads. It was quite a step forward in railroad history when several lines owned by different companies were bought up and made into one through line.

By 1860, although most of the lines were east of the Mississippi, you could go as far as the bend of the Missouri River by rail. From there to the Pacific coast the colorful pony express carried the mail, jolting stagecoaches bumped along with their uncomfortable passengers, and long trains of wagons pulled by oxen crawled overland with supplies for the mining camps and farms. When the first transcontinental railroad was completed, in 1869, the day of the overland freight wagon, stagecoach, and pony express was ended.

The building of this first cross-country road was a tremendous undertaking. Two companies were formed, the Central Pacific to build eastward from Sacramento, and the Union Pacific to build westward from Omaha. Cheap labor was imported; Chinese coolies worked for the Central Pacific and Irish immigrants for the Union Pacific. Supplies for the army of laborers marching west had to be carried overland from Iowa; for those marching east, supplies had to be shipped the long route around Cape Horn, or carried across the Isthmus of Panama (the canal there was not completed until 1914). With unbelievable speed the work was carried on, over plains, rivers, and mountains. An English traveler described the construction work in 1869:

... On they came. A light car, drawn by a single horse, gallops up to the front with its load of rails. Two men seize the end of a rail and start

forward, the rest of the gang taking hold by twos until it is clear of the car. They come forward at a run. At the word of command the rail is dropped in its place, right side up, with care, while the same process goes on at the other side of the car. Less than thirty seconds to a rail for each gang, and so four rails go down to the minute! Quick work, you say, but the fellows on the U. P. are tremendously in earnest. The moment the car is empty it is tipped over on the side of the track to let the next loaded car pass it, and then it is tipped back again; and it is a sight to see it go flying back for another load, propelled by a horse at full gallop at the end of sixty or eighty feet of rope, ridden by a young Jehu who drives furiously. Close behind the first gang come the gaugers, spikers, and bolters, and a lively time they make of it. It is a grand Anvil Chorus that these sturdy sledges are playing across the plains. It is in a triple time, three strokes to a spike. There are ten spikes to a rail, four hundred rails to mile, eighteen hundred miles to San Francisco. That's the sum. What is the quotient? Twenty-one million times are those sledges to be swung—twenty-one million times are they to come down with their sharp punctuation, before the great work of modern America is complete!

This first transcontinental road was shortly followed by others. By 1884 there were four railway lines carrying people and freight between the Mississippi and the Pacific.

Americans were quick to realize that transportation was essential in building up the country. They had helped the railway companies by giving them huge blocks of government-owned land. To the Central Pacific and Union Pacific Congress was particularly generous. Each of these companies was given alternate sections of land stretching twenty miles back on each side of their tracks. In addition, for every mile of track built, Congress gave them a loan of $16,000 to $48,000. (Businessmen knew what they were about when they removed southern planters from control of the government.)

Now the heads of the Union Pacific thought of a scheme whereby they could make some easy money. It worked this way.

The directors of the Union Pacific organized themselves into a construction company called the Crédit Mobilier. Then they awarded the contract for building their road to the Crédit Mobilier—that is, to themselves. So far, so good. Somebody had to build the road. But then, as the construction company, they charged themselves, as heads of the Union Pacific, about $40,000,000 more than it cost to build the road. In the same way the directors of the Central Pacific paid to a construction company $120,000,000 for work which cost $58,-000,000. Capitalists were "cleaning up" on the people's money. Before government land giving was ended, about one hundred and fifty million acres, an area larger than that of all the New England states plus New York, or an area larger than France, was given away to railroad companies. Not for nothing had the Civil War been fought.

Railroads were excellent where they were needed. But in the mad rush for profits through railroad building, many lines were built where they were not needed. In many places there was great duplication of roads—two or three lines where one was enough to do all the business. Then the rival lines would fight one another for the trade.

There would be a price war in which the competing lines would lower their rates to attract customers. This went to such extremes that in 1876 a carload of cattle could be shipped from Chicago to New York—a thousand miles—for only $1. In the same year you could travel all the way from Cleveland to Boston for only six dollars and fifty cents. Today the fare is over three times as much.

Roads which had to cut their freight rates at those points where they had competition tried to make it up by very high rates at those points where there was no competition. Farmers in the West, particularly, were the victims of this crazy system. It worked out something like this: The distance from Fargo to Duluth is one half as great as the distance from Minneapolis to Chicago. You would naturally expect, then, that the rate on wheat from Fargo to Duluth would be one half of the rate from Minneapolis to Chicago. But no. Instead of being one half as much, it was twice as much. No wonder the farmers complained bitterly.

They complained, too, about the way the men who ran the railroads, also ran the courts and legislatures. Western railroads gave free passes to officials in the state governments, to judges, lawyers, ministers, and editors. Evidently southern railroads did likewise, as we learn from this item in the *Progressive Farmer* of Raleigh, North Carolina, for August 14, 1888: "Do they [the railroads] not own the newspapers? Are not all the politicians their dependents? Has not every judge in the State a free pass in his pocket? Do they not control all the best legal talent of the State?"

The United States was a country of great spaces. There were differences of climate, rainfall, and soil (geography again) which helped to cause certain sections to specialize in certain industries. Thus, there was the cattle-raising section of the plains, the cotton-growing section of the South, the corn and wheat belt of the central and western states, and the manufacturing section of the Northeast. Transportation of freight and passengers was necessary between these sections. It was the business of the railroads to furnish that transportation. Since the railroads had been built on government land and helped by government money, many people thought that the aim of the railroads should be to give the country service as cheaply and efficiently as possible. But they were mistaken. In most cases the railroad heads thought it was the first business of the railroads to make money—the more the better. They did not believe in giving the people the most service for the least amount possible.

Not at all. They believed, as one of them frankly said, "in charging all the traffic would bear." Often they misjudged, and the rates they charged were so high that farmers could not afford to pay and were ruined. Nevertheless, the policy of the roads continued to be "all we can get away with."

Not all the railroad heads, of course, were interested primarily in land grabs or get-rich-quick schemes. All of them wanted profits. But some of them realized that profits could be obtained through giving real service. James J. Hill of the Great Northern was one of these men. He, like other western railway men, advertised the wonderful qualities of the land through which his railroad ran. But he didn't stop there. When settlers flocked to the lands along his lines he helped them in every way. The farmers' troubles became his troubles. No small part of the credit due to railroad builders in the successful settling of the Northwest belongs to Hill.

There came a time, of course, when cutthroat competition between railroads was stopped. The many short lines were consolidated into the great trunk lines of today. That was an important step. That it would be attended by more dishonest money-making schemes seemed a certainty to those who had followed the sordid history of the railroads. They performed a necessary service, but the crooked schemes that followed their construction and operation were scandalous. The present plight of the railroads in the United States is due, in no small measure, to their fraudulent unprincipled past.

In agriculture, as in everything else, there were great changes after the Civil War. After 1865, four million colored people were suddenly thrown on their own. They had no land, no homes, and no property. What could they do? They knew how to raise cotton, but they had nothing with which to begin. The great planters, their former masters, were in a very bad way themselves. They had plenty of land but no money with which to pay wages.

So the big plantations were broken up into small farms and rented to white people or Negroes. They either paid their rental in cash or became share tenants or sharecroppers. Share tenants furnished their own farm equipment and animals, and obtained the use of the land by agreeing to pay the owner a fixed share of the produce—one fourth or one third of the crop. The sharecroppers were much worse off. They had neither equipment nor animals, nor, in many cases, even food for themselves and their families. They had nothing but their labor. The share the owner took from them was therefore larger—one half the crop or more.

The owner took out of the crop, too, what he had furnished his tenants and croppers in the way of seed, fertilizer, and food. The tenants and croppers, both white and black, were at the mercy of the landlord. He handled the sale of the crop; he kept the books; he charged what he liked for the food which he supplied out of his own commissary; he usually added an exorbitant interest charge plus a fee for "supervision." It was not surprising, therefore, that when the accounts were settled, the tenants and croppers often found that they were in debt to the owner—if they were lucky they might break even.

The workings of the tenant-cropper system are best illustrated in the following story, one of hundreds of a similar type: "A tenant offering five bales of cotton was told, after some owl-eyed figuring, that this cotton exactly balanced his debt. Delighted at the prospect of a profit this year, the tenant reported that he had one more bale which he hadn't yet brought in. 'Shucks,' shouted the boss, 'why didn't you tell me before? Now I'll have to figure the account all over again to make it come out even.' "

It becomes obvious from this story that the difference between the old slavery and the new tenancy was not very great. It is a little-known fact that today in the South there are more whites than Negroes who are enmeshed in the slavery of the tenant-cropper system.

But the story of the changes in American agriculture after the Civil War is more than the story of a fundamental transformation in southern economy. It is the story of a revolution so great as to change the ways of living of the people not only in America but also in Europe. In the sixteenth century the flow of gold and silver from America to Europe brought with it a price revolution that played an enormous part in shaping the history of the Old World; in the nineteenth century another flow—this time of farm products —brought with it a second revolution in the economy of the Old World.

After the Civil War the United States became a great industrial nation, but it became a great agricultural nation as well. In fact, it was primarily because of the tremendous expansion of agriculture which made America the granary of the world, that the United States was able to become the leading industrial country. Our agricultural surpluses became the farm exports with which we were able to pay for necessary imports, both of goods and money. It was the expansion of agriculture which made it possible for us to pay, in large part, our ever-increasing debts to the capitalists of the Old World.

Just as the Civil War forced the expansion of our railroad system so it forced the expansion of agriculture. Thousands of men were at the front—they had to be fed. Money was needed to carry on the war—it had to be raised. The farms did the trick. In 1860 we exported seventeen million bushels of wheat; in 1863 we exported fifty-eight million bushels. While the export of bales of cotton shrank to almost nothing (because of the northern blockade) the export of bushels of wheat more than tripled. Bread won over cotton —a shorthand way of expressing not only the victory of the North over the South but also the entry of the great western farm lands on the agricultural scene.

What began in the war years continued in the peace years. The Homestead Act of 1862 which gave 160-acre farms in the West to anyone who settled there was a powerful magnet. Immigrants continued to pour into the United States. The thirty-one million people in 1860 had become almost two and a half times that number in 1900. Many of them went into agriculture. The number of farms almost tripled from 1860 to 1900; so did the area under cultivation. The value of the farm property of the country (including land, buildings, machinery, and livestock) was $7,980,000,000 in 1860; in 1900 it was $20,439,000,000.

The table tells the story:

(In thousands)

Year	Population	No. of farms	Improved acreage	Total acreage	Value of farm property
1860	31,443	2,044	163,110	407,212	7,980,493
1870	38,558	2,659	188,921	407,735	8,944,857
1880	50,155	4,008	284,771	536,081	12,180,501
1890	62,947	4,564	357,616	623,218	16,082,267
1900	75,994	5,737	414,498	838,591	20,439,901

Perhaps the best clue to what was happening is contained in the fourth column—the acreage brought under cultivation. The table shows that in the forty-year period, over a quarter of a million acres of improved land was added—an amount greater than the productive area of Italy, Germany, and France together!

What those figures do not show—but what was very important—was that though the *number* of people who went into farming was increasing, the *percentage* of farmers compared to the people in all other gainful occupations was decreasing. In the beginning, farming was the chief occupation of most of our people; by 1860, seven out of every ten American workers were farmers. In 1870, only five out of ten were farmers, and by 1900 the number was down to three and a half.

Percentage distribution of gainfully occupied persons
16 years of age and over, 1870–1900

Occupation group	1870	1880	1890	1900
Agriculture and allied occupations	52.8	48.1	41.2	35.9
Mining	1.5	1.6	1.8	2.1
Manufacturing and mechanical industries	22.0	24.8	26.3	27.5
Trade and transportation ..	9.1	10.7	13.6	16.3
Clerical service	1.7	2.0	2.5	2.8
Domestic and personal service	9.6	8.8	9.7	10.0
Public service not elsewhere classified	.6	.7	.9	1.0
Professional service	2.7	3.3	4.0	4.4
Total	100.0	100.0	100.0	100.0

But though the percentage of farm workers out of the total population was decreasing in this way, nevertheless, more and more farm products were being produced. How could that happen? It happened because at the same time that the percentage of farmers was going down, production per acre and production per person employed were going up. This was made possible, in the main, because of the increasing use of machinery, scientific farming, and the specialization of crops.

The farmer in our country sowed his fields and reaped his crops in very much the same fashion as did the farmer of ancient Egypt. On bended knees or with back bent double the farmer cut his wheat with the ancient hand sickle. It was a slow job. Harvesting just one acre of wheat meant several days of work. The scythe, a lengthened, reshaped sickle, was an improvement. It could be swung with two hands by a man standing up. The cradle was an improvement on the scythe in that it cut the grain with the heads pointing in a single direction. This made gathering the grain and tying it into bundles easier and quicker. The cradle made it possible for a strong man to cut about two acres of grain in one day.

The farmer had only about ten days in which to cut his grain. With none of these hand tools could he cut all he could plant in that short time. As a result, acres and acres of grain had to be left standing to serve as fodder for cattle. Harvest time was hard-work time for every hand that could be put to farm work. That old Yankee spur to quick action, the whisky bottle, was much in evidence during the harvest.

After the grain had been cut by hand, it was bound by hand, then threshed with a flail by hand. Then it was bagged by hand, and carried to market. A long tedious process—too slow to provide enough grain for the growing population of the world. But it was the era of the Industrial Revolution, and machinery solved the problem.

The McCormick reaping machine had its first try in 1831. It was successful. Threshing machines were next invented. Then came improvements—then more improvements. Horses or mules pulled the new machines. In the 1900's, the gasoline tractor was announced as a substitute for horse-pulling power. More improvements. Today, on large up-to-date farms, a tractor "combine" moves across the field, cutting a ten-foot swath. It cuts the wheat, threshes it, and bags it—a factory on wheels! The two men who run it do the work of two hundred working in the old way. The combine has driven armies of farm workers from the fields. In a similar fashion, tractor-drawn gang plows, mechanical potato diggers, mechanical cotton pickers, corn planters, hay loaders, and dozens of other machines have transformed farming methods and released thousands of farm workers, at the same time increasing production enormously. It has been estimated that from 1865 to the present day farm labor has become at least 500 per cent more efficient.

The miracle wrought in agriculture by machines and mechanical power has been described most vividly in this way: "In a section of land there are 640 acres. An active man, in the days before power, might have worked his life long in vain to spade a fraction of it.

If mechanical power had never been invented this man might have begun to spade his section in the year 1432. Today, but not with the same shovel, his great-great and then many times more great, grandchild would just be coming to the end of a five-hundred-year task. But thanks to the thoughtful gentlemen who brought mechanical power into the world, three men with a tractor and gang plows could turn up every inch of that soil within thirty-six hours."

Farming became more efficient for other reasons also. The year 1890 marked the end of the frontier. The end of the frontier marked the end of free land. The rise in the value of land meant that the farmer had to get all he possibly could out of it. It was no longer cheaper to take new land than to manure the old. Now the farmer *had* to interest himself in fertilizers and in every phase of scientific farming. The intelligent farmer began to welcome the help of agricultural school experimentation; he began to send for bulletins of information published by the government Department of Agriculture. With what result? What did labor-saving machinery and scientific methods do to farming?

They made it possible for every farmer to produce much more than ever before in much less time. Output per worker increased while time spent decreased.

Thus it took:

in 1855, 4½ hrs. human labor to produce 1 bu. of corn
in 1895, 2   hrs. human labor to produce 3 bu. of corn;
in 1831, 3   hrs. human labor to produce 1 bu. of wheat,
in 1895, 1   hr. human labor to produce 6 bu. of wheat.

In the case of corn, the time per laborer was cut in half, yet the yield was three times as great. In the case of wheat the time per laborer was cut to one third, yet the yield was six times as great. Improvements since 1895 have helped to increase production and reduce time, per laborer, even further.

In the period after the Civil War the character of farming changed also. Formerly the average farmer was practically self-sufficient. On his own farm he produced the things he needed. Did he want bread? His corn and wheat fields supplied it. Did he want butter, cheese, milk, meat? His cattle supplied them. Did he want clothing? His fields supplied flax for linen, and his sheep supplied wool. Did he want tools? The simple tools that he could not make himself were made by the village blacksmith. The products of his farm went to satisfy his own needs—if anything was left over it was sold to pay his taxes or to buy something fancy that could not be made on the farm. That was production for use.

As time went on, all that was changed. The farmer no longer made everything for himself, but stuck to the production of one or two crops. He was self-sufficient no more. He became a specialist. (Specialization became characteristic of the new manufacturing also.) He became a wheat farmer, or a corn farmer, or a dairy farmer, or a fruit farmer. Then, like the city man, he had to *buy* most of the things he needed. Specialization usually meant a better product and more of it, since he devoted all his time and energy to his specialty. At the same time, it was dangerous; he was "putting all his eggs into one basket"—if the bottom fell out he lost everything. If his crop was a failure he had nothing to sell; if his crop was a big success, he had too much to sell. Specialization was dangerous because it geared him to capitalist economy with all its ups and downs. Production for use was one thing, production for exchange was quite another thing. The specialized farmer learned that lesson.

In addition to specialization, the increasing use of machinery helped to subject the farmer to the economy of capitalism. His old sickle or scythe was inefficient compared to the reaper or combine, but it cost very little (he sometimes made it himself) and it lasted a lifetime; the new machinery was expensive—it took a lot of money to buy it. And he had to buy it—competition by machine-run farms forced him to. More and more capital became a necessity to the farmer.

Now to be a farmer in the American capitalist economy after the Civil War was far different from being an industrialist. The lords of industry were in the saddle—they cracked the whip and the governmental horse did their bidding. For the industrialists there was a high protective tariff which kept up the prices of the goods they sold—the goods which the farmer had to buy. For the farmer there was no high protective legislation for farm produce—the goods which he had to sell. For the industrialists there was the possibility of combining to control prices; for the farmer combination was much more difficult, so farm prices were not controlled. For the industrialists there were all the advantages that came from being in a position to exploit the other fellow; for the farmer there were all the disadvantages that came from being in a position to be exploited by the other fellow.

From the Civil War to the end of the century agriculture was expanding, but profits to the farmer were definitely not expanding. The farmer worked hard for little or no profits. He had his troubles.

The ancient combat between the farmer and the destructive forces of nature continued, of course. The farmer on the plains and prairies of the West was particularly hard hit. Occasionally fierce blizzards raged so violently that men often lost their way and were frozen to death going from their houses to their own barns to feed their cattle. At other times a severe drought would continue for days on end while hot winds withered the crops. A more rare scourge came in the form of grasshopper plagues. The grasshoppers would suddenly appear in huge swarms and eat or destroy every bit of grain in sight. (These grasshoppers have been known to force trains to stop running. So many thousands would cover the tracks that the friction between wheels and track would be eliminated and the train would have to halt.) Blizzards, drought, grasshopper plagues, hail, hot wind—the farmer knew he had to fight these—there was no help for it.

He did object, however, to what he thought were man-made difficulties. He did complain against being exploited, against having others take the major profits of his labor.

He had a grievance against the railroads because of their unfair practices.

He had a grievance against the grain elevator men. They cheated him by unfair grading of his wheat. There might be one grain elevator in his town, to which he had to bring his wheat. There the buyer looked over the wheat and fixed the grade of it. If he called it No. 2 wheat it was No. 2 wheat and the farmer had nothing to say about it. Many farmers knew their wheat was being graded under its real quality, but they could do nothing. The farmer was angry at elevator men who bought his wheat at low-quality prices, and then resold it at the high-quality prices which he should have received.

He had a grievance against the manufacturers who charged him high prices for the things he bought, while he received low prices for the things he sold. The farmer bought in a tariff-protected market, and sold in an open market.

He had a grievance against the money-lender, the banks, the moneyed class in general. They had the capital which he needed so badly and they took advantage of his need. If he wanted a loan of money on his crop they might or might not grant it—if they did, then the rate of interest was sure to be high, too high. Their interest rates on his mortgages were excessive. Low prices for his farm goods made it more and more difficult for him to pay back what he owed—when he couldn't pay, the money lords took his farm away.

The farmer was bitter against the capitalists. He agreed with Mary Elizabeth Lease of Kansas, who said in 1890: "Wall Street owns the country. It is no longer a government of the people, by the people, and for the people, but a government of Wall Street, by Wall Street, and for Wall Street. The great common people of this country are slaves, and monopoly is the master. The West and South are bound and prostrate before the manufacturing East. Money rules. . . . The common people are robbed to enrich their masters. . . . The people are at bay. Let the bloodhounds of money who have dogged us thus far beware."

From the 1870's through to 1896 the farmers translated their grievances into action. They followed the advice of one of their leaders who said, "What you farmers need to do is to raise less corn and more hell."

In some sections of the country they united in politics, organized societies called the Granges, and elected for the state legislatures people who were on their side. Then in 1876 they passed laws which fixed railroad rates, and storage rates for grain, according to what they thought was reasonable. They were swinging into action against the capitalists.

But the capitalists were too strong for them.

Railroad lawyers appeared before the Supreme Court of the United States and argued that the state legislatures had no right to fix railroad rates. The Supreme Court decided with the farmers. Case after case was brought before the court, and every time it decided that the state governments *did* have the right to fix rates; that it was up to the state legislature, and not *to the federal courts*, to fix those rates. The language of the court was plain, "Where property has been clothed with a public interest, the legislature may fix a limit to that which shall be in law reasonable for its use. This limit binds the courts as well as the people. If it has been improperly fixed, the legislature, not the courts, must be appealed to for the change."

But the capitalists continued their fight. Time passed. New judges were appointed to take the place of old ones who had died. A new series of cases was brought before the court and new decisions were made. By 1889, the Supreme Court reversed the decisions of 1876 and thereafter, and decided that it did have the right to decide whether or not rates fixed by state legislatures were reasonable. The capitalists had won out. From that time on, any attack on private property by state legislatures (whose members were *elected* by the people) had to be O.K.'d by the Supreme Court (whose members were *appointed* by the President with the approval of the Senate). Later history proved that the Supreme Court O.K. of an attack on private property was seldom given. The ruling class had a safeguard against attack.

The farmers in parts of the West and South were fighting mad. They were making a last stand for agriculture against the money lords of industry. The platform of their People's party in 1892 will give you an idea of how they felt and what they wanted to do about it:

> The fruits of the toil of millions are boldly stolen to build up colossal fortunes for a few. . . .
> Wealth belongs to him who creates it, and every dollar taken from industry without an equivalent is robbery. If any will not work, neither shall he eat. . . .
> We believe that the time has come when the railroad corporations will either own the people or the people must own the railroads. . . . Transporation being a means of exchange and a public necessity, the government should own and operate the railroads in the interest of the people. . . .

The telegraph and telephone, like the post-office system, being a necessity for the transmission of news, should be owned and operated by the government in the interest of the people. . . .

We demand that the amount of circulating medium be speedily increased to not less than fifty dollars per capita.

We demand a graduated income tax. . . .

We demand that postal savings banks be established by the government for the safe deposit of the earnings of the people. . . .

Their wrath against the railroad abuses was evident. Their remedy was government ownership and operation—as with the post-office system.

Their demand for an increase in the "circulating medium" was the old money-owers' cry for cheap money. The farmers wanted more money to be printed so the dollar would go down in value and the prices they received for their goods would be higher. It was a clear case of money-owers vs. money-lenders. If more money was printed, that would help the money-owers. If more money was not printed, that would help the money-lenders.

Their demand for an income tax was later heeded by Congress in 1894. The law put a 2 per cent tax on all incomes above $4,000— that amount, of course, let the farmer and laborer out. It was a tax on the rich people, and they opposed it. Again the Supreme Court came to the rescue of the wealthy. Although an income tax had been in effect during the Civil War, nevertheless in 1895 the Supreme Court, by a vote of five to four, declared that such a tax was unconstitutional! The *New York Sun,* very much alarmed at the bitter fight of the poor against the rich, rejoiced in the decision. Its editor wrote, "Five to four the court stands like a rock." It took eighteen years of combined effort by farmers and laborers to get at the capitalists secure behind the rock of special privilege which was the Supreme Court. In 1913 the income tax amendment to the Constitution was finally ratified and made the law of the land. Now, at long last, Congress had the right to put a tax on incomes. (But for the very rich, there were loopholes in the income tax laws which were passed. In 1937, Secretary of the Treasury Morgenthau informed the President and Congress of eight ingenious devices "now being employed by taxpayers with large incomes for the purpose of defeating the income taxes which would normally be payable by them.")

In 1892, although the farmers' candidate for the presidency, James Weaver of Iowa, did not win the election, nevertheless he polled more than one million votes. In several western states the People's party swept its candidates into state offices.

The most bitter struggle between the farmers and the capitalists came in the election of 1896. The farmers' organizations threw their support behind William Jennings Bryan, the Democratic candidate, while the money men backed William McKinley, the Republican candidate.

It was a very exciting campaign. Bryan was a wonderful orator. He went up and down the country, thousands of miles, making speeches continually. He spoke to the farmers and laborers of the country. ". . . Upon which side shall the Democratic party fight? Upon the side of the idle holders of idle capital, or upon the side of the struggling masses? . . . The sympathies of the Democratic party . . . are on the side of the struggling masses. . . .

"There are two ideas of government. There are those who believe that if you just legislate to make the well-to-do prosperous, their prosperity will leak through on those below. The Democratic idea has been that if you legislate to make the masses prosperous, their prosperity will find its way up and through every class that rests upon it."

While Bryan was making his six hundred speeches in twenty-nine states on a campaign fund of $300,000, Mark Hanna, a Cleveland capitalist, was busy collecting money from manufacturers and bankers to support McKinley, their candidate. He was a good collector and the capitalists backed McKinley to the tune of over $4,000,000! It was a great deal of money and it performed many services; it paid for tons of leaflets which told the people that the key to prosperity was the election of McKinley; it bought banners, posters, flags, and buttons, which announced that the country needed McKinley; it hired bands to lead McKinley parades; it paid fourteen hundred speakers to promise the workers that the election of McKinley meant a "full dinner pail" (in the same vein, thirty-two years later, Mr. Hoover's backers promised them "a car in every garage and a chicken in every pot"); and it helped to convince small-town newspaper editors that the smart newspaper supported McKinley.

Nor was that all. Capitalists could do more for their cause than merely donate money. Factory owners could terrorize their workers into believing that victory for Bryan would mean that the factory would close and they would lose their jobs; businessmen could order new goods with the announcement that victory for Bryan would mean the order would be canceled; bankers could inform farmers that victory for Bryan would mean the bank would be unable to wait any longer for the money the farmer owed.

Bryan was defeated.

Though the electoral vote was 271 to 176, the popular vote was 7,035,638 to 6,467,946. By a margin of less than 600,000 votes the strongest challenge of the united farmers against the growing power of the capitalists had failed.

Vachel Lindsay has given us an unforgettable picture of the victors in the great struggle:

> Boy Bryan's defeat
> Defeat of western silver.
> Defeat of the wheat.
> Victory of letterfiles
> And plutocrats in miles
> With dollar signs upon their coats,
> Diamond watchchains on their vests
> And spats on their feet.
> Victory of custodians,
> Plymouth Rock,
> And all that inbred landlord stock.
> Victory of the neat.

More Materials, Men, Machinery, Money

★───★

After so many pages devoted to the story of the expansion of agriculture since 1865, it seems a contradiction now to say that this period marked the transformation of the United States from an agricultural to a manufacturing nation. Yet that is exactly what happened. Great as was the revolution in agriculture, the revolution in manufacturing was even greater. After the Civil War the United States became the most powerful industrial nation in the world.

Value of Manufactures (in millions of dollars)

	1860	1894	1929
United Kingdom	2,808	4,263	
France	2,092	2,900	
Germany	1,995	3,357	
United States	1,907	9,498	69,961

While in 1860, the United States ranked fourth among the nations of the world, by 1894 it had jumped to first place. While the value of the manufactures of the United States was almost five times as great in 1894 as it had been in 1860, in none of the other nations had it even doubled.

This table is important for showing the changing position of the United States in relation to the other great manufacturing nations. Equally revealing is another set of figures which gives in more detail the country's startling growth in manufacturing from 1859-1899. In that 40-year period:

the number of establishments ....increased threefold
the number of wage earners ....increased fourfold
the value of mfd. products ....increased sevenfold
the amount of capital invested ....increased ninefold

Growth of Manufactures in the United States
(includes all factories, hand, and neighborhood establishments)
(In thousands)

Year	No. of Establish- ments	Wage Earners	Value of Products	Amount of Capital Invested
1859	140	1,311	1,886,000	1,009,000
1869	252	2,054	3,386,000	2,118,000
1879	254	2,733	5,370,000	2,790,000
1889	355	4,252	9,372,000	....
1899	512	5,306	13,014,000	9,835,000

"By 1890 for the first time, the value of the country's manufactured goods was already greater than that of its agricultural products; in another ten years, manufactured products were worth twice as much as those of the farm, the orchard, and the dairy."

The increasing use of machinery and power was, perhaps, primarily responsible for these enormous strides in manufacturing from the Civil War to the present day.

In the handicraft period the worker was all important. He did the thinking, the designing, and the work that went into the article that he made. The tool was simply an addition to the worker's own skill.

Modern industry has changed all that. Now the tool is all important. The worker has become simply an addition to the tool. The skill of the worker has been transferred to the tool. Instead of a skilled worker plus an unskilled tool, there is now a skilled tool plus an unskilled worker.

At the General Motors plant a worker operates a multiple-spindle machine which drills thirty holes in a Chevrolet motor block in one operation. The accuracy of the drilling does not depend on the skill of the worker, but on the skill of the machine. And the machine does not make mistakes. It does the job of drilling more accurately than the most skilled workman could without it.

Note, too, that in addition to the "transfer of skill" there has been a "transfer of thought" as well. The skilled workman without the machine would have had to think about the proper location of the holes. With the machines no such thought is necessary. It has been done once for all by the toolmaker. The unskilled operator need only push the block into place and the machine does the work.

This is only one of millions of machines that perform similar miracles in the United States every day, and not only in the United

States, but in other industrialized nations of the world also. But it is in the United States that the machine has its most widespread use. And it is in the United States that mass production has reached its zenith.

The story is told of an interesting experiment made by an English manufacturer with three American automobiles all of the same

make—for example, three Chevrolets, or three Fords. He had three of his men drive the cars uphill and downhill over a long stretch of English roads. When the cars were returned after their tour, workmen were told to take them apart and throw the remains into one mixed-up heap. Every screw, nut, wheel, tire, and axle, from each car was taken from its regular place and thrown into the pile. Then the whole mass of parts was jumbled up some more. After that, workmen were told to take parts out of the pile and put together three cars again. They did so. When the cars were assembled, the three chauffeurs jumped in, started immediately, and made the same trip they had made before. The Englishman had demonstrated the first principle of mass production—the making of standard inter-changeable parts.

Eli Whitney, way back in the 1800's, had thought of the idea of standard interchangeable parts and had made muskets for the government that way. But he had none of the wonderful facilities of modern industry. The lathe of his day could be carried on the back of one man. Modern lathes are gigantic affairs which can shape chunks of steel forty feet long and ten feet in diameter.

Standard interchangeable parts means simply that every part must be like every other part. Not nearly like, but *exactly* like. That would not have been possible years ago. But today, with gauges that measure to three millionths of an inch, and with highly accurate machines that make no errors (the human element is taken out of the picture as much as possible), absolutely identical parts are turned out with amazing speed.

Given interchangeable parts, the next step in mass production is to put them together into the finished product—automobile, type-writer, tractor, and so on. In modern plants, assembling has been so systematized that there is a continuous flow of separate parts in a never-ending stream to the main assembly belt along which semi-skilled workmen stand at different stations. Walk through the Ford plant. Watch the chassis of one car after another move steadily along while workers put on the mudguard here, the steering wheel there, the motor, the wheels—every part a snug fit with only a few quick movements necessary to snap it into place. The belt moves on—all the parts of an automobile put together in one hour, eight hundred cars assembled in one plant in one working day! This shows the tempo of modern industry.

Mass production required the standardization of parts. The stand-ardization of parts was made possible only through the development of wonderfully accurate machines. These machines were made pos-sible only through the development of a group of "machine tools." The lathe, the drilling, grinding, boring, and milling machines are the important members of this group. They are the machines which make other machines. And they are the only machines which can re-produce themselves. A cement mixer can mix cement, but it cannot make other cement mixers. Nor could it if it were combined with a power loom. But the machine tools in combination with one another can and do reproduce themselves—make more lathes, more planers, gear cutters, grinders, and borers. They are the basic tools of modern industry.

Hand in hand with the increase in the use of machinery came the increase in the use of power. Some people call this the Power Age. During the fifty-nine years from 1870 to 1929, installed primary power in manufacturing industries increased 2,000 per cent! Here are the figures:

```
1870 .................... 2,000,000 horsepower
1900 .................... 10,000,000     "
1929 .................... 42,000,000     "
```

The graph shows the sources of that power for the year 1929.

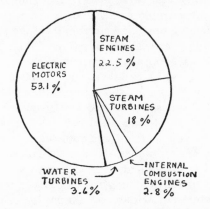

Mass production and the use of power-driven machinery help to explain the tremendous growth of the United States as a manufacturing nation. There were other reasons. You cannot manufacture without raw materials. The United States was rich in materials, particularly those necessary to an industrial country. Its natural resources were unrivaled.

There would be no point in making goods unless people bought them—there must be a market. With constant inpourings of immigrants a domestic market of immense proportions grew up. In only eight years, 1920 to 1928, in spite of the fact that in this period immigration was curtailed by law, just the *increase* in population in the United States was greater than the whole population of Norway, Sweden, and Denmark together! Since 1900 the trade between states in the United States was greater than all of the combined foreign trade of the leading countries of Europe. It was, of course, this great "mass consumption" of goods which made mass production profitable.

Immigrants served in another way to make the United States a great manufacturing nation. They were an endless supply of cheap labor. Northern manufacturers during the Civil War had pushed through Congress a contract immigration law which enabled them to send agents abroad to import laborers, under contract, to work in the mills here with their wages attached until their passage was paid for. The incorporation papers of the American Emigrant Company of Connecticut, gave as its object "to import laborers, especially skilled laborers, from Great Britain, Germany, Belgium, France, Switzerland, Norway and Sweden, for the manufacturers, railroad companies, and other employers of labor in America."

On the West coast, employers helped to solve their labor problem by importing Chinese coolies, Japanese, and Filipinos—to work for low wages. In Texas, Mexicans were the answer.

There were no trade barriers between the states. That was very important. Because Europe is divided into many nations which differ in language and customs, no easy flow of goods is possible. When French goods reach the Italian border, inspectors board the train, examine the goods, and tax them. All along the line, there are inspections and delays which hinder the flow of goods. Not so in the United States. Here manufactured goods from the East could make the long journey through state after state many times the size of some European countries, without any inspection or tax. Here there were no barriers of language or customs, or national prejudice. Between states ours was a tariff-free country. (It is interesting to note, in this connection, that in the depression years of the 1930's, a trend toward the erection of "state tariff walls" was noticeable. Many states were passing laws discriminating against the products of other states.)

A nationwide market needed a nationwide transportation system. Goods were made and had to be distributed to the people who wanted them. It was not an accident that the greatest amount of railroad mileage was found in the greatest manufacturing country.

A high tariff in the beginning, by shutting out foreign competition, helped infant manufacturing plants to get a good start. The high tariff, after their industries were no longer infants, helped manufacturers to make high profits—which attracted more people to the business of manufacturing.

Another great change that helped to swell the volume of manufactured goods was the invention and development of new goods. We ourselves have seen the introduction of the dial telephone, cellophane, the "talkies," and now television. These were unknown a few years ago. Going back as far as 1900, the list of new or improved articles would include radios, rayon, oil-burning furnaces, automobiles, wrist watches, electric refrigerators, electric toasters, electric this and electric that.

Beginning with the twentieth century, invention was no longer an accident. Great industrial firms like the General Electric Company, the American Telephone and Telegraph Company, the Ford Company, and hundreds of others now had as part of their plant equipment scientific laboratories where men did research work all the time. These engineers not only invented new machines, and improved old ones, but they planned more scientific ways of running the factory. Work was expertly divided and rearranged to increase the efficiency of every worker. One person was given one task instead of many; that task was simplified so that it became merely a matter of one or two movements quickly done. According to a report of the United States Public Health Service, "Much of the modern industrial work consists of a constant and rapid repetition of the same movement. A woman worker in one of our munition factories was recently observed to handle during her day's work 24,000 pieces of a shell fuse and put them through a special process. From seven o'clock in the morning until twelve and from one until six she sat at her machine and fed it with the succession of brass pieces." (Incidentally, think of how dull and monotonous such work becomes. Try just *counting* to 24,000 and see how soon you give up.)

In manufacturing industries, as a result of the increase in the use of power-driven machinery, of mass production, and of scientific management, the output per wage earner increased 62 per cent between 1899 and 1929. In other words, every worker in a factory was turning out about one and three-fifths times as much in 1929 as he did in 1899. That was the average for all manufacturing industries. In certain types of work the increase was even more striking. Take automobiles, for example. The same number of men, working the same number of hours in the plants of Ford and General Motors, were turning out three times as many cars in 1929 as they had turned out in 1914. If 1849 be compared with 1929 we find that the average output per worker was quadrupled. "In the textile industry it has been estimated that one man with the help of modern machinery can now produce as much cloth as 45,000 men could in the 1700's."

The chart on the next page pictures the amazing story. With only 5.7 per cent of the land area of the world and only 6.1 per cent of the population, the United States was far and away ahead of every other country in the production of most of the key products listed. The combination of materials, men, machinery, and money had worked wonders.

Such large-scale production required large amounts of money. The United States was too big a theater for small-scale performances. Machinery and big factories were costly. Businessmen needed great sums of money to carry out their ambitious plans. How did they obtain that money?

One man might own and manage his own business. That had been the usual way before the Civil War. But it no longer suited the changing world. One man's money was not enough to carry out great projects.

A partnership of several men might be formed. That, of course, would bring in more money. That, too, was common before the Civil War. But a partnership had one great disadvantage for businessmen. If their firm were successful and there were profits to divide, well and good. But if it were unsuccessful and owed a lot of money, then the partners were in a scrape. According to the law, partners in a business were liable for all its debts, no matter what their share in the business. For example, Jones and Smith form a partnership. Jones invests $10,000, all the money he has. Smith has other interests and puts in only $5,000. Jones is to receive two thirds of the profits and Smith one third. But if there are no profits, if the business of Jones and Smith fails and owes a great deal of money, then what happens? Jones, who has put in every cent he had, can pay none of the debt. Smith, on the other hand, is a wealthy man, and although he has only a one-third share of the business, he must pay *all* the debts of the firm. Naturally, keen businessmen were afraid of partnerships of this sort.

There was a different kind of partnership, however, in which that danger could be avoided—the corporation. The corporation had several unique features which made it particularly suitable to the modern era—so suitable, indeed that it has been called "the mother of large-scale enterprise."

A corporation could raise great sums of money by taking in hun-

ECONOMIC POSITION
United States and the World, 1929

Copyright, 1932, by
National Industrial Conference Board, Inc.
New York City

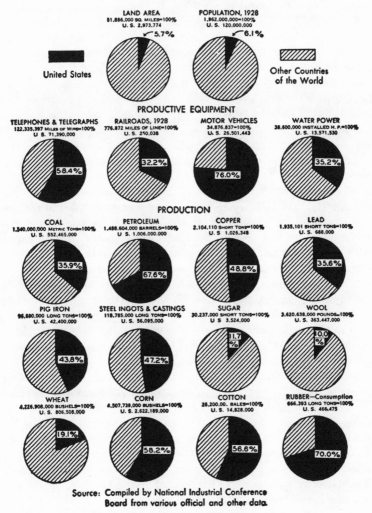

United States

**Other Countries
of the World**

LAND AREA
81,886,000 SQ. MILES=100%
U. S. 2,973,774
5.7%

POPULATION, 1928
1,962,000,000=100%
U. S. 120,000,000
6.1%

PRODUCTIVE EQUIPMENT

TELEPHONES & TELEGRAPHS
122,335,397 MILES OF WIRE=100%
U. S. 71,390,000
58.4%

RAILROADS, 1928
776,872 MILES OF LINE=100%
U. S. 250,038
32.2%

MOTOR VEHICLES
34,876,837=100%
U. S. 26,501,443
76.0%

WATER POWER
38,600,000 INSTALLED H. P.=100%
U. S. 13,571,530
35.2%

PRODUCTION

COAL
1,840,000,000 METRIC TONS=100%
U. S. 552,465,000
35.9%

PETROLEUM
1,488,604,000 BARRELS=100%
U. S. 1,006,000,000
67.6%

COPPER
2,104,110 SHORT TONS=100%
U. S. 1,026,348
48.8%

LEAD
1,935,101 SHORT TONS=100%
U. S. 688,000
35.6%

PIG IRON
96,680,000 LONG TONS=100%
U. S. 42,400,000
43.8%

STEEL INGOTS & CASTINGS
118,785,000 LONG TONS=100%
U. S. 56,095,000
47.2%

SUGAR
30,237,000 SHORT TONS=100%
U S 3,524,000
11.7%

WOOL
3,620,638,000 POUNDS=100%
U. S. 363,447,000
10.0%

WHEAT
4,226,908,000 BUSHELS=100%
U. S. 806,508,000
19.1%

CORN
4,507,739,000 BUSHELS=100%
U. S. 2,622,189,000
58.2%

COTTON
26,200,00 BALES=100%
U. S. 14,828,000
56.6%

RUBBER—Consumption
666,393 LONG TONS=100%
U. S. 466,475
70.0%

Source: Compiled by National Industrial Conference
Board from various official and other data.

dreds of partners. For example, a corporation might issue a thousand shares of stock each worth $100. You might buy two shares, your friend ten shares, Jones one hundred shares, Smith fifty shares, a bank two hundred shares, an insurance company four hundred shares and so on. When all the shares were sold, the corporation would have a thousand times $100 or $100,000.

It was limited liability which made the corporation attractive to the investor. That meant that the partners in the corporation were liable only for the amount of money they put into the business and no more. If Smith put $5,000 in the corporation and the firm failed, all that he lost was $5,000. Even if he were a millionaire he did not have to pay the firm's debts. From the businessman's point of view, this limited liability was a great advantage over the ordinary partnership.

Another advantage was the speed with which ownership in a corporation could be transferred to another person. In the old-style partnership, if a partner wanted to withdraw, it would take him some time to pull out of the business. Not so with the corporation, the new-style partnership. There a partner could get out of the business in a moment—simply by offering his stock for sale on the stock exchange. The fact that businessmen knew that it was so easy to withdraw from a business, meant that they would be more willing to go into it. So they invested their money in corporations.

The corporate form made it possible for the smart investor to lessen his risk by investing not in one or two partnerships but in many. Unlike the farmer who specialized in one crop thus putting all his eggs in one basket, the man with money bought shares in a number of corporations. If one or two went under, he was safe—the rest of his fortune was invested elsewhere.

Still another advantage of the corporation was its perpetual life. Suppose there are twenty of us in a room. We form a corporation. There will then be, in the eyes of the law, twenty-one persons in the room. The corporation, this artificial person created by law, is a being separate from the members who compose it; therefore it lives on after they have died. Not so with the ordinary partnership, in which the death of a partner means that the business must be either liquidated or reorganized. The fact that the corporation had perpetual life was another attraction to the investor.

It was these and other advantages which made the corporation the great capital-raising device it became after the Civil War.

Who managed the affairs of a corporation? Obviously it would be impossible for thousands of people together to manage its business, so the task of running the enterprise was delegated to a board of directors.

With lots of money behind them a hard-working, shrewd board of directors might transform a pygmy corporation into a giant corporation. After the 1880's the United States witnessed the growth of many corporations which grew and grew until in 1932 they were each worth more than $1,000,000,000. It was rightly called the Age of Big Business.

By what means did some of these corporations grow?

Up to the 1880's smart businessmen competed with one another. After the 1880's smart businessmen combined with one another.

They realized that the road to large profits lay in getting control of every product needed in their business. Andrew Carnegie went into the business of making crude steel. In order to make steel—iron, coal, coke, and limestone were needed. In order to transport steel, railroads and boats were needed. The steelmakers of the past would have bought their iron from one man, their coal from another, their coke from a third, and their limestone from a fourth. Each of these men would have tacked on his profit to the cost of what he sold. Mr. Carnegie realized this. He decided to cut out profits one, two, three, and four. How? Instead of buying from four different men and paying each a profit, he decided to buy from only one man and he himself would be that man. So Mr. Carnegie bought his own iron mines, his own coal mines, his own coking plants, and his own limestone properties.

But the iron mines were in Minnesota on the edge of Lake Superior, and the steel mill was in Pittsburgh. Mr. Carnegie's iron had to be carried by a lake steamer to a harbor on Lake Erie, then sent by rail to his steel mill. Mr. Carnegie knew that the owners of the steamer and the owners of the railroad were making a profit in carrying his iron. So he bought the lake steamer and the railroad and no longer paid that profit.

Some of these mineowners and coke-makers and railroad men didn't want to sell, but they did want to join Mr. Carnegie's company. They did that. There was room under Mr. Carnegie's roof for every part of the steelmaking business. He added one company after another. Then, because he owned every process from mine to rolling mill, because he paid no profits to any other company, he was able to say with pride, "Two pounds of ironstone mined upon Lake Superior and transported nine hundred miles to Pittsburgh; one pound and one-half of coal, mined and manufactured into coke, and transported to Pittsburgh; one-half pound of lime, mined and transported to Pittsburgh; a small amount of manganese ore mined in Virginia and brought to Pittsburgh—and these four pounds of materials manufactured into one pound of steel, for which the consumer pays one cent."

He had a right to be proud. It was a glorious achievement. Remember that it was possible only because the Carnegie Steel Company owned every part of the steel business from start to finish. What happened to those steel companies, not organized like Carnegie Steel, which still operated on the old basis of profits to Mr. one, two, three, and four? Of course, they could not sell as cheaply as did Mr. Carnegie, so he captured more and more of their business. Before long the Carnegie Steel Company was doing most of the crude steel business in the United States.

In 1901 Carnegie's company, makers of crude steel, combined with the largest companies making finished steel products. They formed the United States Steel Corporation, the first billion-dollar company in the United States. It had grown so great by 1929 that its sales for that year alone amounted to nearly one and a half billion. Part of its huge properties included one hundred blast furnaces, one hundred and twenty-five steamers, one thousand and four hundred locomotives, three hundred thousand acres of steam and gas coal lands, and from one half to three quarters of all the iron ore deposits in the United States.

Other companies, also, grew like little acorns into giant oaks. In the 1870's, if you were in the oil-refining business, you would have found yourself being slowly but surely pushed to the wall by a hard-hitting competitor. John D. Rockefeller's Standard Oil Company had set for itself the goal of absolute control of the oil industry. It was going to win the fight by fair means or foul. Its history is the story of one refining company after another giving up the fight and selling out—to the Standard Oil Company.

George O. Baslington, one of the partners in the firm of Hanna, Baslington & Company, swore in the court of common pleas, Cuyahoga County, Ohio, that the following story was true: "In the spring of 1869 they [Hanna, Baslington & Company] began the construction of refining works on the west side of the Cleveland and Columbus

Railroad track, and invested in the construction of the works about $67,000, which works were completed. . . . The 1st of June, 1869, and from that time up to about the 1st of July, 1870, the works had netted a profit of $40,000 over all expenses of running said works, being about 60 per cent on the capital invested per annum." Then he goes on to explain that in February, 1872, his firm received a message from the Standard Oil Company that it would like to buy out Hanna, Baslington & Company. Since they were doing an excellent business and making a very high profit, they refused to consider Standard's offer. But they investigated, and to their surprise found that Standard had already obtained control of most of the refineries in Cleveland; that "it had obtained such rates of transportation of crude and refined oil from the different railroads that it was impossible for them [other firms] to compete with it. . . . Mr. Rockefeller . . . said that the Standard Oil Company had such control of the refining business already in the City of Cleveland . . . that there was no use for them to attempt to do business in competition with the Standard Oil Company." Mr. Baslington looked into the matter and found it was true; the railroads would charge his firm more for transportation than they charged Standard Oil. He had his choice of selling out or losing everything. Not only did he have to sell, but he had to take what Standard offered him—$45,000 for a plant that had cost him $67,000 and on which the profit alone for one year was $40,000!

There were others like Baslington. In 1880, George Rice, an independent refiner at Marietta, Ohio, owned one tankcar which brought him crude oil from Macksburg, Ohio. The railroad charged him $.175 a barrel for allowing him the use of its tracks. Suddenly, without any warming, the railroad doubled the freight charge, making it $.35 per barrel. At the same time the railroad charged Standard Oil only $.10 a barrel for the same service. Not was that all. *The railroad paid over to the Standard Oil Company $.25 out of every $.35 which Rice paid for freight.* Even if Rice did *all* the business and Standard did none, it would have made $.25 per barrel on *his* oil. Racketeering is not new, is it?

There is much more to the story of Standard Oil—how independent dealers found it impossible to obtain oil; how they could hire no cars from the railroad in which to ship it; how they could not use the tracks even when they supplied their own cars; how spies reported every move of any competitor of Standard Oil; how prices were cut until the independent had to sell out or quit; how people were slandered and officials bribed; how newspapers unfriendly to Standard Oil were bought by Rockefeller agents and converted into staunch defenders; how courts tried to break up the corporation without real success.

By 1904 the Standard Oil Company controlled over 86 per cent of the refined illuminating oil of the country.

What was happening to steel and oil also happened to sugar, coal, lead, and other products. By 1890, gigantic corporations were in control of each great industry. They have continued to grow. General Motors, Chrysler, and Ford together produce nine out of every ten cars made in the United States. Goodyear, Firestone, U. S. Rubber, and Goodrich account for nearly 93 per cent of the total net sales of the rubber industry. General Electric and Westinghouse, in 1942, had a virtual monopoly over the production and distribution of incandescent lamps. With Hygrade Sylvania, these companies produce and sell virtually all the fluorescent lamps in the country today. Libby-Owens-Ford and the Pittsburgh Plate Glass Co. together make 95 per cent of all the plate glass in the country. The United States Shoe Machinery Co. controls more than 95 per cent of the entire shoe-machinery business in the United States.

To many Americans the increase in the size of corporations spelled an increase in power which was very alarming. One writer thought that,

The larger the corporation, the greater is its power, either for good or for evil, and that makes it especially important that its power be under control.

If I may use a homely illustration, I will take the common house cat, whose diminutive size makes her a safe inmate of our household in spite of her playful disposition and her liking for animal food. If, without the slightest change of character or disposition, she were suddenly enlarged to the dimensions of a tiger, we should at least want her to be muzzled and to have her claws trimmed, whereas if she were to assume the dimensions of a mastodon, I doubt if any of us would want to live in the same house with her. And it would be useless to argue that her nature had not changed, that she was just as amiable as ever, and no more carnivorous than she always had been. Nor would it convince us to be told that her productivity had increased and that she could now catch more mice in a minute than she formerly could in a week. We should be afraid lest, in a playful mood, she might set a paw upon us, to the detriment of our epidermis, or that in her large-scale mouse-catching she might not always discriminate between us and mice.

The people of the United States in the 1880's were aroused to action against the gigantic corporations which, as trusts and monopolies, were getting a stranglehold on American economic life. Farmers, small businessmen, and consumers in general wanted to do something about industrialists' agreements to curtail production, fix prices, divide up the market. They sighed for the good old days of free enterprise and free competition. They read about the enormous profits that were flowing into the pockets of the monopolists and they knew that the prices they were paying for the manufactured goods which they bought were outrageously high. As the trend toward trustification in manufacturing industry became more and more apparent, the hostility to the trusts became more and more bitter. Appeals for relief became demands which Congress heeded. On July 2, 1890, the Sherman Antitrust Act, "An Act to protect trade and commerce against unlawful restraints and monopolies," became a law.

The first two sections contain the meat:

Sec. 1. Every contract, combination in the form of trust or otherwise, or conspiracy, in restraint of trade or commerce among the several States, or with foreign nations, is hereby declared to be illegal. . . .

Sec. 2. Every person who shall monopolize, or attempt to monopolize, or combine or conspire with any other person or persons, to monopolize any part of the trade or commerce among the several States, or with foreign nations, shall be deemed guilty of a misdemeanor. . . .

The law hadn't been on the statute books more than a few years before it became obvious that it was not going to do the job the people wanted done. Perhaps it was because big combinations in industry were inevitable in the American economy of that period and could not be stopped by law; perhaps it was because the language of the Act was too vague, containing no definition of trust, or monopoly, or restraint; or perhaps it was because the enforcement of the law rested finally, with the courts whose judges weren't as quick to recognize trusts as were the people immediately affected by them. In any case, the Sherman Antitrust Act did not stop the formation of big combinations. In fact, some of the biggest, including most of the great corporations of today, were established shortly after it was enacted, in the period from 1897 to 1904.

Holding companies and monopolies were springing up everywhere. Were they "combinations in restraint of trade?" Was the Antitrust Act being violated? As the years rolled by the law enforcement agents of the government didn't show much interest in trying to find the answers to these questions. They did not bring many prosecutions. And often when government lawyers finally did get around to thinking they had caught an offender, they found that the Supreme Court didn't agree with them. What looked like a clear case of restraint of trade, or monopoly, to most people, often looked like something else to the highest judges of the country.

The first case to come before the Supreme Court after the passage of the Act is a good example. It was the case of the United States vs. E. C. Knight Company, decided on January 21, 1895. When the American Sugar Refining Company, which produced 65 per cent of the sugar refined in the United States, bought control of the Knight Company and three other Pennsylvania firms, the government brought suit to cancel the contract of purchase on the ground that it was a violation of the Act. Considering the fact that the purchase of the four additional refineries gave the trust control of 98 per cent of production, it did seem as though the law had been violated. This appeared to be exactly the kind of amalgamation that the people of the country had been clamoring against. If a company that controlled 98 per cent of the refining of sugar wasn't in a position to "restrain trade or commerce," it would be difficult to find one that was. That's what the people thought, that's what the government lawyers thought—but the Supreme Court thought otherwise. It permitted the contracts to stand.

That was the first Supreme Court case. There were others like it. All kinds of trusts and monopolies were found, for one reason or another, to be perfectly legal. But if it was difficult for the judges to find many violators of the Act among the trusts and holding companies in industry, it was easy for the judges to find combinations in restraint of trade in another field—the field of labor.

Congress passed the Sherman Act as a people's weapon against trusts; the courts often interpreted the Sherman Act as an employers' weapon against trade-unions.

CHAPTER XIII

The Have-nots V. The Haves

★───★

Through their trade-unions the men who did the actual work of operating the railroads, mining the coal and iron, building the great cities, and running the machines in the factories—in short, the working class—came to grips with the capitalists.

Nor were they merely battles of words alone. Quite frequently dynamite, bombs, and machine-guns were used. There were murders on both sides. It was a fierce struggle.

Woodrow Wilson hit upon one of the reasons. "Did you never think of it,—men are cheap and machinery is dear; many a superintendent is dismissed for over-driving a delicate machine who wouldn't be dismissed for over-driving an over-taxed man. You can discard your man and replace him; there are others ready to come into his place; but you can't, without great cost, discard your machine and put a new one in its place. . . . It is time that property, as compared with humanity, should take second place, not first place."

Property was first, human life second—that was one reason for the conflict.

Capitalists were interested in making money—the more the better. The smart businessman was the one who paid as little as possible for what he bought, and received as much as possible for what he sold. The first step on the road to high profits was to reduce expenses.

One of the expenses of production was wages to labor. It was therefore to the interest of the employer to pay as low wages as possible. It was likewise to his interest to get as much work out of his laborers as he could. Accordingly, he tried to make the working day as long as possible.

The Industrial Revolution had put the worker at the mercy of the capitalist. The employer owned the factory and the expensive machinery in it. The worker could no longer produce his own food and do his own work. He no longer owned the tools of production. He had to become a wage earner in another man's factory. If that factory was an unhealthful, ill-lighted, poorly ventilated place with no safe-guards on its dangerous machinery, he had to work there, neverthe-less. If the hours were very long, and the wages so low that he could not support himself and his family, he had to work there just the same. There was no way out—work or starve.

That the laborer was not a *thing* like coal or cotton, but a person —a human being like himself—made no difference to the profit seeker. Labor, machinery, raw materials, they were all alike to him—the less they cost him the better. He was interested in profits.

Workers stood this as long as they could. Then they tried to fight back. What could they do?

Alone they could do nothing. Organized together as one group, they could exert pressure on their employers. They banded together and formed unions.

What kind of unions did they form? Were they organized on the basis of craft or industry? Were they local, state, or national? Were they concerned with the here and now or with the utopias of to-morrow? Were they content with the capitalist system, or did they fight to overthrow it? There is no short answer to these questions. Unions arise out of the necessities of the situation and take the form best suited to that situation. They never develop as something separate from the way in which people live and earn their living. There may be a lag—there often is—but in the long run the kind of labor organization that emerges and grows is the one that is forced by the industrial setup. As changes come in the industrial develop-ment of a country, so changes come in the workers' organizations.

That is what happened in the United States. The Declaration of Independence which announced our separation from England was followed soon after by one declaration after another of workmen announcing their separation of interests from the employing class. So, in 1817, the New York printers announced, "This is a society of journeymen printers; and as the interests of the journeymen are separate and in some respects opposite to those of the employers, we deem it improper that they should have any voice or influence in our deliberations."

This was a break with what had prevailed before. In earlier years it had been quite proper that the employers should have a voice in the deliberations of the men who worked for them. It had been

proper because the gulf between the master craftsmen and his journeymen had not been very wide. Journeymen could become masters
fairly easily. The masters worked side by side with the journeymen,
believed the same things, and had the same ideas. Their interests
both social and economic were practically the same. So long as that
was true, the employer and the journeymen could belong to the
same society. Because in 1817 it was no longer true, the New York
printers said so and expelled a member who had become an employer.

In some respects this was similar to what had happened to the
guild system in western Europe centuries ago. It was the expansion
of the market which was the major factor in the breakdown of the
guild system; and it was the expansion of the market which brought
the change here.

To meet the needs of the expanding market in the early nineteenth
century, the merchant-capitalist made his entrance on the American
scene. He brought in large quantities of cheap manufactured goods
from England, stored them in warehouses which dotted the whole
country, and undersold the master craftsmen in the different local
communities. Gradually he took away from the master craftsmen
their marketing function, and before long he was in a position to
force their prices down. Faced with this competition, the master
craftsmen had to find ways and means of cutting their costs. They
tried to lower the wages of their journeymen; they hired young men
to do the skilled jobs before their term of apprenticeship was over;
they sought out and employed workers who would take less than
the old scale of wages. The workers resisted these attempts to lower
their standards. Shoemakers, carpenters, coopers, tailors, and printers
fought back through their own local craft societies. The interests of
employers and workers grew farther apart.

The earliest American unions, then, were not those of oppressed
factory workers: They were unions of highly skilled craftsmen who
were forced to combine in self-defense—to keep their wages up and
hours down, and to prevent the breakdown of the old regulated
conditions of work. Their tactics were the familiar ones of collective
bargaining, the strike, the closed shop, and the boycott. A series of
separate struggles by the separate craft unions made their next step
plain—and before long they took it.

In 1827 fifteen trade societies in Philadelphia joined together to
form the Mechanics' Union of Trade Associations. It was the first
city-wide union of unions in the world. One year later, the year that

Andrew Jackson, "the people's choice," became President, the first Workingmen's party in the world was launched in Philadelphia. It was followed by the formation of other workingmen's parties in almost every state, and the beginning of a labor press—over fifty labor papers were founded at this time. In their political platforms the workers demanded the restriction of child labor, direct election of public officials, abolition of imprisonment for debt, the universal ten-hour day, and free and equal public education (the labor movement was largely responsible for the free public school system in the United States).

The next forty years was a story of ups and downs; first, a period of reaction against political activity, and an increase in the number of trade-unions; more city centrals, further growth—then sudden collapse with the paralysis of industry in the panic of 1837; return to political activity and participation in humanitarian movements of every description—co-operative societies, land reform, utopian communities, etc.; then revival of business, further expansion of the market, further development of transportation and communication, and the formation of craft unions on a national scale; followed the crisis of 1857—a check to industrial enterprise and a general destruction of trade-unions; then the Civil War—expansion of business and revival of old and formation of new unions; establishment again of a labor press—over one hundred daily, weekly, and monthly journals published; after the war, attempts to unite the national unions into a lasting single federation—at first failure, then finally, success.

The growth of Big Business after the Civil War meant that trade-unionism would take tremendous strides. This had to happen because industrial expansion brought with it further concentration of workers into cities, further improvements in transportation and communication so essential to a nationwide organization, and the conditions which made a worker's movement so necessary. Working-class organization grew with capitalist development, which produced both the class and the class sentiment, as well as the physical means of co-operation and communication. At the same time, the difficulties were great; facing the working class in its struggle for unionization was a capitalist class which increased its ruthlessness as it increased its wealth. Capital in the United States after the Civil War did not stand by idly while workers organized; it was fierce in its opposition.

Labor union leaders were not agreed among themselves on the

best way of fighting capital. The Knights of Labor, the American Federation of Labor, and the Industrial Workers of the World went at the problem from different angles. The approach of the first was welfare or "uplift" unionism; of the second, business unionism; and of the third, revolutionary unionism.

The Noble Order of the Knights of Labor was a secret society founded in Philadelphia in 1869, by a small group of clothing cutters. Their leader was Uriah S. Stephens, a tailor, who had been trained for the ministry. Since it was a secret society it was able to grow in a period when open unions were going to pieces because of the depression (there was a "panic" in 1873), or because of the bitter attacks of the employers. Glass workers, iron workers, printers, shoemakers, and other craftsmen who found themselves without a union formed new locals within the Knights of Labor.

But not only skilled workers became members of the Knights— the organization was open to all workers, white and black, men and women, unskilled as well as skilled. Farmers, and even some employers, were eligible for membership. Any person over eighteen "working for wages or who at any time worked for wages" could join. The Knights of Labor was an all-inclusive labor organization to which even members of the middle class could belong. Not, however, all middle-class people—there were some interesting exceptions: "No person who either sells or makes a living, or any part of it, by the sale of intoxicating drink, either as manufacturer, dealer, or agent, or through any member of the family, can be admitted to membership in this order, and no lawyer, banker, professional gambler, or stockbroker can be admitted."

Because the Knights was "one big union" accepting the unskilled as well as the skilled, it is frequently thought of as an industrial union. That is not true. Though it was not organized on craft lines, neither was it organized on the basis of industry. Its local assemblies were of two kinds, trade and mixed. The members of the first were usually those engaged in a single craft; the members of the second were everybody, regardless of occupation. It was not set up to help any single group within labor, but to bring about the union of all labor.

To what end? The Noble Order of the Knights of Labor had the kind of program which one would expect from an organization with such a name. Its leaders announced as their purpose the idealistic aim of elevating the whole laboring class through organization, education, and co-operation. The set of instructions given every new member contained the following:

> Labor is noble and holy. To defend it from degradation; to divest it of the evils to body, mind, and estate which ignorance and greed have imposed; to rescue the toiler from the grip of the selfish—is a work worthy of the noblest and best of our race. . . . We mean no conflict with legitimate enterprise, no antagonism to necessary capital; but men, in their haste and greed, blinded by self-interests, overlook the interests of others and sometimes violate the rights of those they deem helpless. We mean to uphold the dignity of labor, to affirm the nobility of all who earn their bread by the sweat of their brows. . . . We shall, with all our strength, support laws made to harmonize the interests of labor and capital, and also those laws which tend to lighten the exhaustiveness of toil. . . .

Thus early were the new members given their dose of sentimental uplift which was characteristic of the speeches and writings of the leaders of the Knights. Here was no declaration of war on capital, no ringing challenge to the existing order. Nor was there even a recognition of the opposing interests of labor and capital. The creed of the Knights was not employers vs. workers, but employers *and* workers together advancing the cause of humanity. There was "no conflict with legitimate enterprise." Only the selfish—in other writings they are identified as the "money power"—were to be curbed. The way to uphold the dignity of labor was for it to employ itself through "co-operation, of the order, by the order, and for the order" —the Knights believed in and organized producers' co-operatives. The milestones on their path to social reform were to be co-operation, education, and organization.

Their co-operative ventures—some two hundred mines, iron foundries, cooperage works, nail mills, shoe factories, etc.—failed; but they did educate the American workers—largely through their agitation for political reforms such as the income tax, the abolition of child labor, workmen's compensation, labor exchanges for the unemployed, payment of wages by the week and in lawful money, social insurance, the eight-hour day, public ownership of railroads and utilities; and they did succeed, for a time, in organizing the most truly representative labor organization that had yet appeared in America. In 1879, Terence V. Powderly succeeded Stephens as Grand Master Workman of the Order. In 1881, the Knights gave up secrecy. In 1886, the organization had grown from the initial membership of eleven tailors in Assembly No. 1 in Philadelphia, to over seven hundred thousand members in most of the United States.

The chief cause of that growth, however, could not be traced to the leaders' idealistic sentimental program of social uplift. It was to be found, rather, in the fact that the rank and file was militant—it forced strikes and boycotts in spite of the leadership. While Powderly dreamed dreams and talked endlessly of the brotherhood of man, the rank and file translated the slogan of the order, "an injury to one is the concern of all," into concrete action. While Powderly believed that "strikes are deplorable in their effect and contrary to the best interests of the order," and said openly, "I shudder at the thought of a strike and I have good reason," the rank and file did not shudder at strikes, but became more and more aggressive. Had the leadership been less bewildered, had it devoted less time to preaching the principles of the good society and more to perfecting the principles of militant union organization, then its grand conception of one big union embracing all wage earners, skilled and unskilled, of every creed, nationality, race, sex, and craft, might have had even greater success than it did have. As it was, where the Knights of Labor succeeded, it did so largely in spite of its constitution, program, and leadership; where it failed, it did so largely because of them.

The year 1886 was an eventful one in American labor history. In that year the Noble Order of the Knights of Labor reached the height of its power—and began its decline. In that year, out of the Federation of Trades and Labor Unions of the United States and Canada, organized in 1881, the American Federation of Labor was founded.

The Noble Order of the Knights had lost out to an organization entirely opposite in aim, program, membership, and method of struggle. The business unionism of the American Federation of Labor was totally unlike the uplift unionism of the Knights. Where the K. of L. had been idealistic—dreaming of a utopia to come, the A.F. of L. was practical—thinking of better conditions now; where the K. of L. had been unselfish—concerning itself with the interest of all the working class, unskilled as well as skilled, the A.F. of L. was selfish—concerning itself only with the interest of the skilled workers who were in the organization; where the K. of L. had been unbusinesslike—run by the humanitarian Stephens and the windbag Powderly, the A.F. of L. was businesslike—run by the shrewd, matter-of-fact Samuel Gompers.

FACTORY WORKERS

Three years before the A.F. of L. was finally launched, Adolph Strasser, president of the Cigar Makers' Union and founder, with Gompers and P. J. McGuire, of the A.F. of L., was on the stand before the Senate Committee upon Relations between Capital and Labor. His testimony on the aim of his organization was a forerunner of the program of the A.F. of L. "We have no ultimate ends. We are going on from day to day. We are fighting for immediate objects—objects that can be realized in a few years."

The immediate objects for which the A.F. of L. fought were higher wages, shorter hours, better conditions. It was that simple. Though Gompers had flirted with socialism in the past, he was ever anxious to keep reform out of the A.F. of L. picture. The only uplift that was to come to the workers through the A.F. of L. was the uplift that came with higher wages, shorter hours, and better conditions.

The A.F. of L. was essentially a craft organization, a loose federation of national and international (so called because some of them had locals in Canada) craft unions. It was a union of many separate unions, each of them composed of skilled workers and all of them fighting to obtain higher wages, shorter hours, and better conditions. The unskilled workers who had flocked by the thousands to the banner of the Knights of Labor could not obtain admittance into the A.F. of L. The attitude of the leaders of the A.F. of L. toward the unskilled who were left out in the cold was best expressed by one of them who said, as recently as 1934, "We do not want to charter the riffraff or good-for-nothings, or those for whom we cannot make wages or conditions, unless we are compelled to do so by other organizations offering to charter them under any condition."

In membership and aim, then, the A.F. of L. differed from the Knights of Labor. There was an important difference, too, in the structure of the two organizations. "To understand completely the structure and function of the Knights of Labor, it is necessary to read but one constitution. To understand fully the functions and structure of the American Federation of Labor, over a hundred constitutions must be read. The Knights of Labor is a sovereignty, the American Federation of Labor is a federation of sovereignties." Where power in the Knights was centralized in the permanent officers of the General Assembly, in the A.F. of L. power was centralized in the leaders of the various national unions that made up the federation.

While the A.F. of L. unions believed in bargaining with employers to obtain higher wages, shorter hours, and better conditions, while they bent all their efforts to win collective bargaining agreements peaceably, they did not hesitate to fight when it was necessary. But they made certain, whenever possible, that they were entering the fray well armed. Their dues were high enough to enable them to build up a strong fighting fund to be used when they had to resort to strikes or boycotts. The A.F. of L. was aware of the realities of the capitalist system—they knew that there was a struggle going on between capitalists and laborers. But they kept their eyes on immediate goals. They did not plan to overthrow the system. They were quite content to continue in a master-and-servant relationship with capital, but they wanted a bigger share for themselves as servants. Their motto was " a fair day's wage for a fair day's work."

In the "pure and simple trade unionism" philosophy of Samuel Gompers there was no room for the creation by the A.F. of L. of a political party which would represent labor. Despite repeated efforts by some of the members of the A.F. of L. to have the organization form a labor party, Gompers' policy of working within the existing political parties won out. In politics the A.F. of L. has played the game of "rewarding its friends, and punishing its enemies."

By 1900 what was the position of the A.F. of L.? From one point of view it had not done well at all. Despite its practical program of fighting for immediate gains which were the first concern of most American workers, it had grown slowly. The powerful Railway Brotherhoods had not affiliated with it; the unskilled workers had not been invited into its ranks, so they were unorganized; and many, even of the skilled workers whom it had sought out, had not joined up.

From another point of view it had done remarkably well. True, the largest percentage of skilled workers remained outside its ranks, but, nevertheless, its five hundred and fifty thousand members represented more than three times the one hundred and fifty thousand it had begun with in 1886. That was less than the total reached by the Knights of Labor at the height of its power, but it was a different kind of membership—more lasting, more powerful, better disciplined. Its decentralized organization of independent national member unions, following the tactics of business unionism, had stood the test; in a period of fierce opposition by a ruthless employer class, it had managed to hold its own. It had managed to do what no other nonsecret national labor organization had been able to do before in American history—successfully weather the storm of a depression (that of 1893). For its defenders, that it had survived at all was proof of the correctness of its policies.

The Industrial Workers of the World, organized in 1905 with "Big Bill" Haywood as their leader, stood for revolutionary union- ism. They did not believe in the A.F. of L. method of fighting capital. The preamble to their constitution declared that:

The working class and the employing class have nothing in common. There can be no peace so long as hunger and want are found among millions of the working-people, and the few, who make up the employing class, have all the good things of life. Between these two classes a struggle must go on until the workers of the world organize as a class, take possession of the earth and the machinery of production and abolish the wage sy- tem. . . . The trade unions foster a state of affairs which allows one set of workers to be pitted against another set of workers in the same industry, thereby helping to defeat one another in wage wars. Moreover, the trade unions aid the employing class to mislead the workers into the belief that the working class have interests in common with their employers.

Instead of the conservative motto, "a fair day's pay for a fair day's work," we must inscribe on our banner the revolutionary watchword "aboli- tion of the wage system."

It is the historic mission of the working class to do away with capitalism.

The leaders of the I.W.W., unlike those of the A.F. of L., were opposed to making agreements with capitalists. They pointed to the fact that in several A.F. of L. strikes, one group of workmen in an industry—say, the cooks—would be out on strike, while the waiters in the same industry had to continue working because of an agree- ment with the employer. The I.W.W. leaders held that when one set of workers went out on strike, all the workers in that industry should support them by striking also. They were against contracts with capital because they wanted to get rid of capital entirely. They were not interested in immediate gains, but in the final and com- plete victory of labor over capital. They stood for one big union of all the workers, instead of division into craft unions. They made the dues to their organization very low so that all workers, the un- skilled as well as the skilled, could join. They hated the A.F. of L. only a little less than they hated capital. The main points in their program are contained in their song:

PAINT 'ER RED

By Ralph Chaplin

(*Tune:* "Marching through Georgia")

Come with us, you working-men, and join the rebel band;
Come, you discontented ones, and give a helping hand,
We march against the parasite to drive him from the land
    With One Big Industrial Union!

Chorus:

Hurrah: Hurrah! we're going to paint 'er red!
Hurrah! Hurrah! the way is clear ahead—
We're gaining shop democracy and liberty and bread
    With One Big Industrial Union!
We hate their rotten system more than any mortals do.
Our aim is not to patch it up, but build it all anew,
And what we'll have for government, when finally we're through
    Is One Big Industrial Union!

The influence of the I.W.W. was much greater than the total
of its membership at the peak would lead one to believe. At no time,
probably, did it ever have more than seventy-five thousand members,
but in the course of its militant activities it reached hundreds of
thousands of other workers. The unorganized and unskilled, the
many migratory workers who largely made up its rank and file, were
infected with the revolutionary ardor of the leaders. Strikes were
not worrisome to the I.W.W.—on the contrary, it welcomed them.
Its leaders were fearless and magnetic and showed marked ability
in conducting many bitter struggles.

In the course of those struggles oppressed workers received from
them the help which they sorely needed. But the revolutionary program of the I.W.W. did not, in the first quarter of the twentieth century, attract a permanent following. The government cracked down
on the "wobblies" during World War I, and in 1918 over one hundred of their leaders were clapped into jail for conspiracy. By 1924
they were practically out of existence.

Unionists, whether members of the Knights of Labor, the A.F. of
L., or the I.W.W., found the going hard. The employing class saw
in labor unions a challenge to its power. It was, accordingly, opposed
to unions, and it used every means, fair or foul, to destroy them.
Some of the most bitter struggles in American history—struggles in
which thousands of dollars worth of property was destroyed and
scores of lives were lost—were the result, in the last analysis, of the
refusal by the employers to recognize labor unions and bargain collectively with them. That this truth is not more widely accepted is

due to the simple fact that the employers have had control of the opinion-making forces—the press, the schools, the church, etc. The newspapers have printed, the teachers have taught, and the clergymen have preached, in the main, the capitalist side of the struggle.

In addition, in their direct dealings with organized workers, many employers made effective use of their economic power. They formed unions of their own—employers' associations—to present a united front in opposition to unions of workers; they imposed the "ironclad oath" ("yellow-dog" contract), which exacted a promise from the worker that he would not join a union—under penalty of losing his job; they openly discriminated against and discharged known unionists; they made extensive use of the black list against "troublemakers"—*i.e.*, union men—they employed spies to report on the organizing efforts of their employees and to smash the unions; they stuck badges on men, thus converting them into "company police," then gave them clubs and guns to be used on strikers. (It was this ability to obtain workers to fight against their fellow workers that led Jay Gould, a famous capitalist, to boast, "I can hire one-half of the working class to kill the other half.") These employer methods were all very effective—unions had a difficult time.

It was made more difficult for unions when employers discovered that what they could not do for themselves by their own direct economic pressure, they could often get the courts to do for them. The courts could do the most surprising things—so surprising as to excite the envy of a magician.

Congress, in 1890, had put into the legislative hat an antitrust act. Lo, and behold! The courts pulled out an antilabor act! Look, for example, at the government batting average in the courts for the years 1892–1896:

Cases Brought under the Sherman Antitrust Act:

	Total	Won	Lost	Percentage
Against trusts	5	1	4	.200
Against labor	5	4	1	.800

In the list of Sherman Act antilabor cases of this period was the Pullman strike, one of the most famous of labor disputes. Mr. Pullman had built the town of Pullman, in Illinois, for Pullman workers.

Pullman was a very appropriate name for it. The factories belonged to the Pullman Company, the stores belonged to the Pullman Company, the workmen's homes belonged to the Pullman Company, the school belonged to the Pullman Company, the church belonged to the Pullman Company, and the theater belonged to the Pullman Company.

In the spring of 1894 the management of the Pullman Company discharged about one third of its workers and announced a 25 to 40 per cent cut in wages for the others. Did Mr. Pullman also reduce the rent in his houses? Did he lower the prices in his stores? He did not.

In May, 1894, the Pullman workers went out on strike.

Immediately the company shut down its plant and the workers' credit at the stores was stopped. By June, many of the workers' families were starving.

The American Railway Union, organized by Eugene V. Debs, a railway fireman, tried to act as peacemaker, but the Pullman Company management would not see its leaders.

The Railway Union then ordered its members to boycott all Pullman cars attached to the trains on which they worked. In a few days, railway men on roads running west from Chicago refused to handle Pullman cars. The railroad managers refused to allow these cars to be detached and discharged the boycotters.

Then the American Railway Union called all its men out on strike and the trains were stopped. Railway labor all over the country had rallied behind Debs, its standard-bearer. The strike was well organized, and it grew more effective day by day. Trains in every part of the country stood still.

The Pullman Company was not alone in its war on the American Railway Union. The General Managers' Association, whose membership consisted of twenty-four railroad companies, joined forces with the Pullman Company against the union. Debs, in his appeal to the railroad workers to support the boycott of Pullman cars, told them what had happened: " . . . Then the railway corporations, through the General Managers' Association, came to the rescue, and in a series of whereases declared to the world that they would go into partnership with Pullman, so to speak, and stand by him in his devilish work of starving his employees to death. The American Railway Union accepted the gauge of war, and thus the contest is now on between the railway corporation united solidly upon the one hand and the labor forces upon the other. . . ."

So united were the labor forces in the struggle, so effective was their strike against the General Managers' Association, one of the most powerful combinations of capital in the United States, that it looked for a time as though they might win. If they had had to fight the General Managers' Association by itself they might have succeeded. But the combination of the General Managers' Association and the courts and Federal troops was too much for them.

The capitalists appealed to President Cleveland for troops. On July 4, 1894, two thousand United States soldiers moved into Chicago. John Altgeld, then Governor of Illinois, immediately sent a letter of protest to the President, saying that the state of Illinois could handle its own affairs. Cleveland replied that the soldiers were there to protect and move the United States mails. Following the arrival of the troops, trouble started. What had been a comparatively peaceful strike situation became a warring one. Bricks were thrown, trains were overturned, scabs were dragged from their posts and beaten, and railroad property was burned. Though the union officials had begged their men not to break loose—a request which the strikers had heeded up to this time—there was little doubt that union men were responsible for some of the destruction. On the other hand, the strikers claimed that much of the violence was caused by *agents provocateurs*, men hired by the railroad officials who wanted in this way to give the strikers a black eye with the public. There was little doubt that this was true as well. At any rate, the wrecking and burning continued and twelve people were killed.

The man most responsible for the sending of the troops was Mr. Edwin Walker. He was one of the lawyers for the General Managers' Association, and the attorney general of the United States had very obligingly appointed him special counsel for the government as well. Mr. Walker found that he could serve both his clients at the same time quite easily.

He had the troops sent in. And he appeared before the courts and was able to convince the judges that the railroad strike was an unlawful conspiracy *in violation of the Sherman Act*. Then the judges, at his request, issued an injunction, or order, prohibiting the officials of the union from interfering in any way with trains engaged in interstate commerce; or from compelling, or even persuading, the workers on the railways not to do their jobs. It was a "blanket" injunction which meant it covered everybody—not only Debs and the other union officers, but "all other persons whomsoever"; and it forbade practically every activity which the strikers had to engage in to keep the strike effective—even peaceful picketing was now a crime. And all this was based on the law passed to curb the trusts!

Debs and the other leaders carried on in defiance of the injunction. In the middle of July they were arrested for contempt of court. The backbone of the strike was broken. The railway companies, triumphant, refused to take back some of the strikers. Others they hired again on their own terms.

With the help of the government and the courts the capitalists had won a great victory.

They had won more than that. The Pullman strike showed them the effectiveness of a weapon which they had used before but had never really sharpened to a cutting edge. Now they polished it up in great style. The injunction was swift and deadly. From 1895 on the capitalists used it with telling effect. It was a wonderfully efficient strikebreaker.

Employers had only to march into federal or state courts and persuade the judges that unless they restrained the strikers horrible things were about to happen. Irreparable damage was going to be done to their property. Not to their tangible property alone—stuff you could lay your hands on, like the factory, machinery, material, etc.; but to their intangible property as well—stuff you couldn't lay your hands on, like the right to do business, the good will of the public toward the employer and his product, the right to make a profit. The judges were very easily persuaded. There was a deluge of injunctions. They forbade acts which were crimes (which could have been handled by the criminal courts) and acts which were not crimes (which the strikers had a constitutional right to do). Judges have issued injunctions which have prohibited strikers from parading, picketing, assembling near the place where the strike was going on, or distributing pamphlets; strikers have even been prohibited from attending certain churches, or praying and singing on the public highways!

Small wonder that labor spent years in agitating for a law to limit the use of the injunction in labor disputes. In 1932, thirty-eight years after the Pullman strike, such a law was passed—the Norris-La Guardia Act. It read as though it might do the trick, but realist friends of labor were not certain—they remembered that it still remained for the courts to interpret the law. And so long as that was true, then it was wise not to be too optimistic.

They remembered that Sam Gompers had been too optimistic in 1914. In that year a new antitrust act, one supposedly designed to exempt labor unions from the provisions of the Sherman Act, was passed. The Clayton Antitrust Act was hailed by Gompers as labor's "Magna Charta upon which the working people will rear their constitution of industrial freedom." He based his hopes on Section 6, which said in part: "The labor of a human being is not a commodity or article of commerce . . . nor shall such [labor] organizations, or the members thereof, be held or construed to be illegal combinations or conspiracies in restraint of trade, under the anti-trust laws."

Mr. Gompers' enthusiasm was short lived. The Clayton Act, as construed by the courts, did not do what it was supposed to do. On the contrary. There were more suits brought against labor under the Sherman Act in the twenty-four years following the passage of the Clayton Act in 1914, than in the twenty-four years following the passage of the law in 1890!

It had become increasingly clear that laws designed to prevent the growth of trusts were, by court interpretation, being used to prevent the growth of organized labor. It often happened that when a combination of employers was on trial the Supreme Court applied the "rule of reason"—and the employers went free; but when a combination of workers was on trial, then the Supreme Court applied a rule of unreason—and the workers were penalized.

It was all very strange. That was what Justice Brandeis thought in his celebrated dissenting opinion in the Bedford Stone case:

The Sherman Law was held in United States v. United States Steel Corporation . . . to permit capitalists to combine in a single corporation 50 per cent. of the steel industry of the United States, dominating the trade through its vast resources. The Sherman Law was held in United States v. United Shoe Machinery Co. . . . to permit capitalists to combine in another corporation practically the whole shoe machinery industry of the country. . . . It would indeed be strange if Congress had by the same act willed to deny to members of a small craft of working men the right to co-operate in simply refraining from work when that course was the only means of self-protection against a combination of militant and powerful employers. I cannot believe that Congress did so."

But this was a dissenting opinion. The majority of the justices of the Supreme Court thought otherwise. In the long and bitter struggle of the haves v. the have-nots, the courts of the country were on the side of the haves.

From Rags to Riches

Question: How does a law to help Negroes become a law to help corporations?

Answer: When it is interpreted by the Supreme Court.

For fifty years the Supreme Court gave to corporations in the United States a special immunity—freedom from regulation—which corporations in no other great capitalist country enjoyed. It was fine for Big Business, not so good for the people of the country.

Freedom from regulation was given to corporations by the old magician's trick of pulling something else out of the hat. Watch closely.

Congress, after the Civil War, wanted to be certain that the freed Negroes were to be really free with all the privileges of citizenship. So it proposed three amendments to the Constitution which were ratified, in due course, by three fourths of the states. Every child's history of the United States summarizes those amendments in this fashion:

The Thirteenth amendment abolished slavery in the United States forever.

The Fourteenth amendment made the Negro a citizen of the United States, equal before the law to all other citizens.

The Fifteenth amendment gave the Negro the right to vote.

These may seem a far cry from freedom from regulation for corporations. And indeed the Thirteenth and Fifteenth amendments were. But the Fourteenth wasn't—at least not the way in which it was interpreted by the court. This is how Section I of that famous amendment read:

"All persons born or naturalized in the United States and subject to the jurisdiction thereof, are citizens of the United States and of the State wherein they reside. No State shall make or enforce any law which shall abridge the privileges or immunities of citizens of the United States; *nor shall any State deprive any person of life, liberty, or property, without due process of law*; nor deny to any person within its jurisdiction the equal protection of the laws" (my italics).

Read that again—especially the italicized part. It still seems a far cry from freedom of regulation for corporations, doesn't it?

Would you believe that under the "due process" clause of the Fourteenth amendment it would be impossible for the citizens of any state of the United States, through their legally elected state representatives, to pass a law regulating the hours of work in their state; or to pass a law fixing minimum wages; or to pass a law protecting workers in dangerous occupations; or to pass a law giving state utility commissions power to lower rates on electricity and gas; or to pass laws in general protecting the health and safety of the citizens of the state? That is exactly what happened. Under the Fourteenth amendment, the Supreme Court has declared over two hundred and thirty state laws invalid.

How was it done? If you substitute the word "corporation" for the word "person" in the due process clause, you have the key to the riddle. That is what the Supreme Court did. After 1886, whenever any state government tried to pass any laws which benefited its citizens by limiting the power of Big Business in any way, the Supreme Court would come to the rescue of the corporation or corporations affected by the law. It would declare the law unconstitutional because it deprived the "person (*i.e.,* the corporation) of life, liberty, or property, without due process of law." By such interpretations, the business freedom of corporations was made secure— the states could do little to limit their power. Again the rights of private property had a champion in the Supreme Court.

Of course, the law gave protection from "oppressive" state laws to real persons—human beings—as well as to corporations. But the important point was that in most of these state cases decided by the court under the amendment, corporations, not people, were asking for protection—and got it.

Not always, of course. As time went on, as the outcry of the people for necessary protecting legislation grew louder and louder, the court, on occasion, heard—and reversed itself. Every once in a while it did allow a state to pass a welfare law—such as one prohibiting women working more than ten hours, despite the complaint of some corporations that such a law interfered with their women employees' constitutional right to work twelve or fifteen hours a day. Such state regulatory laws were allowed to stand, but not very often.

The Fourteenth amendment was ratified in 1868, but it wasn't until 1886 that a "corporation" became a "person" in the eyes of the court. In the years that followed, this basic principle, affording unique and wonderful protection to corporations, was adhered to. Then, in 1938, it was sharply challenged for the first time. The usual type of case was being decided under the amendment—could the state of California tax the premiums of a Connecticut life insurance company licensed to do business in California? The usual decision was handed down—for California to lay the tax would be to deprive the Connecticut corporation of property without due process of law. That's what eight justices said. But one justice said something else, something extraordinary. Justice Black, in his dissenting opinion, argued that a corporation was not a "person" within the meaning of the Fourteenth amendment: "I do not believe the word 'person' in the Fourteenth Amendment includes corporations. . . . I believe this Court should now overrule previous decisions which interpreted the Fourteenth Amendment to include corporations. . . . The records of the time can be searched in vain for evidence that this amendment was adopted for the benefit of corporations. . . . The history of the amendment proves that the people were told that its purpose was to protect weak and helpless human beings and were not told that it was intended to remove corporations in any fashion from the control of state governments."

Whether the view of Justice Black would, in time, become the majority view, remained for the future to decide. In the past, the contrary view prevailed and corporations had flourished. The percentage of manufactured goods made by corporations was:

1899	66.7%
1919	87.0%
1929	94.0%

At the end of 1929 there were some three hundred thousand non-financial corporations in the United States. There were little corporations and big corporations. There were giant corporations, two hundred of them, which were in a class by themselves. Nearly all of these two hundred corporations—forty-two railroads, fifty-two public utilities, and one hundred and six industrials—had assets of over one hundred million dollars each. Fifteen of them had assets of over one billion dollars each. One of them, the American Telephone and Telegraph Company, with assets of over four billion dollars, controlled "more wealth than is contained within the borders of twenty-one of the states in the country."

These facts and others equally startling are contained in an important book by Berle and Means entitled *The Modern Corporation and Private Property*. The authors tell us that the two hundred dominant corporations—less than seven-hundredths of one per cent—controlled nearly half the wealth of all the corporations in the United States! Here was concentration of control with a vengeance.

Relative Importance of Large Corporations
(On or about January 1, 1930)

Proportion of corporate wealth (other than banking) controlled by the 200 largest corporations	49.2%
Proportion of business wealth (other than banking) controlled by the 200 largest corporations	38.0%
Proportion of national wealth controlled by the 200 largest corporations	22.0%

That parenthesis in the above table (other than banking) simply serves to distinguish the corporations from the great financial houses. It does not mean that bankers had nothing to do with the "non-financial" corporations. On the contrary, bankers had everything to do with them. As business grew it required more and more capital. The bankers were in a position to get the capital so necessary to large-scale business. Increasingly the banks played a more and more important role in the expansion of the mighty corporations. (They did it, of course, with other people's money.) There was a fusion of banking and industry in the concentration of control of American business.

This was already evident to some of the people of the United States at the turn of the century. And they were aware, too, more than a quarter of a century ago, of another astounding fact—not only were powerful corporations in control of most of the industry of the country, but the directors of these different corporations were in many cases the same small body of very rich men. There had grown up an "interlocking directorate." The leaders of the banking, railroad, utilities, and manufacturing industries were all intertwined. What the "muckrakers" of the period were shouting year after year was conclusively proved in the report of the Pujo Committee of the

House of Representatives in 1912, in which it was shown that the partners of J. P. Morgan and Company, and the directors of the Rockefeller-controlled National City Bank and Baker's First National Bank held:

118 directorships in	34	bank and trust companies
30 directorships in	10	insurance companies
105 directorships in	32	transportation systems
63 directorships in	24	producing and trading corporations
25 directorships in	12	public utility corporations

in all, 341 directorships in 112 corporations with a total capitalization of $22,245,000,000.

The frightening fact was already apparent that with each giant corporation master in its field, and a handful of men in control of the corporations, most of the power and money in the country would soon be in their hands. From control of the wealth of the country to control of the government was one short step. Woodrow Wilson, while President of the United States, wrote in 1913: "The facts of the situation amount to this, that a comparatively small number of men control the raw material of this country; that a comparatively small number of men control the water-powers; . . . that the same number of men largely control the railroads; that by agreements handed around among themselves, they control prices, and that that same group of men control the larger credits of the country. . . . The masters of the government of the United States are the combined capitalists and manufacturers of the United States."

They were evidently greater masters of the government than southern planters had been, because they were able to accomplish, in regard to the island of Cuba, what the Southerners had tried and failed to do. Before the Civil War, slaveholders had cast longing eyes on the fertile land of Cuba, where the climate was similar to that in the South. They wanted to add it to the United States as a slave state. Speakers and writers in the South referred to Cuba again and again as a place which of right ought to be part of our country. Southerners in New Orleans, on December 6, 1858, roundly applauded Stephen A. Douglas when he said, "It is our destiny to have Cuba and it is folly to debate the question. It naturally belongs to the American continent."

But try as they would, southern plantation-owners were not able to swing the United States into an invasion of Cuba.

Where they failed in the 1850's, northern capitalists succeeded in 1898.

At that time Cuba was one of the few possessions in the Western Hemisphere still owned by the declining country of Spain. In 1895 the Cubans revolted against her rule, and in the warfare that followed, farms and factories were burned and some of the inhabitants were cruelly treated. Our $100,000,000 annual trade with Cuba was hurt; some of the $50,000,000 worth of property which American capitalists had invested in Cuban business was destroyed by the warring sides. Naturally, our money men wanted action—the government must interfere to save American property. Ministers, preaching sermons describing Spanish cruelties, brought tears to the eyes of their listeners; newspapers, particularly the Hearst press, made sensational appeals for war against Spain; the war fever spread to the people. When the American battleship *Maine* was mysteriously blown up in the harbor of Havana, although there was no proof that any Spaniard had anything at all to do with it, shouts for war grew louder.

Messages were exchanged between the two governments; our minister to Spain discussed the purchase of Cuba by the United States. Spain refused to sell, but agreed to practically all of our demands in an effort to keep peace. President McKinley, however, said nothing of Spain's offer of peace, but instead sent a message to Congress asking it to give him the power to use our army and navy to stop the fighting between Spain and Cuba.

On April 19, 1898, the United States was at war with Spain.

In less than four months Spain was defeated.

The peace treaty provided that the Spanish islands of Puerto Rico, Guam, and the Philippines were to be given to the United States. Twenty million dollars was to be paid to Spain. Cuba was to receive her independence—under certain conditions.

Cuba has since had her own government, but the United States has on several occasions sent its soldiers there to "protect American lives and property." By 1928, American-owned sugar mills, tobacco plantations, mines and railways in Cuba were worth more than $1,000,000,000. In effect, Cuba belonged to us. (That "us" looks as though it refers to the people of the United States; but of course it doesn't, it refers to the rich capitalists.)

Many Americans were dismayed at the thought of the United States owning other countries. Didn't our own Declaration of Independence declare that governments derive "their just powers from the consent of the governed"? Then what right had we to make the Philippines our colony when the people there wanted to be independent? Here was the United States, which had always stood for liberty and freedom, which had itself broken away from a mother country; was it to become a mother country itself? Was there to be an American empire? To some people the whole idea was distasteful. To others, it looked like a desirable step. They agreed with President McKinley, who had seriously thought over the whole matter and had come to this conclusion about our adding the colonies: "There was nothing left for us to do but to take them all, and to educate the Filipinos, and uplift and civilize and Christianize them." Some there were who cared little about making Christians out of heathens, but saw in the addition of colonies a chance to make the United States great and powerful.

After 1898 the die was cast. We joined the other big nations in the scramble for colonies. The United States was to become a world empire.

After 1865 the United States changed from an agricultural to a manufacturing nation. We have already seen that in the wealth of its natural resources the United States had no equal except perhaps Russia. Yet there were some raw materials, very important to our manufacturers, which we did not have at all, or of which we did not have enough. Rubber, silk, jute, tin, nickel, nitrate, cork, manganese, tungsten—these headed a long list. In the field of foodstuffs there were coffee, cocoa, bananas, sugar, olive oil, coconuts, and others—mostly tropical products. All of these things we imported—for all of them there was a market in the United States. American businessmen wanted to control the sources of this natural wealth if they could. There was money in it. Naturally, our businessmen (like those of the other great countries of the world) became very much interested in countries that had these products. Sugar plantations in Haiti, banana plantations in Nicaragua, rubber plantations in Liberia, oil wells in Mexico, nitrate mines in Chile—these were but a few of our capitalists' growing interests.

We wanted to buy raw materials, but we wanted to sell manufactured goods. The increase in the volume of our manufactures was tremendous. As more and more goods were sold, as profits shot skyward, manufacturers increased the size and productive equipment of their plants so they could make more and more goods. (This hap-

WATER MILL

pened in the other great countries of the world, also.) There came
a time when the manufacturers could make more than they could
sell. Then they had to look about for new markets that could absorb
their surplus goods. Their old customers could not buy all that they
had to sell, so they had to find new customers.

American automobiles, typewriters, electrical supplies, safety
razors, moving pictures, bathtubs, fountain pens—to mention only
a few of a very long list—were shipped to the ends of the earth.
They were helping to "Americanize" the whole world.

Not only did American capitalists have surplus goods on their
hands, but they also had surplus capital. When a country is new,
when its lands, mines, and railroads are just beginning to be opened
up, then capitalists of other countries, seeking greater profits than
they can find at home, invest their money in the development of the
new country. This had happened to us from the very beginning of
our history. English capital, later other European capital, was sent
here to be put into railroads, factories, mines, cattle ranches, and
so on. After 1900 it was our turn. American capital began to pene-
trate everywhere, in all directions, to lands near and far. This had
begun to happen in considerable measure before World War I
began. It happened on a larger scale than ever, before the war was
over. World War I marked the ascendancy of the United States as a
dominant capitalist nation.

In 1914, years of imperialist rivalry resulted in the inevitable
clash. The nations of Europe became immersed in war. They needed
food, clothing, munitions, and money. Their own industries could
not meet the demand; factories and farms were shorthanded—labor
was at the front. The United States was ready, willing, and able to
satisfy the needs of the warring powers. It did so. Machines began to
hum twenty-four hours a day; plows quickened their pace.

When hostilities broke out in Europe, both sides, of course, had
their sympathizers in the United States, but most of the American
people wanted to stay out of the war. (Two years after the war began,
in 1916, Woodrow Wilson was re-elected President on the slogan,
"He Kept Us Out of War.") We were quite willing to furnish materials and munitions—at a price—to either side. But we soon discovered that we could not conveniently sell to both sides. England
was mistress of the seas; she established a blockade around German
ports, and American goods headed for Germany had great difficulty
getting there. Only a small part of our output of factory and farm

was sold to the Central Powers; on the other hand, one year after the war began, J. P. Morgan and Company, the purchasing agent for the Allies, was placing orders in the United States to the tune of $10,000,000 a day.

That was a lot of money. It bought a lot of goods which Americans were eager to sell. For their purchases in the first months of the war, the Allies had paid with gold. Then they had paid with the money received from the sale of their American securities. Next American bankers had arranged credits for them. One further step remained. It was taken in August, 1915.

A year before, the American government had put a ban on direct loans to the warring nations. Secretary of State Bryan had informed J. P. Morgan of the government's position: "There is no reason why loans should not be made to the governments of neutral nations, but in the judgment of this government, loans by American bankers to any foreign nation which is at war are inconsistent with the true spirit of neutrality."

That was as true in August, 1915, as it had been in August, 1914. But during that twelve-month period Allied orders to American factories and farms had brought us a taste of prosperity which was very stimulating. Robert Lansing, the new secretary of state, warned the President that we had an economic stake in removing the ban on loans. "Since December 1, 1914, to June 30, 1915, our exports have exceeded our imports by nearly a billion dollars. . . . For the year 1915 the excess will be approximately two and one-half billions of dollars. . . . Can we afford to let a declaration as to our conception of the 'true spirit of neutrality' made in the first days of the war stand in the way of our national interests, which seem to be seriously threatened?"

Apparently we could not "afford" to do so. The ban on loans to belligerents was lifted. The bankers set out full speed ahead. Loan after loan was floated in the United States for the Allied governments. Out of the pockets of Americans came the money which went into the pockets of American manufacturers and farmers in payment for the goods bought by the Allies.

In 1917 things looked black for the Allies. On the military front, the situation was desperate. On the financial front, the situation was hopeless—further borrowing from Americans was impossible. A smashup was in sight. But by this time our own fortunes were so intertwined with those of the Allies that a smashup for them meant a smashup for us. If the crash came, for example, what would happen to our greatly expanded economic plant geared to wartime orders and war-time profits? What would happen to the holders of Allied government bonds, which, if the crash came, would certainly be in default? The collapse of the Allies must not happen. But how avert it? On March 5, 1917, Walter Hines Page, our Anglophile ambassador to Britain, in a confidential cable to the President, supplied the answer, "Perhaps our going to war is the only way in which our present prominent trade position can be maintained and a panic averted."

On April 6, 1917, the Congress of the United States declared war on Germany.

The end of the war found the European nations weak, the United States strong. America had become the greatest financial and political power in the capitalist world. We had changed from a money-owing country to a money-lending country. We had been a debtor nation—we were now a creditor nation. Our surplus capital found investment opportunities in every corner of the globe, in new countries and in old ones.

Canada, our northern neighbor, is part of the British Empire. Yet by 1925 Mr. F. S. Chalmers estimated that "the United States owns one-third of all the industries in Canada and one-third of all the producing mines; it owns a large part of the timber resources not vested in the Crown, and has extensive interests besides in Canadian water-powers, real estate, and other assets. . . . British investments in Canada are roughly $2,000,000,000. . . . United States investments in Canada . . . are close to $2,500,000,000." More United States money than British money in a dominion of Great Britain! By 1930 the Bureau of Foreign and Domestic Commerce estimated our investments in Canada at about $3,942,000,000. Here are its figures in round numbers for American private investments throughout the world in 1930:

Place	Total (in millions of dollars)
Canada	3,942
Europe	4,929
Mexico and Central America	1,000
South America	3,042
West Indies	1,233
Africa	118
Asia	1,023
Oceania	419

When other countries of the world hit back at the high tariff of the United States by putting up high tariff walls of their own, our businessmen set up their establishments within the country itself. Thus in 1929 the Woolworth Company had one hundred and thirty stores in Canada, three hundred and fifty in Great Britain, thirty-five in Germany, and eight in Cuba.

That same year there was one automobile for every five people in the United States. In Europe (without Russia) the ratio was one to eighty-three. American capitalists saw in such a situation an opportunity for investment of surplus capital which must not be muffed simply because of tariff walls. So General Motors bought into the Adam Opel Company which produced nearly half the cars of Germany, and the Ford Company proceeded to set up several plants in some of the countries of Europe. It didn't matter that the labor employed in these American-owned factories had to be European, not American; it didn't matter that the materials used were European, not American; what did matter was that the profits came home—to America.

Capital evidently knew no boundaries. It went everywhere.

Sometimes the invasion of a country by American capital was done peacefully. Occasionally it led to serious trouble. Sometimes our money was followed by our marines, sent to "protect American lives and property." Mr. Borah, Senator from Idaho, protested against this. "We went to Nicaragua in 1910, I believe. In my judgment we never had any sufficient reason for going. Nevertheless, we sent our marines there, landed them, took possession of the country, marched to the capital, killed some 200 Nicaraguans, and placed in control, as the nominal President of Nicaragua, a clerk or employee of a corporation of Pittsburgh."

Senator Borah's account may seem incredible, but that this was the technique used in some of our imperialist ventures was proved by the statement of a man who took an active part in them on many occasions. A few years ago Major General Smedley D. Butler described, in picturesque language, his work as guardian of American Big Business interests in foreign lands:

I spent thirty-three years and four months in active service as a member of our country's most agile military force—the Marine Corps. I served in all commissioned ranks from a second lieutenant to major-general. And during that period I spent most of my time being a high-class muscle man for Big Business, for Wall Street, and for the bankers. In short, I was a racketeer for capitalism. . . .

Thus I helped make Mexico and especially Tampico safe for American oil interests in 1914. I helped make Haiti and Cuba a decent place for the National City Bank boys to collect revenues in. . . . I helped purify Nicaragua for the international banking house of Brown Brothers in 1909–1912. I brought light to the Dominican Republic for American sugar interests in 1916. I helped make Honduras "right" for American fruit companies in 1903. In China in 1927 I helped see to it that Standard Oil went its way unmolested.

During those years I had, as the boys in the back room would say, a swell racket. I was rewarded with honors, medals, promotion. Looking back on it, I feel I might have given Al Capone a few hints. The best he could do was to operate his racket in three city districts. We Marines operated on three continents.

Besides Nicaragua, Cuba, the Philippines, Puerto Rico, and Guam, we own or control Hawaii, Samoa, Panama, Santo Domingo, Haiti, Alaska, and the Virgin Islands. In some of these places we have had trouble, like that in Nicaragua, where both natives and United States marines were killed in small wars. In other countries, not on the above list, our capitalists conquered with little or no trouble at all. The more modern imperialist technique of invading a weak country without fanfare, without bugles, was successfully employed. These countries became "spheres of influence" for the United States through the quiet but highly effective penetration of surplus capital.

Should the "flag follow the dollar"?

If American capitalists get control of a country through their large ownership of its railroads, mines, land, and so on, then if a George Washington of that country raises an army to free his native land from American capitalist rule, should the United States Government send marines there to protect the property of its businessmen? This was a hotly debated question, not yet settled. It was an ever-recurring question, because after World War I the economy of the United States was such that our capitalists, like those of other countries, found it necessary to seek for control of the raw materials of the earth, for available markets for surplus goods, for opportunities for profitable investment of surplus capital.

In 1900 the wealth of the United States was estimated at $86,000,000,000.

In 1929 the wealth of the United States was estimated at $361,-000,000,000.

The period from the Civil War to 1900 was one of great expansion. But the expansion from 1900 to 1929 was so tremendous as to make it appear that in the previous period the country had been standing still. Look, for example, at these figures showing the percentage of gain, in value added by manufacture, in a few outstanding industries between 1899 and 1927:

Chemicals, etc. 239%
Leather and products 321%
Textiles and products 449%
Food products 551%
Machinery 562%
Paper and printing 614%
Steel and products 780%
Transportation and equipment 969%

Those are the figures for a few selected industries. For manufacturing as a whole, the following table is equally revealing:

Growth of Manufactures in the United States *
(in thousands)

Year	No. of Establishments	Wage-Earners	Value of Products	Value Added by Manufacture
1899	208	4,713	11,407,000	4,831,000
1914	273	7,024	24,217,000	9,858,000
1929	207	8,822	69,961,000	31,783,000

* These census figures for 1899 and 1914 relate to factories (excluding hand and neighborhood establishments) whose products were valued at more than $500; for 1929, factories whose products were valued at more than $5,000.

At the turn of the century the United States was already the leading manufacturing country in the world. Twenty-nine years later, no other country was even within hailing distance of it. Nor was it in manufacturing alone that the United States led the world in 1929. It occupied first place in practically every other field as well. The three hundred years from the time of the first settlements until 1929 had been years of economic expansion—years in which there had been a continual increase in the amount of goods and services available to the people of the country. The steady rise in the standard of living had reached its topmost peak in the 1920's, a period of unparalleled prosperity.

The America of the early seventeenth century was very different from the America of the golden year 1929. What had been a wilderness inhabited only by savages and wild animals had become the richest country the world had ever seen. The transformation which had taken place during those three hundred years was a success story which would have delighted the old-time writer of thrillers. He would probably have given the story the appropriate title of "From Rags to Riches."

WE, THE PEOPLE

Part II

From Riches to Rags

★————————————————————————————————————★

After October, 1929, the title of the story would have had to be turned around to read, "From Riches to Rags." In the terrible depression years of 1930–32, the richest country in the world was "a stricken nation."

Every section of the United States was in distress. Workers, farmers, professional people, all were hard hit.

In the big cities, increasing millions tramped the streets looking for jobs that did not exist. Bread lines everywhere.

On the farms, crops piled high, prices low. Famine in the face of plenty.

One bank after another closed its doors—on the hopes and dreams of millions who had gone without in order to save for the future. In 1932, at the bottom of the depression, banks were failing at the rate of forty a day.

Charitable organizations did what they could, but they could not do enough. A committee of the Senate listened to their tales of woe. Two reports were from Philadelphia:

J. Prentice Murphy, Executive Director of the Children's Bureau: ". . . but certainly if the modern state is to rest upon a firm foundation its citizens must not be allowed to starve. Some of them do. They do not die quickly. You can starve for a long time without dying."

Dorothy Kahn, Executive Director of the Jewish Welfare Society: "Only the other day a case came to my attention in which a family of ten had just moved in with a family of five in a three-room apartment. However shocking that may be to the members of this committee, it is almost an everyday occurrence in our midst. Neighbors do take people in. They sleep on chairs, they sleep on the floor. There are conditions in Philadelphia that beggar description. There is

scarcely a day that calls do not come to all of our offices to find some-
how a bed or a chair. The demand for boxes on which people can
sit or stretch themselves is hardly to be believed."

In 1932, a Chicago committee wrote a report on its investigation
of nine city garbage dumps. This was part of its report: "Around
the truck which was unloading garbage and other refuse were about
thirty-five men, women, and children. As soon as the truck pulled
away from the pile all of them started digging with sticks, some with
their hands, grabbing bits of food and vegetables."

A farmer, in 1932, told his story, one of many like it: "I have
fed and marketed 430 head of fat cattle. The meat that I put on those
cattle would amount to 135,000 pounds of beef. That is enough beef
to last 2076 people one year. And I haven't a bit of meat in the
house, and nothing to buy any with.

"I have raised and marketed 1200 head of hogs. That would make
240,000 pounds of pork. That is enough pork to last 3000 people
one year, and I am out of pork, lard, and money."

All these stories show what the depression meant to the United
States in terms of human beings. There's another way of showing
what the depression meant to the United States—statistics. Though
totals and averages are always misleading, in that they cover up
the extent of the suffering of those who are worst off, nevertheless
a valuable clue to what happened can be obtained from a glance at
some key statistics. All kinds of statistics: national income, industrial
production, factory employment, pay rolls, construction, foreign
trade. They all add up to the same thing—crisis. The figures show
in unmistakable terms the breakdown of the American economy.

The net value of the commodities produced (food, clothing,
houses, cars, steel rails, locomotives, etc.) plus the services rendered
(services of doctors, nurses, lawyers, beauticians, barbers, waiters,
etc.) is what economists call the "national income produced." The
amount actually distributed as wages, salaries, dividends, interest,
and so forth is what economists call the "national income paid out."

In 1929 the national income produced was eighty-one billion
dollars.

In 1932 the national income produced was forty billion dollars.

The production of goods and services had shrunk, in value, to less
than half of what it had been.

In 1929 national income paid out was seventy-eight and a half
billion dollars.

In 1932 it was forty-nine billions—a drop of more than a third.

To understand more fully what such a drop in the national income means, let us look at the losses suffered by the two major groups, workers and farmers. What happened to labor and agriculture is illustrated in the graphs below.

An important thing to remember is that in the first graph, "Salaries and Wages" includes the salaries of the men at the top as well as the wages of the workers at the bottom—and the men at the top, in spite of the depression, continued to pay themselves "a living wage" of thousands of dollars per week.

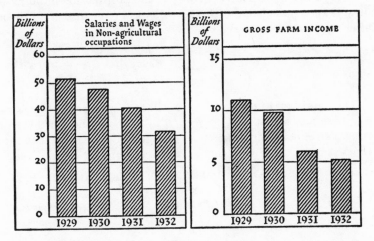

The United States *Statistical Abstract* breaks down these income figures further. If we take the wages of a group of selected industries alone (including mining, manufacturing, steam railroads, Pullman, railway express, and water transportation), we find that wages fell from $17,093,000,000 in 1929 to $7,243,000,000 in 1932, a drop of nearly 60 per cent.

Another key to our prosperity or poverty is how much our industries produce, that is, the output of our factories and mines. With 1923-25 equal to 100, the index of our industrial production was 119 in 1929, 64 in 1932. This means that, in 1932, our factories and mines were turning out just a little more than half of what they produced in 1929.

The indices of employment and pay rolls in manufacturing industries (admittedly not comprehensive) proclaim the same story.

With 1923–25 equal to 100, the index of employment, which was 106 in 1929, fell to 66 in 1932, a drop of nearly 40 per cent, even though those who were working only part time were counted as employed.

Even more striking was the drop in the index of pay rolls:

$$1929 = 110$$
$$1932 = 47.$$

Another important economic indicator is the index of the value of construction contracts awarded, because the building industry is both a large employer of labor itself and one of the chief customers of heavy industry as a whole. How far the props of the building industry were pulled out with the collapse of the real-estate boom after 1929 is shown in the table:

1923–25 = 100

Year	Total	Residential	All Others
1929	117	87	142
1932	28	13	40

The figures on foreign trade give still another clue to the crisis in our national economy. The year 1929 was not the peak year in American exports and imports, yet foreign trade was more than three times as great in value in that year as in 1932:

EXPORTS AND IMPORTS OF MERCHANDISE
(IN MILLIONS OF DOLLARS)

Year	Exports	Imports
1929	5,241	4,399
1932	1,611	1,322

Wherever we turn we find the same picture. The level of economic activity reached its peak about 1929—it fell at an unprecedented rate and to an unprecedented extent, from 1929 to 1932. In no other country was the collapse so great, because in no other country had expansion been so rapid and so spectacular. And with collapse came disillusionment and suffering.

The America of 1932 was a vastly different place from the America of 1929. The hopes of the postwar decade had received a shattering blow. The high priests of private enterprise had become a public laughingstock. Where were the high wages, "the chicken in every pot," and "the car in every garage" of which they had boasted? The economic system which had made America the richest country in the world in 1929 had bogged down. The American dream of a never-ending and growing prosperity had become an exploded myth.

Understand, there was nothing wrong with the American worker. His ability to produce goods was, in fact, greater than ever before and increasing all the time. The productive plant and the natural resources of the country were still available. The people's desire for the good things of life was greater, not less. Yet machinery was idle, materials were rotting in disuse while people were starving for lack of them, money was idle because the few who had it could not turn its use to profit, and fourteen million workers walked the streets looking for jobs that did not exist.

All over the country people were undergoing hardship and in-security. They waited in vain for that prosperity which their business and political leaders had assured them was "just around the corner." It didn't come.

What was wrong? What had happened that America, the dream-land of the starving European peasant and the oppressed European worker, had been smitten with the same disease as other lands? It was not that depressions were new to the United States. There had been "bad times" before, particularly in the seventies and the nineties, and in the first decade of the twentieth century. But those bad times had been temporary. The United States was then an expanding country. Now, like England, France, and Germany, it was an ex-panding country no longer.

The economic system had become senile. It had performed its gigantic task of liberating and developing the forces of production to a point never before reached—and it had nowhere else to go. It could no longer continue on its own momentum. The drive for more profits, more capital, more profits, more capital . . . had reached the stage where it became harder and harder to make more profits and invest more capital. There was no way out in these terms of more and more for the sake of more and more. The economic system had performed its function. It had exhausted its potentialities.

What were the causes of the crisis in 1929? *There was only one cause—the system of production.* All explanations in terms of the monetary system, speculation, distribution of wealth, technological progress, the disappearance of the frontier, the aftereffects of World War I, and the hundred and one others which economists spend their time concocting, miss the main point. They mistake the symptoms for the disease. Yes, there was something wrong with the monetary system. Certainly there had been too much speculation. Income was indeed badly distributed. No doubt technological progress had taken place at an unheard-of rate. True, the frontier had been closed (for more than a generation). Sure, the war had left a headache. But no doctor dares to tell you, when you have a fever, that it is due to your white tongue or high temperature—if he does, you show him the door. There was only one disease America was suffering from —capitalism in its most acute and highly developed form.

America was the richest country in the world. American banks and corporations were the biggest in the world. Nowhere else was Big Business more firmly entrenched. Nowhere else had the process of concentration gone further. Nowhere else had such large fortunes been amassed.

And with Dives went Lazarus.

The richest country in the world had slums which could compete with the worst hovels of the Old World. The Negroes—almost one tenth of the population—were as badly off in the large towns as they were on the farms and plantations, where slavery was still more than a memory. Labor was continually being pushed to working harder for the same or lower wages. Hunger and poverty existed in American industrial centers just as they existed in English, French, and German industrial centers. Pittsburgh, Chicago, and Detroit hardly differed from Sheffield and Lyons and Essen.

It was the same disease.

In 1929 there were over 300,000 nonbanking corporations in the United States. Some were giants, some were pygmies. There were "Two Hundred" out of the 300,000 which were giants, but giants so large that they outstripped the other 299,800 all put together.

Of all the 300,000 nonfinancial corporations in 1929, the Two Hundred:

> paid out 56.8 per cent of the interest
> paid out 55.4 per cent of the cash dividends
> earned 56.8 per cent of the net profit
> saved 69.3 per cent of the savings

Maybe this was just an accident? Not at all. The Two Hundred's 1929 slices of the corporate pie were thicker than in 1920; and their 1933 slices were proportionately bigger than in 1929.

Just think of it: The Two Hundred had total assets of ninety-eight billion dollars—an amount equal to the combined wealth of the whole United Kingdom.

Yet all this understates the degree of centralization and concentration. In addition to the Two Hundred in the nonfinancial group there were Fifty in the financial group which stood out. As we have seen, the distinction between financial and nonfinancial corporations must not be taken literally. Finance and industry are so closely intertwined that, so far as corporations are concerned, it is difficult to say where finance ends and industry begins. They are tied together by interlocking directorates and all manner of legal, financial, and commercial devices. They are linked together by chains of gold.

They are not giants standing alone but groups of giants operating together. The giant nonfinancial corporations of the Two Hundred are clustered in bunches around the biggest of the big financial houses of the Fifty. A government report separates these bunches into eight "interest groups," showing which of the Two Hundred are bound to or "closely associated with" which of the Fifty; for obvious reasons five of these groups are called after Morgan, Rockefeller, Kuhn-Loeb, Mellon, and du Pont. Thus to the banking houses of J. P. Morgan and Company and the First National Bank of New York (the Morgan-First National "interest group") are assigned:

13 industrial corporations with assets of	$ 3,920	millions
12 utility corporations with assets of	12,191	millions
5 major railroad systems and one other road	9,678	millions
5 banks	4,421	millions
TOTAL	30,210	millions

A few names under each category will show the nature of the corporations under the partial control of Morgan-First National: General Electric Company (four Morgan-First National representatives in its management), United States Steel Corporation (three representatives), American Telephone and Telegraph Company, Consolidated Gas Company of New York, New York Central System, Guaranty Trust Company.

Whereas the Morgan-First National group is based on partial control through "long-standing financial relations," the Mellon group, "probably the best integrated and most compact of all the interest groups considered . . . is based on a solid core of industrials and banks which are closely held by members of the Mellon family and a small number of close associates. . . ."

The Mellon list is as follows:

Industrials:
  Closely held:
    Gulf Oil Corporation
    Koppers Co.
    Aluminum Co. of America
    Pittsburgh Coal Co.
  Probably Mellon dominated:
    Westinghouse Electric & Manufacturing Co.
  Allied:
    Jones & Laughlin Steel Corporation
    American Rolling Co.
    Crucible Steel Co. of America
    Pittsburgh Plate Glass Co.
Rails:
  Virginian Ry. Co.
Utilities:
  United Light & Power Co.
  Brooklyn Union Gas Co.
Banks (closely held) :
  Mellon National Bank
  Union Trust Co.

Total assets of the Mellon group are as follows:

	Millions of dollars
Industrials	$1,648
Utilities	859
Rails	153
Banks	672
TOTAL	3,332

It must not be thought that the division of the Two Hundred and the Fifty into eight golden clusters means that each of the groups is unrelated to any of the others. Not at all. They overlap and interconnect. One of the corporations which the du Ponts control is General Motors, in which they hold about 25 per cent of the voting stock. Yet "three high representatives of Morgan-First National are directors of General Motors. . . . Additionally, the Morgan firms are chief bankers and underwriters for the du Pont interests."

What does capitalism in this most acute and highly developed form mean for the people of America?

It means that a few persons have the key controls of the most important part of the economy. It means that, as long as they continue their control, they will fight to maintain their profits at all costs—by lowering wages, increasing efficiency, squeezing out competition, pegging prices, competing ever more keenly for foreign markets.

It means that industry develops more rapidly than, and at the expense of, agriculture. Large-scale production does not develop to anywhere near the same extent in agriculture as in industry. Farmers are exploited both at the selling and the buying end, so rural standards of living are much lower than urban. About a quarter of the population of the United States lives on farms, but even in the best years they never get within hailing distance of a quarter of the national income.

It means not only that agriculture is out of step with industry—but that different industries are out of step with each other. Fluctuations in production are most marked in the heavy goods industries—too much expansion in good times, too much contraction in bad times. The cogs don't mesh.

It means that industries are run by remote control, by men who are preoccupied with the money-making side of business rather than with the producing side. In its turn this means that there is an intensified drive toward speculative orgies, which have less and less connection with underlying economic realities. For the easiest way to make money for the people who have the controls is financial manipulation. This means the construction of a crazy patchwork of holding companies, pyramiding one phony company on top of another (for example, Insull), until the inevitable day of reckoning comes, when the losers are not the Big Boys at the controls, but the workers who, through no fault of their own, lose their jobs and see their earnings slashed; the farmers who bear the brunt of a fall in prices; the small investors who have been taken in by the promoters; the homeowners who are suddenly called on to meet their mortgages; anybody and everybody—except those responsible for an expansion which cannot be sustained.

It means that the drive for improved methods of production and for increasing the productivity of labor will cause more and more to be produced with less and less labor. Machines and systems of efficiency turn workers into the streets while production shoots upward. The average rise in output per man hour in fifty-nine industries from 1919 to 1929 was between 40 and 50 per cent. In 1932, Sidney Hillman, then president of the Amalgamated Clothing Workers, told a Senate committee that "it takes 50 per cent of the people to produce as many garments today as it did in 1915." When profits are falling, the pressure to push labor harder and to use more labor-saving machinery is all the greater. Professor Schumpeter of Harvard summed it up in a line ". . . the depression acted as an efficiency expert. . . ."

It means that a larger proportion of the national income goes to corporate savings and to a dwindling number of people in the high-income brackets. It means that it becomes ever more difficult to invest the huge surpluses and savings that the corporations and the men at the top accumulate. It means that the hold of the Two Hundred on production gives them a hold on distribution, too. The economy's production base outruns its consumption base, that is, more is produced—not than is needed—but than can be sold at a profit. The way to make profits is to keep costs low. The way to keep costs low is to use as little labor and to pay as little for it as possible. But the less labor gets in wages, the less it can buy. In other words, making profits is a self-defeating process. It is a game the capitalists cannot always go on winning—but they must.

People need bread, clothing, shoes, apartments. They want automobiles, radios, electric refrigerators. But they have no money to buy these things. This was true even in the golden year of 1929, our peak prosperity year. It was indeed a prosperity year—but only for a few. For the many, even the richest year in the richest country of the world was anything but prosperous.

This is proven beyond a doubt by three sets of figures. The first is part of a message from President Roosevelt to Congress. It gives the lie to the widely held notion that large dividends from the ownership of stocks were going to the masses of the people. "The

year 1929 was a banner year for distribution of stock ownership.
But in that year three-tenths of one percent of our population received 78 percent of the dividends reported by individuals. This
has roughly the same effect as if, out of every 300 persons in our
population, one person received 78 cents out of every dollar of
corporate dividends while the other 299 persons divided up the
other 22 cents between them."

The second set of figures is even more striking. "In 1929 there
were 504 supermillionaires at the top of the heap who had an
aggregate net income of $1,185,000,000. That is 504 people. These
persons could have purchased with their net income the entire wheat
and cotton crops of 1930. In other words, there were 504 men who
made more money in that year than all the wheat farmers and all
the cotton farmers in this great land of democracy. Out of the
two chief crops, 1,300,000 wheat farmers, and 1,032,000 cotton farmers—2,300,000 farmers raising wheat and cotton—made less than
these 504 men."

The third set of figures is the most comprehensive. It gives us a
complete picture of the incomes of American families in 1929.

DISTRIBUTION OF INCOME IN THE UNITED STATES
IN 1929 (*Approximate*)

Income Class (*In dollars*)	Number of families (*In thousands*)	Cumulative percent of total number of families	Cumulative percent of income received
0 to 1,000	5,899	21.5	4.5
1,000 to 1,500	5,754	42.5	13.0
1,500 to 2,000	4,701	59.6	23.6
2,000 to 2,500	3,204	71.2	32.9
2,500 to 3,000	1,988	78.4	40.0
3,000 to 5,000	3,672	91.8	57.9
5,000 to 10,000	1,625	97.7	72.0
10,000 and over	631	100.0	100.0
All classes	27,474	100.0	100.0

This table is adapted from a much more complete one in *America's Capacity to Consume*, published by the Brookings Institution.
The authors tell us that the 27,474,000 families in the United States

consisted of two or more persons each and "the average number of persons per family was just a fraction over four." Let us see what a breakdown of the figures tells us about the distribution of income to American families in 1929:

About six million families, or over 21 per cent of the total number, had incomes of less than $1000 for the year.

Another six million families had incomes of less than $1500 a year.

Taken together these twelve million families were 42.5 per cent of the total number of families. Yet they received only 13 per cent of the total income.

And with Lazarus went Dives.

There were thirty-six thousand families at the top of the economic ladder. These thirty-six thousand families were one tenth of one per cent of all the families. Yet their share of the national income was also about 13 per cent.

In other words:

Twelve million families, 42 per cent of the total, received 13 per cent of the national income.

Thirty-six thousand families, 0.1 per cent of the total, received 13 per cent of the national income.

Thirty-six thousand families had as much to eat, drink, and be merry on as twelve million families.

The $1500 income (or less) of these twelve million families was not enough to supply the minimum essentials of living. The Brookings experts tell us that at 1929 prices a family income of $2000 a year was "sufficient to supply only basic necessities." A glance at the table shows that almost 60 per cent of the American people did not get as much as $2000 a year—which means that 60 per cent of the American people in 1929, the richest year in our history up to that time, did not get enough to buy even the bare necessities of life, let alone the luxuries. The share of most American families, at the bottom of the economic ladder, was too small; the share of a small group of families, at the top of the economic ladder, was too large.

For a while it was possible to postpone the day of reckoning. We disposed of surplus savings and at the same time, by lending them money, made it possible for countries abroad to purchase our exports. Our export trade expanded as they bought goods from the United States for which they paid with money borrowed from the United States. In the domestic market the gap between production and consumption was bridged for a time by the system of large-scale installment selling. This was especially true of those industries that were still expanding, such as the automobile, radio, and electrical products industries. The demand for durable consumption goods and housing continued to increase on the basis of this increased borrowing.

But it could not go on indefinitely. Expansion contains the seeds of its own contraction, and the greater the expansion, the greater the subsequent contraction. The explanation for the collapse of 1932 is the crash of 1929, and the explanation for the crash of 1929 is the preceding boom. The sequence of more profits, more ac-

cumulation, more profits, more accumulation . . . was bound to snap. The chain was sure to break at its weakest link. It did. The weakest link happened to be the speculative orgy on the stock market, but this was not the basic factor. The basic factor was that the capitalist system depends for its continuance on permanent expansion, on an indefinite unleashing of productive forces—but in its operation it automatically sets up barriers to permanent expansion. And when it cannot expand, it contracts.

The system in Europe had already entered into the phase of general crisis in 1919. The United States was ten years behind. In 1929 it caught up—with a vengeance. In 1929 the United States left behind it forever the period when capitalism could still expand. Henceforth it was to be concerned not with generating expansion, but with keeping contraction to a minimum.

When the depression hit the United States, Herbert Hoover was President. To Mr. Hoover the cure for the crisis was to help the big fellows, in the hope that some measure of prosperity would trickle down to the little fellows. But that did not happen.

When the elections of November, 1932, rolled around, the country was worse off than it had ever been. All of Mr. Hoover's "cures" could not put vigor into the dying patient. Labor was ravaged by unemployment; the farmers were ravaged by the crisis in agriculture; the middle class had lost its savings in bank crashes and was fearful of its economic security.

On November 8, 1932, the American people elected Franklin D. Roosevelt, President of the United States.

"*No One Should Be Permitted to Starve*"

★————————————————————————————————★

Mr. Roosevelt's New Deal has been called a revolution. It was—and it wasn't. It was a revolution in ideas, but it was not a revolution in economics.

It did not change the system of private ownership of the means of production in which the primary object is the making of profit —the United States is still a capitalist country. It did not bring the overthrow of one class by another—the employers are still in their accustomed places, the workers in theirs. "No one in the United States believes more firmly than I do in the system of private business, private property and private profit. . . . It was this Administration which saved the system of private profit and free enterprise after it had been dragged to the brink of ruin. . . ." These were the words of Mr. Roosevelt, three years after he became President. They were the truth—the New Deal was not a revolution in economics.

But though "the system of private profit and free enterprise" was saved, much of the baggage that had always accompanied it was thrown overboard and new tackle was substituted. Gone was the businessman's doctrine of *laissez-faire,* "let us alone" was out—in its place came the idea of government intervention, of "help us or we are ruined"; gone was the acceptance of the policy of employer war on trade-unionism—in its place came the idea of the legal right of labor to self-organization; gone was the unregulated system of banking which resulted in one crash after another—in its place came the idea of a banking structure in which deposits were insured; gone was the principle, in the sale of securities, of "let the buyer beware"— in its place came the idea of "let the seller beware"; gone was the traditional idea of "rugged individualism" with its attendant insecurity —in its place came the idea of security; gone was the doctrine that the poor must be helped by charity alone—in its place came Mr. Roosevelt's idea that "while it isn't written in the Constitution, nevertheless, it is the inherent duty of the Federal Government to keep its citizens from starvation." The New Deal was a revolution in ideas.

These ideas did not spring full fledged out of the minds of the President and his "Brain Trust." They arose out of the necessities of the situation. They were translated into laws to meet definite needs.

The period between the election of Franklin D. Roosevelt in November, 1932, and his inauguration on March 4, 1933, was a period of deepening crisis. The financial structure of the nation was in ruins —the banks everywhere had been forced to close their doors. About fourteen million persons were out of work—a number actually as well as proportionately greater than that of any country in the world. These unemployed people with their dependents totaled a population greater than that of the United Kingdom. Social unrest was sweeping the country. The ruling class felt itself definitely threatened; it had lost confidence in its ability to govern. In his inaugural address the incoming President summed up the situation:

. . . Let me assert my firm belief that the only thing we have to fear is fear itself—nameless, unreasoning, unjustified terror which paralyzes needed efforts to convert retreat into advance. . . . Our distress comes from no failure of substance. . . . Plenty is at our doorstep, but a generous use of it languishes in the very sight of the supply. Primarily this is because rulers of the exchange of mankind's goods have failed through their own stubbornness and their own incompetence, have admitted their failure, and have abdicated. Practices of the unscrupulous money changers stand indicted in the court of public opinion, rejected by the hearts and minds of men. . . . The money changers have fled from their high seats in the temple of our civilization. We may now restore that temple to the ancient truths. . . . Our greatest primary task is to put people to work. . . . I am prepared under my constitutional duty to recommend the measures that a stricken Nation in the midst of a stricken world may require.

It was well that the new President was prepared. There was no time to wait. He didn't wait. He went into action immediately. The most urgent problem facing the new administration was the collapse of the whole banking system. Inauguration Day came on a Saturday. On Sunday, March 5, the President called Congress into extraordinary session for the following Thursday. On Monday, March 6, at one o'clock in the morning (using the power conferred on the

President through a resurrected wartime "Trading with the Enemy Act"), he proclaimed a national bank holiday for the four days through the Thursday when Congress was to meet. On that Thursday he was ready with a message asking for blanket authority over the banks—and with the bill which was to grant it. Congress made the bill into law on the same day. The Emergency Banking Act, in addition to conferring upon the President the authority he sought, gave him the power to control the movement of gold and other currency, and all foreign-exchange transactions. It gave him also the right to reopen, when he saw fit, those banks that were in sound condition, and to reorganize those banks that needed reorganization (that is, government credit) to put them on a sound basis for reopening.

Yet all these powers would have been to no avail if the President had not been able to win back the confidence of the people. Those bank depositors who in February and the first days of March had rushed to get their money out of the collapsing banks (thus bringing further collapse) had to be reassured. Only if their confidence was restored, would they re-store their money in the banks. The President was able to restore their confidence. His decisive emergency measures were the first step. They were followed on Sunday, March 12, by a masterly radio address—the first of a series of famous "fireside chats"—in which he convinced the people of the country that the situation was well in hand, that there was no need for further panic, that the banks which would be reopened the next day and the days following were now in good condition. He turned the trick. The people's fear vanished. Hoarded gold was taken out of its hiding place and brought to the banks. The queues of people in front of bank doors were no longer waiting to take their money out—they were waiting for a chance to put their money in.

The way Mr. Roosevelt handled this extreme emergency was an indication of what was to come. He could be depended upon to act and act quickly. He would make a bad state of affairs better. But beyond that he would not go. He could have socialized the banking system. He had the chance to introduce government ownership and operation of the mechanisms of banking, credit, and investment. He chose not to do so. "The money changers had," indeed, "fled from their high seats in the temple." Mr. Roosevelt, with the use of public credit, had ably performed the necessary task of restoring the temple. But he had restored the money-changers in their high seats as well. True, their powers were diminished, their opportunities for further wrongdoing in the old ways lessened. But they were back. The New Deal was not a revolution in economics.

The banking emergency over, Mr. Roosevelt now turned his attention to the tasks still remaining—the tasks of Relief, Recovery, and Reform, the three R's of the New Deal. They were, of course, intertwined, and the measures taken to deal with any one helped the others, too. Priority, however, was given to the task of relief. Americans were told in the first "fireside chat" of 1934: "I have continued to recognize three related steps. The first was relief because the primary concern of any Government dominated by the humane ideals of democracy is the simple principle that in a land of vast resources no one should be permitted to starve. Relief was and continues to be our first consideration."

Mr. Roosevelt's "simple principle" was a new one for the United States. People had been permitted to starve before. Government relief for the needy had, indeed, been given by President Hoover. But it had been relief for needy railroads, banks, insurance companies. To the cries for government relief which came from distressed people, Mr. Hoover had turned a deaf ear. To give government aid to the poor, he argued, was to destroy their moral fiber, their spirit of self-reliance, their self-respect. He never thought it necessary to explain why his Reconstruction Finance Corporation, established in January, 1932, to give aid to down-and-out financial institutions, was not destructive of the moral fiber, etc., of the stockholders of those institutions. Mr. Hoover was willing, through his RFC, to give government subsidies to the rich; he was not willing to give necessary government help to the poor. Mr. Roosevelt's simple principle that government money must be used to serve all of the people instead of only the favored few was a significant break with the past.

But for the New Deal Administration to recognize the fact that the unemployed were in distress through no fault of their own, and to be willing to aid them, was not enough. Every other advanced industrial nation in the world had some social-insurance system, some way of handling national relief. Not so the United States. Here, where the need was the greatest, suitable machinery for doing the job had yet to be created. It was not easy. There were important questions to be answered. Should there be unemployment insurance as in England? And should there also be straight relief for those not insured? And if so, should relief payments be made only for work

COTTON SHIPPING

done? And if for work, what kind of work? Was it possible to create useful jobs for the unemployed which would not interfere with private industry?

There was no simple answer to these questions. The relief program was, of necessity, an experimental one. It was made up of many parts, each of which was constantly being changed to fit new conditions. Relief was administered by charitable agencies, by cities, states, and the Federal Government, all acting separately in some phases of the program, collectively in others.

Distress relief formed one part of the program. Agencies were set up to make outright gifts of cash to the needy; to buy surplus foods from down-and-out farming areas for distribution to the distressed in cities; to take surplus stocks of clothing from the shelves of manufacturers' warehouses to be handed out to the poor; to move destitute farm families from submarginal land to good land.

Work relief was without doubt the most important part of the program. From the outset, the principle of relief for work done rather than a dole was preferred by the Administration and the people.

Most important, most extensive, and most severely criticized of the work-relief agencies was the Works Progress Administration (WPA). It was not just another effort to aid the needy—it was a well-conceived plan organized by people with true social vision and real understanding of the nature of the whole problem of relief. Their aim was the admirable one of putting the unemployed to work on jobs for which their training and experience had fitted them. From one to three million men and women a year were employed at "security wages" (enough for subsistence but not as much as ordinary wages paid in normal employment) ranging from $19 per month for unskilled workers in the South to $103.40 per month for technical workers in the North. A list of the accomplishments of this vast army of employed unemployed would be pages long—an incomplete summary shows the construction of hundreds of thousands of miles of highways, roads, and streets; thousands of bridges, parks, public buildings, schools, and hospitals; hundreds of airports, playgrounds, swimming pools, recreation grounds. Not only were schools and recreation centers built under WPA—they were used to a greater extent than ever before to meet needs long neglected. In a single month more than one million people were in attendance in over one hundred thousand classes in adult education, workers' education, the elimination of illiteracy, nurseries—and this was only part of the gigantic educational program. In the field of recreation a trained personnel operated over nine thousand community centers and assisted in the operation of six thousand others.

Of especial significance, because of its outstanding character, was the contribution to the cultural life of the nation made by WPA writers, artists, actors, and musicians. To have written books, painted pictures, produced plays, and made music for millions of listeners would have been enough. They did more. They won the praise of the country's most competent critics by the top-notch quality of their work. They ventured into paths never before trod, and, through their successful experimentation with new forms, broadened the horizon of the arts. A magnificent performance.

In spite of the fine achievements of the WPA program, the charge was frequently made that the work was useless, and the workers lazy and incompetent. The causes of this continual sniping at WPA works and workers by the comfortable were simple—WPA cost money, which was raised by increased and more progressive taxes; and it supported the wage level by preventing an indiscriminate scramble for jobs at almost any wage by the large army of the unemployed. The very people who in 1933 had shouted the loudest against a "dole" were the ones who, six years later, led the pack in calling for the abolition of WPA work relief and a change to direct relief (or no relief at all). It did not matter to them that their old arguments against supporting the unemployed in idleness—demoralization, loss of self-respect, etc.—were still valid; it did not matter to them that relief workers had created public assets of permanent value; it did not matter to them that the work-relief projects helped to stimulate private industry to an extent not possible by idle relief. What did matter to them was that work relief cost more than idle relief, and that wages were not so easily slashed. The choice lay between a humane, enlightened program of work relief which was of great economic and social benefit to the nation but involved higher federal taxes on the rich, and an inhuman unenlightened program of idle relief which would result in severe economic dislocation and widespread suffering but would lower the tax burden for those who could afford to pay higher taxes. The snipers at WPA had made their choice—they were trying to shoot down the former and set up the latter.

The truth of the matter was that not too much but too little was spent on relief. Millions who were in need were never taken care of at all—they could not get either distress relief or work relief. Those who were fortunate enough to be chosen had to submit to an inquisition on their needs and resources which was degrading. The money paid to the wretched on relief was admittedly just enough to keep them alive. Standards of decent living conditions were not in the picture at all. The extent to which the health and strength of the needy on and off relief were affected could not be measured. But one thing was certain. A truly adequate program would have cost the nation many more millions; it would have saved the nation many billions.

Another important part of the program was debt relief. A series of emergency measures was passed setting up agencies with billions of dollars at their disposal to bring immediate aid to debtors—particularly farmers and homeowners. By October 22, 1933, the President was able to say in his fourth fireside chat to the nation: ". . . if there is any family in the United States about to lose its home or about to lose its chattels, that family should telegraph at once either to the Farm Credit Administration or the Home Owners Loan Corporation in Washington requesting their help."

This announcement by the President was meant to inform those farmers and homeowners who had not already heard the good news, that the government was in the money-lending business. For the time being, at least, the familiar thud of the auctioneer's hammer sounding the forced sale of farm property need no longer be feared by the farmer; the burden of excessively high farm interest payments was now lightened considerably—the government was in the money-lending business. In the four-year period from May, 1933, to September, 1937, the Farm Credit Administration made loans of over two billion dollars to more than half a million farmers. Through its refinancing program, thousands of farms that had been in imminent danger of foreclosure were saved; thousands of farmers who had been groaning under the weight of high interest rates of 6, 8 and even 12 per cent were now breathing easier with interest charges of from 5 to 3½ per cent on their government loans—a total saving to the borrowers of over $70,000,000 per year; in about one third of all relieved cases, the FCA was able to force through a scaling down of the debt owed by the farmers—a total of over $200,000,000 was lopped off in scale-downs.

Was all this accomplished at the expense of the creditors? Did the money saved by the poor come out of the pockets of the rich? No, the New Deal was not a revolution in economics. Debt relief was cheering news not only to impoverished farmers but also to worried creditors—mainly insurance companies and banks. They were supposed to get 6 to 12 per cent interest on the money they had lent to the farmers, but for several years they had not been getting it. Foreclosure was not much good to them. The drop in land values meant that after foreclosing they would have on their hands property worth less than the amount of the loan. Sales at auction had ended in disaster—the embattled farmers often banded together to see to it that no bidder made the mistake of shouting a bid ap-

proaching even a quarter of what the property was worth. Debt relief, therefore, meant creditor relief as well. To be able to exchange a practically worthless high-interest mortgage paper for a government-guaranteed low-interest bond was good fortune indeed.

The same opportunity was given to the holders of mortgages on nonfarm homes whose owners were in distress. In signing the "Home Owners Loan Act of 1933" the President stated: "The Act extends the same principle of relief to home-owners as we have already extended to farm-owners. Furthermore, the Act extends this relief not only to people who have borrowed money on their homes but also to their mortgage creditors."

The New Deal was a revolution in ideas. As early as 1891 Germany had set up an old-age insurance scheme, but as late as August, 1935, the United States, the richest country in the world, had made no permanent provision for its needy old people. As early as 1911 England had introduced a national unemployment insurance scheme, but as late as August, 1935, the United States, the country with the largest number of unemployed in the world, had made no permanent provision for workers who lost their jobs. Permanent provision for old age and unemployment insurance came to the United States for the first time with the signing on August 14, 1935, of the Social Security Act, a New Deal measure. Mr. Roosevelt had reason to boast in a broadcast speech on the third anniversary of the Act: "If the people, during these years, had chosen a reactionary administration or a 'do nothing' Congress, social security would still be in the conversational stage, a beautiful dream which might come true in the dim distant future."

Old-age security and unemployment compensation were the main features of the Social Security Act, but provisions were also made in it for aid to the blind, aid to dependent and crippled children, maternal and child health services, public health, and vocational rehabilitation. The Social Security Board was created to administer the most important parts of the Act; the others were to be administered by existing federal agencies already in the field. Only old-age insurance was to be the direct responsibility of the Federal government; all the other types of aid were to be the joint responsibility of the federal and state governments in co-operation, with power given to the Social Security Board to approve federal grants to states, outline policies, and set standards.

Between old- age assistance and old-age insurance there was a difference. In the first, dependent old people, whether wage earners or not, were to receive cash allowances from the state—approximately one half of the money being paid out of local and state funds, the other half a federal grant. Public assistance of this type, granted on the basis of need, was not new in America. Old-age insurance, on the other hand, was new in America. Its benefits were based on previous earnings and were paid as a matter of right. Under the insurance scheme, both workers and employers paid equal amounts into a fund, which, from 1940 on, was to be drawn on for monthly benefits for the workers after they had reached the age of sixty-five. The benefits ranged from $10 to $85 per month, depending upon the total amount of wages previously earned by the worker. The plan went into effect on January 1, 1937, and fifteen months later over thirty-eight million social-security accounts were in the files. Not all workers were eligible—not covered were agricultural labor, domestic servants, casual labor, maritime labor, employees in nonprofit-making institutions (for example, teachers, religious workers), and government employees.

The same groups of workers were exempted from the provisions of the unemployment-insurance scheme. Under the law, qualified workers who were laid off or lost their jobs were to receive weekly payments, not equal in amount to their regular pay, but based on it. Since unemployment insurance, unlike old-age insurance, was not a national system but a federal-state system, the provisions for the amount and duration of benefits and for the waiting period varied. Benefits were, however, usually equal to about 50 per cent of the worker's weekly wage, with a maximum of $15 and a minimum of $5, and they generally ran for about sixteen weeks. By July 1, 1937, every state in the Union had an approved unemployment-compensation law. In 1938 three and a half million workers had received benefits under the law amounting to $400,000,000.

The Social Security Act was a step in the right direction. But it was only a step. It was badly drawn and in some parts unworkable. It left millions of needy people unprotected. But most serious of all, this act, supposedly designed to meet the challenge of insecurity, fell far short of its aim. Here was an "insurance" program which insured a low standard of living, nothing more. The New Deal was a revolution in ideas. It was not a revolution in economics.

"To Put People Back to Work"

★————————————————————————————★

It is the doctor's first job to ease the pain of his patient. His next task is to do what he can to make him recover. Relief had eased the patient's pain. The New Deal medicines for recovery were labeled AAA, NRA, and PWA.

The history of the case was interesting. One item of great importance commanded attention. It appeared that even when the patient had been in the best of health—in the vigorous twenties—he had had trouble with his breadbasket. Now with the patient flat on his back, the diagnosis showed a cancer had developed. In 1932 "the largest farm population in the nation's history had the smallest farm cash income" on record.

Of the many contributing causes of the disease, one was quickly apparent—the decline of the foreign market. During World War I the farmers in the United States had taken advantage of their opportunities to feed the warring nations of the world. The slogan "Food will win the war" was sweet music in the farmers' ears. To help win the war—and line their own pockets—they added some forty million acres of grasslands to their already cultivated area. That was not too much—during the war. But after the war the added bushels of wheat, pounds of tobacco, and bales of cotton found fewer buyers—and the prices dropped. Sales to foreign countries brought American farmers almost $3,500,000,000 in 1920; five years later that figure was down to a little over $2,000,000,000; and in 1932, it was only $662,000,000.

The fact that they were not selling as much of their goods abroad as they had in the past did not mean that the farmers produced less. They continued to produce in as great quantities as before, and the result was a mountain of unsold produce—farm surpluses. As long as these export surpluses existed, the prices of farm goods on the domestic market had to go down. And go down they did. When the depression came, the domestic market was weakened further. The people in the United States had less money than ever before to buy the cotton, tobacco, hides, wheat, etc., which the farmer produced. Nevertheless, the farmers continued to produce as much as formerly. The lower prices went, the more the farmers felt they had to produce in order to pay their high fixed charges—interest, taxes, etc.

The desperate plight of the farmers did not go unnoticed by Mr. Hoover. In 1929 the Federal Farm Board was set up with a fund of $500,000,000 to be used to increase farm prices. The Farm Board tried—and failed. It bought millions of bushels of surplus wheat and millions of bales of surplus cotton. It asked the farmers to reduce their acreage. The farmers did not do so. The result was that while the slump in prices was checked for a little while, it did not stay checked. After a few years of operation, the Federal Farm Board was licked. Its warehouses were full of unsold farm products which finally had to be dumped on the market at prices far below cost. The Federal Treasury stood the loss. Mr. Hoover's method had ended in collapse.

The New Deal Administration, too, turned its attention to the serious problem of too much farm produce at too low prices. Salvation for the farmers was an important part of his recovery program, Mr. Roosevelt told his listeners in the fourth fireside chat on October 22, 1933:

How are we constructing the edifice of recovery—the temple . . . dedicated to and maintained for a greater social justice, a greater welfare for America—the habitation of a sound economic life? We are building, stone by stone, the columns which will support that habitation. . . .

We all know that immediate relief for the unemployed was the first essential of such a structure. . . .

Another pillar in the making is the Agricultural Adjustment Administration. I have been amazed by the extraordinary degree of co-operation given to the Government by the cotton farmers in the South, the wheat farmers of the West, the tobacco farmers of the Southeast, and I am confident that the corn-hog farmers of the Middle West will come through in the same magnificent fashion.

There was a reason for "the extraordinary degree of co-operation" given by the farmers to the Agricultural Adjustment Administration (AAA). With this New Deal agency for handling the problem of farm recovery, Mr. Roosevelt wanted to do what Mr. Hoover's Federal Farm Board had tried to do—raise the prices of farm products.

NEGRO FIELD HAND

But the AAA did not make the Farm Board's mistake of attempting to raise prices without at the same time controlling production. The AAA realized that *both* prices and production had to be controlled or the scheme would fall through. Where the Farm Board had *asked* the farmers to reduce acreage, the AAA *paid* them for doing so. The result was that what the farmers did not do for the Federal Farm Board they did do for the AAA.

Under the terms of the Agricultural Adjustment Act, signed by the President on May 12, 1933, voluntary agreements to curtail production were to be signed by the farmers. To those who signed the agreements to reduce their acreage or otherwise limit their production to a stipulated amount, the Federal Government would give a subsidy. At first, benefit payments were made only on seven basic commodities—wheat, cotton, corn, hogs, rice, tobacco, milk. Later cattle, peanuts, rye, barley, flax, sugar beets, and sugar cane were added. The commodities first selected were chosen because our farmers produced a surplus for export of nearly all of them, and also because they had to go through some manufacturing process before they came to the consumer's table. That was important since the money for the benefit payments was raised through a "processing tax." On every hog slaughtered, every bushel of wheat milled, every pint of milk canned, every pound of cotton spun, the processors (that is, the meat packers, millers, canners, etc.) paid a tax. This tax money was the money that went to the farmers in the form of benefit payments. Of course the tax did not really come out of the pockets of the processors. They promptly added the amount of the tax to the cost of the goods, so that it was, in reality, the consumers who paid.

That part of the Act disturbed many people, but it was the reduction feature which brought the most hostile criticism. Once the plan was under way, crop limitation could be planned ahead before actual planting began. But in the spring of 1933 cotton already planted and pigs already grown had to be destroyed. Some four million bales of cotton from crops then growing were removed from production, about 20 per cent of the wheat crop was not raised, and over six million young pigs were slaughtered (the pork was later distributed to relief families). People who had never before been aware of the way the capitalist system operated were now aroused. Severe condemnation came from every quarter when the policy of "killing little pigs" and "plowing under cotton" was put into effect.

Denunciation of the program by those people who believed in a system of production for use was justified. They had a right to point to the bitter irony of destroying food and clothing in a period of starvation. But believers in the capitalist system had no right to criticize. For profitability was the touchstone of capitalist economy and the goal of the AAA planners was to restore profitability. Theirs was not a new method. They were following the pattern set for them by monopoly manufacturers—the pattern of gearing production to effective demand, the pattern of raising prices through scarcity. Manufacturers had long followed the practice of turning their workers into the streets and letting their machines lie idle when their products could not be sold at a profit. What was that but a policy of deliberate limitation? The AAA was simply trying to help the farmers do what the industrialists had learned to do for themselves.

As Mr. Roosevelt put it: "We have been producing more of some crops than we can consume or can sell in a depressed world market. The cure is not to produce so much. Without our help the farmers cannot get together and cut production, and the Farm Bill gives them a method of bringing their production down to a reasonable level and of obtaining reasonable prices for their crops."

Within the framework of the profit system there was nothing wrong with the policy of "plowing under." It would have made more sense, of course, if the New Deal had embarked, instead, on a long-range program of crop expansion rather than curtailment, on a policy of feeding all the hungry and clothing all the naked. But such a program would have involved far-reaching changes in every direction—the substitution of production for use for production for profit. To replace capitalism with socialism was not, however, the goal of the Roosevelt Administration. The New Deal was not a revolution in economics.

Did the AAA crop-reduction program help the farmers along the road to recovery? Probably. It was difficult to determine exactly to what extent because Nature, a much more effective crop-reducer than the AAA, had put in a few hard licks, too. Whether the drought which came in 1934 and again in 1936 deserved more or less credit than the AAA for the improved position of the farmers could not be proven. But what could be proven was that the farmers were better off than they had been before the New Deal—and they continued to be better off after the drought was over. The figures were conclusive:

ESTIMATED ANNUAL CASH INCOME
(IN MILLIONS OF DOLLARS)

Year	From Sale of Farm Products	Government Payments	Total
1932	4,328	0	4,328
1933	4,955	162	5,117
1934	5,792	556	6,348
1935	6,507	583	7,090
1936	7,657	287	7,944
1937	8,233	367	8,600

The patient was back on his feet. The growth of the cancer was checked. Every year of the New Deal had meant more money for the farmers, until, by 1937, their cash income was almost twice what it had been in 1932! Higher prices for their goods were one of the factors which were responsible for their greater income. But if the farmers had also to pay higher prices for the things they bought, then they would be no better off. In fact, the stated aim of the AAA was not simply to increase farm prices but rather "to re-establish prices to farmers at a level that will give agricultural commodities a purchasing power with respect to articles that farmers buy, equivalent to the purchasing power of agricultural commodities in the base period. The base period in the case of all agricultural commodities except tobacco shall be the pre-war period, August 1909–July 1914." (Base period for tobacco, 1919–29.)

Put more simply, this meant that it was the purchasing power of the farmer's dollar that was to be increased—until it was equal to what it had been in 1909–14; that, if in 1910 it took two bushels of the farmer's wheat to get him a monkey wrench, the AAA wanted it to take two bushels in 1933, not four bushels or five. The real test, then, of whether or not the New Deal program had brought recovery to the farmer was in the ratio of the prices he received for the goods he sold to the prices he paid for the goods he bought. The index number told the story of the steady climb of the farmer's dollar toward greater purchasing power.

Year	Ratio (%) of Prices Received to Prices Paid
1909–1914	100 (Base period)
1932	61
1933	64
1934	73
1935	86
1936	92
1937	93

There was no doubt, from the figures, that a good measure of recovery had come to the farmers. What was not clear from the figures, however, was how much increased income went to which people. For the word "farmers" is a very broad term—it includes not only agricultural landlords and big commercial farmers, but also tenants, sharecroppers, and farm laborers. The figures showed that annual cash income had almost doubled. But the figures did not show that that increased cash income was distributed equally among all the farmers. Recovery had, indeed, come to the landlords and large owners who received most of the increased farm income; it may or may not have come to the tenants, sharecroppers, and laborers who received least of the increased farm income.

But if only a beginning was made in the task of salvaging impoverished humans, a sizable step was taken in the salvaging of impoverished land. And impoverished the land was—some two hundred million acres, according to a government survey, were badly deteriorated through overcropping and overgrazing. Much of the land was already ruined by erosion and more would be unless protected immediately. A tall story from the West made plain what was happening to the land in some areas:

"A Kansas farmer stopped at a bank to see if he could get a loan on his farm. 'It might be arranged,' said the banker. 'I'll drive out with you and appraise it.'

" 'You needn't bother,' said the farmer, noticing a huge cloud of dust rolling down the road. 'Here it comes now.' "

A soil-conservation program on a nationwide scale was needed. It became government policy with the signing of the Soil Conservation and Domestic Allotment Act, on February 29, 1936. A month earlier the Agricultural Adjustment Act had been declared unconstitutional by the Supreme Court. The Soil Conservation Act was, in effect, the old Act in new dress with the emphasis on soil conservation and more scientific use of the land. Benefit payments were to go to those farmers who planted soil-conserving crops in place of soil-depleting crops. This really meant crop reduction old style since the soil-depleting crops which were to be taken out of cultivation were wheat, corn, cotton, tobacco—crops of which there was a surplus.

Had the AAA merely asked the farmers to co-operate in saving their soil, it is doubtful whether much progress would have been made. But as it was, the government authorities were in a position to pay them for their co-operation. The happy result was that the soil was being built up, the farmers were being paid for doing it, and AAA was still in the saddle driving toward recovery with its production-control program.

But a big hurdle would have to be leaped before the goal could be reached. Agriculture and industry were intertwined. Recovery could not come to agriculture unless it came to industry as well. And industry was in a state of collapse. There were more materials, men, machinery, and money idle than ever before in the country's history. What to do?

Businessmen had an answer—help business. In this depression, as always, "fair" competition had become "unfair" competition. There were fewer consumers' dollars and the fight to get them had become a real war. Manufacturers had tried to cut costs by lengthening hours and cutting wages. Sweatshops had thrived. Prices had tumbled until in some industries goods were even sold below cost. Unfair competition had become "cutthroat" competition. Business needed help.

Workers had an answer—help the workers. In this depression, as always, workers had suffered most. Many of them had lost their jobs. Those who were lucky enough to keep their jobs found they had to work longer hours for less pay. Their standard of living had dropped down and down until it had become a standard of dying. Their unions were crumbling to pieces. Workers needed help.

The President's "Brain Trust" had an answer—help both employers and workers. The National Industrial Recovery Act (NIRA) was the New Deal scheme for bringing recovery to industry. Its purpose was described by the President on June 16, 1933: "The law I have just signed was passed *to put people back to work*, to let them buy more of the products of farms and factories and start our business at a living rate again. . . .

"Throughout industry, the change from starvation wages and starvation employment to living wages and sustained employment can, in large part, be made by an industrial covenant to which all employers shall subscribe. . . .

"We are relaxing some of the safeguards of the anti-trust laws . . . we are putting in place of old principles of unchecked competition some new Government controls. . . . Their purpose is to free business, not to shackle it."

The emergency situation had brought forth an emergency measure —a plan for control by the government of the entire industrial structure of the United States. A plan which was designed to give both employers and workers what they wanted. Employers wanted the right to do openly what some monopolists had succeeded in doing secretly—to get together in every industry to put an end to cutthroat competition, overproduction, and resultant low prices. The antitrust laws were in the way. NIRA "suspended" the antitrust laws.

Workers wanted more jobs, more money, shorter hours, and the right to organize into unions to protect these gains once they had them. NIRA abolished child labor—to make more jobs for men and women; it established minimum wages and maximum hours; it gave workers legal protection in the right to organize.

To administer the provisions of NIRA the National Recovery Administration (NRA) was set up. It asked the employers in every industry to get together in their trade associations and draft a "code of fair competition" which was to govern each industry. As soon as a code was submitted, NRA held public hearings to give consumers and workers and any other interested persons a chance to approve or disapprove the provisions of the code, and suggest additions. After the code in its final form was approved by the President or the NRA administrator, it became a law applicable to the whole industry. Then, for its enforcement, a Code Authority was set up. Usually, since NRA believed in the principle of "self-government in industry," the members of the Code Authority were trade-association representatives of the employers.

The codes submitted for the different industries varied in detail, but all of them contained some provisions dealing with trade practices and labor. Since the employers themselves drafted the codes, the provisions generally were those the employers wanted. In one way or another, in the trade-practice provisions, the employers made certain that production was controlled and prices raised.

The labor provisions differed for different industries. Where labor in a certain industry was strongly organized, it could, at the public hearing, fight for and win for itself higher minimum wages and a shorter work week. Where labor in a certain industry was not strong, the employers had a field day—minimum wages were low and the work week long. But every code under NIRA had to contain Section 7a, which gave the workers "the right to organize and bargain collectively through representatives of their own choosing."

There was no doubt that NRA helped, along with the other accomplishments of the New Deal, to change the mood of the country from despair to hope. Even if the performance did not equal the promise, it did, nevertheless, achieve a partial success. NRA did not make business thrive, but it helped to put it back on its feet; it did not begin to solve the problem of unemployment, but it did increase employment some: it did not give all workers "the wages of decent living," but it did raise the wages of the lowest paid; it did not enforce the provisions of Section 7a, but it did help the organization of labor.

NRA was designed to promote recovery. Did it succeed or fail? Unfortunately this could not be determined precisely. Recovery did, indeed, come during the period of its operation. But that recovery was due, more certainly, not to that part of NRA which has been discussed so far, but rather to Title II of NIRA—the part which created the Public Works Administration (PWA).

Billions of dollars of government money were provided to finance the largest single construction program the United States (or, in fact, the world) had ever seen. In the forty-eight states that make up the United States of America there are 3071 counties. Four years after it was launched, PWA had furnished funds for over 26,000 construction projects in every state, in all but three counties. About three fifths of the projects were federal—carried on by federal agencies themselves with direct allotments of over one billion five hundred million dollars. Even more money was allotted to the remaining projects, which were nonfederal—carried on by municipalities with loans or outright gifts from PWA. Eighty per cent of all public construction in the United States in this four year period was made possible by PWA.

This is what the recovery agency meant in terms of useful projects of lasting value to the nation:

Public buildings
Slum clearance
Water conservation
Flood control
River and harbor improvements
Coast defense
Vessels
Bridges
Reclamation projects
Post offices
Hospitals
Schools
Housing projects
Power projects
Dams

The PWA design for recovery was plain. Men were idle. Machines were idle. Private industry was flat on its back. The government could revive industry through large-scale spending on public works. Government spending would prime the pump of business activity. To carry through to completion the thousands of government construction projects, men and materials would be needed. Direct employment on government projects would indirectly create employment in private industry, which would supply the materials. (Experience proved that employment resulting indirectly from the PWA program was two and one-half times as great as the direct employment). In addition to the prevailing wages paid to the workers on the government projects, there would be the wages paid to the workers in the stimulated private industries (plus the wages paid to relief workers on WPA). Money would be in circulation again. Workers with money in their pay envelopes would do what idle workers could not do—buy consumers' goods. They would have purchasing power—the wherewithal to pay for the things they needed. The products of farm and factory would be sold again.

It happened. Recovery came. The country felt it. The statistics proved it. And the statistics also proved that it was the government spending program which was chiefly responsible. For when, toward the end of 1936 and early in 1937, government expenditures were sharply curtailed, another depression set in. The drop in industrial production, more precipitous even than that of 1929, showed how sensitive a plant recovery was.

The same picture shows up in other key statistics, such as employment and pay rolls in manufacturing industries, freight car loadings, etc. The same picture in the stomachs and minds of the people. Government spending had made jobs. Government spending had put money into people's pockets. Government spending had brought about what economists called "consumer recovery." When government spending was slashed, the recovery movement was slashed.

Not all had eyes to see, however. The poor could see—government spending had given them jobs, money, food, clothing, shelter, hope.

The rich could not see—government spending, to them, was ruining the country. To get the billions of dollars which went into government spending for public works and relief, the government resorted to borrowing. The lending-spending program which had primed the pump of business activity was a borrowing program on a

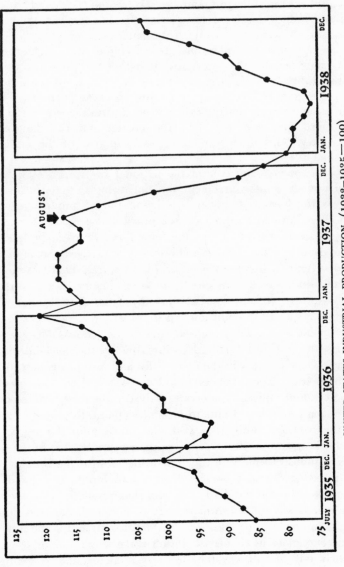

UNITED STATES INDUSTRIAL PRODUCTION (1923–1925=100)

large scale. And such borrowing meant an increase in the national debt and—horror of horrors!—an "unbalanced budget." And an "unbalanced budget" surely meant inflation, and loss of credit, and bankruptcy, and a host of other dreadful calamities.

The argument was plausible. It convinced—and frightened—a great many people. They were told that they had only to consider their own financial dealings to see how dangerous was the government's program of borrowing for lending-spending purposes. When their income was greater than their expenditures they were well off. The more they got into debt the greater was the danger of bankruptcy. This, they were told, was also true of the national government.

It was, however, not true of the national government. The real point was what the government was borrowing the money for. As long as the borrowed money was being put to productive uses, then there was no danger of bankruptcy. Some of the borrowed money had been used to save the homes and farms of the people of the country. Part of that money would be returned. Some of the borrowed money had been spent on public works. That was money not thrown away but invested—in power plants, dams, tunnels, schools, bridges, decent houses. What the critics of the government program neglected to point out was that there were two sides to the government books. They pointed only to the red-ink side—the liabilities, the cost. But balanced against this was the black-ink side— the assets, the increase in the real wealth and income of the people.

The rich who could not—or would not—see, had no criticism of a corporation of capitalists in private industry when it embarked on a borrowing program to build, to expand its plant, to produce goods. On the contrary. This, they said, was an occasion for rejoicing, for throwing caps in the air, for singing hymns of praise to the captains of industry who were thus providing jobs for the people. But when the government borrowed money to build, to expand its plants, to raise the standard of living, thus providing jobs for the people, that was a different matter. That, they said, was an occasion for gloom, for hanging crape on the door, for attending the funeral of the once-glorious country. It didn't make sense.

Their talk of runaway inflation was nonsense, too. A brilliant young economist made that clear: ". . . they tell us that an increasing government debt is the high road to disastrous inflation . . .

they fail to explain that all the runaway inflations on record either accompanied or followed a period of war during which national wealth and human resources were both wantonly destroyed."

Our national debt was increasing. True. But in relation to national income it was still only about one fourth of the British national debt; and our debt per capita (adding together state, local, and national) was less than two thirds of the British per capita debt. Moreover, the important question is not so much the absolute size of the debt, but rather how much does the interest on the debt cost us per year in dollars and cents of taxes, *i.e.*, what is the debt burden? Again, the facts were conclusive. Long before World War II the British taxpayer was paying four times as much as the American to meet the burden of debt interest. Yet our "inflation bugs" did not, then, notice any sign of inflation in England—or, if they did, they conveniently kept it to themselves.

And in spite of all the cries of alarm about the blows to our government's credit because of its huge borrowings, the Federal Treasury was able to dispose of government bonds at lower rates of interest than ever before in the country's history. That was an important fact, since it tended to indicate that the rich—the loudest critics—did not themselves believe their own talk of the disaster to come because of the spending program. They were eager to put their money into government bonds. There was little doubt that much of their criticism came from political rather than immediate economic considerations. They hated Roosevelt. They were out to discredit him and scrap the New Deal program, and any stick was good enough to beat him with.

The public spending program was not perfect. Far from it. But the criticism to be made of it was precisely the opposite of what had been made. It was inadequate not because the government borrowed and spent too much but rather because the government did not borrow and spend enough. It is true that it was Congress that was responsible for the cuts made in the spending program. Nevertheless, it is also true that at no time did the President even *ask for* an amount that was anywhere near what was needed. Mr. Roosevelt had failed by his own standard, set in the second fireside chat of 1934:

"I stand or fall by my refusal to accept as a necessary condition of our future a permanent army of unemployed. On the contrary, we must make it a national principle that we will not tolerate a large army of unemployed and that we will arrange our national economy to end our present unemployment as soon as we can and then to take wise measures against its return. I do not want to think that it is the destiny of any American to remain permanently on relief rolls."

These were brave words. But they pointed to a goal which had not been reached. Despite all of Mr. Roosevelt's worth-while efforts,

"a large army of unemployed" continued to exist throughout his first two terms in office. It never numbered less than eight million people. It would have been greater but for the public spending program. It would have been smaller had that spending program been truly adequate.

The New Dealers looked upon unemployment as an emergency condition, so they thought of public spending as an emergency program. That was a mistake. The breakdown of the profit system meant that it was to be the destiny of many Americans to be permanently unemployed. What was needed was immediately to launch a permanent program of public spending on a gigantic scale—a program which would make full use of the nation's human and material resources; and ultimately to abolish the profit system. What the New Deal did, however, was to take only a halting step in the direction of alleviation of the unemployment problem. It was not a revolution in economics.

"Let the Seller Also Beware"

★——★

Relief and Recovery were not enough. To remedy an existing bad situation was only one part of the job that faced Mr. Roosevelt. To cope with the evils that had led to the situation in the first place was another. Those New Deal measures which aimed at correcting old abuses are considered here under the heading of Reform.

In actual practice, as we have seen, the program of the New Deal was not separated into the three distinct parts—Relief, Recovery, and Reform. WPA, for example, was both a relief and a recovery measure, while PWA construction and Soil Conservation were often a combination of all three. So with the other parts of the New Deal program. The major purpose of some measures was relief or recovery or reform, but often one or both of the other purposes were also served.

The housing program was a good illustration. It began as part of PWA. It was thought of as an aid to recovery. It was that—and more. The eradication of slums and the construction of low-cost housing were, without question, reform measures as well.

It was paradoxical that the richest country in the world should have worse slums than most of the world, but it was a fact. In his second inaugural address in 1937, Mr. Roosevelt pointed out that, while gains had undoubtedly been made, much still remained to be done: "Let us ask again: Have we reached the goal of our vision of that fourth day of March 1933? Have we found our happy valley?

"I see a great nation upon a great continent blessed with a great wealth of natural resources. . . .

"But here is a challenge to our democracy: In this nation I see tens of millions of its citizens—a substantial part of its whole population —who at this very moment are denied the greater part of what the very lowest standards of today call the necessities of life. . . .

"I see one-third of a nation ill-housed, ill-clad, ill-nourished."

Mr. Roosevelt saw correctly. One third of the nation was ill housed. There was no dispute about the fact. It was plain to people in their own cities; it was obvious to any passenger looking out of a window on a railroad train. Slum dwellers everywhere. Millions of people living under indecent, unhealthful conditions. There was need for reform. There was need for a program of rehousing which would move people out of the slums into decent low-rent houses. Such a program for slum clearance would mean the saving of human lives. And what was less important but equally true—it would mean the saving of money. Slums were disease and crime breeders. Municipalities paid dearly for their neglect of the slum problem in extra costs for added hospitals, added policemen, added jails. One investigation after another in town and country, North, South, East, and West, proved the point:

Jacksonville, Florida—"nearly one-third of all major crimes were committed in a slum section covering less than 2 percent of the city's area."

Detroit, Michigan—"a 50-block area, chosen for clearance and re-housing, shows a crime rate seven and one-half times the city average, a juvenile delinquency rate more than ten times the city average, and a tuberculosis rate six and one-half times the city average."

New York City—"a five-year study disclosed that three out of four babies in the tenement population had rickets."

Birmingham, Alabama—"1933 survey showed that the city spent in nine slum areas six times as much as it received in taxes from those areas."

And the figures for rural areas showed that housing conditions in the country districts were even worse than in the cities!

European nations faced with the slum problem had embarked on public housing programs immediately after World War I, but in the United States practically nothing had been done.

When the RFC was set up under Mr. Hoover in 1932, it was given the right to make loans on housing projects. It made only one. Then came the New Deal—and the job of clearing the slums and providing decent homes for low-income families was at last begun.

In 1937, the United States Housing Authority (USHA) was set up to carry on the work along the lines proven successful in European countries. Under USHA, the Federal Government did no building itself. Instead, it made loans and grants to local housing authorities established by city or county governments. Of the amount needed for construction USHA loaned up to 90 per cent, and the remainder was to be raised by the local authority. In addition, annual contributions were made by both the local authority and USHA in the ratio of 1 to 5 to keep the rentals in the projects within reach of the "lowest-income group." This annual contribution of the local authority was usually made by granting tax exemption to the project.

USHA's program of government-assisted, low-rent housing was strikingly successful. Construction costs were restricted by law to $1000 a room or $4000 a dwelling unit (in cities of over 500,000, the limitation was $1250 and $5000). Rents in USHA housing developments ranged from $2.00 to $5.25 per room per month. For "decent, safe, and sanitary dwellings" these rentals were lower than had ever before been achieved by either public or private builders. Eight dollars per month for a four-room house or flat was within the reach of slum dwellers whose income might be as low as $450 a year. The USHA program was moving people from substandard dwellings to decent homes. It was clearing the slums.

But it was not clearing them fast enough. As with most other New Deal measures, a step in the right direction—but only a step—had been taken. Slum clearance in Great Britain was also moving slowly but because the problem there had been tackled as far back as 1918, over one million new low-rent dwelling units had been constructed under the government-assisted local authority plan. That meant rehousing for 4,500,000 people or 10 per cent of the population. In contrast, USHA's appropriation of $800,000,000 for a three-year program would move only half a million people from slums to decent houses. With "one-third of the nation ill-housed" that was nothing more than a drop in the bucket.

If the New Deal merely scratched the surface in its program for slum clearance, it went considerably deeper in its program for the regional development of the Tennessee Valley. For years there had been a bitter dispute in the country concerning the government plant at Muscle Shoals on the Tennessee River in Alabama. Originally acquired in 1918, as a wartime measure, for the production of nitrates, the dam, powerhouse, and nitrate plants had lain idle while the friends and foes of government operation carried on their debate in Congress. Twice the advocates of government operation led by the great Senator Norris of Nebraska had succeeded in having bills passed providing for government production and distribution of power and the manufacture of fertilizers at Muscle Shoals. On both occasions the foes of government operation had succeeded in blocking the measure through presidential vetoes—in 1928 by Mr. Coolidge, and in 1931 by Mr. Hoover. In his veto message to the Senate on March 3, 1931, the "engineer President" voiced his horror at the thought of government invasion of the private power companies' field. For the Federal Government to enter the business of producing and distributing power and manufacturing fertilizer was "to break down the initiative and enterprise of the American people; it is destruction of equality of opportunity of our people; it is the negation of the ideals upon which our civilization is based."

But Mr. Roosevelt was not alarmed. The only thing wrong with the plan, as he saw it, was that it was too narrow. Where Mr. Hoover saw breakdown of the enterprise of the people, Mr. Roosevelt saw an opportunity for the regeneration of the whole Tennessee Valley area. On April 10, 1933, he asked Congress to widen the scope of the scheme: "It is clear that the Muscle Shoals development is but a small part of the potential public usefulness of the entire Tennessee River. Such use, if envisioned in its entirety, transcends mere power development; it enters the wide fields of flood control, soil erosion, afforestation, elimination from agricultural use of marginal lands, and distribution and diversification of industry. In short, this power development of war leads logically to national planning for a complete river watershed involving many States and the future lives and welfare of millions. It touches and gives life to all forms of human concerns."

Mr. Roosevelt boldly asked the Congress to create a Tennessee Valley Authority (TVA) to plan for the proper use of the land and the waters of the seven states in the basin of the Tennessee—an area about the size of England and Scotland. One month later Congress passed the Tennessee Valley Authority Act and the greatest experiment in regional planning in the history of the country was begun.

The key questions in any planning program are three: What do we have to work with? What do we need? What can we do with what we have to get what we need?

TVA had a great river—the fourth largest in volume of flow in the country—draining twenty-six million acres of land on which three quarters of the population were engaged in farming. It was a mighty river, but its wild strength was uncontrolled. Its great volume of water, pouring into the Ohio, frequently forced that river to overflow its banks, causing flood damage to the extent of almost two million dollars annually. Its periods of winter floods were followed by periods of summer drought, when the waters ran low and navigation was impossible. Its tremendous power resources were largely wasted. The farms and the farmers in the Valley were poor. The land on more than one third of the total acreage had already been partially or wholly destroyed through erosion.

What was needed was a method of saving the soil, conserving the resources, and increasing the wealth of the region. What was needed was a method of aiding the farmers to get more out of their land, to provide better means of transportation for their products, to encourage old industries and bring new ones into the Valley.

TVA had a plan for doing what was needed. The most important part of the plan was to tame the mighty river, to harness its wild energy so that it would perform the necessary tasks. Engineers were called in, and construction was begun on a series of storage dams on the tributaries of the river, and of high navigation dams on the Tennessee itself.

The dams served a threefold purpose—flood control, navigation, and power production. The water was stored up during floodtime and released when the flow in the river was scanty. The project has more than paid back its cost by the role it played in the reduction of floods in 1936 and 1937 and the winter of 1942 (and particularly in the production of much-needed power during World War II). The leveling off of seasonal fluctuations of the river was part of the plan for providing a great system of all-year-round navigation—the river was made into a highway carrying huge amounts of freight, and helping the inhabitants of the Valley directly by making it easier for them to sell their own goods and buy the goods of others.

The power-production phase of the projects was most familiar to Americans because of the bitter opposition to it by the private utility companies. The reason for their fierce attack was apparent —measured by the TVA "yardstick," they were charging far too much for electricity. Government production and distribution of power did not have the dire results predicted by Mr. Hoover and echoed by utility spokesmen—"the initiative and enterprise of the American people" were not broken down. What did happen was simply that government production and distribution of power brought cheaper electric current and more of it to the American people in the Valley. TVA rates per kilowatt-hour were just about half private power-company rates—2.14 cents average for Valley consumers compared to 4.21 cents average for the country.

What followed was interesting and important. Lowered rates per kilowatt-hour meant more electrical appliances bought and more kilowatt-hours used. The average number of kilowatt-hours used per year in the United States was 850 in 1939. But the average for the Valley's 340,000 users of TVA power was 1179 kilowatt-hours. As rates went down for TVA customers, they bought more refrigerators, toasters, washing machines, milking machines, etc. The sale of electrical appliances to TVA customers was $114,942 for August 1938. For August 1939, it was $912,231. The private power companies had run their business on the principle of selling less power at high rates; TVA had demonstrated that the exact opposite —selling more power at low rates—was better business. And behind the figures showing increased purchases of electrical appliances and the use of more electricity per consumer in the Valley than elsewhere in the United States was a picture of people relieved from drudgery. Electricity was a wonderful servant. Its increased use meant a better life for the inhabitants of the Valley.

This was particularly true of the farmers. In 1933, one Mississippi farm out of a hundred had electricity; in Georgia, one out of thirty-six; in Tennessee, one out of twenty-five. Ten years later one out of every five farmers in the TVA region had electricity (the region had become the second largest producer of power in the United States). Electricity meant even more on the farm than it did in city homes. It meant, for example, so necessary a service as running water in place of the old pump-and-carry system. The old power companies had not been interested in furnishing electric service to the rural inhabitants of the Valley, and such service when it was obtained was too expensive for most farmers. TVA changed all that. It was especially interested in providing cheap electricity to farmers. It brought the rural inhabitants conveniences they had never before enjoyed.

The success or failure of TVA had, in fact, to be measured by whether or not it was bringing prosperity to the farmers in its area. By that test, it was plain after a few years of operation that TVA was succeeding. Less well known than the power program to most people, but of great importance to the inhabitants of the Valley, was TVA's work in saving the soil. Erosion had started just after the Civil War. TVA checked it and began the difficult task of restoring millions of acres. It needed and obtained the voluntary co-

BLAST FURNACE

operation of thousands of farmers in its soil-conservation program. They have experimented with, and kept records of the performance of, metaphosphate—a remarkable new concentrated superphosphate developed by TVA engineers to solve the problem of producing a healthful plant food. The farmers needed no urging to co-operate with TVA. They had seen for themselves that from its laboratories were coming valuable aids in developing new and improving old farm practices. They observed that engineers were constantly at work on new industrial processing of farm products, on inventions particularly suited to the Valley's agricultural needs. TVA planning was improving their lot and they knew it.

The record of TVA in other fields was equally impressive. Its unified river management was able to serve the interests of the whole region, providing benefits in addition to flood control, navigation, and power production. By reducing water pollution it improved the quality of the water supply. Its lakes and public parks, intelligently managed and carefully looked after, made ideal vacation spots for camping, bathing, boating, and fishing. Its safety record on construction work, its labor relations, its general all-round efficiency gave the lie to the too-frequent charges that government operation must of necessity be badly administered.

TVA was America's great experiment in regional planning. It worked.

Another New Deal reform measure of which the same comforting words—"it worked"—could be written was the plan to protect depositors from loss by bank failures. The need had long been obvious for some sort of insurance scheme which would save the savings of the people in a country where bank crashes had been an everyday occurrence even before the depression. Efforts in that direction had been made by Congress as early as 1886, but nothing had come of them. The New Deal succeeded where previous administrations had failed.

Its banking legislation checked the wave of bank crashes. Then its Federal Deposit Insurance Corporation (FDIC) gave insurance against loss to depositors in those banks which finally went under in spite of everything that could be done to keep them solvent. The sign, DEPOSITS INSURED BY THE FEDERAL DEPOSIT INSURANCE CORPORATION, WASHINGTON, D. C., in his bank window was assurance to every depositor that, come what might, he was protected to the extent of $2500 (the limit was later raised to $5000). On January 1, 1934, the day that deposit insurance first became effective, 98 per cent of the 50,000,000 depositors in the 14,214 banks which were FDIC members were fully protected by the $2500 limitation.

What this reform meant to the great mass of people with small bank accounts was illustrated during the next three years when 166 insured banks found themselves "in difficulties." The old picture was one of terror and despair as queues of white-faced depositors stood about anxiously hoping against hope that the closed doors would open and their hard-earned savings would be restored. The new picture was different. Reorganization by FDIC officials. No weeping and wailing before closed bank doors. Often no closed doors at all. No interruption of services. Not a penny lost by the poor. Of the 259,000 depositors in the 166 banks, less than 600 were not fully protected against loss. The FDIC was the New Deal method of insuring depositors against loss by bank failures. It worked.

Efforts were made to protect the investing public, too. President Roosevelt called for reform in the conduct of the financial markets in a recommendation to Congress on March 29, 1933: "In spite of many State statutes the public in the past has sustained severe losses through practices neither ethical nor honest on the part of many corporations selling securities. . . .

"There is . . . an obligation upon us to insist that every issue of new securities to be sold in interstate commerce shall be accompanied by full publicity and information, and that no essentially important element attending the issue shall be concealed from the buying public.

"This proposal adds to the ancient rule of *caveat emptor,* the further doctrine of 'Let the seller also beware.' It puts the burden of telling the whole truth on the seller. It should give impetus to honest dealing in securities and thereby bring back public confidence."

The President's proposals were made into law with the passage of the Securities Act of 1933. The law attempted to give protection to the American investor in a manner similar to that afforded the English investor by the British Companies Act. It was not designed to stop the investor from taking risks. Nor did it give him insurance against loss. Its purpose was merely to protect him to the extent of letting him really know what he was buying. It did nothing more to the issuer of securities than require him to tell the whole truth about what he was selling. Before a new security issue could be offered to the investing public, the issuer had to register it with the

Securities and Exchange Commission (SEC) with full information concerning the issue and the house offering it for sale. In addition, a prospectus with the same detailed information in condensed form was to be given the prospective buyer. If in the opinion of SEC the information was false or misleading, then registration could be denied and the issue could not be floated.

Wall Street opposed the law. Bankers, brokers, corporation officials —our leading citizens—found a great many things wrong with it. These people would have been enraged if they had found that a sweater they had purchased was not 100 PER CENT WOOL as the tag indicated. Yet they were not even willing to put a tag on their own wares. They were asked to do nothing more than tell the truth—but they protested. It was very odd.

To provide still further protection to investors against the grosser frauds of 1929, SEC was given control over the stock exchanges of the country, with wide powers to correct unfair practices such as the making of "pools," the rigging of the market, manipulation by insiders—all the various tricks of the trade by which the "lambs were shorn" and the wolves waxed fat. The old notion that the members of stock exchanges, brokers, and corporation officials had the right to carry on their business with the public according to their own rules was replaced by the idea of proper regulation by SEC to the end that shady and destructive practices be eliminated.

That such regulation was essential was known to thousands of investors through sad experience; it was made obvious to the whole country through the criminal acts of Richard Whitney, one-time member of the Committee on Business Conduct and former president of the New York Stock Exchange. SEC investigated the Whitney case and wrote a report which contained a scathing attack on the dangerous philosophy which had dominated the affairs of the Exchange. "This attitude," the report ran, "that the Exchange was more of a private club than a public institution and that its responsibilities were to its members rather than to the nation of investors it served has had a long history. It was a well-entrenched customary attitude. But although it can thus be explained, it cannot be permitted to continue. Hence, we can properly condemn, and we do, the traditions which may explain that conduct."

SEC was aimed at reforming some of the abuses in the system of selling securities to investors. It worked.

From the wreck of the NRA (declared unconstitutional by the

Supreme Court on May 27, 1935) the New Dealers managed to salvage two other items of reform, important in the field of labor. Section 7a had declared that workers had the right to organize; and minimum wages, maximum hours, and the abolition of child labor had been written into the codes. These provisions, beneficial to labor, had been largely ineffective because under NRA they depended for their success on the "voluntary co-operation" of the employers. After the sinking of NRA by the Supreme Court, the labor provisions were enacted into laws and compulsion took the place of co-operation. The National Labor Relations Act—commonly called the Wagner Act—made specific the "unfair labor practices" of employers which were violations of labor's right to organize. The Fair Labor Standards Act of 1938—commonly called the Wage and Hour Law—was designed to abolish child labor and eliminate substandard conditions in industry. Both laws were needed.

The National Labor Relations Act (NLRA), signed by the President on July 5, 1935, was perhaps the most important of all New Deal legislation. It began with the recognition of the fact that "The denial by employers of the right of employees to organize, and the refusal by employers to accept the procedure of collective bargaining, lead to strikes and other forms of industrial strife or unrest which have the intent or the necessary effect of burdening or obstructing commerce. . . ." The theory behind the law was that protection of labor's right to organize and bargain collectively through representatives of its own choosing would serve to eliminate a major cause of industrial conflict. The heart of the Act was in Section 7 which, modeled after 7a of NIRA, *guaranteed* employees that right.

Unlike 7a, however, NLRA *specified* the practices of employers which had made that right empty in the past:

Section 8. It shall be an unfair labor practice for an employer
(1) To interfere with, restrain, or coerce employees in the exercise of the rights guaranteed in section 7.
(2) To dominate or interfere with the formation or administration of any labor organization or contribute financial or other support to it. . . .
(3) By discrimination in regard to hire or tenure of employment or any term or condition of employment to encourage or discourage membership in any labor organization. . . .
(4) To discharge or otherwise discriminate against an employee because he has filed charges or given testimony under this Act.
(5) To refuse to bargain collectively with the representatives of his employees, subject to the provisions of section 9 (a).

The representatives duly chosen by a majority of the workers were given the exclusive representation of the employees in a unit appropriate for collective bargaining. What that unit was to be—whether employer, craft, plant, or any subdivision of these—was to be determined by the National Labor Relations Board. This agency, consisting of three members appointed by the President, was to administer the law.

No New Deal measure has been so bitterly criticized as the National Labor Relations Act; no New Deal agency has been so bitterly attacked as the National Labor Relations Board. Nor did the employers who were in opposition stop at criticism and abuse alone. The record of their violations of the NLRA is ample proof that these upholders of law and order were themselves flagrant lawbreakers. Ordinarily, when an act is passed by Congress and duly signed by the President, it is the law of the land unless and until it is declared unconstitutional by the Supreme Court. But our best citizens reversed this procedure. Acting on the advice of fifty-eight Liberty League lawyers, they proceeded on the assumption that the law was unconstitutional. They did everything possible, through injunctions and legal entanglements of every kind, to sabotage enforcement of the Act by the board. It was only after April 12, 1937, when the Supreme Court upheld the constitutionality of the Act, that the board was able to make real headway.*

The charge was frequently made that the Act was "one-sided," that it gave everything to the employees and tied the hands of the employers completely. This was not true. The Act restricted employers' conduct in only one respect—where it was in conflict with the workers' right of self-organization and collective bargaining. The employer still dominated his employees in every other way. He could still discriminate against any of his workers, cut wages, introduce the speed-up, extend the working day, shut down the plant and move to another city—do any or all of these things for any reason, *except antiunionism.* (Where there was a union agreement in effect, the employer might be prohibited from doing most of these things, but it would be the union agreement, *not* the law, which stopped

* What antiunion employers failed to do for themselves after 1935, a reactionary Congress did for them twelve years later with the passage of the Taft-Hartley Bill which "altered" the act beyond recognition. "This bill would go far toward weakening our trade union movement," said President Truman in his veto message to Congress. It was passed over his veto on June 23, 1947.

him.) The Act did not regulate the whole field of employer-worker relationships. It did nothing more than give to workers legal protection of their rights to self-organization and collective bargaining.

From a reading of the sugared statements of our captains of industry it was difficult to understand why a law giving legal protection to the workers in their efforts to organize had to be passed at all. No dispute between capital and labor was ever complete without a pretty speech by the employer that he was not at all opposed to unionization or collective bargaining. But what these employers *said* and what they *did* were quite different matters.

What they *said* was always in terms of the "partnership of capital and labor." What they *did* was reflected in the statistics of the United

States Department of Labor, which showed that, in most of the strikes called in this country from 1934 through 1937, the major issues were not wages and hours, but matters pertaining to union organization and recognition.

What they *said* was illustrated by the silken phrases of Mr. Alfred P. Sloan, Jr. "The management of General Motors holds that there is no real conflict of interests between employers and employees. . . . Enlightened employers and enlightened employees realize that they have a mutuality of interests such as to dictate the wisdom of maintaining the highest degree of co-operation and harmonious relations."

What they *did* was illustrated by the fact that this "mutuality of interests" was not so great as to prevent this "enlightened employer," the General Motors Corporation, from paying almost a million dollars to spy agencies in a two-and-a-half-year period for reports on the union activities of its "enlightened employees."

What they *said* was that they were "always ready to talk things over with their men."

What they *did* was told in the decision of Chief Justice Hughes in the NLRB vs. Jones & Laughlin case. "Refusal to confer and negotiate has been one of the most prolific causes of strife. This is such an outstanding fact in the history of labor disturbance that it is a proper subject of judicial notice and requires no citation of instances."

Two years after the passage of the Wagner Act union membership was doubled. The jump in membership from 10 per cent of the organizable workers in 1935 to twice that figure in 1937 was traceable only in part to the NLRA. It was due, in great measure, to the appearance on the trade-union scene of the Congress of Industrial Organizations (CIO), and its emphasis on industrial unionism in place of the traditional craft-unionism policy of the American Federation of Labor. The wave of new unionism which came to Britain in 1889 was paralleled here after 1935.

It was long overdue. Organization of the skilled alone may have been suited to the industrial setup of the nineteenth century, but it was definitely not suited to the industrial setup of the fourth decade of the twentieth century. The increased use of machinery and the resultant leveling of skills had rendered strict adherence to the old craft-union policy obsolete. In the mass-production industries the belt system had almost entirely wiped out the boundaries within which the various skills had formerly been confined. To what extent skill had been eliminated as an essential factor in production was indicated by Henry Ford in his book, "My Life and Work," in which he stated that 43 per cent of all the jobs in his plant required not more than one day's training, 36 per cent from a day to a week, 20 per cent between a week and a year, and only 1 per cent not less than a year. The implications which these changes in industry had for the organizational technique and policy of trade-unions should have been plain to union leaders.

They were plain—to a few. These few submitted a minority resolution at the 1935 convention of the A. F. of L. which read in part: "We declare the time has arrived when common sense demands the organization policies of the American Federation of Labor must be molded to meet present day needs. In the great mass production industries and those in which the workers are composite mechanics, specialized and engaged upon classes of work which do not fully qualify them for craft union membership, industrial organization is the only solution. . . . Jurisdictional claims over small groups of workers in these industries prevent organization by breeding a fear

that when once organized the workers in these plants will be separated, unity of action and their economic power destroyed by requiring various groups to transfer to National and International Unions
organized upon craft lines."

The signers of the minority resolution were not guessing. They
knew what they were talking about. A halfhearted effort to organize
the unorganized in the mass-production industries had been made,
and it had failed. It had failed because the purpose behind the
"drive" had been not to organize powerful unions where they did
not exist but rather to get additional members for the already existing craft unions. The method employed was to put the workers in
the mass-production industries into federal locals, affiliated directly
with the A. F. of L. and controlled by its executive council. These
federal locals were looked upon by the A. F. of L. leaders as incubators
for the craft unions. When, through the efforts of hard-working rank-
and-file organizers, a brood of union members had been hatched
within a federal local, then craft officials would raid the local and
divide the membership on the basis of craft jurisdiction. The result
was disastrous—the federal local was broken up; the transferred members, disillusioned, withdrew from "their" new craft union; and
newly organized workers were again unorganized.

At the 1935 convention one delegate after another told the same
story. Delegate Lilly, Gas Distribution Workers Union, No. 15268:
". . . We come along and we organize our industry, and then your
crafts have come along and demanded their pound of flesh. I had
the experience with myself as president of my local. We had organized
these men and then the crafts came along and demanded that these
men be turned over to them within three months' time. Not one of
them that they took away from my union belonged to any union,
but they killed my union."

Delegate Addes, International Union, United Automobile Workers of America: "When we first organized our local we got into a dispute with the machinists. We worked together for a while until they
wanted to take everybody over and leave us the sweepers in the
plants. When we turned men over to the machinists' union, what
happened? There isn't a member that is in good standing with the
local union."

Delegate Mortimer, United Automobile Workers: ". . . It is all
well enough for certain craft unions who insist upon certain procedure which they have followed ever since Columbus discovered

America, but things have changed and things we held good thirty or forty years ago do not hold good today. None of you gentlemen would think of coming here in an ox-cart, but that is what you expect us to do. Make no mistake about it, gentlemen, the automobile industry is going to be organized, if not by us, then by somebody else because the economic pressure in the industry is so great, it is so terrific, it is inexorably driving all the workers into the organization. They will not go into craft organizations because they believe—and I believe they are right—that craft unionism means confusion in the industry."

These delegates, one after another, were trying to point out that the A. F. of L. policy of organization on craft-union lines did not work for mass-production industries. They were appealing for the right to organize all workers in an industry into one union, irrespective of the jobs they did, the tools they used, or the materials they worked with. They were pleading the case for industrial unionism. They were beseeching the leaders of the A. F. of L. to change their type of organization to suit the change which had come in industry.

As a matter of fact, it was A. F. of L. theory more than practice which had to be changed. For the A. F. of L. was not, and had not been for some time, an exclusively craft organization. Many A. F. of L. unions had found in the past that in order to exist at all they had to adopt some form of industrial organization. As long ago as 1915, a study by Mr. Theodore Glocker revealed that of some 133 national unions, most of which were affiliated with the A. F. of L., only 28 could rightly be called pure craft unions. Another study, made in 1939 by Mr. David J. Saposs, chief economist for the NLRB, showed that only 12 of 85 national A. F. of L. unions (17 others, consisting of government employees, railroad employees, and air-line pilots, were not examined because the board had no jurisdiction over them) could be classified as strictly craft organizations. Among these were the American Wire Weavers' Protective Association, the International Union of Journeymen Horseshoers of the United States and Canada, and the Sheep Shearers' International Union of North America. The total membership of these 12 unions, a mere 25,800, pointed to the fact that craft of itself was no longer of any importance in modern industry.

The other 73 unions represented every stage of development ranging from multiple craft (for example, the Bricklayers, Masons and Plasterers International Union of America), through semi-industrial (for example, the International Brotherhood of Electrical Workers), to industrial (for example, the Tobacco Workers International Union). The membership figures for 1938 were:

Multiple Craft	458,300
Semi-Industrial	814,800
Industrial	815,600

But though the leaders of the A. F. of L. had found it necessary to compromise with the industrial-union principle, they still thought in terms of craft-union philosophy. At the 1935 convention, Mr. Daniel J. Tobin, head of the Teamsters International, expressed the feeling of the old-line leadership in these words: "To us was given a charter—a charter from the American Federation of Labor, and Gompers, McGuire, Duncan . . . and the other men said: 'Upon the rock of trades autonomy, craft trades, you shall build the church of the labor movement, and the gates of hell nor trade industrialism shall not prevail against it.' "

It did not matter that "the church of the labor movement" was in danger of schism and collapse. It did not matter that, in practice, in some measure, many of the most powerful of the A. F. of L. unions had abandoned "the rock of trades autonomy, craft trades," for the more realistic rock of industrial unionism. The leadership still clung doggedly to its craft-union ideology. Why? The reason for so adamant a refusal to throw overboard a philosophy which could no longer be of service to the labor movement was that its craft-union philosophy served the interests of the entrenched leadership controlling the A. F. of L. To put it quite simply—the old-line leaders had good jobs and they wanted to keep them. Whether consciously or unconsciously, they were more concerned for their positions as jobholders than for their functions as organizers of the workers. Their power and security were clearly jeopardized by industrial unionism and a great influx of new members in new unions not under their control. Craft unions would be no match for giant industrial unions in the voting at the annual A. F. of L. conventions. These leaders would have had no objection whatsoever to the organization of millions of workers on industrial lines in their unions or subject to their control; what they were worried about and what they fought against was the possibility of millions of workers being organized in unions not under their control. Had they been less concerned with their own vested interests and more concerned with the needs of American workers, they would have not shrunk from the task of organizing the unorganized.

Fortunately there were some old, able, and experienced leaders who did not shrink from that task. They saw that organization of the unorganized was necessary and possible; they were shrewd enough to understand that unless that job was done the strength and security of the existing unions would be undermined; they were imaginative enough to change their policies and tactics to fit the changing times. These leaders of the industrial-union bloc fought a valiant battle for their cause in the 1935 convention. They tried to arouse the delegates to action through their resolution showing the failure that had resulted from inaction: "The fact that after fifty-five years of activity and effort we have enrolled under the banner of the American Federation of Labor approximately three and one-half millions of members of the thirty-nine millions of organizable workers is a condition that speaks for itself."

But the reactionary leadership won the day. The minority resolution calling for an aggressive organization campaign on industrial-union lines in the mass-production industries was defeated by a vote of 18,024 to 10,933.

But the men who believed in industrial unionism refused to accept defeat. If the reactionary leadership of the A. F. of L. would not go along on the job of organization that was crying to be done, then they would do it themselves. Three weeks after the convention adjourned, on November 10, 1935, they announced the formation of the Committee for Industrial Organization.

The first official pronouncement of the committee gave as its purpose "encouraging and promoting the organization of the unorganized workers in mass-production and other industries upon an industrial basis . . . to further in every way the efforts of groups of workers in autos, aluminum, radio, and many other mass-production industries to find a place within the organized labor movement as represented by the American Federation of Labor."

The CIO was born. A new era in American labor history was begun.

Workers in rubber, autos, glass, steel, radio, packing houses, cement, had been clamoring for organization. Now, at long last, they were to get it. They joined the CIO.

Workers in industries where unionism had never even been thought of before now flocked into unions of their own choosing within the CIO. White-collar workers, agricultural workers, retail clerks, professional workers—all were swept up in the wave of militant unionism and joined the CIO.

Steel towns, textile towns, rubber towns—places where the companies had owned the factories, the stores, the houses, the churches, the schools, the newspapers, the politicians—were transformed. Labor was speaking in a mighty voice—a voice loud enough to be heard: *Join the CIO*.

Nothing like it had ever been seen before in America. The movement took on the character of a crusade: *Join the CIO*.

The CIO set out to organize the unorganized, to bring unionism to the mass-production workers. It did. The hitherto unconquerable strongholds of antiunionism—steel, auto, rubber—were stormed—and conquered.

In 1935, before CIO, of some eight hundred thousand workers in the steel mills, only ninety-two hundred were organized; in 1937, after CIO, five hundred thousand were organized.

In 1935, before CIO, of some five hundred thousand auto workers, only thirty-five thousand were organized; in 1937, after CIO, three hundred and seventy-five thousand were organized.

In 1935, before CIO, of some one hundred and twenty thousand rubber workers, only thirty-five hundred were organized; in 1937, after CIO, seventy-five thousand were organized.

When the Committee for Industrial Organization was first set up in November, 1935, it had hoped to organize on industrial lines *within the A. F. of L.* It had no desire to set up a separate movement apart from the A. F. of L. But the executive council of the A. F. of L. wouldn't have it that way. It attempted first to "discipline" the committee, then suspended it, and finally expelled it.

Efforts to patch up the quarrel were made by some leaders on both sides, but nothing came of them. In 1938, in Pittsburgh, the unions affiliated with the CIO called their first constitutional convention. There they changed their name from the Committee for Industrial Organization to the Congress of Industrial Organizations.

The change of name was significant. It meant CIO leaders no longer thought of themselves as a committee within the A.F. of L. The split had widened. They were now a separate organization. The house of labor was divided.

Continued attempts were made to bring the two organizations together, but they failed. The leaders could not agree on the terms under which the CIO unions would be accepted into the A.F. of L. The separation was distressing to friends of labor and to the rank and file of both organizations; the task of organizing the unorganized in the face of employer opposition was difficult enough for both groups without adding to it a war on each other.

But in spite of the split, labor gained increased membership. What the believers in industrial unionism had predicted came true —the labor movement as a whole was strengthened by the organization of the unskilled.

The success of the CIO had the effect of a call to action on the leaders of the A.F. of L.—they had to bestir themselves. They had to do now what they were unwilling to do before—pay attention to unskilled as well as to skilled workers and organize on industrial lines as well as on craft lines. They had to change their methods to fit the changes that had come in industry.

So membership in the A.F. of L. increased because of the CIO. In 1939, for the first time since 1920, its peak year, the A.F. of L. reported over four million members.

The figures in the table below shout the story of the growth of the American Labor Movement since 1935.

	1935	1937	1945
Organizable Workers	37,000,000	38,000,000	50,000,000
In the A.F. of L.	3,000,000	3,000,000	7,000,000
In the CIO	———	4,000,000	6,000,000
In the Railroad Brotherhoods and Independent unions	700,000	500,000	1,700,000*
Total of organized workers	3,700,000	7,500,000	14,700,000
Per cent of workers organized ..	10%	20%	30%

* Of this number, 600,000 were members of the United Mine Workers which became an independent union in 1942 when John L. Lewis took it out of the CIO. In January, 1946, the United Mine Workers went back again into the A.F. of L. which it had left when the CIO was set up.

In the benefits it brought to the workers of the country, the Wage-Hour Law was almost as important as the Wagner Act. Thousands of children of school age labored in field, mine, and factory; hundreds of thousands of workers were working long hours at starvation wages. Employers in those progressive states which had enacted decent labor laws often found themselves undersold in the market by unscrupulous sweatshop operators who moved into backward states where there were no restrictions. The Wage-Hour Law, by setting "fair labor standards" for the whole country, remedied the situation to some extent in those industries engaged in interstate commerce.

The law established a floor for wages and a ceiling for hours. Minimum wages for the first year, October 24, 1938 to October 24, 1939, were set at twenty-five cents an hour, for the next six years at thirty cents, and thereafter at forty cents.

Maximum hours for the first year were set at forty-four per week, for the second year at forty-two per week, and thereafter at forty per week. Longer hours could be worked, but they were to be paid for at the rate of time and a half for overtime.

The employment of children under sixteen years of age in any occupation, and of children between sixteen and eighteen in occupations declared hazardous or detrimental to health, was made illegal.

It was a good law as far as it went but, as usual, it did not go far enough. It did not cover all workers. Since Congress had the right to make laws pertaining only to those workers engaged in interstate commerce, those in intrastate commerce would have to wait for protection until the passage of state Wage and Hour laws—probably a long wait. In addition, there were broad exemptions which further reduced the number of workers who were to benefit from the Act. Among those exempt from both the hours and wages provisions of the law were: seamen, fishermen, executives, agricultural workers (including even children above fourteen), and persons employed "within the area of production" in handling, canning, or preparing agricultural or horticultural products for market. Thus the very people perhaps most in need of the law's benefits—the agricultural workers—were denied protection.

Enforcement was a difficult problem. Some eleven million workers were covered by the law. The staff which was to handle the complaints of violations by chiseling employers was, at first, woefully inadequate. They had their hands full. In addition to those employers who had no intention of obeying the law, there were others who tried in every way possible to force exemptions for themselves.

There were some employers who thought they would be forced out of business by having to pay the 25-cent minimum, but who would in reality be forced simply to reorganize their business on more efficient lines. As long as they paid low wages they could run their plants inefficiently and make a profit. The penalty for paying higher wages was, in their case, a little better planning, nothing more.

There were some employers who were in a position to pay the minimum but would not do so. The tobacco industry was an example. Profits were high, wages were low. Some of the biggest fortunes in America had come out of the tobacco industry, yet tobacco companies were not willing to raise the wages of their workers to twenty-five cents an hour. They preferred to shut down their plants and fight for exemption on a legal technicality. The New York *Times* of October 25, 1938, reported:

30,000 TOBACCO WORKERS OUT

RALEIGH, N.C., Oct. 24 (AP).—The Federal Wages and Hours Law resulted today in the closing of many tobacco stemming plants. Those thrown out of work were unofficially estimated at 30,000.

Throughout the flue-cured tobacco belt, plants suspended operations rather than pay the minimum wage under the law.

An attorney said tobacconists would contend, in a petition to wage-hour officials, that stemming and redrying was part of preparation of an agricultural product for market, and hence exempt from interstate commerce provisions.

Would paying the minimum wage have resulted in ruin for these companies? Would giving their workers twenty-five cents an hour even have cut into their profits tremendously? Not according to a report of the Women's Bureau of the United States Department of Labor, which had made a study of "Hours and Earnings in Tobacco Stemmeries" in 1934. According to this report: "Labor cost is comparatively such a small part of the total production costs that *the wage levels could be raised without making an appreciable difference to the industry.*" One stemmery with two thousand employees had produced in one week "something over 3,000,000 pounds of strips, or enough tobacco for a billion cigarettes, the cost of these operations being less than a penny a pound of prepared tobacco or less than a mill [one tenth of a cent] per package of 20 cigarettes."

What was the stupendous amount which employers fought so bitterly to avoid paying? Twenty-five cents an hour. For forty-four hours that meant a wage of $11 per week. If the worker was lucky enough to have all-year-round employment, that came to $572 a year. This was less than a third of the amount that government experts had estimated was necessary to feed, clothe, and shelter a family decently.

The immediate effect of the law showed how necessary a reform it was. Millions of workers were not covered by the law. Other millions were exempt from its provisions. Nevertheless, it was estimated that in its first year of operation some seven hundred and fifty thousand workers who had been receiving less than twenty-five cents an hour had their pay increased; some one million five hundred thousand workers who had been working more than forty-four hours a week had their hours lessened. If it did nothing more, at least that much was to its credit.

The Wage-Hour Law and the Wagner Act were part of the explanation for the support the plain people had given to Mr. Roosevelt throughout his two terms in office. For the President had, from the very beginning, aimed at more than merely making capitalism work. He wanted to make it work more tolerably for the vast majority of the population. The rich backed him on the first aim and fought him on the second. The poor backed him on both. The big industrialists supported those New Deal laws (for instance, NRA) which helped to restore property values; they attacked those New Deal laws (for instance, Social Security) which helped to restore human values. By 1935 they had recovered their breath and shouted their opposition to the New Deal from the housetops. By the time of the 1936 election campaign they did everything in their power to defeat the administration which had saved them—but had dared, at the same time, to initiate labor and social reform laws. In his opening speech of the 1936 campaign on September 29, Mr. Roosevelt told a parable which summed up the situation:

Most people in the United States remember today the fact that starvation was averted, that homes and farms were saved, that banks were reopened, that crop prices rose, that industry revived, and that the dangerous forces subversive of our form of government were turned aside.

A few people—a few only—unwilling to remember, seem to have forgotten those days.

In the summer of 1933, a nice old gentleman wearing a silk hat fell off the end of a pier. He was unable to swim. A friend ran down the pier, dived overboard and pulled him out; but the silk hat floated off with the tide. After the old gentleman had been revived he was effusive in his thanks. He praised his friend for saving his life. Today, three years later, the old gentleman is berating his friend because the silk hat was lost.

The overwhelming victory of the New Deal in the 1936 elections proved that "most people in the United States" did, indeed, remember that Mr. Roosevelt had sought to improve their conditions. Their millions of votes were evidence that they were behind him in his defiant utterance on the eve of the election: "We have only just begun to fight."

"The Epidemic of World Lawlessness is Spreading"

★——★

After 1933 world affairs were more disturbed and hectic than at any time since 1918. War was no longer a blurred memory of the distant past or a vague dread of the remote future but something you expected to read about in your paper and hear reported over your radio, morning, noon, and night. And though America was removed from the immediate scenes of conflict by two comfortingly broad oceans, it was tied by a thousand ties to the events which were plunging the people of two continents into war. America's foreign policy was now a matter of vital concern not only to the whole world but also to itself.

In the eyes of the American people the main issue in foreign policy was the question: What is the best way to keep America out of war? As in other countries the postwar years had witnessed a growing wave of antiwar sentiment. The lessons of the last war had made a deep impression on the American people. War had become identified with profiteering and professional patriotism. The rise of fascism in Italy and Germany and the growing international anarchy from 1933 to 1940 only redoubled the determination of the American people to stay out of war.

One solution popular in certain quarters was isolationism—having as little as possible to do with Europe and the Far East. There was a great deal to be said for this view. Involvement in the last war had not done the American people any good. Our former allies had reneged on their debts. They had imposed a peace settlement which was partly responsible for later tragic events. The Nye Committee had once and for all exposed in all their nakedness the manipulations of the arms manufacturers and financial interests which had had so much to do with bringing us into war in 1917. The propaganda techniques of foreign powers in the early years of the last war had been publicized to an extent which increased the native skepticism of Americans with regard to foreign affairs.

Any program of co-operation with foreign powers was bound to be viewed with suspicion when these powers were themselves suspect. The obstacles in the way of working together with England and France were enhanced by their conduct of foreign affairs, which made Americans wonder what they were really up to. Here were countries which stood directly in the line of attack, which ostensibly had everything to gain and nothing to lose from a concerted effort to curb the aggressors. Yet not only did they do nothing to resist aggression, they actually encouraged it. Professor Arnold Toynbee, the noted specialist of the Royal Institute of International Affairs of London, summed up the objective of Anglo-French policy in the crucial years after 1933 as follows: ". . . the democratic Powers wanted to retain intact the whole of their own great possessions. . . . In practice the pacific Powers went far along the road towards connivance, or even positive collusion, with the predatory Powers in a tacit policy of keeping the peace between all the Great Powers by virtually licensing aggression at the expense of weaker third parties; and in their anxious cult of Peace they sacrificed on her altar both new principles and old traditions."

What was the good of trying to do anything when the countries which had most to gain from a united bloc against aggression were least willing to come into it and were only too ready to knife us in the back for our efforts?

And finally, the isolationists argued, we had plenty of problems to cope with at home without burning our fingers abroad. We had millions of unemployed. We had a chronic agrarian crisis. Our economy badly needed a thorough overhauling. Europe and Asia were hopeless. It was no use trying to save them. Let us mind our own business and save ourselves.

But there was a powerful case on the other side, too. America could never isolate itself completely from what was happening in the rest of the world. The world was too much of an integrated economic and social unit for us to be able to cut ourselves off from it just like that. What happened abroad was bound to affect America. We had foreign investments. We had a foreign trade which could not be discarded without intensifying our own economic problems. Isolation would not help cure our economic ills, it might make them worse.

However much we might want to isolate ourselves from the world, the world would not isolate itself from us. Aggression, if it went unchecked, might end by threatening our own security. It might be easier to stop war by taking the lead in a rational peace program than to keep out of war once it started. And it might involve less expenditure of effort and energy to stop war than to counteract its adverse repercussions once it broke out.

In addition, the argument ran, we were in a better position to take the lead than anybody else. We had less to risk. The chances of our getting involved in a war were less. Our enormous economic power could be used as an instrument for confining aggression without our having to worry about recourse to military action. Here was a weapon which would make aggressors and potential aggressors think twice if not thrice. If they knew in advance that their exports would be excluded from the United States market, that they would be denied the products of United States industry, that in itself would constitute a powerful deterrent. And if the victims and potential victims of aggression could count on our economic support, they would be immeasurably fortified in their resistance. Help from us to Loyalist Spain might save the day for democracy and change the history of Europe.

Moreover, it might not be correct to assume that nothing we could do would affect the policies of England and France. After all, there were many groups in these countries which were more than dissatisfied with their governments' supine and treacherous foreign policies. A lead from us would undoubtedly increase the pressure on Chamberlain and Daladier to mend their ways—or quit. Neither Chamberlain nor Daladier could afford to let it appear to the English and French peoples that they were pursuing a course diametrically opposed to America's. Even they had to pay lip service to President Roosevelt's splendid statements.

And finally, if Europe and Asia were hopeless, might we not be hopeless too? Did the laws of God and man operate in a different way on the American continent? Were not wars in Europe and Asia the result of causes which operated here also? Maybe the cause of progress there was the cause of progress here, and it was merely enlightened self-interest to initiate and apply the kind of program that was best designed to keep us at peace.

Here were the rational alternatives. Either to attempt to withdraw from world affairs as much as we possibly could; or consciously and actively to participate in them with the declared objective of making it as hard as we could for the aggressors—short of war—and as easy as we could for the "aggressees."

We did neither.

Our foreign policy was the product of a whole complex of conflicting forces. Neither labor on the one hand nor business on the other consistently supported any clear-cut program. Some business interests wanted us to go much further than we ever did in curbing Japanese power; others stood to gain too much from their trade with Japan to be prepared to support such measures. Most, though not all, business interests were lukewarm, if not opposed, to concerted attempts to resist Fascist expansion in Europe. American investors were antagonistic to the Good Neighbor policy because it might endanger their investments in Latin American countries, but at the same time they welcomed the administration's attempts to increase our trade with those countries.

Labor's attitude ranged from indifference to a strong desire to help preserve world peace by concerted action. Labor recognized fascism as its eternal enemy but was not certain as to the best way of opposing it. The more politically conscious elements in the trade-unions were favorable to assistance to Spain and to a meaningful Good Neighbor policy in Latin America. The farmers were predominantly isolationist—they were absorbed by their own acute economic problems almost to the exclusion of everything else.

The State Department was traditionally pro-British and was willing to be tied to England's apron strings. There was another complication. The actual carrying out of policy was in the hands of the Executive—that is, the President and the State Department; but the State Department was not always in sympathy with the President's announced objectives. More important was the fact that Congress had a real voice in determining the direction of our foreign policy and it did not always see eye to eye with the Executive.

The constellation of groupings inevitably varied on almost every single issue. That is why it is a mistake to believe that the division between isolationists and non-isolationists corresponded to that between reactionaries and progressives or to suppose that any simple formula can be found to cover the New Deal's conduct of foreign affairs.

The outstanding characteristic of New Deal foreign policy was its comparative ineffectiveness. Most of the time the New Deal wanted to stop aggression. But while it willed the ends, it did not will the means. At close range, the picture that emerges is that of a Hamlet, conscious of the gigantic and vital tasks that confront him, conscious of the way in which these tasks might be performed, but a Hamlet whose will power and energy did not match his understanding and strength.

At longer range the ineffectiveness of the New Deal foreign policy arose not from the subjective motivations at work within the administration but from the objective interests of American imperialism in the contradictory and shifting alignments of the world powers. Our commercial interests sought the protection of our markets against the incursions of Germany, Japan, and England. But the immediate push for the redivision of the world arose not from England, but from Germany, Italy, and Japan. Such a redivision would be to the disadvantage of American imperialism. But so, in the last analysis, was determined resistance to piecemeal Fascist aggression. Was the safest bet to trail inglorious clouds behind England, waiting till England's imperialist and class interests could finally be synthesized into a struggle against German imperialism and the Soviet Union? Only the future could tell.

New Deal foreign policy was its weakest point. It was neither fish, flesh, nor fowl. It vacillated, moving first in one direction, then in another. It was long on rhetoric, short on deeds.

President Roosevelt's statements of principles on foreign affairs were a constant reminder of the utterances of the man who was President of the United States when World War I broke out. No other statesman anywhere in the world, since Woodrow Wilson, was able to reflect so vividly the hopes and fears of the people of all countries. For that reason the impotence of American foreign policy in most of its *actions* during the period of the New Deal was all the more startling.

On March 4, 1933, President Roosevelt, in his first inaugural address, asserted: "In the field of world policy, I would dedicate this Nation to the policy of the good neighbor—the neighbor who resolutely respects himself and, because he does so, respects the rights of others—the neighbor who respects his obligations and respects the sanctity of his agreements in and with a world of neighbors." But the world of 1933 and after was a world of bad neighbors,

neighbors who indulged in cutthroat economic competition, persecuted racial, religious, and national minorities, piled up armaments against each other, broke their treaties, and committed aggression on weaker countries—neighbors who, intent on redividing the world, were rapidly turning it into a shambles. It needed more than the assertion of good-neighborliness to avert war and lay a solid foundation for peace.

The United States itself was clearly not an aggressor. Its dominant interests were the maintenance of peace and the expansion of its export trade. The correct principles ensuing from its interests were plainly stated by the President and the Secretary of State on numerous occasions. On October 5, 1937, in a historic speech at Chicago, the President put his finger on the cause of the rapid degeneration in world affairs, and for all practical purposes named the responsible parties:

The present reign of terror and international lawlessness began a few years ago. It began through unjustified interference in the internal affairs of other nations or the invasion of alien territory in violations of treaties [Italy in Ethiopia, Germany and Italy in Spain, Japan in China] and has now reached a stage where the very foundations of civilization are seriously threatened. . . .

Without a declaration of war and without warning or justification of any kind, civilians, including women and children, are being ruthlessly murdered with bombs from the air.

In times of so-called peace, ships are being attacked and sunk by submarines without cause or motive. Nations are fomenting and taking sides in civil warfare in nations that have never done them any harm. . . .

The peace-loving nations must make a concerted effort in opposition to those violations of treaties and those ignorings of humane instincts which today are creating a state of international anarchy and instability from which there is no escape through mere isolation or neutrality. . . .

It seems to be unfortunately true that the epidemic of world lawlessness is spreading.

When an epidemic of physical disease starts to spread, the community approves and joins in a quarantine of the patients in order to protect the health of the community against the spread of the disease. . . .

There must be positive endeavors to preserve peace.

America hates war. America hopes for peace. Therefore America actively engages in the search for peace.

This speech is quoted at some length because it directly and explicitly described the international malady, diagnosed its symptoms and causes, and proposed a specific remedy. It prescribed a program of foreign policy in accordance with the general tenor of New Deal philosophy. However, the words spoke louder than the actions.

In July, 1936, a rebellion broke out in Spain. The rebellion could not have been carried on without extensive German and Italian aid in the form of men, money, and supplies. It was a revolt of the most reactionary elements in Spain against a democratically and legally elected government which was *not* a radical government. We had diplomatic and treaty relations with this government. Its overthrow might embolden the forces of fascism in Latin America. Our neutrality legislation did not cover civil wars. Yet in spite of plain self-interest, in spite of our repeated holier-than-thou proclamations of our adherence to international law, and in spite of our treaty obligations, in January, 1937, we put an embargo on the export of arms to *either* side in a war which was civil only in a Pickwickian sense. The pretext was that we shouldn't take sides. We must do nothing to help either Franco or the Spanish Government.

But we did take sides. Instead of quarantining the aggressor, we actually quarantined the "aggressee." We helped Franco. We helped him by continuing to export arms—to Germany and Italy—arms which were used by Franco to fight the legally constituted democratic government and to bomb and shoot women and children. These countries had not declared war on Spain, but they were at war. Here was a plain case for applying the neutrality legislation to belligerent countries. But we did not do it. We played our part in the ghastly farce of nonintervention which England and France were perpetrating to the greater glory of Hitler and Mussolini. We allowed ourselves to be used by Chamberlain, who could point to what we were doing and not doing as an excuse for his own actions and inactions. We joined in the assassination of the first really democratic government Spain had ever known.

One excuse that was offered was that, though the President was eager to help the Spanish Government, with twenty million Catholics in the United States and with the American people divided in its sympathies, he could not take the risk of endangering support for his progressive domestic policies by "taking sides." This excuse was not substantiated by the facts. According to the Gallup poll of public opinion in February, 1937, 65 per cent of those having an opinion sympathized with the legal Spanish Government. In December, 1938, the figure rose to 75 per cent. Moreover, a surprisingly large minority (42 per cent) of Catholics expressed their sympathy not for Franco but for the Loyalists. The President's fine words about quarantining the aggressor bore fruit in the polls of public opinion and hardly at all in deeds.

We were used as a pawn by England in her policy of "appeasing" the Fascist powers. England was letting Germany and Italy get away with Spain. And we trailed behind. The President even went out of his way to praise Chamberlain's "Gentleman's Agreement" with Mussolini in March, 1938, when the English Opposition was vehemently condemning it, and when it was becoming harder for Chamberlain to defend his policy of appeasement.

In January, 1939, the President himself admitted that our policy had worked—in reverse. The aggressor, not the victim, had been aided: "At the very least, we can and should avoid any action, or any lack of action, which will encourage, assist, or build up an aggressor. We have learned that when we deliberately try to legislate neutrality, our neutrality laws may operate unevenly and unfairly—may actually give aid to an aggressor and deny it to the victim. The instinct of self-preservation should warn us that we ought not to let that happen any more."

But in spite of these fine words about avoiding "any action, or any lack of action, which will encourage, assist, or build up an aggressor," the United States proceeded to recognize General Franco with unseemly haste soon after the betrayal of Madrid in March, 1939, and only a little later extended to his government a credit of thirteen million dollars with which to purchase American cotton. By the first action the United States encouraged, and by the second assisted and built up, the aggressor. Our Spanish policy was the blackest mark in the whole record of the New Deal, a crime which nothing can condone or extenuate.

The record in the Far East was not as bad, but it was bad enough.

Since the beginning of the twentieth century the Far Eastern situation had been dominated by the emergence and rapid expansion of Japan as an imperialist world power. With the invasion of Manchuria in 1931, Japan announced to the world that it regarded the Far East as its special domain of exploitation, and that other countries had better prepare to clear out. England was reluctant to co-operate with the United States in resisting Japanese expansion because she was not averse to the strengthening of Japan's position in China relative to the Soviet Union. The United States recognized Soviet Russia in November, 1933—at the beginning of the seventeenth year of its existence. Not because the Roosevelt Administration felt friendly toward the Soviet Union—our relations with her since recognition have seldom been warm, and have at times been frigid—but because it felt the need for coming to some understanding with another major power in the Far East, if only as a warning to Japan that the possibility of a combination of powers against her still existed. This point of view was not confined to the administration. It was shared by Senator Borah, the leading Republican expert on foreign affairs, who had for several years been clamoring for recognition of the U.S.S.R.

China was one of the few remaining vast undeveloped markets of the world. It was a country whose unification would greatly strengthen the cause of peace in the Pacific. The main threat to its unification and unfettered economic development came from Japan, which ever since 1895 had treated China as a colonial country.

The climax of Japanese aggression against China came in July, 1937, when Japan openly went to war to conquer China and make her a colonial appendage of the Japanese Empire. The fact that she would not declare war, that she called her invasion the "China incident," fooled nobody. This time she bit off more than she could chew. The China of 1937 was not the China of 1931. The National Liberation Movement had grown stronger, and the Chinese people showed a capacity for heroic resistance which took the Japanese militarists, and indeed the whole world, by surprise.

Japan was waging a bloody and ruthless war on an independent sovereign state with which we had ties of friendship. It was flagrantly violating America's treaty rights in the Far East. Now, if ever, was the time for the administration to suit its action to its words. The American people, roused by indiscriminate bombings, burnings, and atrocities of the Japanese invaders, was only too glad to support measures which would help China and hurt Japan. A poll of public opinion in September, 1937, indicated that 47 per cent of the American people were sympathetic to China and 51 per cent were neutral. But in June, 1939, 74 per cent were pro-Chinese and 24 per cent neutral. Perhaps of greater significance was the fact that, while not more than 37 per cent of the American people expressing an opinion were in favor of a boycott of Japanese goods in October, 1937, 66 per cent were in favor of a boycott in June, 1939. Thus there could be little doubt that a popular basis for a really purposeful program of aid for China existed. The administration could plead neither that its hands were tied by events elsewhere, as could England and France, nor that it would be running ahead of its people if it did something. Something could have been done. We exported to Japan more than half of her essential war materials. From her sale of silk to us—more than 50 per cent of all our Japanese imports—she derived invaluable foreign exchange. It would have been a relatively simple matter to put an embargo on our export of Japan's sinews of war and our imports of her sinews of foreign exchange. But the ever-increasing sentiment for a boycott was not strong enough to prevail over the business interests which would suffer if such a boycott were imposed.

We read Japan lofty sermons about the brutalities of her invasion of China, at the same time that we continued to provide her with the wherewithal to inflict such brutalities.

In July, 1939, the United States gave six months' notice of the termination of the 1911 commercial treaty with Japan. This step implied no immediate reduction of our exports or imports. It was a warning in stronger language than our notes that we *might* take such action in the future if Japan did not mend her ways.

One late development in America's Far Eastern policy had an ominous twist to it. After the Soviet-German pact of August, 1939, our government began to fear the possibility of a similar pact between Japan and Russia. The international balance of forces had changed. In 1933 the United States had recognized Russia so as to use her as a counterweight to Japan. Now what the government wanted was to use Japan as a counterweight to Russia. The wheel was turning full circle. That was why at last the State Department was beginning to take a strong line with Japan. That was why it was wooing her alternately with threats and promises.

A good explanation of what was happening was given by Walter Lippmann. In his column in the New York *Herald Tribune* on November 30, 1939, he let the cat out of the bag. Here's the threat: ". . . The Japanese will be well advised if they realize that making a pact with Russia in order to extend their conquests in the Pacific would cause opinion in this country to move in favor of making more secure the position in the Atlantic with a view to making more certain the eventual return of a British fleet to Singapore. Then, with an American fleet at Hawaii, the conquests that Japan might make now would be temporary conquests. . . ."

And here's the promise: ". . . They will find this country very ready to meet them half-way in a general effort to establish a genuine new order in Asia. Though some Americans would object, the majority would support a project of peace in China which, while restoring Chinese sovereignty in China proper, would recognize the special position of Japan. They would find, if they explored it, a willingness here to induce the Chinese to negotiate a settlement of this sort. . . ."

Wherever we turn, the record is the same. Fine words, some progressive actions, and, on occasions, reaction.

Take Latin America. The New Deal Administration had gone on record as having abandoned "dollar diplomacy" for the Good Neighbor policy. It had made much of its withdrawal of American troops from the Central American republics, yet it was the previous administration which, whatever its motives, initiated this reversal of traditional policy. In 1933, the marines sent by Mr. Coolidge in 1927 to protect American property in Nicaragua were recalled—by Mr. Hoover. In 1934 President Roosevelt followed suit in Haiti.

Even Hoover had not recognized butcher Martínez of Salvador. But Roosevelt obliged when the Salvador government made a settlement on its foreign debt of which the United Fruit Company was the chief beneficiary.

Cuba is the classic land of dollar diplomacy. United States investments in Cuba totaled close to a billion dollars, and the paramount influence in Cuban economics and politics was the Chase National Bank of New York. In August, 1933, a revolution broke out in Cuba and the bloody tyrant Machado was overthrown and replaced, first by Dr. de Céspedes, then, in September, by the liberal Grau San Martín regime. The new president committed several unpardonable errors. He raised wages and lowered hours in the sugar fields—American sugar interests were infuriated. He ordered a cut in the rates for electricity—American utility interests were incensed. He would not recognize a loan of eighty million dollars made by Machado—American banking interests were ruffled. Our government's response was to make a naval display of thirty warships outside Havana—just for moral effect. The United States refused to recognize the new government. In November, 1933, Grau asked for the recall of Sumner Welles, special American ambassador to Cuba, who, he charged, had "held communication and dealings with the enemies of the government." But Welles was not recalled. Two months later Grau was overthrown and the more palatable Colonel Carlos Mendieta took office as provisional president. The new government was given recognition in five days. And it was only after this new "safe" government was in power that the United States proceeded to abandon the Platt Amendment of 1903 by which we had been entitled to intervene, and had intervened, in Cuban affairs.

In Mexico the story was different—and much better.

In 1938 the liberal Mexican Government nationalized the foreign oil companies' properties. It took this action only after the companies had refused to comply with a Federal Labor Board order upholding the workers in a labor dispute. The government did not confiscate the oil properties; it nationalized them, promising indemnification in the future. Naturally the oil companies were furious. They clamored for diplomatic pressure and intervention. What was the United State government's response? It was that of the Good Neighbor. It did not follow the precedent set by previous administrations. It did not send an army to restore law and order in Mexico, or bomb Veracruz. It tried to let Mexico solve its domestic problems in its own way. To this extent New Deal words and actions were in accord.

Nevertheless, our Mexican policy was not all of a piece. We embittered our political relations with our southern neighbor and strengthened the reactionary anti-Cárdenas forces by terminating our agreement with the Mexican Government to purchase Mexican silver. Yet at the same time we continued to purchase Mexican silver —at a lower price. The oil companies struck back at Mexico by boycotting the purchase of Mexican oil. And not only did they refuse to carry the oil in their own ships but they also used their economic strength to frighten away foreign tankers. In fact they all but drove the progressive Mexican Government into the arms of the totalitarian states, which were eager to buy the Mexican oil that the democracies blacklisted.

In recent years the Pan-American conferences have become glorified junketing parties. In many ways these conferences were an elaborate hoax. The Latin-American countries were predominantly colonial countries run by local dictatorships for the benefit of the large landlords in collusion with foreign financial and industrial interests. But at these conferences the United States actively participated in spreading the myth that they were genuine democracies ruled by and for their peoples. The President himself joined in the myth making. At Buenos Aires in 1936, he said:

"Three centuries of history sowed the seeds which grew into our

Nations; the fourth century saw those Nations become equal and free and brought us to a common system of constitutional government."

When in Rio de Janeiro, he went out of his way to pat Vargas on the back: ". . . it was two people who invented the New Deal—the President of Brazil, and the President of the United States." Vargas, the President of Brazil, seized and maintained power by a series of putsches. Trujillo of Santo Domingo, Martínez of Salvador, Ubico of Guatemala, were ruthless military dictators maintaining their rule by blood and iron. Peru, Nicaragua, Haiti, Paraguay, Bolivia, were countries where democracy was conspicuous by its absence, and Argentina and Uruguay had only the semblance of democracy. But that did not affect our friendship for them.

On the contrary. It seemed that the one way by which Latin-American countries could undermine amicable relations with our State Department was by becoming more democratic. Its attitude toward the Grau San Martín regime in Cuba was a case in point. Our difficulties with Mexico arose primarily from the fact that the Cárdenas government was trying to lay the economic basis for political democracy. Since 1938 Chile has been following the Mexican path of an attempt at genuine democracy. It remains to be seen how good-neighborly we will be toward Chile if it continues along that road.

When you have billions of dollars of investments in the Latin-American countries and when your day-to-day relations with them are run by career diplomats familiar with the ways of dollar diplomacy, friendly to Big Business, and steeped in an essentially undemocratic tradition, the Good Neighbor policy is going to have hard going. However sincere and laudable the intentions of President Roosevelt, his Good Neighbor policy was not too rich in positive accomplishments. It was, however, a distinct improvement on the policy of his predecessors.

Even in the conduct of its international commercial and monetary relations, where the New Deal had done something, it had not much to show. Secretary of State Hull's great contribution to world peace was the trade-agreement program. Mr. Hull was a simon-pure nineteenth-century Cobdenite in a world which had little place for Cobdenism. He was a doctor with one prescription—free trade. If other countries were compelled to resort more and more to higher tariffs, import quotas, export subsidies, clearing agreements, currency depreciation, exchange controls, and crude barter, Doctor Hull's answer was—free trade. If all the world was rearming on a scale which could only spell WAR, Doctor Hull had one remedy— free trade. If certain countries were flagrantly violating treaties and openly invading other countries whose only crime was their weakness, Doctor Hull prescribed—free trade. Faced with an outbreak of a pneumonia epidemic, Doctor Hull revived a dubious and outworn treatment for the common cold.

Make no mistake. The trade-agreement program was designed to open contracting foreign markets to American trade, and the key was to be mutual tariff concessions. It was initiated in 1934 (renewed again in 1937 and 1940), in an act giving the President special power to negotiate reciprocal trade treaties and to reduce tariffs by as much as 50 per cent. This step was a reversal both of the seventy-year-old trend in American commercial policy of raising tariffs to protect America's domestic market from foreign competition, and of the dominant tendency in almost all countries of the world to increase restrictions on foreign trade.

By December 1, 1939, twenty-one reciprocal-trade agreements were concluded with countries as commercially important as Canada, the United Kingdom, and Brazil and as unimportant as Nicaragua, Honduras, and Finland. They involved mutual concessions on goods of varying economic significance. These agreements all included a most-favored-nation clause, in which both parties agreed to give each other the benefits of any concessions subsequently granted to other countries. Thus a concession granted to a country with which we were making an agreement automatically extended to any country with which we had a most-favored-nation understanding—which happened to be every country in the world except Germany. As a matter of fact, too much stress should not be laid on this most-favored-nation clause. Trade agreements were drawn up with minute care on both sides in such a way as to confine the main benefits to the two countries immediately involved. They entailed prolonged negotiations and horse trading between the two countries, and also within each of them. Domestic groups that thought they were going to be harmed by any concession their government intended to make raised a tremendous howl, and often succeeded in keeping such concessions to a minimum. The net result was that the trade agreements covered a much smaller area of international trade than State Department publicity led us to expect.

It is not easy to weigh the actual economic results of the Hull trade-agreement program. The ballyhoo both for and against was so loud that the facts were obscured. It was true that in years of recovery our foreign trade with trade-agreement countries had increased more than that with nontrade-agreement countries, and that in years of depression it had fallen less. But the most that could be safely inferred was that the trade-agreement program did probably raise our trade with certain countries though probably not to the extent that had been claimed for it. It served to provide the administration with an alibi for the absence of a truly constructive foreign policy. It was the fact that it was an alibi that gave it its greatest political significance. It was a cover-up, an excuse. If people were restless about the foreign situation and the little the United States was doing to improve it, the government could proudly point to "the achievements" of its trade-agreement program. Which is exactly what Hull did.

The fundamental weakness of American commercial policy was that it was not used nearly as effectively as it might have been as a political instrument. The United States market was a first-rate economic consideration to many leading trading countries, and our exports in turn often played a vital part in their economies. Here we had a tremendous bargaining weapon, which could have been employed, both in the threat and the execution, to curb the expansion of fascism. Instead, for most of the time we did nothing and when we did act, it was on a petty and ineffectual scale. Though we had reason, cause, and legal ground to do so four or five years earlier, we did not impose countervailing duties on German exports to the United States, which were subsidized by the German Government, until March 1939, after the occupation of Czechoslovakia. Similar failure in the case of Japan has already been noted.

That the political use made of our economic power was in no way commensurate with it was true in matters of monetary as well as of commercial policy. Here we were with more than half the world's monetary gold, with more gold than we could ever possibly use. It would have been the easiest thing in the world to make extensive gold loans to Latin-American countries, for instance, in amounts which would have absorbed barely a small fraction of our immense holdings, but for which we could have obtained a big return in political good will and mutual economic advantage. We could have halted the inroads into Latin-American trade made by the Fascist countries, and thus prevented them from using their trade in this area as a base for political intrigue and for the encouragement of ultrareactionary systems of government in this hemisphere. But we didn't. Midas, Pecksniff, and Caspar Milquetoast had their way.

With the outbreak of the Second World War between England and France against Germany in September, 1939, the twists and turns in our foreign policy became a thing of the past, and we marched forward in a straight line.

Sympathy for the Allies and hatred for the Fascists had grown as it became apparent that aggression and war and hideous brutality were not a necessary expedient but part and parcel of Fascist philosophy. To an increasing number of Americans that philosophy became more and more repulsive.

As a matter of fact there had never been any doubt as to which side most Americans preferred in the struggle waging in Europe and the Far East. The debate that had raged throughout the country had centered solely on the question of our keeping out of war. The American people had an unmistakable will to peace. Their purpose, from the first, was to maintain the peace if at all possible. If not, then our purpose was to stay out of the war.

But with the fall of France and the bombing of Britain it became apparent that the choice of peace or war was no longer ours to make. We could continue to hope that we would not get involved, but our own security was now threatened. Our next move must be to defend ourselves. Six days after the Nazis began their invasion of France, on May 16, 1940, the President sent a message to Congress asking for the production of fifty thousand planes in one year. (Called "fantastic" when it was first announced, in a few years this goal was exceeded.) In September, 1940, the Selective Service Act was passed, and in the same month the United States traded fifty destroyers to Great Britain in exchange for leases of naval and air bases on British islands in this hemisphere.

On September 27, 1940, the union of the Fascist powers for the conquest of Europe and Asia was formally announced when Japan signed the Pact of Berlin recognizing "the leadership of Germany and Italy in the establishment of a new order in Europe." In turn, Germany and Italy recognized "the leadership of Japan in the establishment of a new order in Greater East Asia." Of great significance for the United States was one article in the treaty in which the three Fascist countries agreed "to assist one another with all political, economic, and military means if one of the three Contracting Powers is attacked by a Power at present not involved in the European War or in the Chinese-Japanese conflict."

Confronted by the menace of war on two fronts, it was clearly our best strategy to stave off invasion of our own shores by preventing the collapse of Britain. To do that, we must supply her with the materials of war of which she was in desperate need. The President pointed this out in a fireside chat on December 29, 1940:

> The Nazi masters of Germany have made it clear that they intend not only to dominate all life and thought in their own country, but also to enslave the whole of Europe, and then to use the resources of Europe to dominate the rest of the world. . . . If Great Britain goes down, the Axis powers will control the continents of Europe, Asia, Africa, Australasia and the high seas—and they will be in a position to bring enormous military and naval resources against this hemisphere. It is no exaggeration to say that all of us, in all the Americas, would be living at the point of a gun—a gun loaded with explosive bullets as well as military. . . .
>
> The people of Europe who are defending themselves do not ask us to do their fighting. They ask us for the implements of war, the planes, the tanks, the guns, the freighters which will enable them to fight for their liberty and for our security. Emphatically we must get these weapons to them in sufficient volume and quickly enough, so that we and our children will be saved the agony and suffering of war which others have had to endure. . . . In a military sense Great Britain and the British Empire are today the spearhead of resistance to world conquest. . . .
>
> We must be the great arsenal of democracy.

With the passage of the Lend-Lease Bill by Congress in March, 1941, we were able to supply the victims of Fascist aggression with some of "the planes, the tanks, the guns, the freighters" which they needed. After the Nazi invasion of Russia on June 22, 1941, the part of the swelling stream of Lend-Lease supplies which went to that country played an important part in her heroic struggle, just as it did with Britain. Lend-Lease supplies were expensive—but so was the war. "Three years of Lend-Lease cost the United States thirty billion dollars, but every month of fighting in 1944 cost this country alone eight billion dollars." (Lend-Lease aid at the end of the war totaled about forty-six billion dollars.)

Part of the reason for the high cost of the supplies is contained in a 1941 report made for the Senate Temporary National Economic Committee: "Speaking bluntly, the government and the public are 'over a barrel' when it comes to dealing with business in time of war or other crisis. Business refuses to work except on terms which it dictates. It controls the natural resources, the liquid assets, the strategic position in the country's economic structure, and its technical equipment and knowledge of processes.

"The experience of the [first] World War, now apparently being repeated, indicates that business will use this control only if it is 'paid properly.' In effect this is blackmail, not too fully disguised. . . . It is in such a situation that the question arises: What price patriotism?"

Our strategy for defense against Fascist aggression took different forms in Europe and Asia. In Europe we supplied the Allies in ever-increasing amounts with the essential materials of war; in Asia we stopped supplying essential materials of war to Japan. For several years our policy in regard to Japan had been the contradictory one of protesting against her brutalities in China, while at the same time supplying her with oil, cotton, iron, steel and other war materials which made her invasion possible. This policy had been dictated by the assumption that our interests would best be served by a stalemate in the Far East. We did not want Japan to be completely victorious in China because that would shut us out of the market there; on the other hand, we did not want Japan to be defeated because we regarded her as a buffer against the Soviet Union.

But when the Nazis attacked the Soviet Union in June, 1941, we mistakenly assumed that the Soviet Union would be crushed in short order—and therefore our need for Japan as a buffer was gone. Thus, when the Japanese occupied French Indo-China and threatened the Philippines and Southeast Asia, then, in July, 1941, we froze the Japanese assets with which she conducted her business in America, and restricted the export of oil and other war goods. We went further. By buying up the strategic raw materials in Latin America we made it impossible for Japan to secure what she needed. Without oil and the other essentials, Japanese war industries had to slow down.

On Sunday afternoon, December 7, 1941, in a surprise raid, 105 Japanese bombing planes crippled the ships and destroyed most of the airplanes belonging to the United States Pacific Fleet in Pearl Harbor. "Yesterday, December 7, 1941—a date which will live in infamy—the United States of America was suddenly and deliberately attacked by naval and air forces of the Empire of Japan," President Roosevelt told Congress the next day. "I ask that the Congress declare that, since the unprovoked and dastardly attack by Japan on Sunday, December 7, a state of war has existed between the United States and the Japanese Empire." With only one dissenting vote, Congress declared war on Japan.

Four days later, on December 11, 1941, Germany and Italy declared war on the United States.

We were in it again—the second time in a quarter of a century.

On December 23, 1941, the leaders of the American Federation of Labor and the Congress of Industrial Organizations gave a voluntary pledge to the President of the United States that organized labor would give up its legal right to strike for the duration, on condition that membership in unions would be protected and prices would not be allowed to rise out of proportion to wages. In the war years that followed, they kept their pledge—not one single strike was authorized by either of these two labor organizations. Though rising prices and unsettled grievances did result in some "wildcat" strikes, which were given highly dramatized and exaggerated publicity in the press, the amazing record was portrayed in the official figures of the U. S. Bureau of Labor Statistics—from December, 1941, to August, 1945, these stoppages resulted in a loss of only "slightly over *a tenth of 1 percent* of the available working time."

More important than anything else in the first period of our entrance into the war was the battle of production. More than ever before, we had to be the "arsenal of democracy." How well labor and management fulfilled its responsibility was shown in the figures —one year after the sneak attack on Pearl Harbor, our production of war material was equal to the combined production of Germany, Italy, and Japan.

The many problems concerned with the distribution of war material to Britain and the Soviet Union had been among the topics discussed by President Roosevelt and Britain's Prime Minister Churchill at a meeting on American and British warships anchored off Newfoundland, in August, 1941. (Other policy-shaping meetings of great significance were held later by the President with China's Generalissimo Chiang Kai-shek, and with Premier Stalin of the Soviet Union and Prime Minister Churchill.) At this first meeting a declaration called the "Atlantic Charter" was agreed upon which

COAL MINE

outlined "certain common principles" in the national policies of the United States and Britain "on which they base their hopes for a better future for the world."

The purposes and principles of the Atlantic Charter were later endorsed by representatives of 26 governments hostile to the Axis in a declaration of alliance signed in Washington on January 1, 1942. The Atlantic Charter was thus transformed into a world charter. In their Declaration of Washington, each of the United Nations pledged its "full resources" to carrying on the war, and "not to make a separate armistice or peace with the enemies." Three years later, on April 25, 1945, delegates from the United Nations (then numbering fifty countries) met in San Francisco for the purpose of creating an international authority to preserve and promote peace. Like its predecessor, the League of Nations, the United Nations grew out of a wartime coalition. But unlike the League, the United Nations was created while the war was still being fought.

There was a difference, too, in the attitude of the United States toward participation in an international organization to preserve peace. We refused to join the League of Nations; it took the United States Senate only three weeks to decide to approve the charter of the United Nations Organization.

While the delegates were debating the terms of the Charter in San Francisco, the most devastating of all wars was approaching the end. On May 7, 1945, Germany surrendered.

Victory in the Far East did not come until three months later. On August 6, 1945, the deadliest weapon ever known to man was dropped on the city of Hiroshima in Japan. It was a small atom bomb—packed with the destructive force of twenty thousand tons of TNT.

Japan was beaten before the atom bomb was dropped and the Japanese knew it. They were hoping, however, that their enemies— the United States, Britain, and the Soviet Union—would fall out among themselves. That hope was blasted two days later when the Soviet Union declared war on Japan and the Red Army swarmed into Manchuria, Korea and Sakhalin. On the same day, August 8, 1945, a second atom bomb was dropped on the Japanese city of Nagasaki.

The atom bombs plus the Russian entry into the war brought

Japan to her knees. On August 14, 1945, the Japanese Government announced its acceptance of the surrender terms.

World War II was ended.

Amidst the rejoicing of the peoples all over the world, there was a note of sadness. America's greatest soldier had not lived to see the final victory. On April 12, 1945, Franklin Delano Roosevelt died in his home at Warm Springs, Georgia.

The common man, everywhere, mourned his loss.

On March 4, 1933, Franklin Delano Roosevelt took office as the thirty-second President of the United States. He remained in office (re-elected by overwhelming majorities in 1936, 1940, and 1944) until his death twelve years later.

When he first assumed the presidency, the nation had suffered three and a half years of the worst crisis in its history. The ruling class had lost confidence in its ability to govern and was willing to accept any leadership which could salvage the existing system. The people were ready neither for a basic transformation of American society nor for a passive acceptance of things as they were. The leadership which President Roosevelt and the New Deal Administration provided was, on the whole, admirably fitted to this situation. The President made it clear, again and again, that he was a reformer, not a revolutionist. He strove to save the capitalist system by eliminating its existing evils, ignoring the fact that those evils were the inevitable product of that system. In his own person he brilliantly reflected, and sometimes anticipated, the political development of the American people. That, in essence, constituted his greatness.

The New Deal philosophy was derived from the pressure of economic forces on the working class and the middle class and, to a smaller extent, on a few comparatively enlightened capitalists. The middle class was discontented with the old way of living, without knowing where, exactly, to turn. Its position was essentially crystallized in the New Deal. It wanted change, but not too much change. It wanted reforms which came easy, it dreaded reforms which came hard. Because it wanted some change, its interests coincided—at least temporarily—with those of the mass of the people. But the New Deal was not prepared to go more than a prescribed distance, in fact, no further than it was compelled to go; and, in critical situations, it was apt to fall back upon the guidance of the reactionaries. It did not provide the leadership for solving *basically* the problems set by the collapse of the American economy at home or by the chaos abroad.

The New Deal was a vital stage in the education of the American people. It was a revolution in ideas.

The New Deal was a reshuffle of the old deck of cards. It was not a revolution in economics.

Jobs and Peace

★——★

The same fears that plagued the people before World War II remained to plague them after the war was over. The American people were not crying for the moon. In an economy capable of providing plenty, they asked only for enough. They wanted job security and peace.

But these wants were precisely what the economic system had been unable to satisfy after World War I. It began to look, after World War II, as though the economic system would again be unable to deliver the goods.

Monopoly capitalism throughout the world had tried to survive, since the breakdown in 1929, in one of two ways. Either it had been put on a war footing, or it had been kept going by government expenditures on public works, relief, aid to agriculture, etc. In either case it was government economic activity that, for the time being, kept the patient alive.

The first medicine was tried in Germany, Italy, and Japan. Its base was gigantic government orders for war materials. The whole economy was geared to war. It functioned, and could only function, as a war economy. It involved the partial or complete suppression of civil liberties, the imposition of increasing sacrifices on the largest sectors of the population for the benefit of a dwindling number of monopoly capitalists and their parasitic political apparatus, and the immeasurably intensified search for markets for their products. It speeded up the drive toward war. (The big war came in September, 1939.) Under whatever name it disguised itself, it was nothing more nor less than fascism—the last, most decadent, most brutal form of capitalism.

The second medicine was government spending of such a character as not only to maintain the stream of profits for the giant corporations but at the same time to relieve some of the more glaring social and economic evils. This treatment was tried in the United States—haltingly, tentatively, jerkily—under the form of the New Deal. The New Deal was the social philosophy of those who thought capitalism might be made a going concern by government spending to increase the contracting volume of purchasing power of the masses.

But even this temporary palliative was obnoxious to the men on top as soon as they recovered from the hang-over of 1932. They hated the three R's of Relief, Recovery, and Reform, and they loathed the fourth R—Roosevelt—because he was the personification of the unholy trinity. As they regained their self-confidence and profits, they grew tired of spending and turned on their savior.

When they came to power in the Congressional elections of 1946, they envisaged success at home in terms of balancing the budget at the expense of the American working people, of restricting and curbing labor unions, of cutting government expenditures on useful things and increasing them on weapons of war. Their domestic success could only end in a black night of reaction.

The magnitude of the amount they were prepared to spend on armaments was a measure of their attitude toward peace. Expenditures for "national defense" were by far the largest single item in their budget—thirty cents out of every dollar. They did their utmost to change the American people's deep feeling of friendship and admiration for the Soviet Union which had grown during the war, into one of suspicion and distrust. They acted on the underlying assumption that the United States and Russia would inevitably have to go to war—the only question for the American nation, in their minds and actions, was not "should we" but "when."

Their solution for the problem of what to do with Germany was the one that had been tried before World War II—build up her war industries as a bulwark against the Soviet Union.

In the other European countries American monopoly capitalism did its utmost to restore the economic and social *status quo* of before the war. It was a difficult task since the one thing the peoples of Europe were certain about was that they wanted a future unlike their past. But dollar diplomacy—giving much needed credits here, denying them there—was resorted to in our capitalists' effort to serve as the last and strongest bulwark of things as they were.

Perhaps more disturbing than any of these developments was what was happening to atomic power. As long as the secret of atomic power was kept by the military alone, it was a safe bet that it would be used in the only way the military knew—for war and destruction. The hope that this potentially greatest boon to humanity ever developed by science might one day be used to serve all of mankind began to diminish as the Big Boys put on a drive for the maintenance of private patents in atomic energy.

Did the drive toward reaction at home and war abroad come about because capitalists were selfish? Was that why the paramount problem of jobs and peace for the American people went unsolved? Not at all. "The trouble," as our foremost sociologist put it, "is not that business men as a class are 'wicked,' 'greedy,' or 'irresponsible,' but that the dynamic system in which their lives are enmeshed and which determines their actions is not set up to serve collective democratic ends. . . . What is called for is a broad coherent policy dominated by the public interest as democratically defined, and this is precisely what capitalism has not been able to achieve."

On April 29, 1938, the President of the United States, in a message to Congress, called the attention of the people of the country to a grave danger which threatened their liberties and their form of government.

The menace was not communism. On the contrary, it was capitalism itself.

Among us today a concentration of private power without equal in history is growing. . . . Today many Americans ask the uneasy question: Is the vociferation that our liberties are in danger justified by the facts? . . . Their answer is that if there is that danger it comes from that concentrated private economic power which is struggling so hard to master our democratic government. . . .

That heavy hand of integrated financial and management control lies upon large and strategic areas of American industry. The small business man is unfortunately being driven into a less and less independent position in American life. You and I must admit that.

Private enterprise is ceasing to be free enterprise and is becoming a cluster of private collectivisms; masking itself as a system of free enterprise after the American model, it is in fact becoming a concealed cartel system after the European model. . . .

No people, least of all a people with our traditions of personal liberty, will endure the slow erosion of opportunity for the common man, the oppressive sense of helplessness under the domination of a few, which are overshadowing our whole economic life.

The President was both right and wrong. He was right in his analysis of the effect of concentrated private economic power on our liberties and democratic government. He was wrong in his statement that "private enterprise is ceasing to be free enterprise." The tense of the verb was badly chosen. The truth of the matter was that private enterprise *had ceased* to be free enterprise long before. Exactly fifty years before this president so forcefully pointed to the ominous cloud on our economic horizon, another President in another message to another Congress had, with equal vigor, already flown the storm signals. Said Grover Cleveland on December 3, 1888:

> As we view the achievements of aggregated capital, we discover the existence of trusts, combinations, and monopolies, while the citizen is struggling far in the rear or is trampled to death beneath an iron heel. Corporations, which should be carefully restrained creatures of the law and the servants of the people, are fast becoming the people's masters.

And thirty-seven years before President Franklin Delano Roosevelt spoke so eloquently about the dangers of monopoly capitalism, another President Roosevelt began to make so big a noise about the evils of trusts and what he would do to them that he was headlined as the "trust-buster." This was inaccurate billing for the great showman. When the final curtain had been lowered, it was the opinion of the critics that Roosevelt I had bungled the part—instead of "speaking softly and carrying a big stick," he had spoken loudly and carried a small stick. The noise continued—and so did the trusts.

There was no doubt about it. Private enterprise had ceased to be free enterprise long ago.

The concentration of control in the hands of a few was intensified during World War II. So Harry S. Truman, successor to President Roosevelt, reported to Congress in January, 1947:

> The [Temporary National Economic] Committee's study showed that, despite half a century of anti-trust law enforcement, one of the gravest threats to our welfare lay in the increasing concentration of power in the hands of a small number of giant organizations.
> During the war, this long-standing tendency toward economic concentration was accelerated. As a consequence, we now find that to a greater extent than ever before, whole industries are dominated by one or a few large organizations which can restrict production in the interest of higher profits and thus reduce employment and purchasing power.

The question of jobs and peace is thus intimately related to our monopoly structure and the profit system. The issue is not whether we are for or against "free enterprise." The issue is whether our economy is to be run by monopoly capitalism for its own private ends, or by the people for their own welfare.

The common man must not forget the New Deal. It was a valuable experience. It gave the workers and farmers a sense of their own power. They learned that in order to be able to get any of the things they wanted they had to organize both politically and economically. And today, when the New Deal is rapidly becoming a memory, they must remember that lesson. They must redouble their economic and political activities. They want jobs and peace. They must take the initiative in getting them. And they will learn through their struggles that jobs and peace are attainable only under a system of production for use, not for profit.

Appendix

★————————————————————————————————★

Grateful acknowledgment is made to the publishers of the books listed below for permission to use the material cited.

CHAPTER I

Page 4. *Gentleman's Magazine*, Vol. II, April, 1732, p. 727.

Page 5. Mittelberger, Gottlieb, *Reise nach Pennsylvanien im Jahre 1750 und Ruckreise nach Deutschland im Jahre 1754.*

Quoted in Diffenderffer, Frank R., *The German Immigration into Pennsylvania*, Pennsylvania German Society. Proceedings, Vol. X, p. 176.

Page 7. Steiner, Edward A., *On the Trail of the Immigrant*, pp. 35, 36. New York, Fleming H. Revell Co., 1906.

Steerage Conditions, pp. 13-23; Reports of U. S. Immigration Commission, XXXVII, 1911.

Page 7. Warne, Frank Julian, *The Immigrant Invasion*, p. 49. New York, Dodd, Mead & Company, 1913.

Page 9. Mittelberger, Gottlieb, *op. cit.*, pp. 64, 65.

Page 10. Roberts, Peter, *The New Immigration*, p. 11. New York, The Macmillan Company, 1912.

Page 12. Beard, Charles A., and Mary R., *The Rise of American Civilization*, one-volume edition, pp. 103, 104. New York, The Macmillan Company, 1930.

Page 14. Walsh, Reverend Robert, *A Cargo of Black Ivory*, 1829.

Quoted in Hart, A. B., *American History Told by Contemporaries*, Vol. III, pp. 615-617. New York, The Macmillan Company, 1901.

Warne, Frank Julian, *op. cit.*, p. 10.

CHAPTER II

Page 16. Adapted from Smith's *General Historie Book IV*, in *Narratives of Early Virginia 1606-1625*, pp. 393-395. New York, Charles Scribner's Sons, 1907.

Page 17. Earle, A. M., *Home Life in Colonial Days*, pp. 5, 6. New York, The Macmillan Company, 1898.

Bruce, P. A., *Social Life of Virginia in the 17th Century*, p. 212. Richmond (Va.), Whittleb and Shepperson, 1907.

Page 18. Mason, Captain John, *A Brief History of the Pequot War*, pp. 268, 269. Boston, Kneeland & Green, 1736.

Adapted from Bradford, William, *History of Plymouth Plantation*, p. 78, in Massachusetts Historical Society, Vol. III of the 4th series. (Emphasis mine.)

Page 20. "Observations by George Percy," in *Narratives of Early Virginia 1606-1625*, pp. 20, 21. New York, Charles Scribner's Sons, 1907.

Page 27. Log Book No. 15 in Nantucket Whaling Museum.

Page 28. Morison, S. E., *Maritime History of Massachusetts*, pp. 325, 326. Boston, Houghton Mifflin Company, 1921.

(Quotation within the quotation from Melville, Herman, *Moby Dick*.)

CHAPTER III

Page 37. Wertenbaker, T. J., *The First Americans*, p. 75. New York, The Macmillan Company, 1927.

CHAPTER IV

Page 53. Schlesinger, A. M., *The Colonial Merchants and the Revolution 1763-1776*, p. 43, footnote. New York, Columbia University Press, 1918.

Paragraph following above quotation is adapted from the same source, pp. 39, 40.

Page 56. Story of colonies "passing the buck" is adapted from Beer, G. L., *British Colonial Policy, 1754-1765*, pp. 263, 264. New York, The Macmillan Company, 1907.

Page 62. *The Correspondence of General Thomas Gage with the Secretaries of State, 1763-1775*, edited by Carter, C. E., pp. 78, 79. New York, Yale University Press, 1931.

Page 65. Schlesinger, A. M., *op. cit.*, pp. 179, 180.

Page 66. *Gaspee* story adapted from above, pp. 252, 253.

Page 70. *Ibid.*, p. 276.

Page 71. Story of solidarity between New York and Boston craftsmen is adapted from Hacker, Louis M., *The American Teacher*, September–October, 1936.

CHAPTER V

Page 76. Quoted in Hart, A. B., *op. cit.*, Vol. II, pp. 561, 569, 571.

Page 77. "Providence" story adapted from Jameson, J. Franklin, *The American Revolution Considered as a Social Movement*, pp. 104, 105. Princeton University Press, 1926.

Page 78. Beard, Charles A., and Mary R., *op. cit.*, p. 276.

Page 79. General Howe story adapted from Becker, Carl L., *Beginnings of the American People*, p. 256. Boston, Houghton Mifflin Company, 1915.

Page 82. Jameson, J. Franklin, *op. cit.*, pp. 33, 36.

Page 88. Knox letter quoted in Beard, Charles A., *An Economic Interpretation of the Constitution of the United States*, p. 59. New York, The Macmillan Company, 1913. (Emphasis mine.)

Page 91. Legislature story adapted from above, p. 231.

CHAPTER VI

Page 93. Carter, C. E., *op. cit.*, p. 279.

Dunmore quotation in Henderson, Archibald, *Conquest of the Old Southwest,* frontispiece. New York, The Century Co., 1920.

Page 95. McMaster, J. B., *History of the People of the United States,* Vol. IV, pp. 384, 385, 387. New York, Appleton & Co., 1895.

Page 97. Hall, James, *Letters from the West,* pp. 87, 88. London, Henry Colburn, 1828.

Page 98. McMaster, J. B., *op. cit.,* p. 386.

Traveler story adapted from Hall, James, *op. cit.,* pp. 346-348.

Page 99. Peck, J. M., *A New Guide for Emigrants to the West,* 2nd ed., pp. 119-121. Boston, Gould, Kendall and Lincoln, 1837.

Page 100. Description of moving frontier line adapted from Turner, F. J., *The Frontier in American History.* New York, Henry Holt & Company, Inc., 1920.

Cooper story quoted in Hart, A. B., *op. cit.,* Vol. III, p. 97.

Page 101. Account of care of ax adapted from Drake, Daniel, *Pioneer Life in Kentucky,* p. 42. Cincinnati, Robert Clarke & Company, 1870.

Page 102. *Ibid.,* p. 92.

Page 103. *Ibid.,* pp. 54-56.

McMaster, J. B., *op. cit.,* Vol. V, pp. 158-159.

Page 105. Hall, James, *op. cit.,* p. 124.

Account of pioneer life in wilderness adapted from Turner, F. J., *op. cit.,* pp. 3, 4.

Page 107. *Salem Mercury,* November 4, 1788.

Page 109. Turner, F. J., *Rise of the New West,* p. 100. New York, Harper & Brothers, 1906.

Page 113. Flint, Timothy, *Recollections of the Last Ten Years in the Valley of the Mississippi,* p. 103. Boston, Cummings, Hilliard & Company, 1826.

Page 114. Twain, Mark, *Life on the Mississippi,* p. 21. New York, Harper & Brothers, 1927.

Page 117. Account of steamboat fatalities adapted from Eskew, G. L., *The Pageant of the Packets,* p. 73. New York, Henry Holt & Company, Inc., 1929.

Page 118. Story of steamboat race adapted from Quick, H. and E., *Mississippi Steamboatin',* pp. 207-210. New York, Henry Holt & Company, Inc., 1926.

CHAPTER VII

Page 123. Quoted in Paxson, F. L., *History of the American Frontier,* pp. 459, 460. New York, Houghton Mifflin Company, 1924.

Page 125. Webb, W. P., *The Great Plains,* p. 9. New York, Ginn and Company, 1931.

Description of Plains Indian as a fighter adapted from above, p. 67.

Page 126. Irving, Washington, *The Adventures of Captain Bonneville,* Vol. I Putnam's 1895 edition, p. 7. New York, G. P. Putnam's Sons.

Ibid., p. 20.

Page 127. *Ibid.,* pp. 92-98.

Ibid., pp. 228-230; Vol. II, p. 119.

Page 129. Gregg, Josiah, *Commerce of the Prairies,* pp. 188, 189. Vol. XIX of "Early Western Travels 1748-1846," edited by Thwaites, R. G., Cleveland, Arthur Clark Co., 1905.

Ibid., pp. 195, 219.

Page 130. Beard, Charles A., and Mary R., *op. cit.,* p. 588.

Page 131. Quoted in Chittenden, H. M., *The American Fur Trade of the Far West,* Vol. III, p. 972. New York, Francis Harper, 1902.

Page 132. Statement made by John Sinclair relative to the rescue of the Donner Party in *Some Pioneer Recollections of George Lathrop and Luke Voorhees,* Philadelphia, Jacobs & Company, 1927.

Page 133. Quoted in Beard, Charles A., and Mary R., *op. cit.,* p. 606.

Page 136. Gregg, Josiah, *op. cit.,* p. 264.

Page 139. "Diagram of a Herd on Trail" from Dale, E. E., *The Range Cattle Industry,* p. 66. University of Oklahoma Press.

Page 143. Wind story adapted from Webb, W. P., *op. cit.,* p. 22.

Page 144. Rölvaag, O. E., *Giants in the Earth,* pp. 29, 37. New York, Harper & Brothers, 1927.

Chapter VIII

Page 145. Quoted in Tryon, R. M., *Household Manufacture in the United States 1640-1860,* p. 101. University of Chicago Press, 1917.

Page 146. Adapted from Bogart, E. L., *Economic History of the American People,* pp. 390, 391. New York, Longmans, Green and Co., 1930.

Page 147. "Betsy" story adapted from Beard, Charles A., and Mary R., *op. cit.,* p. 661.

Quotation in Bogart, E. L., *op. cit.,* p. 249.

Page 148. Warden, D. B., *Statistical, Political, and Historical Account of the United States.* Edinburgh, Constable & Co., 1819.

Page 149. Franklin, Benjamin, *Canadian Pamphlet,* 1760.

Ware, Caroline F., *Early New England Cotton Manufacture,* p. 23. New York, Houghton Mifflin Company, 1931.

Martineau, Harriet, *Society in America.* London, Saunders and Otley, 1837.

Page 150. Ware, Caroline F., *op. cit.,* p. 199.

Page 151. Chevalier, Michael, *Society, Manners and Politics in the United States.* Boston, Weeks, Jordan & Co., 1839.

Page 152. Rearranged from Whitworth and Wallis, *Official Reports to the British Government, 1854,* quoted in Callender, G. S., *Economic History of the United States,* pp. 482-484. New York, Ginn and Company, 1909.

Page 154. Ware, Caroline F., *op. cit.,* p. 264.

Ibid., p. 268.

Chapter IX

Page 156. Helper, Hinton Rowan, *The Impending Crisis of the South,* p. 22. New York, Burdick Bros., 1857.

Page 158. From the *Georgia Courier,* October 11, 1827, quoted in Phillips, Ulrich B., *Plantation and Frontier,* Vol. I, of the *Documentary History of*

American Industrial Society, edited by Commons, John R., pp. 283-285. Cleveland (Ohio), Arthur Clark Company, 1910.

Page 160. Plantation description adapted from above, pp. 71-73.

Cairnes, *The Slave Power.* New York, Foster & Co., 1862.

Page 162. Buckingham, J. S., *The Slave States of America,* Vol. I, pp. 132, 133. London, Fisher, Son and Company, 1842.

Quoted in Olmsted, F. L., *A Journey in the Back Country,* p. 60. New York, Mason Bros., 1860.

Page 163. Quoted in Buckingham, J. S., *op. cit.,* p. 173.

Page 164. Quoted in Hammond, M. B., *The Cotton Industry,* p. 83. Published for the American Economic Association. New York, The Macmillan Company, 1897.

Page 165. Quoted in Olmsted, F. L., *A Journey in the Seaboard Slave States,* p. 289. New York, Dix and Edwards, 1856.

Page 166. Hammond, M. B., *op. cit.,* pp. 54, 55.

Olmsted, F. L., *A Journey in the Seaboard Slave States, op. cit.,* p. 55.

Account of Gadsen sale adapted from Bancroft, Frederic, *Slave Trading in the Old South,* pp. 340, 341. Baltimore, J. H. Furst Co., 1931.

Ibid., p. 344.

Page 167. Table of Slaveholders in Helper, H. R., *op. cit.,* p. 146.

Page 168. Quoted in Olmsted, F. L., *A Journey in the Back Country, op. cit.,* pp. 329, 330.

Ibid., p. 33.

Page 169. *Ibid.,* p. 259.

Page 170. Table of prices from *Bureau of Agriculture Investigation,* quoted in Hammond, M. B., *op. cit.,* p. 90.

Page 171. Description of auction quoted from *Chambers' Journal* for October, 1853, in Olmsted, F. L., *A Journal in the Seaboard Slave States, op. cit.,* p. 38.

Newspaper advertisement quoted in Bancroft, Frederic, *op. cit.,* footnote, p. 28.

Ibid., footnote, p. 210.

Page 172. Martineau, Harriet, *Retrospect of Western Travel,* p. 270. London, Saunders and Otley, 1838.

Quoted in Olmsted, F. L., *A Journey in the Seaboard Slave States, op. cit.,* pp. 118, 119. (Emphasis mine.)

Chapter X

Page 177. Hart, A. B., *Slavery and Abolition,* p. 245. New York, Harper & Brothers, 1906.

Page 178. Speech by Senator Hammond in the *Congressional Globe,* March 6, 1858.

Quoted in Buckingham, J. S., *op. cit.,* Vol. I, pp. 213, 214.

Quoted in Beard, Charles A., *Captains Uncourageous,* p. 504, *Virginia Quarterly Review,* 1931.

Page 179. Quoted in McMaster, J. B., *op. cit.,* Vol. V, p. 267.

Page 180. Quoted in Channing, Edward, *A History of the United States,* Vol. VI, p. 3. New York, The Macmillan Company, 1925.

McMaster, J. B., *op. cit.,* p. 268. Helper, H. R., *op. cit.*

Page 182. Adapted from Webb, W. P., *op. cit.,* pp. 184-202.

Beard, Charles A. and Mary R., *op. cit.,* p. 636.

CHAPTER XI

Page 192. Quoted in Paxson, F. L., *The Last American Frontier,* pp. 329, 330. New York, The Macmillan Company, 1910.

Page 193. Quoted in Hicks, John D., *The Populist Revolt,* pp. 70, 71. University of Minnesota Press.

Page 195. Johnson, C. S., Embree, E. R., and Alexander, W. W., *The Collapse of Cotton Tenancy,* University of North Carolina Press, Chapel Hill, 1935, p. 9.

Page 196. Adapted from Hacker, Louis M., "The Farmer is Doomed," *Modern Monthly,* March, 1933, p. 72.

World Almanac, 1938, pp. 244, 346.

Page 197. *Cf. Recent Social Trends,* Whittlesey House, New York, 1934, one-volume edition, p. 284.

Page 199. Hodgins, Eric, and Magoun, F. Alexander, *Behemoth, The Story of Power,* New York, Doubleday, Doran & Company, Inc., 1932, p. 3.

Page 202. Quoted in Hicks, John D., *op. cit.,* p. 160.

Page 204. Quoted in Commager, H. S., Editor, *Documents of American History,* Crafts, New York, 1934, Vol. II, pp. 143-145.

Page 205. Commager, H. S., *op. cit.,* p. 177.

Page 206. Lindsay, N. Vachel, *Collected Poems of Nicholas Vachel Lindsay,* Macmillan, New York, 1923, p. 103.

CHAPTER XII

Page 207. Table (excluding 1929 figure) from Mulhall, Michael G., *Industries and Wealth of Nations,* 1896, New York, Longmans, Green & Co., p. 32.

Page 208. Hacher, Louis M., and Kendrick, B. V., *The United States Since 1865,* Crofts, New York, 1932, p. 186.

Page 210. Automobile story adapted from Hendrick, B. J., *The Age of Big Business,* p. 173. Yale University Press, 1919.

Page 211. Population comparison adapted from Alexander, M. W., *The Economic Evolution of the United States,* p. 22. Published by the National Industrial Conference Board.

Page 212. Beard, Mary R., *The American Labor Movement: A Short History,* Macmillan, New York, 1928, pp. 71, 72.

Page 219. Baslington story adapted from affidavit of George O. Baslington. "In the case of the Standard Oil Company *vs.* William C. Scofield *et al.* in the Court of Common Pleas, Cuyahoga County, Ohio," quoted in Tarbell, Ida M., *The History of the Standard Oil Company,* Appendix No. 7. New York, The Macmillan Company, 1925.

George Rice story story adapted from Lloyd, Henry D., *Wealth Against Commonwealth,* p. 206. New York, Harper & Brothers, 1894. (Emphasis mine.)

Page 220. Committee on Small Business, House of Representatives, *United*

States Versus Economic Concentration and Monopoly, U. S. Government Printing Office, Washington, D. C., 1946, pp. 104, 105, 108, 123, 133.

Carver, T. N., *Essays in Social Justice,* p. 332. Harvard University Press, 1925.

Page 221. *U. S. Statutes at Large,* Vol. XXVI, p. 209.

CHAPTER XIII

Page 223. Wilson, Woodrow, *The New Freedom,* Doubleday, Page & Co., New York, 1913, p. 275.

Page 224. Beard, Mary, *op. cit.,* p. 17.

Page 227. Cummins, E. E., *The Labor Problem in the United States,* Van Nostrand, New York, 1935, p. 130.

Page 228. Faulkner, H. U., *American Economic History,* Harper, New York, 1931, p. 557.

Page 229. *Ibid.*

Fine, Nathan, *Labor and Farmer Parties in the United States, 1828-1928,* Rand School of Social Science, New York, 1928, p. 121.

Page 231. Faulkner, H. U., *op. cit.,* p. 564.

Levinson, Edward, *Labor on the March,* Harper, New York, 1935, pp. 13-14.

Hoxie, R. F., *Trade Unionism in the United States,* Appleton, New York, 1920, p. 90.

Page 233. U. S. Senate Doc. No. 870, 62nd Congress, 2nd Session, Government Printing Office, Washington, D. C., 1912, pp. 63, 64.

Page 234. *From Songs to Fan the Flame of Discontent,* 14th ed., reprinted by Brissenden, Paul F., *The I.W.W.: A Study of American Syndicalism,* Appendix 9, Columbia University Press, New York, 1919.

Page 235. Ware, Norman J., *Labor in Modern Industrial Society,* Heath, New York, 1935, p. 277.

Page 236. Yellen, Samuel, *American Labor Struggles,* Harcourt, Brace, New York, 1936, pp. 101 ff.

Page 237. *Ibid.,* pp. 115, 116.

Page 239. *American Federationist,* November, 1914, p. 971.

Page 240. Bedford Cut Stone Co. *v.* Journeymen Stone Cutters Association, 274 U. S. 37 (1927).

CHAPTER XIV

Page 243. Connecticut General Life Insurance Co. *v.* Johnson, Supreme Court, No. 316, October Term, 1937, pp. 3, 4.

Page 244. Berle, Adolf A., and Means, Gardiner C., *The Modern Corporation and Private Property,* The Macmillan Company, New York, 1933, p. 19.

Ibid., p. 32.

Page 245. Quoted in Lundberg, Ferdinand, *America's 60 Families,* Vanguard, New York, 1937, pp. 104, 105.

Page 250. Quoted in Beard, Charles A., *The Devil Theory of War,* Vanguard, New York, 1936, p. 39.

Ibid., pp. 82, 87.

Page 251. *Ibid.*, p. 96.

U. S. Department of Commerce, Trade Information Bulletin, Nos. 767 and 731.

Page 252. *Congressional Record*, Proceedings and Debates of the Session of the 67th Congress, Vol. LXII, p. 8941.

Page 253. Butler, Smedley D., in *Common Sense*, November, 1935.

Page 254. Hacker and Kendrick, *op. cit.*, p. 617.

CHAPTER XV

Page 259. Hearings before a Sub-Committee of the Committee on Manufactures, U. S. Senate, Dec. 28-30, 1931, Jan. 4-9, 1932, Government Printing Office, Washington, D. C., 1932, p. 55.

Page 260. *Ibid.*, p. 75.

Davis, Jerome, *Capitalism and Its Culture*, Farrar and Rinehart, New York, p. 149.

Ibid., p. 465.

Page 261. U. S. Department of Commerce, Bureau of the Census, Statistical Abstract of the United States, 1938, Government Printing Office, Washington, D. C., 1939, p. 302. It is true that the cost-of-living index also fell during this period, but it declined only half as much as national income paid out.

Ibid., pp. 302, 616.

Federal Reserve Bulletin, November, 1939, p. 1004.

Page 262. Statistical Abstract, 1938, p. 324.

Ibid., p. 834.

Ibid., p. 439.

Page 265. *The Structure of the American Economy, Part 1, Basic Characteristics*, National Resources Committee, Government Printing Office, Washington, D. C., 1939, p. 284.

Berle and Means, *op. cit.*, pp. 36-37.

Stamp, Josiah C., *The National Capital*, King, London, 1937, p. 30.

The Structure of the American Economy, op. cit., p. 311.

Page 266. *Ibid.*, p. 312.

Page 267. *Ibid.*, p. 314.

Page 268. Magdoff, Harry, "The Purpose and Method of Measuring Productivity," *Journal of the American Statistical Association*, June, 1939, Vol. XXXIV, p. 316.

Hearings before a Sub-Committee of the Committee on Manufactures, U. S. Senate, 1932, p. 347.

Schumpeter, J. A., *Business Cycles*, McGraw-Hill, New York, 1939, Vol. II, p. 928.

Page 269. Senate Doc. No. 173, 75th Congress, 3rd Session.

Congressional Record, 72nd Congress, 1st Session, Apr. 4, 1932.

Adapted from Leven, M., Moulton, H. G., and Warburton, C., *America's Capacity to Consume*, Brookings Institution, Washington, D. C., 1934, p. 54.

Page 270. *Ibid.*, p. 56.

Chapter XVI

Page 273. Roosevelt, Franklin D., *The Public Papers and Addresses of Franklin D. Roosevelt,* compiled and collated by Samuel I. Rosenman, Random House, New York, 1938, Vol. V (1936), pp. 534, 587.

Page 274. *Ibid.,* Vol. II (1933), pp. 356-357.

Ibid., Vol. II (1933), pp. 11-15.

Page 276. *Ibid.,* Vol. III (1934), p. 313.

In July 1932, after three years of depression, when it was apparent even to a child that local bodies and states could no longer cope with the relief problem, the RFC was authorized to *lend* up to $300,000,000 to states and municipalities for relief! But so hard did the Hoover tradition die that by January 1, 1933, only $80,000,000 of the RFC fund had been disbursed.

Page 280. *Ibid.,* Vol. II (1933), p. 422.

Page 281. *Ibid.,* Vol. II (1933), p. 233.

Page 282. New York *Times,* Aug. 16, 1938.

Chapter XVII

Page 284. Report of AAA for 1935, quoted in Lindley, Ernest, K., *Half Way with Roosevelt,* Viking, New York, 1936, p. 115.

Page 285. Roosevelt, Franklin D., *op. cit.,* Vol. II (1933), pp. 421-423.

Page 288. *Ibid.,* p. 298.

Page 289. Statistical Abstract of the United States, 1938, p. 616.

Emergency Agricultural Act, U. S., 73rd Congress, 1st Session, Public Act No. 10, Section 2.

Statistical Abstract, 1938, p. 621.

Page 290. Gould, Kenneth M., *Windows on the World,* Stackpole, New York, 1938, p. 206.

Page 291. Roosevelt, Franklin D., *op. cit.,* Vol. II (1933), pp. 251-253.

Page 294. *Cf.* Ickes, Harold, "Projects of Reconstruction," in *The Federal Government Today* (pamphlet), American Council on Public Affairs, New York, p. 26.

Page 297. Sweezy, Paul M., "The Power of the Purse," *New Republic,* Feb. 8, 1939, p. 7.

Page 298. Roosevelt, Franklin D., *op. cit.,* Vol. III (1934), p. 420.

Chapter XVIII

Page 301. New York *Times,* Jan. 21, 1937.

9 Questions and 9 Answers, pamphlet, United States Housing Authority, Government Printing Office, Washington, D. C., p. 10.

Ibid.

Ibid.

"Housing and Your Community," leaflet, United States Housing Authority, Government Printing Office, Washington, D. C., p. 2.

Page 303. "Message from the President of the United States," March 3, 1931, Government Printing Office, Washington, D. C.

Roosevelt, Franklin D., *op. cit.,* Vol. II (1933), p. 122.

Page 305. *Cf.* "To Keep the Water in the Rivers and the Soil on the Land," Government Printing Office, Washington, D. C., 1938. Also pamphlets issued by Tennessee Valley Authority.

Lilienthal, David E., *TVA: Democracy on the March,* Harper & Brothers, New York, 1944, pp. 18, 19.

Page 308. Roosevelt, Franklin D., *op. cit.,* Vol. II (1933), p. 93.

Page 309. New York *Times,* Nov. 2, 1938.

Page 312. Hearings before a Sub-Committee of the Committee on Education and Labor, U. S. Senate, 75th Congress, 1st Session, Part 7, Government Printing Office, Washington, D. C., 1937, p. 2509.

Cf. Huberman, Leo, *The Labor Spy Racket,* Modern Age, New York, 1937, p. 6.

Page 313. NLRB *v.* Jones & Laughlin, 301 U. S. 1.

Ford, Henry, in collaboration with Crowther, Samuel, *My Life and Work,* Doubleday, Page, New York, 1926, p. 110.

Page 314. *Reports of the Proceedings of the Fifty-Fifth Annual Convention of the American Federation of Labor,* 1935, pp. 523, 524.

Ibid., p. 724.

Ibid., p. 732.

Page 315. *Ibid.,* p. 734.

Saposs, David J., "Structure of A. F. of L. Unions," *Labor Relations Reporter,* May 15, 1939, p. 6 ff.

Page 316. A. F. of L. *Proceedings, op. cit.,* p. 659.

Page 317. *Ibid.,* p. 523.

A. F. of L. vs. CIO, the Record, pamphlet, American Federation of Labor, Washington, D. C., November, 1939, p. 8.

Page 319. Huberman, Leo, *The Truth About Unions,* Reynal & Hitchcock, New York, 1946, p. 113.

Page 322. "Hours and Earnings in Tobacco Stemmeries," United States Department of Labor, Bulletin of the Women's Bureau, No. 127, Government Printing Office, Washington, D. C., p. 18. (My italics.)

Page 323. Roosevelt, Franklin D., *op. cit.,* Vol. V (1936), p. 385.

CHAPTER XIX

Page 325. Toynbee, A. J., *Survey of International Affairs, 1937,* Oxford, London, 1938, Vol. I, p. 50.

Page 328. Roosevelt, Franklin D., *op. cit.,* Vol. II (1933), p. 14.

Page 329. New York *Times,* Oct. 6, 1937.

Page 330. *Public Opinion Quarterly,* Vol. III, No. 4, Oct., 1939, p. 20 (published by School of Public Affairs, Princeton University).

Page 331. New York *Times,* Jan. 5, 1939.

Page 332. *Public Opinion Quarterly,* Oct., 1939, p. 19.

Page 333. "Japan's Ability to Finance Purchase of War Materials," Special Study No. 1, by the Chinese Council for Economic Research, Washington, D. C., March, 1938, Part 1, p. 14.

Page 334. *Cf.* "Mr. Roosevelt's Foreign Policy," in *Propaganda Analysis,* Bulletin of the Institute for Propaganda Analysis, New York, Nov. 15, 1939, Vol. III, No. 2, p. 4.

Page 336. Roosevelt, Franklin D., *op. cit.,* Vol. V (1936), p. 609.

Page 340. Shugg, Roger W., and De Weerd, Major H. A., *World War II,* The Infantry Journal, Washington, 1946, p. 97.

Ibid., p. 99.

Page 341. Temporary National Economic Committee, 76th Congress, 3rd Session; Monograph No. 26, pp. 172, 173. U. S. Government Printing Office, Washington, D. C., 1941.

Page 342. Bulletin No. 878, U. S. Bureau of Statistics, p. 6. U. S. Government Printing Office, Washington, D. C., 1946.

Shugg and De Weerd, *op. cit.,* p. 134.

CHAPTER XX

Page 349. Lynd, Robert S., *The Nation,* December 28, 1946, p. 749. Message from President Franklin D. Roosevelt to Congress, Senate Doc. No. 173, 75th Congress, 3rd Session.

Page 350. Fourth Annual Message, Dec. 3, 1888, Misc. Doc. 210, Part 8, 53rd Congress, 2nd Session, House of Representatives.

New York Times, Jan. 7, 1947.

Index

MONTHLY REVIEW

AN INDEPENDENT SOCIALIST MAGAZINE

EDITED BY PAUL M. SWEEZY & HARRY MAGDOFF

Business Week: "...a brand of socialism that is thorough-going and tough-minded, drastic enough to provide a sharp break with the past that many left-wingers in the underdeveloped countries see as essential. At the same time they maintain a sturdy independence of both Moscow and Peking....Their analysis of the troubles of capitalism is just plausible enough to be disturbing."

Wall Street Journal: "...a leading journal of radical economic analysis. Sweezy is the 'dean' of radical economists."

L'Espresso (Italy's *Time*): "The best Marxist journal not only in the United States, but in the world."

NACLA (North American Congress on Latin America): "It is hard to adequately express what MR has meant to us in *NACLA* and as individuals over the years, but I don't think it is an exaggeration to say that we cut our eye-teeth on Marxism in the publications of MR."

Village Voice: "The *Monthly Review* has been for many years a resolute and independent exponent of Marxist ideas, with regular analysis of what is happening in the economy. Paul Sweezy is a renowned Marxist economist. ...Harry Magdoff is similarly esteemed for his economic writings..."